Self Portraits

Self Portraits

A collection of writings by people who lived ordinary lives in extraordinary times.

SPECIAL EDITION
Edited by Gary Brin

Standish Press

Spelling errors and publishing mistakes found in the original versions were corrected or adjusted when necessary for this edition. Incorrect spelling of biographical and geographical names mentioned was adjusted whenever possible as well. Original text was left intact to preserve the historical accuracy of existing writings. A complete list of titles used for this edition can be found at the end pages.

Original versions of all titles used for this collection can be found online in downloadable PDF copies from scanned images.

www.nancyhankslincolnpubliclibrary.org

BOOKS USED FOR THIS EDITION HAS BEEN REFORMATTED FROM THE ORIGINAL PUBLISHED VERSIONS

Cover design and book layout © 2021 by Standish Press
Compilation © 2021 by Standish Press

FIRST EDITION

ALL NEW MATERIAL AND CORRECTIONS
Copyright © 2021 by Standish Press

All rights reserved. No part of this book may be reproduced by any means whatsoever without written permission from the publisher.

For more information about reprint rights please visit
www.standishpress.com

ISBN—978-1-945510-05-2

Library of Congress Control Number
2021946343

MANUFACTURED IN THE UNITED STATES OF AMERICA

In Remembrance of

Anne Frank
Chief Joseph
Frederick Douglass
Harriet Tubman
Henry Whiteley
Martha Mitchell
Martin Luther King Jr.
Marvella Bayh
Nancy Hanks Lincoln
Nathan Hale
Pocahontas
Princess Diana
Sacajawea
William Bradford

They achieved a notable place in history without trying to be anyone else other than themselves.

Contents

Page 9
Foreword

Page 11
Edward Winslow

Page 11
William Bradford

Page 31
John Knight

Page 43
John Slover

Page 56
Daniel Boone

Page 77
George Washington

Page 86
Tobias Lear

Page 91
Henry Whiteley

Page 115
Abraham Lincoln

Page 135
Martha Morgan

Page 159
James Akin Jr.

Page 173
Frances Sawyer

Page 196
James Richey
Page 202
Chief Joseph
Page 224
Nancy Hunt
Page 239
Frederick Walker
Page 252
Frank Allen McCurdy
Page 252
John Kirk McCurdy
Page 277
Harold Bride
Page 286
Kate Evelyn Luard
Page 357
Afterword
Page 372
Source Notes
Page 376
About the Series Editor

Chapters are in order of when events took place from the landing of the Pilgrims to the First World War.

Foreword

The biographical collection in this book is taken from previously published material available online at the Nancy Hanks Lincoln Public Library in their original editions. Nevertheless, most, if not all, are out of print presently. So, the idea of bringing together a selection of works such as these into one volume has only one objective for Standish Press—and that is to make available to a wider audience the words of people who lived previously in a time long gone but nevertheless left an important legacy behind through their vivid recollections and notes.

Each of the books in this collection lets the reader relive the thoughts and experiences through the eyes of the author, seeing what they saw and felt at that particular moment. In many cases descriptions of events and places seem almost impossible to believe that just a short century or two (maybe three or four) previously someone actually lived in a time that seems much closer to fiction than actual reality from our perspective. Words can be powerful even when written in the simplest of ways and the writings in this collection of memoirs tells a story that even the best fiction can't duplicate perfectly. The fact that those who lived these lives are no longer around to tell us their stories is something to be reminded of every day when we think of our own mortality. But despite knowing they are no longer able to speak to us in person, their words remain to remind us of how much selected events changed from one era to another and how life evolved—as one incredible year passed and another began.

Whether famous or not, everyone has a story to tell, and through writing many things can be learned not only about the writer but also of specific events mentioned. In a time when video did not exist, the vivid details of everyday life through someone's writings can present a visual history of the past. I can clearly remember being in fourth grade and listening to a book being read out loud by my teacher focusing upon details of the landing of the Pilgrims in Massachusetts* which caused my mind to wander back several centuries as I imagined standing besides the people in the story, seeing what they saw. So powerful were the words I heard back in fourth grade that decades later I still love reading about lives lived previously—knowing that history is only a page away from being discovered and explored as only a book can do for one's imagination since time travel remains elusive.

*Margaret Pumphrey's Pilgrim Stories Revised and Expanded Edition by Elvajean Hall. Originally published (1961) by Rand McNally and Company.

Gary Brin
Series Editor

Edward Winslow and William Bradford

Excerpt from *Cape Cod Journal of the Pilgrim Fathers* (1920)
Reprinted from *Mourt's Relation* (1622)

Wednesday, the sixth of September, the wind coming east northeast, a fine small gale, we loosed from Plymouth, having been kindly entertained and courteously used by divers friends there dwelling and after many difficulties in boisterous storms, at length, by God's Providence, upon the ninth of November following, by break of the day we espied land, which we deemed to be Cape Cod, and so afterward it proved.

And the appearance of it much comforted us, especially seeing so goodly a land, and wooded to the brink of the sea, it caused us to rejoice together, and praise God that had given us once again to see land. And thus we made our course south southwest, purposing to go to a river ten leagues to the south of the Cape—but at night the wind being contrary—we put round again for the bay of Cape Cod and upon the 11th of November we came to an anchor in the bay, which is a good harbor and pleasant bay, circled round, except in the entrance, which is about four miles over from land to land—compassed about to the very sea with oaks, pines, juniper, sassafras, and other sweet wood—it is a harbor wherein a thousand sail of ships may safely ride. There we relieved ourselves with wood and water, and refreshed our people, while our shallop was fitted to coast the bay to search for a habitation. There was the greatest store of fowl that ever we saw. And every day we saw whales playing hard by us, of which in that place, if we had instruments and means to take them, we might have made a very rich return, which, to our great grief, we wanted. Our master, and his mate, and others experienced in fishing, professed we might have made three or four thousand pounds worth of oil. They preferred it before Greenland whale fishing, and purpose the next winter to fish for whale here. For cod we assayed, but found none—there is good store, no doubt, in their season. Neither got we any fish all the time we lay there—but some few little ones on the shore.

    We found great mussels, and very fat and full of sea pearl but we could not eat them, for they made us all sick that did eat as well sailors as passengers—they caused to cast and scour—but they were soon well again. The bay is so round and circling, that before we could come to anchor, we went round all the points of the compass. We could not come near the shore by three quarters of an English mile, because of shallow water, which was a great prejudice to us, for our people, going on shore, were forced to wade a bowshot or two in going inland, which caused many to get colds and coughs, for it was many times freezing cold weather. This day, before we came to harbor, observing some not well affected to unity and concord, but gave some appearance of faction, it was thought good there should be an association and agreement that we should combine together in one body, and to submit to such government and governors as we should by common consent agree to make and choose, and set our hands to this that follows, word for word in the name of God. Amen. We, whose names are underwritten, the loyal subjects of our dread sovereign Lord King James, by the grace of God, of Great Britain, France, and Ireland, king, defender of the faith and etc. Having undertaken for the glory of God and advancement of the Christian faith, and honor of our king and country, a voyage to plant the first colony in the northern parts of Virginia, do by these presents solemnly and mutually, in the presence of God and one of another, covenant and combine ourselves together into a civil body politic, for our better ordering and preservation, and furtherance of the ends aforesaid and by virtue hereof to enact, constitute, and frame such just and equal laws, ordinances, acts, constitutions, offices from time to time, as shall be thought most meet and convenient for the general good of the colony—unto which we promise all due submission and obedience. In witness whereof we have hereunder subscribed our names, Cape Cod, 11th of November, in the year of the reign of our sovereign Lord King James of England, France, and Ireland 18th, and of Scotland 54th, Anno Domini 1620. The same day, so soon as we could, we set ashore 15 or 16 men, well-armed, with some to fetch wood, for we had none left—as also to see what the land was, and what inhabitants they could meet with.

They found it to be a small neck of land on this side where we lay, is the bay, and the further side the sea, the ground or earth, sand hills, much like the downs in Holland, but much better, the crust of the earth, a spit's depth, excellent black earth all wooded with oaks, pines, sassafras, juniper, birch, holly, vines, some ash, walnut—the wood for the most part open and without underwood—fit either to go or ride in. At night our people returned, but found not any person, nor habitation—and laded their boat with juniper, which smelled very sweet and strong, and of which we burnt the most part of the time we lay there.

Monday, the 13th of November, we unshipped our shallop and drew her on land to mend and repair her, having been forced to cut her down in bestowing her betwixt the decks, and she was much opened with the people's lying in her which kept us long there, for it was 16 or 17 days before the carpenter had finished her. Our people went on shore to refresh themselves, and our women to wash, as they had great need. But whilst we lay thus still, hoping our shallop would be ready in five or six days at the furthest, but our carpenter made slow work of it, so that some of our people, impatient of delay, desired for our better furtherance to travel by land into the country (which was not without appearance of danger, not having the shallop with them, nor means to carry provision but on their backs) to see whether it might be fit for us to seat in or no, and the rather, because, as we sailed into the harbor, there seemed to be a river opening itself into the mainland. The willingness of the persons was liked, but the thing itself, in regard of the danger, was rather permitted than approved and so with cautions, directions, and instructions, sixteen men were set out with every man his musket, sword, and corslet, under the conduct of Captain Miles Standish unto whom was adjoined for counsel and advice, William Bradford, Stephen Hopkins, and Edward Tilley. Wednesday, the 15th of November, they were set ashore and when they had ordered themselves in the order of a single file and marched about the space of a mile, by the sea they espied five or six people with a dog coming towards them, who were savages, who, when they saw them, ran into the wood and whistled the dog after them and etc.

First they supposed them to be Master Jones—the master and some of his men—for they were ashore and knew of their coming—but after they knew them to be Indians, they marched after them into the woods, lest other of the Indians should lie in ambush. But when the Indians saw our men following them, they ran away with might and main, and our men turned out of the wood after them—for it was the way they intended to go—but they could not come near them. They followed them that night about ten miles by the trace of their footings, and saw how they had come the same way they went, and at a turning perceived how they run up a hill to see whether they followed them.

At length night came upon them, and they were constrained to take up their lodging. So they set forth three sentinels, and the rest, some kindled a fire, and others fetched wood, and there held our rendezvous that night. In the morning, so soon as we could see the trace, we proceeded on our journey, and had the track until we had compassed the head of a long creek, and there they took into another wood and we after them supposing to find some of their dwellings. But we marched through boughs and bushes, and under hills and valleys, which tore our very armor in pieces, and yet could meet with none of them, nor their houses, nor find any fresh water, which we greatly desired and stood in need of—for we brought neither beer nor water with us, and our victuals was only biscuit and Holland cheese, and a little bottle of aqua vitae, so as we were sore athirst. About ten o'clock we came into a deep valley full of brush, wood gaile, and long grass, through which we found little paths or tracts and there we saw a deer, and found springs of fresh water, of which we were heartily glad, and sat us down and drunk our first New England water with as much delight as ever we drunk drink in all our lives. When we had refreshed ourselves we directed our course full south, that we might come to the shore, which within a short while after we did, and there made a fire, that they in the ship might see where we were (as we had direction), and so marched on towards this supposed river.

And as we went in another valley, we found a fine clear pond of fresh water—being about a musket shot broad—and twice as long there grew also many small vines—and fowl and deer haunted there—there grew much sassafras. From thence we went on and found much plain ground, about fifty acres, fit for the plow, and some signs where the Indians had formerly planted their corn. After this some thought it best, for nearness of the river, to go down and travel on the sea sands, by which means some of our men were tired and lagged behind. So we stayed and gathered them up, and struck into the land again, where we found a little path to certain heaps of sand, one whereof was covered with old mats, and had a wooden thing like a mortar whelmed on the top of it, and an earthen pot laid in a little hole at the end thereof. We, musing what it might be, digged and found a bow, and, as we thought, arrows, but they were rotten. We supposed there were many other things but because we deemed them graves, we put in the bow again, and made it up as it was, and left the rest untouched, because we thought it would be odious unto them to ransack their sepulchers. We went on further and found new stubble of which they had gotten corn this year and many walnut trees full of nuts—and great store of strawberries, and some vines. Passing thus a field or two, which were not great, we came to another, which had also been new gotten, and there we found where a house had been, and four or five old planks laid together. Also we found a great kettle, which had been some ship's kettle and brought out of Europe.

There was also an heap of sand, made like the former, but it was newly done (we might see how they had paddled it with their hands), which we digged up, and in it we found a little old basket full of fair Indian corn and digged further and found a fine great new basket full of very fair corn of this year with some 36 goodly ears of corn, some yellow, and some red, and others mixed with blue, which was a very goodly sight. The basket was round and narrow at the top. It held about three or four bushels, which was as much as two of us could lift up from the ground, and was very handsomely and cunningly made. But whilst we were busy about these things, we set our men sentinel in a round ring, all but two or three which digged up the corn. We were in suspense what to do with it and the kettle, and at length after much consultation, we concluded to take the kettle and as much of the corn as we could carry away with us—and when our shallop came, if we could find any of the people and come to parley with them, we would give them the kettle again and satisfy them for their corn. So we took all the ears, and put a good deal of the loose corn in the kettle for two men to bring away on a staff.

Besides they that could put any into their pockets filled the same. The rest we buried again—for we were so laden with armor that we could carry no more. Not far from this place we found the remainder of an old fort or palisado, which, as we conceived, had been made by some Christians. This was also hard by that place which we thought had been a river unto which we went, and found it so to be, dividing itself into two arms by a high bank standing right by the cut or mouth, which came from the sea. That which was next unto us was the less—the other arm was more than twice as big, and not unlike to be a harbor for ships but whether it be a fresh river, or only an indraught of the sea, we had no time to discover for we had commandment to be out but two days. Here also we saw two canoes, the one on the one side, the other on the other side. We could not believe it was a canoe, till we came near it. So we returned, leaving the further discovery hereof to our shallop, and came that night back again to the fresh water pond and there we made our rendezvous that night, making a great fire, and a barricade to windward of us, and kept good watch with three sentinels all night, everyone standing when his turn came, while five or six inches of match was burning. It proved a very rainy night. In the morning we took our kettle and sunk it in the pond, and trimmed our muskets, for few of them would go off because of the wet, and so coasted the wood again to come home, in which we were shrewdly puzzled and lost our way. As we wandered we came to a tree, where a young sprit was bowed down over a bow, and some acorns strewed underneath. Stephen Hopkins said it had been to catch some deer. So as we were looking at it, William Bradford being in the rear, when he came looked also upon it, and as he went about it, it gave a sudden jerk up, and he was immediately caught by the leg.

It was a very pretty device, made with a rope of their own making, and having a noose as artificially made as any roper in England can make, and as like ours as can be, which we brought away with us. In the end we got out of the wood, and were fallen about a mile too high above the creek, where we saw three bucks, but we had rather have had one of them. We also did spring three couple of partridges and as we came along by the creek, we saw great flocks of wild geese and ducks, but they were very fearful of us. So we marched some while in the woods, some while on the sands, and other while in the water up to the knees till at length we came near the ship and then we shot off our pieces—and the long boat came to fetch us. Master Jones and Master Carver being on the shore, with many of our people, came to meet us. And thus we came both weary and welcome home and delivered in our corn into the store to be kept for seed, for we knew not how to come by any, and therefore were very glad purposing, so soon as we could meet with any of the inhabitants of that place, to make them large satisfaction. This was our first discovery, whilst our shallop was in repairing. Our people did make things as fitting as they could, and time would, in seeking out wood, and helving of tools, and sawing of timber to build a new shallop. But the discommodiousness of the harbor did much hinder us, for we could neither go to nor come from the shore but at high water—which was much to our hindrance and hurt—for oftentimes they waded to the middle of the thigh, and oft to the knees, to go and come from land. Some did it necessarily, and some for their own pleasure but it brought to the most, if not to all, coughs and colds (the weather proving suddenly cold and stormy), which afterwards turned to the scurvy, whereof many died. When our shallop was fit (indeed before she was fully fitted for there was two days work after bestowed on her) there was appointed some 24 men of our own, and armed, then to go and make a more full discovery of the rivers before mentioned.

    Master Jones was desirous to go with us and took such of his sailors as he thought useful for us, so as we were in all about 34 men. We made Master Jones our leader, for we thought it best herein to gratify his kindness and forwardness. When we were set forth—it proved rough weather and cross winds—so as we were constrained, some in the shallop, and others in the long boat, to row to the nearest shore, the wind would suffer them to go unto and then to wade out above the knees. The wind was so strong as the shallop could not keep the water, but was forced to harbor there that night. But we marched six or seven miles further, and appointed the shallop to come to us as soon as they could. It blowed and did snow all day and night, and froze withal. Some of our people that are dead took the original of their death here.

    The next day about 11 o'clock our shallop came to us and we shipped ourselves—and the wind being good—we sailed to the river we formerly discovered, which we named *Cold Harbor* to which when we came—we found it not navigable for ships—yet we thought it might be a good harbor for boats, for it flows there twelve foot at high water. We landed our men between the two creeks, and marched some four or five miles by the greater of them, and the shallop followed us. At length, night grew on, and our men were tired with marching up and down the steep hills and deep valleys, which lay half a foot thick with snow.

Master Jones, wearied with marching, was desirous we should take up our lodging, though some of us would have marched further. So we made there our rendezvous for that night under a few pine trees, and as it fell out, we got three fat geese and six ducks to our supper—which we eat with soldiers stomachs, for we had eaten little all that day. Our resolution was next morning to go up to the head of this river—for we supposed it would prove fresh water. But in the morning our resolution held not, because many liked not the hilliness of the soil and badness of the harbor. So we turned towards the other creek that we might go over and look for the rest of the corn that we left behind when we were here before. When we came to the creek, we saw the canoe lie on the dry ground, and a flock of geese in the river at which one made a shot and killed a couple of them—and we launched the canoe and fetched them, and when we had done, she carried us over by seven or eight at once. This done, we marched to the place where we had the corn formerly, which place we called *Cornhill* and digged and found the rest of which we were very glad. We also digged in a place a little further off and found a bottle of oil. We went to another place which we had seen before—and digged and found more corn and etc.

Two or three baskets full of Indian wheat and a bag of beans with a good many of fair wheat ears. Whilst some of us were digging up this—some others found another heap of corn which they digged up also—so as we had in all about ten bushels which will serve us sufficiently for seed. And sure it was God's good Providence that we found this corn, for else we know not how we should have done for we knew not how we should find or meet with any of the Indians, except it be to do us a mischief.

Also, we had never in all likelihood seen a grain of it, if we had not made our first journey, for the ground was now covered with snow, and so hard frozen that we were fain with our curtlaxes and short swords to hew and carve the ground a foot deep, and then wrest it up with levers, for we had forgot to bring other tools. Whilst we were in this employment, foul weather being towards, Master Jones was earnest to go aboard but sundry of us desired to make further discovery and to find out the Indians habitations. So we sent home with him our weakest people, and some that were sick, and all the corn and 18 of us stayed still, and lodged there that night, and desired that the shallop might return to us next day, and bring us some mattocks and spades with them. The next morning we followed certain beaten paths and tracts of the Indians into the woods, supposing they would have led us into some town or houses. After we had gone a while, we light upon a very broad beaten path, well nigh two foot broad. Then we lighted all our matches, and prepared ourselves, concluding we were near their dwellings. But in the end we found it to be only a path made to drive deer in, when the Indians hunt, as we supposed. When we had marched five or six miles into the woods and could find no signs of any people, we returned again another way and as we came into the plain ground, we found a place like a grave, but it was much bigger and longer than any we had yet seen. It was also covered with boards, so as we mused what it should be, and resolved to dig it up where we found first a mat, and under that a fair bow, and there another mat, and under that a board about three quarters long, finely carved and painted, with three tines or broaches on the top like a crown—also between the mats we found bowls, trays, dishes, and such like trinkets. At length we came to a fair new mat, and under that, two bundles, the one bigger, the other less. We opened the greater, and found in it a great quantity of fine and perfect red powder and in it the bones and skull of a man. The skull had fine yellow hair still on it, and some of the flesh unconsumed. There was bound up with it a knife, a pack needle, and two or three old iron things. It was bound up in a sailor's canvas cassock and a pair of cloth breeches. The red powder was a kind of embalmment, and yielded a strong but no offensive smell—it was as fine as any flour. We opened the less bundle likewise, and found of the same powder in it, and the bones and head of a little child. About the legs and other parts of it were bound strings and bracelets of fine white heads. There was also by it a little bow, about three quarters long, and some other odd knacks. We brought sundry of the prettiest things away with us, and covered the corpse up again. After this we digged in sundry like places, but found no more corn, not anything else but graves. There was variety of opinions amongst us about the embalmed person. Some thought it was an Indian lord and king. Others said, the Indians have all black hair, and never any was seen with brown or yellow hair.

Some thought it was a Christian of some special note, which had died amongst them, and they thus buried him to honor him. Others thought they had killed him, and did it in triumph over him. Whilst we were thus ranging and searching, two of the sailors which were newly come on the shore, by chance espied two houses, which had been lately dwelt in, but the people were gone. They having their pieces and hearing nobody, entered the houses, and took out some things, and durst not stay, but came again and told us. So some seven or eight of us went with them, and found how we had gone within a flight shot of them before. The houses were made with long young sapling trees bended and both ends stuck into the ground. They were made round like unto an arbor and covered down to the ground with thick and well wrought mats, and the door was not over a yard high, made of a mat to open. The chimney was a wide open hole in the top, for which they had a mat to cover it close when they pleased. One might stand and go upright in them. In the midst of them were four little truncheons knocked into the ground, and small sticks laid over, on which they hung their pots and what they had to seethe. Round about the fire they lay on mats, which are their beds. The houses were double matted for as they were matted without, so were they within, with newer and fairer mats. In the houses we found wooden bowls, trays, and dishes, earthen pots, hand baskets made of crab shells wrought together—also an English pail or bucket—it wanted a bail handle—but it had two iron ears—there was also baskets of sundry sorts, bigger and some lesser, finer and some coarser—some were curiously wrought with black and white in pretty works—and sundry other of their household stuff. We found also two or three deer heads, one whereof had been newly killed, for it was still fresh. There was also a company of deer's feet stuck up in the houses, harts (deer) horns, and eagles claws, and sundry such like things, there was also two or three baskets full of parched acorns, pieces of fish, and a piece of a broiled herring. We found also a little silk grass, and a little tobacco seed, with some other seeds which we knew not. Without was sundry bundles of flags, and sedge, bulrushes, and other stuff to make mats. There was thrust into an hollow tree two or three pieces of venison—but we thought it fitter for the dogs than for us. Some of the best things we took away with us, and left the houses standing still as they were.

So it growing towards night, and the tide almost spent, we hasted with our things down to the shallop and got aboard that night, intending to have brought some beads and other things to have left in the houses in sign of peace and that we meant to truck with them, but it was not done by means of our hasty coming away from Cape Cod. But so soon as we can meet conveniently with them, we will give them full satisfaction. Thus much of our second discovery, having thus discovered this place, it was controversial amongst us what to do touching our abode and settling there. Some thought it best, for many reasons, to abide there. As first, that there was a convenient harbor for boats, though not for ships, secondly good corn ground ready to our hands, as we saw by experience in the goodly corn it yielded, which would again agree with the ground and be natural seed for the same. Thirdly, Cape Cod was like to be a place of good fishing—for we saw daily great whales of the best kind for oil and bone, come close aboard our ship and in fair weather swim and play about us. There was once one, when the sun shone warm, came and lay above water as if she had been dead, for a good while together, within half a musket shot of the ship at which two were prepared to shoot to see whether she would stir or no. He that gave fire first, his musket flew in pieces, both stock and barrel, yet, thanks be to God, neither he nor any man else was hurt with it, though many were there about. But when the whale saw her time, she gave a snuff and away. Fourthly, the place was likely to be healthful, secure, and defensible. But the last and especial reason was, that now the heart of winter and unseasonable weather was come upon us, so that we could not go upon coasting and discovery without danger of losing men and boat, upon which would follow the overthrow of all, especially considering what variable winds and sudden storms do there arise. Also, cold and wet lodging had so tainted our people (for scarce any of us were free from vehement coughs), as if they should continue long in that estate, it would endanger the lives of many and breed diseases and infection amongst us. Again, we had yet some beer, butter, flesh, and other such victuals left, which would quickly be all gone, and then we should have nothing to comfort us in the great labor and toil we were like to undergo at the first. It was also conceived, whilst we had competent victuals, that the ship would stay with us, but when that grew low, they would be gone, and let us shift as we could. Others, again, urged greatly the going to Anguum, or Angoum, a place twenty leagues off to the northwards, which they had heard to be an excellent harbor for ships, better ground, and better fishing. Secondly, for anything we knew, there might be hard by us a far better seat and it should be a great hindrance to seat where we should remove again. Thirdly, the water was but in ponds, and it was thought there would be none in summer, or very little. Fourthly, the water there must be fetched up a steep hill. But to omit many reasons and replies used hereabouts, it was in the end concluded to make some discovery within the bay, but in no case so far as Angoum. Besides, Robert Coppin, our pilot, made relation of a great navigable river and good harbor in the other headland of the bay—almost right over against Cape Cod being a right line—not much above eight leagues distant, in which he had been once, and because that one of the wild men with whom they had some trucking stole a harping iron from them, they called it *Thievish Harbor*. And beyond that place they were enjoined not to go, whereupon a company was chosen to go out upon a third discovery. Whilst some were employed in this discovery, it pleased God that Mistress White was brought a birth of a son, which was called Peregrine. The fifth day we, through God's mercy, escaped a great danger by the foolishness of a boy, one of John Billington's sons, who, in his father's absence, had got gunpowder, and had shot off a piece or two, and made squibs, and there being a fowling piece charged in his father's cabin, shot her off in the cabin, there being a little barrel of powder half full, scattered in and about the cabin, the fire being within four foot of the bed between the decks, and many flints and iron things about the cabin, and many people about the fire, and yet, by God's mercy, no harm done. Wednesday, the sixth of December, it was resolved our discoverers should set forth, for the day before was too foul weather, and so they did, though it was well over the day ere all things could be ready. So ten of our men were appointed who were of themselves willing to undertake it, to wit, Captain Standish, Master Carver, William Bradford, Edward Winslow, John Tilley, Edward Tilley, John Howland, and three of London, Richard Warren, Stephen Hopkins, and Edward Doty, and two of our seamen, John Allerton and Thomas English. Of the ship's company there went two of the master's mates, Master Clarke and Master Coppin, the master gunner, and three sailors, the narration of which discovery follows, penned by one of the company. Wednesday, the sixth of December, we set out, being very cold and hard weather.

  We were a long while after we launched from the ship before we could get clear of a sandy point, which lay within less than a furlong of the same. In which time two were very sick, and Edward Tilley had like to have sounded with cold. The gunner also was sick unto death (but hope of trucking made him to go) and so remained all that day and the next night. At length we got clear of the sandy point, and got up our sails, and within an hour or two we got under the weather shore, and then had smoother water and better sailing. But it was very cold—for the water froze on our clothes, and made them many times like coats of iron. We sailed six or seven leagues by the shore, but saw neither river nor creek. At length we met with a tongue of land, being flat off from the shore, with a sandy point. We bore up to gain the point, and found there a fair income or road of a bay, being a league over at the narrowest, and some two or three in length, but we made right over to the land before us, and left the discovery of this income till the next day. As we drew near to the shore, we espied some ten or twelve Indians very busy about a black thing—what it was we could not tell—till afterwards they saw us, and ran to and fro, as if they had been carrying something away. We landed a league or two from them, and had much ado to put ashore anywhere, it lay so full of flat sands. When we came to shore, we made us a barricade, and got firewood, and set out sentinels, and betook us to our lodging, such as it was. We saw the smoke of the fire which the savages made that night about four or five miles from us. In the morning we divided our company, some eight in the shallop, and the rest on the shore went to discover this place. But we found it only to be a bay, without either river or creek coming into it. Yet we deemed it to be as good a harbor as Cape Cod, for they that sounded it found a ship might ride in five fathom water. We on the land found it to be a level soil, but none of the fruitfullest. We saw two becks of fresh water, which were the first running streams that we saw in the country, but one might stride over them. We found also a great fish, called a grampus, dead on the sands. They in the shallop found two of them also in the bottom of the bay, dead in like sort.

  They were cast up at high water, and could not get off for the frost and ice. They were some five or six paces long and about two inches thick of fat, and fleshed like a swine. They would have yielded a great deal of oil, if there had been time and means to have taken it. So we, finding nothing for our turn both we and our shallop returned. We then directed our course along the sea sands to the place where we first saw the Indians. When we were there, we saw it was also a grampus which they were cutting up. They cut it into long rands or pieces about an ell long and two handful broad. We found here and there a piece scattered by the way, as it seemed, for haste. This place the most were minded we should call the *Grampus Bay* because we found so many of them there. We followed the tract of the Indians bare feet a good way on the sands. At length we saw where they struck into the woods by the side of a pond. As we went to view the place, one said he thought he saw an Indian house among the trees—so went up to see. And here we and the shallop lost sight one of another till night, it being now about nine or ten o'clock. So we light on a path, but saw no house, and followed a great way into the woods. At length we found where corn had been set, but not that year. Anon, we found a great burying place, one part whereof was encompassed with a large palisado, like a churchyard with young spires four or five yards long, set as close one by another as they could, two or three foot in the ground. Within it was full of graves, some bigger and some less. Some were also paled about and others had like an Indian house made over them, but not matted. Those graves were more sumptuous than those at Cornhill yet we digged none of them up, but only viewed them and went our way. Without the palisado were graves also, but not so costly. From this place we went and found more corn ground, but not of this year. As we ranged, we light on four or five Indian houses, which had been lately dwelt in but they were uncovered—and had no mats about them—else they were like those we found at Cornhill but had not been so lately dwelt in. There was nothing left but two or three pieces of old mats, a little sedge, also a little further we found two baskets full of parched acorns hid in the ground which we supposed had been corn when we began to dig the same—we cast earth thereon again and went our way—all this while we saw no people. We went ranging up and down till the sun began to draw low and then we hasted out of the woods, that we might come to our shallop, which, when we were out of the woods, we espied a great way off and called them to come unto us—the which they did as soon as they could, for it was not yet high water. They were exceeding glad to see us, for they feared because they had not seen us in so long a time, thinking we would have kept by the shore side. So being both weary and faint—for we had eaten nothing all that day—we fell to make our rendezvous and get firewood, which always cost us a great deal of labor. By that time we had done and our shallop come to us, it was within night and we fed upon such victuals as we had, and betook us to our rest, after we had set out our watch.

About midnight we heard a great and hideous cry and our sentinel called "*Arm! Arm!*" So we bestirred ourselves, and shot off a couple of muskets, and noise ceased. We concluded that it was a company of wolves or foxes—for one told us he had heard such a noise in Newfoundland. About five o'clock in the morning we began to be stirring, and two or three, which doubted whether their pieces would go off or no, made trial of them and shot them off, but thought nothing at all. After prayer we prepared ourselves for breakfast and for a journey—and it being now the twilight in the morning, it was thought moot to carry the things down to the shallop. Some said it was not best to carry the armor down, others said, they would be readier. Two or three said they would not carry theirs till they went themselves, but mistrusting nothing at all. As it fell out, the water not being high enough, they laid the things down upon the shore, and came up to breakfast. Anon, all upon a sudden, we heard a great and sudden cry, which we knew to be the same voices, though they varied their notes. One of our company, being abroad, came running in, and cried "They are men! Indians! Indians!" and withal their arrows came flying amongst us. Our men ran out with all speed to recover their arms as by the good Providence of God they did. In the meantime, Captain Miles Standish, having a snaphance ready, made a shot, and after him another.

After they two had shot, other two of us were ready, but he wished us not to shoot till we could take aim, for we knew not what need we should have—and there were four only of us which had their arms there ready, and stood before the open side of our barricade, which was first assaulted. They thought it best to defend it, lest the enemy should take it and our stuff, and so have the more vantage against us. Our care was no less for the shallop but we hoped all the rest would defend it. We called unto them to know how it was with them and they answered "Be of good courage!" We heard three of their pieces go off, and the rest called for a firebrand to light their matches. One took a log out of the fire on his shoulder and went and carried it unto them—which was thought did not a little discourage our enemies.

The cry of our enemies was dreadful, especially when our men ran out to recover their arms. Their note was after this manner "*Woath woach ha ha hach woach.*" Our men were no sooner come to their arms, but the enemy was ready to assault them. There was a lusty man, and no witless valiant, who was thought to be their captain, stood behind a tree within half a musket shot of us, and there let his arrows fly at us. He was seen to shoot three arrows, which were all avoided, for he, at whom the first arrow was aimed saw it, and stooped down, and it flew over him. The rest were avoided also. He stood three shots of a musket. At length one took, as he said, full aim at him, after which he gave an extra ordinary cry, and away they went all.

We followed them about a quarter of a mile—but we left six to keep our shallop, for we were careful of our business.

Then we shouted all together two several times, and shot off a couple of muskets, and so returned. This we did that they might see we were not afraid of them, nor discouraged. Thus it pleased God to vanquish our enemies and give us deliverance. By their noise we could not guess that they were less than thirty or forty, though some thought that they were many more.

Yet, in the dark of the morning, we could not so well discern them among the trees, as they could see us by our fire side. We took up 18 of their arrows, which we have sent to England by Master Jones—some whereof were headed with brass, others with harts horn, and others with eagles claws. Many more no doubt were shot, for these we found were almost covered with leaves, yet, by the especial Providence of God, none of them either hit or hurt us, though many came close by us and on every side of us, and some coats which hung up in our barricade were shot through and through. So after we had given God thanks for our deliverance, we took our shallop and went on our journey, and called this place the *First Encounter*. From hence we intended to have sailed to the aforesaid Thievish Harbor if we found no convenient harbor by the way. Having the wind good we sailed all that day along the coast about 15 leagues—but saw neither river nor creek to put into. After we had sailed an hour or two, it began to snow and rain, and to be bad weather. About the midst of the afternoon the wind increased, and the seas began to be very rough and the hinges of the rudder broke, so that we could steer no longer with it, but two men with much ado were fain to serve with a couple of oars. The seas were grown so great that we were much troubled and in great danger and night grew on. Anon, Master Coppin bade us be of good cheer, he saw the harbor. As we drew near, the gale being stiff, and we bearing great sail to get in, split our mast in 3 pieces, and were like to have cast away our shallop. Yet, by God's mercy recovering ourselves, we had the flood with us, and struck into the harbor.

Now he that thought that had been the place, was deceived, it being a place where not any of us had been before and coming into the harbor, he that was our pilot did bear up northward, which if we had continued, we had been cast away. Yet still the Lord kept us, and we bare up for an island before us and recovering of that island, being compassed about with many rocks, and dark night growing upon us, it pleased the divine Providence that we fell upon a place of sandy ground, where our shallop did ride safe and secure all that night, and coming upon a strange island, kept our watch all night in the rain upon that island. And in the morning we marched about it, and found no inhabitants at all—and here we made our rendezvous all that day, being Saturday, 10th of December, on the Sabbath day we rested and on Monday we sounded the harbor, and found it a very good harbor for our shipping. We marched also into the land, and found divers cornfields, and little running brooks, a place very good for situation. So we returned to our ship again with good news to the rest of our people, which did much comfort their hearts. On the fifteenth day we weighed anchor to go to the place we had discovered—and coming within two leagues of the land, we could not fetch the harbor, but were fain to put room again towards Cape Cod, our course lying west, and the wind was at northwest. But it pleased God that the next day, being Saturday the 16th day, the wind came fair, and we put to sea again, and came safely into a safe harbor and within half an hour the wind changed, so as if we had been letted but a little, we had gone back to Cape Cod. This harbor is a bay greater than Cape Cod, compassed with a goodly land and in the bay 2 fine islands uninhabited, wherein are nothing but wood, oaks, pines, walnut, beech, sassafras, vines, and other trees which we know not. This bay is a most hopeful place—innumerable store of fowl, and excellent good—and cannot but be of fish in their seasons—skate, cod, turbot, and herring, we have tasted of—abundance of mussels, the greatest and best ever we saw—crabs and lobsters in their time infinite. It is in fashion like a sickle—or fish hook.

Postscript

Following the events mentioned above, the Pilgrims endured a harsh winter of which many died tragically. The following spring their encounters with nearby Indians increased of which led to legendary friendships with Squanto, Samoset, and Massasoit. It is because of these associations that the Pilgrims were able to survive their first year in the New World. Today the picturesque town of Plymouth serves as a must-visit tourist destination for devoted history buffs. Many prominent Americans from the past claim Pilgrim blood in their veins including John Adams, Humphrey Bogart, Amelia Earhart, George Eastman, Thomas Edison, Sally Field, Jane Fonda, Marilyn Monroe, Laura Ingalls Wilder and the Wright brothers to name a few.

John Knight

Excerpt from *Narratives of a Late Expedition Against the Indians* first published in 1783. The horrifying experiences of John Knight and John Slover were recounted in their own words—compiled and edited by noted historian Hugh Henry Brackenridge. It has been reprinted several times.

About the latter end of the month of March or the beginning of April of the present year, the western Indians began to make incursions upon the frontiers of Ohio, Washington, Yohogania, and Westmoreland Counties, which has been their constant practice ever since the commencement of the present war between the United States and Great Britain. In consequence of these predatory invasions the principal officers of the abovementioned counties, namely, Colonels Williamson and Marshall tried every method in their power to set on foot an expedition against the Wyandot towns, which they could affect no other way than by giving all possible encouragement to volunteers. The plan proposed was as follows—every man furnishing himself with a horse, a gun, and one month's provision should be exempted from two tours of militia duty. Likewise, that everyone who had been plundered by the Indians, should, if the plunder could be found at their towns, have it again, proving it to be his property—and all horses lost on the expedition by unavoidable accident were to be replaced by horses taken in the enemy's country. The time appointed for the rendezvous or general meeting of the volunteers was fixed to be on the 20th of May, and the place, the old Mingo town on the west side of the river Ohio about forty miles below Fort Pitt by land—and I think about 75 by water. Colonel Crawford was solicited by the general voice of these western counties and districts to command the expedition. He accordingly set out as a volunteer and came to Fort Pitt two days before the time appointed for the assembling of the men. As there was no surgeon yet appointed to go with the expedition Colonel Crawford begged the favor of General Irvine to permit me to accompany him (my consent having been previously asked) to which the general agreed provided Colonel Gibbon did not object. Having obtained permission of the Colonel I left Fort Pitt on Tuesday, May 1st, and the next day about one in the afternoon arrived at the Mingo bottom. The volunteers had not all crossed the river until Friday morning the 24th, they then distributed themselves into eighteen companies, choosing their captains by vote. There were chosen, also, one colonel commandant, four field and one brigade major. There were four hundred and sixty-five who voted. We began our march on Saturday May 25th, making almost a due west course, and on the fourth day reached the old Moravian town, upon the Muskingum River about 60 miles from the Ohio River. Some of the men having lost their horses on the night preceding, returned home.

    Tuesday the 28th in the evening, Major Brenton and Captain Bean went some distance from camp to reconnoiter, having gone about one quarter of a mile they saw two Indians, upon whom they fired, and then returned to camp. This was the first place in which we were discovered, as we understood afterwards. On Thursday the fourth of June, which was the eleventh day of our march, about one o'clock we came to the spot where the town of Sandusky formerly stood. The inhabitants had moved 18 miles lower down the creek nearer the lower Sandusky, but as neither our guides or any who were with us had known anything of their removal we began to conjecture there were no Indian towns nearer than the lower Sandusky, which was at least 40 miles distant. However, after refreshing our horses we advanced on in search of some of their settlements, but had scarcely got the distance of three or four miles from the old town when a number of our men expressed their desire to return, some of them alleging that they had only five days provision—upon which the field officers and captains, determined, in council, to proceed that afternoon and no longer. Previous to the calling of this council, a small party of light horse had been sent forward to reconnoiter. I shall here remark, by the way, that there are a great many extensive Plains in that country—the woods in general grow very thin and free from brush and underwood so that light horsemen may advance a considerable distance before an army without being much exposed to the enemy. Just as the council ended, an express returned from the above mentioned party of light horse with intelligence, "that they had been about three miles in front, and had seen a large body of Indians running towards them." In a short time we saw the rest of the light horse, who joined us, and having gone one mile further met a number of Indians who had partly got possession of a piece of woods before us, whilst we were in the Plains, but our men alighting from their horses and rushing into the woods soon obliged them to abandon that place. The enemy being by this time reinforced flanked to the right and part of them coming in our rear quickly made the action more serious. The firing continued very warm on both sides from four o'clock until the dusk of the evening—each party maintaining their ground. Next morning about six o'clock some guns were discharged at the distance of two or three hundred yards, which continued till day, doing little or no execution on either side. The field officers then assembled and agreed as the enemy were every moment increasing and we had already a number wounded, to retreat that night. The whole body was to form into three lines, keeping the wounded in the center. We had four killed and twenty-three wounded, of the latter, seven very dangerously, on which account as many biers were got ready to carry them—most of the rest were slightly wounded and none so bad but they could ride on horseback. After dark the officers went on the outposts and brought in all the men as expeditiously as they could. Just as the troops were about to form, several guns were fired by the enemy, upon which some of our men spoke out and said our intention was discovered by the Indians who were firing alarm guns. Upon which some in front hurried off and the rest immediately followed—leaving the seven men that were dangerously wounded—some of whom however got off on horseback by means of some good friends who waited for and assisted them. We had not got a quarter of a mile from the field of action when I heard Colonel Crawford calling for his son John Crawford, his son-in-law Major Harrison, Major Rose and William Crawford, his nephews, upon which I came up and told him I believed they were before us—he asked was that the doctor? I told him it was—he then replied they were not in front and begged of me not to leave him—I promised him I would not.

We then waited and continued calling for these men till the troops had passed us. The Colonel told me his horse had almost given out—that he could not keep up with the troops and wished some of his best friends to remain with him—he then exclaimed against the militia for riding off in such an irregular manner and leaving some of the wounded behind—contrary to his orders. Presently there came two men riding after us—one of them an old man—the other a lad. We inquired if they had seen any of the above persons? They answered they had not.

By this time there was a very hot firing before us, and, as we judged, near where our main body must have been. Our course was then nearly southwest, but changing it we went north about two miles, the two men remaining in company with us. Judging ourselves to be now out of the enemy's lines, we took a due east course, taking care to keep at the distance of fifteen or twenty yards apart, and directing ourselves by the North Star. The old man often lagged behind and when this was the case never failed to call for us to halt for him. When we were near the Sandusky Creek he fell one hundred yards, and bawled out, as usual, for us to halt. While we were preparing to reprimand him for making a noise I heard an Indian halloo, as I thought one hundred and fifty yards from the man and partly behind him. After this we did not hear the man call again—neither did he ever come up to us anymore. It was now past midnight, and about daybreak Colonel Crawford's and the young man's horses gave out and they left them. We pursued our journey eastward, and about two o'clock fell in with Captain Biggs who had carried Lieutenant Ashley from the field of action, who had been dangerously wounded. We then went on about the space of an hour, when a heavy rain coming on we concluded it was best to encamp, as we were encumbered with the wounded officer.

We then barked four or five trees—made an encampment and a fire and remained there all that night. Next morning we again prosecuted our journey, and having gone about three miles found a deer which had been recently killed. The meat was sliced from the bones and bundled up in the skin with a tomahawk lying by it. We carried all with us and in advancing about one mile further, espied the smoke of a fire. We then gave the wounded officer into the charge of the young man, desiring him to stay behind whilst the colonel, the captain, and myself, walked up as cautiously as we could toward the fire. When we came to it, we concluded from several circumstances some of our people had encamped there the preceding night. We then went about roasting the venison, and when just about to march observed one of our men coming upon our tracks. He seemed at first very shy, but having called to him he came up and told us he was the person who had killed the deer, but upon hearing us come up, was afraid of Indians, hid it in a thicket and made off. Upon this we gave him some bread and roasted venison, proceeded altogether on our journey and about two o'clock came upon the paths by which we had gone out. Captain Biggs and myself did not think it safe to keep the road, but the colonel said the Indians would not follow the troops farther than the Plains, which we were then considerably past. As the wounded officer rode Captain Biggs's horse I lent the captain mine—the Colonel and myself went about one hundred yards in front, the Captain and the wounded officer in the center—and the two young men behind. After we had traveled about one mile and a half, several Indians started up within fifteen or twenty steps of the Colonel and me. As we at first discovered only three, I immediately got behind a large black oak, made ready my piece and raised it up to take fight, when the colonel called to me twice not to fire—upon that one of the Indians ran up to the Colonel and took him by the hand. The Colonel then told me to put down my gun, which I did. At that instant one of them came up to me whom I had formerly seen very often, called me doctor and took me by the hand. They were Delaware Indians of the Wingenim tribe. Captain Biggs fired amongst them but did no execution. They then told us to call these people and make them come there, else they would go and kill them, which the Colonel did, but they got four off and escaped for that time. The Colonel and I were then taken to the Indian camp, which was about half a mile from the place where we were captivated. On Sunday evening five Delawares who had posted themselves at some distance further on the road brought back to the camp, where we lay, Captain Biggs's and Lieutenant Ashley's scalps, with an Indian scalp which Captain Biggs had taken in the field of action—they also brought in Biggs's horse and mine. They told us the two other men got away from them. Monday morning the tenth of June we were paraded to march to Sandusky, about 33 miles distant—they had eleven prisoners of us and four scalps, the Indians being seventeen in number.

Colonel Crawford was very desirous to see a certain Simon Girty, who lived with the Indians, and was on this account permitted to go to town the same night, with two warriors to guard him, having orders at the same time to pass by the place where the Colonel had turned out his horse, that they might if possible, find him. The rest of us were taken as far as the old town which was within eight miles of the new. Tuesday morning the 11th, Colonel Crawford was brought out to us on purpose to be marched in with the other prisoners. I asked the Colonel if he had seen Mr. Girty? He told me he had, and that Girty had promised to do everything in his power for him, but that the Indians were very much enraged against the prisoners, particularly Captain Pipe, one of the chiefs. He likewise told me that Girty had informed him that his son-in-law Colonel Harrison and his nephew William Crawford, were made prisoners by the Shawanese, but had been pardoned. This Captain Pipe had come from the towns about an hour before Colonel Crawford and had painted all the prisoners faces black. As he was painting me he told me I should go to the Shawanese towns and see my friends. When the Colonel arrived he painted him black also—told him he was glad to see him—and that he would have him shaved when he came to see his friends at the Wyandot town. When we marched, the Colonel and I were kept back between Pipe and Wingenim, the two Delaware chiefs, the other nine prisoners were sent forward with another party of Indians. As we went along we saw four of the prisoners lying by the path tomahawked and scalped, some of them were at the distance of half a mile from each other. When we arrived within half a mile of the place where the Colonel was executed we overtook the five prisoners that remained alive—the Indians had caused them to sit down on the ground—as they did also the Colonel and me at some distance from them I was there given in charge to an Indian fellow to be taken to the Shawanese towns. In the place where we were now made to sit down, there was a number of squaws and boys who fell on the five prisoners and tomahawked them. There was a certain John McKinley amongst the prisoners, formerly an officer in the 13th Virginia regiment—whose head on old squaw cut off and the Indians kicked it about upon the ground. The young Indian fellows came often where the Colonel and I were and dashed the scalps in our faces. We were then conducted along toward the place where the Colonel was afterwards executed when we came within about half a mile of it Simon Girty met us with several Indians on horseback. He spoke to the Colonel, but as I was about one hundred and fifty yards behind I could not hear what passed between them. Almost every Indian we met struck us either with sticks or their fists. Girty waited till I was brought up and asked was that the doctor? I told him, yes, and went toward him reaching out my hand but he bid me begone and called me a damned rascal upon which the fellow who had me in charge pulled me along. Girty rode up after me and told me I was to go to the Shawanese towns. When we were come to the fire the Colonel was stripped naked, ordered to sit down by the fire and then they beat him with sticks and their fists. Presently after, I was treated in the same manner. They then tied a rope to the foot of a post about fifteen feet high, bound the Colonel's hands behind his back and fastened the rope to the ligature between his wrists. The rope was long enough either for him to sit down or walk round the post once or twice and return the same way.

    The Colonel then called to Girty and asked if they intended to burn him? Girty answered, yes. The Colonel said he would take it all patiently. Upon this Captain Pipe, a Delaware chief, made a speech to the Indians, about thirty or forty men, sixty or seventy squaws and boys. When the speech was finished they all yelled a hideous and hearty assent to what had been said. The Indian men then took up their guns and shot powder into the Colonel's body, from his feet as far up as his neck. I think not less than seventy loads were discharged upon his naked body. They then crowded about him, and to the best of my observation, cut off his ears. When the throng had dispersed a little I saw the blood running from both sides of his head in consequence thereof. The fire was about six or seven yards from the post to which the colonel was tied. It was made of small hickory poles, burnt quite through in the middle, each end of the poles remaining about fix feet in length. Three or four Indians by turns would take up, individually, one of these burning pieces of wood and apply it to his naked body, already burnt black with the powder. These tormentors presented themselves on every side of him, so that whichever way he ran round the post they met him with the burning faggots and poles. Some of the squaws took broad boards upon which they would put a quantify of burning coals and hot embers and throw on him, so that in a short time he had nothing but coals of fire and hot embers to walk upon.

In the midst of these extreme tortures he called to Simon Girty and begged of him to shoot him but Girty making no answer he called to him again. Girty then, by way of derision, told the Colonel he had no gun, at the same time turning about to an Indian who was behind him, laughed heartily, and by all his gestures seemed delighted at the horrid scene. Girty then came up to me and bade me prepare for death. He said, however, I was not to die at that place, but to be burnt at the Shawanese towns. He swore by G—d I need not expect to escape death, but should suffer it in all its extremities. He then observed that some prisoners had given him to understand that if our people had him they would not hurt him, for his part, he said, he did not believe it, but desired to know my opinion of the matter. But being at that time in great anguish and distress for the torments the Colonel was suffering before my eyes, as well as the expectation of undergoing the same fate in two days I made little or no answer. He expressed a great deal of ill will for Colonel Gibson and said he was one of his greatest enemies, and more to the same purpose to all which I paid very little attention. Colonel Crawford at this period of his sufferings besought the Almighty to have mercy on his soul, spoke very low, and bore his torments with the most manly fortitude. He continued in all the extremities of pain for an hour and three quarters or two hours longer, as near as I can judge, when at last being almost spent, he lay down on his belly. They then scalped him and repeatedly threw the scalp in my face, telling me "that was my great captain." An old squaw (whole appearance every way answered the ideas people entertain of the devil) got a board, took a parcel of coals and ashes and laid them on his back and head after he had been scalped. He then raised himself upon his feet and began to walk round the post. They next put a burning stick to him as usual, but he seemed more insensible of pain than before. The Indian fellow who had me in charge now took me away to Captain Pipe's house, about three quarters of a mile from the place of the Colonel's execution.

I was bound all night and thus, prevented from seeing the last of the horrid spectacle. Next morning, being June 12th, the

Indian untied me, painted me black, and we set off for the Shawanese town, which he told me was somewhat less than forty miles from that place. We soon came to the spot where the Colonel had been burnt, as it was partly in our way. I saw his bones laying amongst the remains of the fire, almost burnt to ashes, I suppose after he was dead they had laid his body on the fire. The Indian told me that was my Big Captain and gave the scalp halloo. He was on horseback and drove me before him.

    I pretended to this Indian I was ignorant of the death I was to die at the Shawanese town—effected as cheerful a countenance as possible and asked him if we were not to live together as brothers in one house when we should get to the town? He seemed well-pleased, and said, yes. He then asked me if I could make a wigwam? I told him, I could—he then seemed more friendly—we went that day as near as I can judge about 25 miles, the course partly southwest—the Indian told me we should next day come to the town the sun being in such a direction pointing nearly south. At night when we went to rest I attempted very often to untie myself but the Indian was extremely vigilant and scarcely ever shut his eyes that night. About daybreak he got up and untied me—he next began to mend up the fire and as the gnats were troublesome I asked him if I should make a smoke behind him? He said, yes. I then took the end of a dogwood fork which had been burnt down to about 18 inches long.

    It was the longest stick I could find, yet too small for the purpose I had in view—then I picked up another smaller stick and taking a coal of fire between them went behind him—then turning suddenly about, I struck him on the head with all the force I was master of which so stunned him that he fell forwards with both his hands into the fire, but seeing him recover and get up, I seized his gun while he ran off howling in a most fearful manner. I followed him with a determination to shoot him down, but pulling back the cock of the gun with too great violence I believe I broke the main spring. I pursued him, however, about thirty yards still endeavoring to fire the gun but could not—then going back to the fire I took his blanket—a pair of new moccasins—his hoppes—powder horn—bullet bag (together with the gun) and marched off—directing my course toward the five o'clock mark.

About half an hour before sunset I came to the Plains which I think are about sixteen miles wide. I laid me down in a thicket till dark and then by the assistance of the North Star made my way through them and got into the woods before morning. I proceeded on the next day and about noon crossed the paths by which our troops had gone out. These paths are nearly east and west but I went due north all that afternoon with a view to avoid the enemy. In the evening I began to be very faint, and no wonder, I had been six days a prisoner, the last two days of which I had eaten nothing and but very little the first three or four. There were wild gooseberries in abundance in the woods, but being unripe required mastication, which at that time I was not able to perform on account of a blow received from an Indian on the jaw with the back of a tomahawk. There was a weed that grew plentifully in that place, the juice of which I knew to be grateful and nourishing. I gathered a bundle of the same, took up my lodging under a large spreading beech tree and having sucked plentifully of the juice, went to sleep. Next day I made a due east course which I generally kept the rest of my journey. I often imagined my gun was only wood bound and tried every method I could devise to unscrew the lock but never could effect it having no knife nor anything fitting for the purpose. I had now the satisfaction to find my jaw began to mend and in four or five days could chew any vegetable proper for nourishment, but finding my gun only a useless burden left her in the wilderness. I had no apparatus for making fire to sleep by so that I could get but little rest for the gnats and mosquitoes. There are likewise a great many swamps in the beech ridge which occasioned me very often to lie wet—this ridge through which I traveled is about 20 miles broad, the ground in general very level and rich, free from shrubs and brush. There are, however, very few springs, yet wells might easily be dug in all parts of that ridge. The timber on it is very lofty, but it is no easy matter to make a straight course through the same, the moss growing as high upon the south side of the trees as on the north. There are a great many white oaks, ash and hickory trees that grow among the beech timber. There are likewise some places on the ridge, perhaps for three or four continued miles where there is little or no beech—and in such spots, black, white oak, ash and hickory abound.

Sugar trees grow there also to a very great bulk. The soil is remarkably good, the ground a little ascending and defending with some small rivulets and a few springs. When I got out of the beech ridge and nearer the Muskingum River the lands were more broken but equally rich with those before mentioned, and abounding with brooks and springs of water. There are also several small creeks that empty into that river, the bed of which is more than a mile wide in many places, the woods consist of white and black oaks, walnut, hickory and sugar tree in the greatest abundance. In all parts of the country through which I came the game was very plenty, that is to say, deer, turkeys and pheasants. I likewise saw a great many vestiges of bears and some elks.

I crossed the Muskingum River about three or four miles below Fort Laurens, and crossing all paths aimed for the Ohio River. All this time my food was gooseberries, young nettles, the juice of herbs, a few serviceberries, and some May apples, likewise, two young blackbirds and a terrapin, which I devoured raw. When my food sat heavy on my stomach, I used to eat a little wild ginger which put all to rights. I came upon Ohio River about five miles below Fort McIntosh, in the evening of the 21st day after I had made my escape, and on the twenty second, about seven o'clock in the morning, being the fourth day of July, arrived safe, though very much fatigued, at the fort.

John Slover

Excerpt from *Narratives of a Late Expedition Against the Indians* first published in 1783. The horrifying experiences of John Knight and John Slover were recounted in their own words—compiled and edited by noted historian Hugh Henry Brackenridge. It has been reprinted several times.

Having in the last war been a prisoner amongst the Indians many years, and so being well-acquainted with the country west of the Ohio I was employed as a guide in the expedition under Colonel William Crawford against the Indian towns on or near the Sandusky River. It will be unnecessary for me to relate what is so well-known, the circumstances and unfortunate event of that expedition—it will be sufficient to observe—that having on Tuesday the fourth of June fought the enemy near Sandusky, we lay that night in our camp, and the next day fired on each other at the distance of three hundred yards, doing little or no execution. In the evening of that day it was proposed by Colonel Crawford, as I have been since informed, to draw off with order—but at the moment of our retreat the Indians (who had probably perceived that we were about to retire) firing alarm guns, our men broke and rode off in confusion, treading down those who were on foot and leaving the wounded men who supplicated to be taken with them. I was with some others on the rear of our troops feeding our horses in the glade, when our men began to break. The main body of our people had passed by me a considerable distance before I was ready to set out. I overtook them before they crossed the glade, and was advanced almost in front. The company in which I was had separated from me—and had endeavored to pass a morass—for coming up I found their horses had stuck fast in the morass—and endeavoring to pass—mine also in a short time stuck fast. I ought to have said, the company of five or six men with which I had been immediately connected, and who were some distance to the right of the main body, had separated from me and etc. I tried a long time to disengage my horse, until I could hear the enemy just behind me and on each side—but in vain. Here then I was obliged to leave him.

The morass was so unstable that I was to the middle in it and it was with the greatest difficulty that I got across it but which having at length done, I came up with the six men who had left their horses in the same manner I had done—two of these, my companions, having lost their guns. We traveled that night making our course towards Detroit, with a view to shun the enemy, who we conceived to have taken the paths by which the main body of our people had retreated. Just before day we got into a second deep morass—and were under the necessity of detaining until it was light to see our way through it. The whole of this day we traveled toward the Shawnee towns, with a view of throwing ourselves still farther out of the search of the enemy.

About ten o'clock this day we sat down to eat a little having tasted nothing from Tuesday, the day of our engagement until this time which was on Thursday—and now the only thing we had to eat was a scrap of pork to each. We had sat down just by a warrior's path which we had not suspected, when eight or nine warriors appeared. Running off hastily we left our baggage and provisions, but were not discovered by the party for skulking sometime in the grass and bushes, we returned to the place and recovered our baggage. The warriors had hallooed as they passed, and were answered by others on our flanks. In our journey through the glades, or wide extended dry meadows about twelve o'clock this day we discovered a party of Indians in front, but skulking in the grass and bushes were not perceived by them. In these glades we were in great danger, as we could be seen at a great distance. In the afternoon of this day there fell a heavy rain, the coldest I ever felt. We halted while it rained, and then traveling on we saw a party of the enemy about two hundred yards before us, but hiding ourselves in the bushes, we had again the good fortune not to be discovered. This night we got out of the glades, having in the night crossed the paths by which we had advanced to Sandusky. It was our design to leave all these paths to the right and to come in by the Tuscarawas.

We should have made a much greater progress had it not been for two of our companions who were lame—the one having his foot burnt—the other with a swelling in his knee of a rheumatic nature. On this day, which was the second after the retreat, one of our company, the person affected with the rheumatic swelling, was left behind some distance in a swamp.

Waiting for him some time we saw him coming within one hundred yards as I sat on the body of an old tree mending my moccasins—but taking my eye from him I saw him no more. He had not observed our tracks, but had gone a different way. We whistled on our chargers and afterwards hallooed for him, but in vain. Nevertheless he was fortunate in missing us, for he afterwards came safe into Wheeling. We traveled on until night, and were on the waters of Muskingum from the middle of this day. Having caught a fawn this day we made a fire in the evening, and had a repast, having in the meantime eat nothing but the small bit of pork I mentioned before. We set off at break of day. About nine o'clock the third day we fell in with a party of the enemy about twenty miles from the Tuscarawas, which is about 135 miles from Fort Pitt. They had come upon our tracks, or had been on our flanks and discovered us, and then having got before had way laid us, and fired before we perceived them. At the first fire one of my companions fell before me, and another just behind, these two had guns, there were six men in company, and four guns, two of these rendered useless by reason of being wet when coming through the swamp the first night. We had tried to discharge them, but could not. When the Indians fired I ran to a tree, but an Indian presenting himself fifteen yards before me desired me to deliver myself up and I should not be hurt.

My gun was in good order, but apprehending the enemy behind might discharge their pieces at me, I did not risk firing, which I had afterwards reason to regret, when I found what was to be my fate—and that the Indian who was before me and presented his gun—was one of those who had just before fired. Two of my companions were taken with me in the same manner, the Indians assuring us we should not be hurt. But one in company, James Paul, who had a gun in order, made his escape, and has since come into Wheeling. One of these Indians knew me, and was of the party by whom I was taken in the last war.

He came up and spoke to me calling me by my Indian name, and upbraiding me for coming to war against them. I will take a moment here to relate some particulars of my first captivity, and my life since. I was taken from New River in Virginia by the Miami, a nation of Indians by us called the Picts, amongst whom I lived six years—afterwards being sold to a Delaware, and by him put into the hands of a trader, I was carried amongst the Shawnee, with whom I continued six years so that my whole time amongst these nations was twelve years, that is, from the eighth to the twentieth year of my age. At the treaty at Fort Pitt in the fall preceding what is called Dunmore's War, which, if I am right was in the year 1773, I came in with the Shawnee nation to the treaty, and meeting with some of my relations at that place was by them solicited to relinquish the life of a savage, which I did with some reluctance, this manner of life having become natural to me, inasmuch as I had scarcely known any other. I enlisted as a soldier in the Continental Army at the commencement of the present war, and served fifteen months. Having been properly discharged I have since married, have a family, and am in communion with the church. To return, the party by whom we were made prisoners had taken some horses, and left them at the glades we had passed the day before. They had followed on our tracks from these glades—on our return to which we found the horses and rode. We were carried to Wachatomakak, a town of the Mingo and Shawnee. I think it was on the third day we reached the town, which when we were approaching, the Indians, in whose custody we were, began to look sour, having been kind to us before, and given us a little meat and flour to eat, which they had found or taken from some of our men on their retreat.

This town is small, and we were told was about two miles distant from the main town to which they meant to carry us. The inhabitants from this town came out with clubs and tomahawks, struck, beat and abused us greatly. One of my two companions they seized, and having stripped him naked blacked him with coal and water—this was the sign of being burnt—the man seemed to surmise it, and shed tears. He asked me the meaning of his being blacked, but I was forbidden by the enemy in their own language to tell him what was intended. In English, which they spoke easily, having been often at Fort Pitt, they assured him he was not to be hurt. I know of no reason for making him the first object of their cruelty, unless it was that he was the oldest. A warrior had been sent to the greater town to acquaint them with our coming, and prepare them for the frolic—for on our coming to it, the inhabitants came out with guns, clubs and tomahawks.

We were told that we had to run to the council house about three hundred yards. The man that was blacked was about twenty yards before us—in running the gauntlet they made him their principal object, men, women and children beating him, and those who had guns firing loads of powder on him as he ran naked, putting the muzzles of the guns to his body, shouting, hallooing and beating their drums in the meantime. The unhappy man had reached the door of the council house, beaten and wounded in a manner shocking to the fight—for having arrived before him we had it in our power to view the spectacle—it was indeed the most horrid that can be conceived—they had cut him with their tomahawks, shot his body black, burnt it into holes with loads of powder blown into him, a large wadding had made a wound in his shoulder whence the blood gushed. Agreeable to the declaration of the enemy when he first set out, he had reason to think himself secure when he had reached the door of the council house. This seemed to be his hope, for coming up with great struggling and endeavor he laid hold of the door but was pulled back and drawn away by them—finding they intended no mercy, but putting him to death he attempted several times to snatch or lay hold of some of their tomahawks, but being weak could not affect it. We saw him borne off and they were a long time beating, wounding, pursuing and killing him.

That same evening I saw the dead body of this man close by the council house. It was mangled cruelly and the blood mingled with the powder was rendered black. The same evening I saw him, after he had been cut into pieces and his limbs and his head about two hundred yards on the outside of the town put on poles. That evening also I saw the bodies of three others in the same black and mangled condition. These I was told had been put to death the same day and just before we had recalled the town. Their bodies as they lay were black, bloody, burnt with powder, two of these were [William] Harrison and young [William] Crawford. I knew the visage of Colonel Harrison and I saw his clothing and that of young Crawford at the town. They brought horses to me and asked if I knew them? I said they were Harrison's and Crawford's. They said they were. The third of these men I did not know, but believe to have been Colonel [John] McClelland, the third in command on the expedition.

The next day the bodies of these men were dragged to the outside of the town, and their carcasses being given to the dogs, their limbs and heads were stuck on poles. My surviving companion shortly after we had reached the council house was sent to another town, and I presume he was burnt or executed in the same manner. In the evening the men assembled in the council house—this is a large building about fifty yards in length and about twenty five yards wide—and about sixteen feet in height—built of split poles covered with bark—their first object was to examine me—which they could do in their own language inasmuch as I could speak the Miami, Shawnee, and Delaware languages which I had learned during my early captivity in the last war, I found I had not forgotten these languages, especially the two former, as well as my native tongue. They began with interrogating me concerning the situation of our country.

What were our provisions? Our numbers? The state of the war between us and Britain? I informed them Cornwallis had been taken, which next day, when Matthew Elliott with James Girty came—he affirmed to be a lie—and the Indians seemed to give full credit to his declaration. Hitherto I had been treated with some appearance of kindness—but now the enemy began to alter their behavior towards me. Girty had informed them, that when he asked me how I liked to live there I had said that I intended to take the first opportunity to take a scalp and run off. It was—to be sure—very probable that if I had such intention—I would communicate it to him. Another man came to me and told me a story of his having lived on the south branch of Potomac in Virginia—and having three brothers there—he pretended he wanted to get away—but I suspected his design—nevertheless he reported that I had contented to go. In the meantime I was not tied, and could have escaped, but having nothing to put on my feet, I waited some time longer to provide for this. I was invited every night to the war dances, which they usually continued until almost day. I could not comply with their desire, believing these things to be the service of the devil. The council lasted fifteen days—from fifty to one hundred warriors being usually in council and sometimes more. Every warrior is admitted to these councils but only the chiefs or head warriors have the privilege of speaking. The head warriors are accounted such from the number of scalps and prisoners they have taken. The third day [Alexander] McKee was in council, and afterwards was generally present. He spoke little, and did not ask any questions or speak to me at all. He lives about two miles out of the town, has a house built of squared logs with a shingled roof—he was dressed in gold laced cloths I had seen him at the former town through which I passed. I think it was on the last day of the council, save one, that a speech came from Detroit, brought by a warrior who had been counseling with the commanding officer at that place. The speech had been long expected, and was in answer to one sometime before sent from the town to Detroit—it was in a belt of Wampum, and began with addressing them "My children" and inquiring why they continued to take prisoners? "Provisions are scarce—when prisoners are brought in we are obliged to maintain them, and still some of them are running away, and carrying tidings of our affairs. When any of your people fall into the hands of the rebels they show no mercy—why then should you take prisoners? Take no more prisoners, my children, of any fort, man, woman or child." Two days after a party of every nation that was near being collected, it was determined on to take no more prisoners of any fort. They had held a large council, and the determination was that if it were possible they could find a child of a span or three inches long, they would show no mercy to it. At the conclusion of the council it was agreed upon by all the tribes present, the Ottawa, Chippewa, the Wyandot, the Mingo, the Delaware, the Shawnee, the Munsee, and a part of the Cherokees, that should any of the nations who were not present take any prisoner, these would rise against them, take away the prisoners and put them to death. In the course of these deliberations I understood what was said perfectly. They laid plans against our settlements of Kentucky, the Falls, and towards Wheeling. These it will be unnecessary for me to mention in this narrative, more especially as the Indians finding me to have escaped, and knowing that I would not fail to communicate these designs, will be led to alter their resolutions. There was one council held at which I was not present. The warriors had sent for me as usual, but the squaw with whom I lived would not suffer me to go, but hid me under a large quantity of skins. It may have been from an unwillingness that I should hear in council the determination with respect to me, that I should be burnt. About this time twelve men were brought in from Kentucky, three of whom were burnt on this day—the remainder was distributed to other towns—and all, as the Indians informed me, were burnt. This was after the speech came from Detroit. On this day also I saw an Indian who had just come into town, and who said that the prisoner he was bringing to be burnt, and who he said was a doctor, had made his escape from him. I knew this must have been Dr. Knight, who went as surgeon of the expedition. The Indian had a wound four inches long in his head, which he acknowledged the doctor had given him. He was cut to the skull. His story was, that he had untied the doctor, being asked by him to do so, the doctor promising that he would not go away—that while he was employed in kindling the fire, the doctor snatched up the gun, had come behind and struck him—that he then made a stroke at the doctor with his knife, which he laid hold of, and his fingers were cut almost off, the knife being drawn through his hand—that he gave the doctor two stabs, one in the belly, the other in the back—said the doctor was a great, big, tall, strong man. Being now adopted in an Indian family, and having some confidence for my safety, I took the liberty to contradict this, and said that I knew the doctor, who was a weak, little man. The other warriors laughed immoderately, and did not seem to credit him. At this time I was told that Colonel Crawford was burnt, and they greatly exulted over it. The day after the council I have mentioned, about forty warriors accompanied by George Girty came early in the morning round the house where I was.

  The squaw gave me up, I was sitting before the door of the house, they put a rope round my neck, tied my arms behind my back, stripped me naked, and blacked me in the usual manner. George Girty as soon as I was tied, damned me, and said that I now should get what I had deserved many years. I was led away to a town distant about five miles, to which a messenger had been dispatched to desire them to prepare to receive me. Arriving at this town I was beaten with clubs and the pipe ends of their tomahawks, and was kept for some time tied to a tree before a house door. In the meanwhile the inhabitants set out to another town about two miles distant, where I was to be burnt, and where I arrived about three o'clock in the afternoon. Here also was a council house, part of it covered and part of it without a roof. In the part of it where no cover was, but only sides built up there stood a post about sixteen feet in height, and in the middle of the house around the post, there were three piles of wood built about three feet high and four feet from the post. Being brought to the post my arms were tied behind me, and the thong or cord with which they were bound was fastened to the post—a rope also was put about my neck—and tied to the post about four feet above my head. During the time they were tying me, piles of wood were kindled and begin to flame. Death by burning, which appeared to be now my fate, I had resolved to sustain with patience. The divine grace of God had made it less alarming to me, for on my way this day I had been greatly exercised in regard to my latter end. I knew myself to have been a regular member of the church, and to have sought repentance for my sins—but though I had often heard of the faith of assurance, had known nothing of it, but early this day, instantaneously by a change wrought upon me, sudden and perceivable as lightning, an assurance of my peace made with God, sprung up in my mind.

The following words were the subject of my meditation "In peace thou shalt see God. Fear not those who can kill the body. In peace shalt thou depart." I was on this occasion by a confidence in mind not to be resisted, fully assured of my salvation. This being the case, I was willing, satisfied, and glad to die. I was tied to the post, as I have already said, and the flame was now kindled. The day was clear, not a cloud to be seen, if there were clouds low in the horizon, the sides of the house prevented me from seeing them, but I heard no thunder, or observed any sign of approaching rain. Just as the fire of one pile began to blaze, the wind rose, from the time they began to kindle the fire and to tie me to the post, until the wind began to blow, was about fifteen minutes. The wind blew a hurricane, and the rain followed in less than three minutes. The rain fell violent and the fire, though it began to blaze considerably, was instantly extinguished. The rain lasted about a quarter of an hour.

When it was over the savages stood amazed, and were a long time silent. At last one said, we will let him alone till morning, and take a whole day's frolic in burning him. The sun at this time was about three hours high. It was agreed upon, and the rope about my neck was untied, and making me sit down, they began to dance around me. They continued dancing in this manner until eleven o'clock at night—in the meantime, beating, kicking, and wounding me with their tomahawks and clubs. At last one of the warriors, the Half Moon, asked me if I was sleepy. I answered, yes. The head warrior then chose out three men to take care of me. I was taken to a blockhouse—my arms were tied until the cord was hidden in the flesh—they were tied in two places, round the wrist and above the elbows. A rope was fastened about my neck, and tied to a beam of the house, but permitting me to lie down on a board. The three warriors were constantly harassing and troubling me, saying, "How will you like to eat fire tomorrow—you will kill no more Indians now." I was in expectation of their going to sleep when at length, about an hour before daybreak, two laid down, the third smoked a pipe, talked to me, and asked the same painful questions. About half an hour after he also lay down—and I heard him begin to snore.

Instantly I went to work, and as my arms were perfectly dead with the cord, I laid myself down upon my right arm which was behind my back, and keeping it fast with my fingers, which had still some life and strength, I slipped the cord from my left arm over my elbow and my wrist. One of the warriors now got up and stirred the fire, I was apprehensive that I should be examined, and thought it was over with me, but my hopes revived when now he lay down again. I then attempted to unloose the rope about my neck, tried to gnaw it but in vain, as it was as thick as my thumb and as hard as iron, being made of a buffalo hide, I wrought with it a long time, gave it out, and could see no relief. At this time I saw daybreak and heard the cock crow. I made a second attempt almost without hope, pulling the rope by putting my fingers between my neck and it, and to my great surprise it came easily untied, it was a noose with two or three knots tied over it. I stepped over the warriors as they lay, and having got out of the house looked back to see if there was any disturbance. I then ran through the town into a cornfield. In my way I saw a squaw with four or five children lying asleep under a tree—going a different way into the field I untied my arm which was greatly swelled and turned black—having observed a number of horses in the glade as I ran through it, I went back to catch one, and on my way found a piece of an old rug or quilt hanging on a fence which I took with me—having caught the horse—the rope with which I had been tied serving for a halter I rode off. The horse was strong and swift, and the woods being open and the country level, about ten o'clock that day I crossed the Scioto River at a place by computation fifty full miles from the town. I had rode about twenty five miles on this side Scioto by three o'clock in the afternoon, when the horse began to fail and could no longer go on a trot. I instantly left him and on foot ran about twenty miles farther that day, making in the whole the distance of near one hundred miles. In the evening I heard hallooing behind me and for this reason did not halt until about ten o'clock at night, when I sat down, was extremely sick and vomited but when the moon rose which might have been about two hours after, I went on and traveled until day. During the night I had a path, but in the morning judged it prudent to forsake the path and take a ridge for the distance of fifteen miles, in a line at right angles to my course, putting back as I went along, with a stick, the weeds which I had bended, lest I should be tracked by the enemy. I lay the next night on the waters of Muskingum, the nettles had been troublesome to me after my crossing the Scioto, having nothing to defend myself but the piece of a rug which I had found, and which while I rode I used under me by way of saddle—the briars and thorns were now painful to and prevented me from traveling in the night until the moon appeared. In the meantime I was hindered from sleeping by the mosquitoes, for even in the day I was under the necessity of traveling with a handful of bushes to brush them from my body. The second night I reached Cushakim, next day came to Newcomer's Town, where I got about seven raspberries, which were the first thing I ate from the morning in which the Indians had taken me to burn me until this time, which was now about three o'clock the fourth day. I felt hunger very little—but was extremely weak. I swam Muskingum River at Oldcomer's Town—the river being about two hundred yards wide having reached the bank I sat down, looked back and thought I had a start of the Indians if any should pursue. That evening I traveled about five miles, next day came to Stillwater a small river—in a branch of which I got two small crawfish to eat.

Next night I lay within five miles of Wheeling, but had not slept a wink during this whole time—being rendered impossible by the mosquitoes—which it was my constant employment to brush away. Next day came to Wheeling and saw a man on the island in the Ohio opposite to that post, and calling to him and asking for particular persons who had been on the expedition, and telling him I was Slover, at length, with great difficulty, he was persuaded to come over and bring me across in his canoe.

Daniel Boone

Foreword

This brief memoir is the only known writings by Daniel Boone. His brief autobiography first published in 1784—covers a portion of his life concentrating on his legendary quest to settle the Kentucky frontier. Boone had planned to write a complete account of his life but for whatever reasons never got around to completing a published version detailing his famed exploits. Apparently according to one well-known story told mostly by Daniel Boone himself when he was older—he mentions an autobiographical version about his life and times he wrote that was supposedly lost in a canoe mishap of which is mentioned in several biographies about Boone. According to other accounts, a second attempt at writing a full-length autobiography in his later years with a ghostwriter ended when Boone lost interest in completing the book, and the project was scrapped. Many biographies have been written about Boone—but few have had personal insight into his true character and world. His own words—dictated to historian John Filson offer a personal look at Boone's life and his adventures in Kentucky. This slim memoir is his legacy—one that allows him to achieve immortality through his own words—not imagined events created by sloppy biographers—carelessly blending fact and fiction together and passing it off as truth which too often has been the results of numerous so-called truthful accounts of Boone's exploits.

Autobiography of Daniel Boone

Dictated to writer and historian John Filson and first published in 1784 as part of a book about the settling of Kentucky and of Boone's legendary skirmishes with Indians titled *Discovery, Settlement and Present state of Kentucke*. Daniel Boone would later say of the material when questioned about its authenticity concerning his memoir *"it is every word true."*

Curiosity is natural to the soul of man, and interesting objects have a powerful influence on our affections. Let these influencing powers actuate, by the permission of disposal of Providence, from selfish or social views, yet in time the mysterious will of heaven is unfolded, and we behold our conduct, from whatsoever motives excited, operating to answer the important designs of heaven. Thus we behold Kentucky lately an howling wilderness, the habitation of savages and wild beasts become a fruitful field—this region, so favorably distinguished by nature, now become the habitation of civilization—at a period unparalleled in history, in the midst of a raging war, and under all the disadvantages of emigration to a country so remote from the inhabited parts of the continent. Here where the hand of violence shed the blood of the innocent—where the horrid yells of savages, and the groans of the distressed sounded in our ears. We now hear the praises and adorations of our Creator—where wretched wigwams stood, the miserable abodes of savages, we behold the foundations of cities laid, that, in all probability, will rival the glory of the greatest upon earth. And we view Kentucky situated on the fertile banks of the great Ohio, rising from obscurity to mine with splendor, equal to any other of the stars of the American hemisphere. The settling of this region well deserves a place in history. Most of the memorable events I have myself been exercised in, and, for the satisfaction of the public will briefly relate the circumstances of my adventures, and scenes of life from my first movement to this country until this day.

It was on the first of May, in the year 1769, that I resigned my domestic happiness for a time, and left my family and peaceable habitation on the Yadkin River, in North Carolina, to wander through the wilderness of America, in quest of the country of Kentucky, in company with John Finley, John Stewart, Joseph Holden, James Monay, and William Cool. We proceeded successfully, and after a long and fatiguing journey through a mountainous wilderness, in a westward direction, on the seventh day of June following, we found ourselves on Red River, where John Finley had formerly been trading with the Indians, and, from the top of an eminence, saw with pleasure the beautiful level of Kentucky. Here let me observe, that for some time we had experienced the most uncomfortable weather as a prelibation of our future sufferings. At this place we encamped and made a shelter to defend us from the inclement season, and began to hunt and reconnoiter the country. We found everywhere abundance of wild beasts of all sorts, through this vast forest. The buffaloes were more frequent than I have seen cattle in the settlements, browsing on the leaves of the cane, or cropping the herbage on those extensive Plains, fearless, because ignorant, of the violence of man. Sometimes we saw hundreds in a drove, and the numbers about the salt springs were amazing. In this forest the habitation of beasts of every kind natural to America, we practiced hunting with great success until the twenty-second day of December following. This day John Stewart and I had a pleasing ramble, but fortune changed the scene in the close of it. We had passed through a great forest, on which stood myriads of trees, some gay with blossoms, others rich with fruits.

Nature was here a series of wonders, and a fund of delight. Here she displayed her ingenuity and industry in a variety of flowers and fruits, beautifully colored, elegantly shaped, and charmingly flavored and we were diverted with innumerable animals presenting themselves perpetually to our view. In the decline of the day, near Kentucky River, as we ascended the brow of a small hill, a number of Indians rushed out of a thick cane brake upon us, and made us prisoners. The time of our sorrow was now arrived, and the scene fully opened. The Indians plundered us of what we had, and kept us in confinement seven days, treating us with common savage usage. During this time we discovered no uneasiness or desire to escape, which made them less suspicious of us—but in the dead of night, as we lay in a thick cane brake by a large fire, when sleep had locked up their senses, my situation not disposing me for rest, I touched my companion and gently awoke him. We improved this favorable opportunity, and departed, leaving them to take their rest, and speedily directed our course towards our old camp, but found it plundered, and the company dispersed and gone home.

    About this time my brother, Squire Boone, with another adventurer, who came to explore the country shortly after us, was wandering through the forest, determined to find me, if possible, and accidentally found our camp. Notwithstanding the unfortunate circumstances of our company, and our dangerous situation, as surrounded with hostile savages, our meeting so fortunately in the wilderness made us reciprocally sensible of the utmost satisfaction. So much does friendship triumph over misfortune, that sorrows and sufferings vanish at the meeting not only of real friends, but of the most distant acquaintances, and substitutes happiness in their room. Soon after this, my companion in captivity, John Stewart, was killed by the savages, and the man that came with my brother returned home by himself. We were then in a dangerous, helpless situation, exposed daily to perils and death amongst savages and wild beasts, not a white man in the country but ourselves. Thus situated, many hundred miles from our families in the howling wilderness, I believe few would have equally enjoyed the happiness we experienced. I often observed to my brother, you see now how little nature requires to be satisfied. Felicity, the companion of content, is rather found in our own breasts than in the enjoyment of external things. And I firmly believe it requires but a little philosophy to make a man happy in whatsoever state he is. This consists in a full resignation to the will of Providence and a resigned soul finds pleasure in a path strewed with briars and thorns. We continued not in a state of indolence, but hunted every day, and prepared a little cottage to defend us from the winter storms. We remained there undisturbed during the winter and on the first day of May, 1770, my brother returned home to the settlement by himself, for a new recruit of horses and ammunition, leaving me by myself, without bread, salt or sugar, without company of my fellow creatures, or even a horse or dog. I confess I never before was under greater necessity of exercising philosophy and fortitude. A few days I passed uncomfortably.

  The idea of a beloved wife and family, and their anxiety upon the account of my absence and exposed situation, made sensible impressions on my heart. A thousand dreadful apprehensions presented themselves to my view, and had undoubtedly disposed me to melancholy, if further indulged. One day I undertook a tour through the country, and the diversity and beauties of nature I met with in this charming season, expelled every gloomy and vexatious thought. Just at the close of day the gentle gales retired, and left the place to the disposal of a profound calm. Not a breeze shook the most tremulous leaf. I had gained the summit of a commanding ridge, and, looking round with astonishing delight, beheld the ample plains, the beauteous tracts below. On the other hand, I surveyed the famous river Ohio that rolled in silent dignity, marking the western boundary of Kentucky with inconceivable grandeur. At a vast distance I beheld the mountains lift their venerable brows, and penetrate the clouds. All things were still. I kindled a fire near a fountain of sweet water, and feasted on the loin of a buck, which a few hours before I had killed. The sullen shades of night soon overspread the whole hemisphere, and the earth seemed to gasp after the hovering moisture. My roving excursion this day had fatigued my body, and diverted my imagination. I laid me down to sleep, and I awoke not until the sun had chased away the night. I continued this tour, and in a few days explored a considerable part of the country, each day equally pleased as the first. I returned again to my old camp, which was not disturbed in my absence. I did not confine my lodging to it, but often reposed in thick cane brakes, to avoid the savages, who, I believe, often visited my camp, but fortunately for me, in my absence. In this situation I was constantly exposed to danger, and death. How unhappy such a situation for a man tormented with fear, which is vain if no danger comes, and if it does, only augments the pain. It was my happiness to be destitute of this afflicting passion, with which I had the greatest reason to be affected. The prowling wolves diverted my nocturnal hours with perpetual howling and the various species of animals in this vast forest, in the daytime, were continually in my view. Thus I was surrounded with plenty in the midst of want. I was happy in the midst of dangers and inconveniences. In such a diversity it was impossible I should be disposed to melancholy. No populous city, with all the varieties of commerce and stately structures, could afford so much pleasure to my mind, as the beauties of nature I found here. Thus, through an uninterrupted scene of sylvan pleasures, I spent the time until the 27th day of July following, when my brother, to my great felicity, met me, according to appointment, at our old camp.

  Shortly after, we left this place, not thinking it safe to stay there longer, and proceeded to Cumberland River, reconnoitering that part of the country until March, 1771, and giving names to the different waters. Soon after, I returned home to my family with a determination to bring them as soon as possible to live in Kentucky, which I esteemed a second paradise, at the risk of my life and fortune. I returned safe to my old habitation, and found my family in happy circumstances. I sold my farm on the Yadkin, and what goods we could not carry with us and on the twenty fifth day of September, 1773, bade a farewell to our friends, and proceeded on our journey to Kentucky, in company with five families more, and forty men that joined us in Powell Valley, which is one hundred and fifty miles from the now settled parts of Kentucky. This promising beginning was soon overcast with a cloud of adversity—for upon the tenth day of October, the rear of our company was attacked by a number of Indians, who killed six and wounded one man. Of these my eldest son was one that fell in the action. Though we defended ourselves, and repulsed the enemy, yet this unhappy affair scattered our cattle, brought us into extreme difficulty, and so discouraged the whole company, that we retreated forty miles, to the settlement on Clinch River. We had passed over two mountains, Powell's and Wallen's, and were approaching Cumberland Mountain when this adverse fortune overtook us. These mountains are in the wilderness, as we pass from the old settlements in Virginia to Kentucky, are ranged in a southwest and northeast direction, are of a great length and breadth, and not far distant from each other. Over these, nature hath formed passes, that are less difficult than might be expected from a view of such huge piles. The aspect of these cliffs is so wild and horrid, that it is impossible to behold them without terror. The spectator is apt to imagine that nature had formerly suffered some violent convulsion and that these are the dismembered remains of the dreadful shock—the ruins, not of Persepolis or Palmyra, but of the world. I remained with my family on Clinch until the sixth of June, 1774, when I and one Michael Stoner were solicited by Governor Dunmore, of Virginia, to go to the Falls of the Ohio, to conduct into the settlement a number of surveyors that had been sent thither by him some months before—this country having about this time drawn the attention of many adventurers. We immediately complied with the Governor's request and conducted in the surveyors, completing a tour of eight hundred miles through many difficulties in sixty-two days. Soon after I returned home I was ordered to take the command of three garrisons during the campaign which Governor Dunmore carried on against the Shawanese Indians. After the conclusion of which the militia was discharged from each garrison and I being relieved from myself was solicited by a number of North Carolina gentlemen, that were about purchasing the lands lying on the south side of Kentucky River from the Cherokee Indians to attend their treaty at Watauga in March 1775 to negotiate with them, and, mention the boundaries of the purchase. This I accepted, and at the request of the fame gentlemen, undertook to mark out a road in the best passage from the settlement through the wilderness to Kentucky, with such assistance as I thought necessary to employ for such an important undertaking. I soon began this work, having collected a number of enterprising men, well-armed. We proceeded with all possible expedition until we came within fifteen miles of where Boonesborough now stands, and where we were fired upon by a party of Indians that killed two, and wounded two of our number. Yet, although surprised and taken at a disadvantage, we stood our ground. This was on the twentieth of March, 1775. Three days after, we were fired upon again, and had two men killed, and three wounded. Afterwards we proceeded on to Kentucky River without opposition and on the first day of April began to erect the fort of Boonesborough at a salt lick about sixty yards from the river on the south side.

On the fourth day, the Indians killed one of our men. We were busily employed in building this fort until the fourteenth day of June following without any farther opposition from the Indians—and having finished the work I returned to my family on Clinch. In a short time I proceeded to remove my family from Clinch to this garrison where we arrived safe without any other difficulties than such as are common to this passage—my wife and daughter being the first white women that ever stood on the banks of Kentucky River. On the twenty-fourth day of December following we had one man killed and one wounded by the Indians who seemed determined to persecute us for erecting this fortification. On the fourteenth day of July, 1776, two of Colonel Callaway's daughters, and one of mine, were taken prisoners near the fort. I immediately pursued the Indians with only eight men and on the sixteenth overtook them, killed two of the party, and recovered the girls. The same day on which this attempt was made, the Indians divided themselves into different parties and attacked several forts, which were before this time erected, doing a great deal of mischief. This was extremely distressing to the new settlers. An innocent husbandman was shot down, while busily cultivating the soil for his family's supply. Most of the cattle around the stations were destroyed. They continued their hostilities in this manner until the fifteenth of April 1777, when they attacked Boonesborough with a party of above one hundred in number, killed one man, and wounded four. Their loss in this attack was not certainly known to us. On the fourth day of July following, a party of about two hundred Indians attacked Boonesborough, killed one man, and wounded two.

They besieged us forty-eight hours, during which time seven of them were killed, and at last, finding themselves not likely to prevail, they raised the siege, and departed. The Indians had disposed their warriors in different parties at this time, and attacked the different garrisons to prevent their assisting each other, and did much injury to the distressed inhabitants.

On the nineteenth day of this month, Colonel Logan's fort was besieged by a party of about two hundred Indians.

During this dreadful siege they did a great deal of mischief, distressed the garrison in which were only fifteen men, killed two, and wounded one. The enemy's loss was uncertain, from the common practice which the Indians have of carrying off their dead in time of battle. Colonel Harrod's fort was then defended by only sixty-five men, and Boonesborough by twenty two, there being no more forts or white men in the country, except at the Falls, a considerable distance from these, and all taken collectively, were but a handful to the numerous warriors that were everywhere dispersed through the country intent upon doing all the mischief that savage barbarity could invent.

Thus, we passed through a scene of sufferings that exceeds description. On the twenty-fifth of this month a reinforcement of forty-five men arrived from North Carolina, and about the twentieth of August following, Colonel Bowman arrived with one hundred men from Virginia. Now we began to strengthen, and from hence, for the space of six weeks, we had skirmishes with Indians in one quarter or other almost every day. The savages now learned the superiority of the Long Knife as they call the Virginians by experience—being outgeneraled in almost every battle. Our affairs began to wear a new aspect and the enemy, not daring to venture on open war, practiced secret mischief at times. On the first day of January, 1778, I went with a party of thirty men to the Blue Licks, on Licking River, to make salt for the different garrisons in the country. On the seventh day of February as I was hunting to procure meat for the company I met with a party of one hundred and two Indians, and two Frenchmen, on their march against Boonesborough, that place being particularly the object or the enemy. They pursued, and took me—and brought me on the eighth day to the Licks, where twenty-seven of my party were, three of them having previously returned home with the salt. I knowing it was impossible for them to escape, capitulated with the enemy, and, at a distance in their view gave notice to my men of their situation with orders not to resist but surrender themselves captives. The generous usage the Indians had promised before in my capitulation was afterwards fully complied with, and we proceeded with them as prisoners to old Chillicothe, the principal Indian town, on Little Miami, where we arrived after an uncomfortable journey in very severe weather on the eighteenth day of February and received as good treatment as prisoners could expect from savages. On the tenth day of March following, I, and ten of my men were conducted by forty Indians to Detroit where we arrived the thirtieth day, and were treated by Governor Hamilton, the British commander at that post with great humanity. During our travels, the Indians entertained me well and their affection for me was so great, that they utterly refused to leave me there with the others, although the Governor offered them one hundred pounds Sterling for me on purpose to give me a parole to go home. Several English gentlemen there, being sensible of my adverse fortune, and touched with human sympathy, generously offered a friendly supply for my wants, which I refused, with many thanks for their kindness—adding, that I never expected it would be in my power to recompense such unmerited generosity. The Indians left my men in captivity with the British at Detroit and on the tenth day of April brought me towards Old Chillicothe, where we arrived on the twenty-fifth day of the same month. This was a long and fatiguing march through an exceeding fertile country, remarkable for fine springs and streams of water. At Chillicothe I spent my time as comfortably as I could expect—was adopted, according to their custom, into a family where I became a son, and had a great share in the affection of my new parents, brothers, sisters, and friends. I was exceedingly familiar and friendly with them, always appearing as cheerful and satisfied as possible, and they put great confidence in me. I often went a hunting with them, and frequently gained their applause for my activity at our shooting matches. I was careful not to exceed many of them in shooting, for no people are more envious than they in this sport. I could observe in their countenances and gestures the greatest expressions of joy when they exceeded me—and, when the reverse happened, of envy. The Shawanese king took great notice of me, and treated me with profound respect, and entire friendship, often entrusting me to hunt at my liberty. I frequently returned with the spoils of the woods, and as often presented some of what I had taken to him, expressive of duty to my sovereign. My food and lodging was, in common, with them, not so good indeed as I could desire, but necessity made everything acceptable. I now began to meditate an escape, and carefully avoided their suspicions, continuing with them at Old Chillicothe until the first day of June following, and then was taken by them to the salt springs on Scioto, and kept there, making salt, ten days. During this time I hunted some for them, and found the land for a great extent about this river to exceed the soil of Kentucky, if possible, and remarkably well-watered.

When I returned to Chillicothe, alarmed to see four hundred and fifty Indians, of their choicest warriors, painted and armed in a fearful manner, ready to march against Boonesborough, I determined to escape the first opportunity. On the sixteenth, before sunrise I departed in the most secret manner and arrived at Boonesborough on the twentieth, after a journey of one hundred and sixty miles, during which, I had but one meal. I found our fortress in a bad state of defense, but we proceeded immediately to repair our flanks, strengthen our gates and posterns—and form double bastions—which we completed in ten days. In this time we daily expected the arrival of the Indian army—and at length—one of my fellow prisoners, escaping from them, arrived, informing us that the enemy had an account of my departure and postponed their expedition three weeks. The Indians had spies out viewing our movements and were greatly alarmed with our increase in number and fortifications.

The Grand Councils of the nations were held frequently and with more deliberation than usual. They evidently saw the approaching hour when the Long Knife would dispossess them of their desirable habitations and anxiously concerned for futurity determined utterly to extirpate the whites out of Kentucky. We were not intimidated by their movements, but frequently gave them proofs of our courage. About the first of August, I made an incursion into the Indian country, with a party of nineteen men, in order to surprise a small town up Scioto, called Paint Creek Town. We advanced within four miles thereof, where we met a party of thirty Indians, on their march against Boonesborough, intending to join the others from Chillicothe. A smart fight ensued between us for some time. At length the savages gave way, and fled. We had no loss on our side. The enemy had one killed, and two wounded. We took from them three horses, and all their baggage and being informed, by two of our number that went to their town, that the Indians had entirely evacuated it, we proceeded no further, and returned with all possible expedition to assist our garrison against the other party. We passed by them on the sixth day, and on the seventh, we arrived safe at Boonesborough.

On the eighth, the Indian army arrived, being four hundred and forty-four in number, commanded by Captain Duquesne, eleven other Frenchmen, and some of their own chiefs, and marched up within view of our fort, with British and French colors flying—and having sent a summons to me, in his Britannic Majesty's name, to surrender the fort, I requested two days confederation, which was granted. It was now a critical period with us. We were a small number in the garrison. A powerful army before our walls, whose appearance proclaimed inevitable death, fearfully painted, and marking their footsteps with desolation. Death was preferable to captivity and if taken by storm, we must inevitably be devoted to destruction. In this situation we concluded to maintain our garrison, if possible.

We immediately proceeded to collect what we could of our horses, and other cattle, and bring them through the posterns into the fort. And in the evening of the ninth, I returned answer, that we were determined to defend our fort while a man was living. "Now," said I to their commander, who stood attentively hearing my sentiments, "we laugh at all your formidable preparations, but thank you for giving us notice and time to provide for our defense. Your efforts will not prevail for our gates shall forever deny you admittance." Whether this answer affected their courage, or not, I cannot tell, but, contrary to our expectations, they formed a scheme to deceive us, declaring it was their orders, from Governor Hamilton, to take us captives, and not to destroy us, but if nine of us would come out, and treat with them, they would immediately withdraw their forces from our walls, and return home peaceably. This sounded grateful in our ears and we agreed to the proposal. We held the treaty within sixty yards of the garrison, on purpose to divert them from a breach of honor, as we could not avoid suspicions of the savages. In this situation the articles were formally agreed to, and signed, and the Indians told us it was customary with them, on such occasions, for two Indians to shake hands with every white man in the treaty, as an evidence of entire friendship.

We agreed to this also, but were soon convinced their policy was to take us prisoners. They immediately grappled us, but, although surrounded by hundreds of savages, we extricated ourselves from them, and escaped all safe into the garrison, except one that was wounded, through a heavy fire from their army. They immediately attacked us on every side, and a constant heavy fire ensued between us day and night for the space of nine days. In this time the enemy began to undermine our fort, which was situated sixty yards from Kentucky River. They began at the water mark, and proceeded in the bank some distance, which we understood by their making the water muddy with the clay—and we immediately proceeded to disappoint their design by cutting a trench across their subterranean passage. The enemy discovering our countermine, by the clay we threw out of the fort, desisted from that stratagem. And experience now fully convincing them that neither their power nor policy could affect their purpose, on the twentieth day of August they raised the siege, and departed. During this dreadful siege, which threatened death in every form, we had two men killed, and four wounded, besides a number of cattle. We killed of the enemy thirty-seven, and wounded a great number. After they were gone, we picked up one hundred and twenty-five pounds weight of bullets, besides what stuck in the logs of our fort, which certainly is a great proof of their industry. Soon after this I went into the settlement and nothing worthy of a place in this account passed in my affairs for some time. During my absence from Kentucky, Colonel Bowman carried on an expedition against the Shawanese, at Old Chillicothe with one hundred and sixty men in July 1779. Here they arrived undiscovered and a battle ensued, which lasted until ten o'clock, AM when Colonel Bowman, finding he could not succeed at this time, retreated about thirty miles. The Indians, in the meantime, collecting all their forces, pursued and overtook him, when a smart fight continued near two hours, not to the advantage of Colonel Bowman's party. Colonel Harrod proposed to mount a number of horses, and furiously to rush upon the savages, who at this time fought with remarkable fury.

  This desperate step had a happy effect, broke their line of battle, and the savages fled on all sides. In these two battles we had nine killed, and one wounded. The enemy's loss uncertain, only two scalps being taken. On the twenty-second day of June, 1780, a large party of Indians and Canadians, about six hundred in number, commanded by Colonel Byrd, attacked Ruddles and Martin's Stations, at the Forks of Licking River, with six pieces of artillery. They carried this expedition so secretly, that the unwary inhabitants did not discover them until they fired upon the forts and not being prepared to oppose them, were obliged to surrender themselves miserable captives to barbarous savages, who immediately after tomahawked one man and two women and loaded all the others with heavy baggage, forcing them along toward their towns, able or unable to march. Such as were weak and faint by the way, they tomahawked. The tender women and helpless children fell victims to their cruelty. This, and the savage treatment they received afterwards is shocking to humanity and too barbarous to relate. The hostile disposition of the savages and their allies caused General Clark, the commandant at the Falls of the Ohio, immediately to begin an expedition with his own regiment, and the armed force of the country, against Pecaway, the principal town of the Shawanese, on a branch of Great Miami, which he finished with great success, took seventeen scalps, and burnt the town to ashes, with the loss of seventeen men. About this time I returned to Kentucky with my family, and here, to avoid an inquiry into my conduct, the reader being before informed of my bringing my family to Kentucky, I am under the necessity of informing him that, during my captivity with the Indians, my wife, who despaired of ever seeing me again, expecting the Indians had put a period to my life, oppressed with the distresses of the country, and bereaved of me, her only happiness, had, before I returned, transported my family and goods, on horses, through the wilderness, amidst a multitude of dangers to her father's house in North Carolina.

    Shortly after the troubles at Boonesborough, I went to them, and lived peaceably there until this time. The history of my going home, and returning with my family, forms a series of difficulties, an account of which would swell a volume, and being foreign to my purpose, I shall purposely omit them. I settled my family in Boonesborough once more, and shortly after, on the sixth day of October 1780, I went in company with my brother to the Blue Licks, and, on our return home, we were fired upon by a party of Indians. They shot him, and pursued me, by the scent of their dog three miles, but I killed the dog, and escaped. The winter soon came on and was very severe which confined the Indians to their wigwams. The severity of this winter caused great difficulties in Kentucky. The enemy had destroyed most of the corn the summer before. This necessary article was scarce, and dear, and the inhabitants lived chiefly on the flesh of buffaloes. The circumstances of many were very lamentable. However, being a hardy race of people, and accustomed to difficulties and necessities, they were wonderfully supported through all their sufferings, until the ensuing fall, when we received abundance from the fertile soil. Towards spring, we were frequently harassed by Indians, and, in May 1782, a party assaulted Ashton's Station, killed one man, and took a Negro prisoner. Captain Ashton, with twenty-five men, pursued, and overtook the savages, and a smart fight ensued, which lasted two hours, but they being superior in number, obliged Captain Ashton's party to retreat, with the loss of eight killed, and four mortally wounded, their brave commander himself being numbered among the dead.

The Indians continued their hostilities, and, about the tenth of August following, two boys were taken from Major Hoys station. This party was pursued by Captain Holder and seventeen men who were also defeated with the loss of four men killed and one wounded. Our affairs became more and more alarming.

Several stations which had lately been erected in the country were continually infested with savages, stealing their horses and killing the men at every opportunity. In a field, near Lexington, an Indian shot a man, and running to scalp him, was himself shot from the fort, and fell dead upon his enemy.

Every day we experienced recent mischief. The barbarous savage nations of Shawanese, Cherokees, Wyandots, Tawas, Delawares, and several others near Detroit, united in a war against us, and assembled their choicest warriors at Old Chillicothe to go on the expedition in order to destroy us and entirely depopulate the country. Their savage minds were inflamed to mischief by two abandoned men, Captains McKee and Girty. These led them to execute every diabolical scheme and on the fifteenth day of August commanded a party of Indians and

Canadians of about five hundred in number, against Bryan's Station, five miles from Lexington. Without demanding a surrender, they furiously assaulted the garrison, which was happily prepared to oppose them, and, after they had expended much ammunition in vain, and killed the cattle round the fort, not being likely to make themselves matters of this place, they raised the siege, and departed in the morning of the third day after they came, with the loss of about thirty killed, and the number of wounded uncertain. Of the garrison four were killed, and three wounded. On the eighteenth day Colonel Todd, Colonel Trigg, Major Harlan, and myself, speedily collected one hundred and seventy-six men, well-armed, and pursued the savages.

They had marched beyond the Blue Licks to a remarkable bend of the main fork of Licking River, about forty-three miles from Lexington, as it is particularly represented in the map where we overtook them on the nineteenth day. The savages observing us, give way, and we, being ignorant of their numbers passed the river. When the enemy saw our proceedings, having greatly the advantage of us in situation, they formed the line of battle as represented in the map from one bend of Licking to the other, about a mile from the Blue Licks. An exceeding fierce battle immediately began, for about fifteen minutes, when we, being overpowered by numbers, were obliged to retreat, with the loss of sixty-seven men—seven of whom were taken prisoners. The brave and much lamented Colonels Todd and Trigg, Major Harlan and my second son, were among the dead. We were informed that the Indians, numbering their dead, found they had four killed more than we, and therefore, four of the prisoners they had taken, were, by general consent ordered to be killed in a most barbarous manner, by the young warriors, in order to train them up to cruelty, and then they proceeded to their towns.

On our retreat we were met by Colonel Logan, hastening to join us with a number of well-armed men. This powerful assistance we unfortunately wanted in the battle for notwithstanding the enemy's superiority of numbers—they acknowledged that if they had received one more fire from us they should undoubtedly have given way. So valiantly did our small party fight, that, to the memory of those who unfortunately fell in the battle, enough of honor cannot be paid. Had Colonel Logan and his party been with us, it is highly probable we should have given the savages a total defeat. I cannot reflect upon this dreadful scene but sorrow fills my heart. A zeal for the defense of their country led these heroes to the scene of action, though with a few men to attack a powerful army of experienced warriors.

When we gave way, they pursued us with the utmost eagerness, and in every quarter spread destruction. The river was difficult to cross and many were killed in the flight, some just entering the river, some in the water, others after crossing, in ascending the cliffs. Some escaped on horseback, a few on foot, and, being dispersed everywhere, in a few hours, brought the melancholy news of this unfortunate battle to Lexington. Many widows were now made. The reader may guess what sorrow filled the hearts of the inhabitants, exceeding anything that I am able to describe. Being reinforced, we returned to bury the dead, and found their bodies strewed everywhere, cut and mangled in a dreadful manner. This mournful scene exhibited a horror almost unparalleled. Some torn and eaten by wild beasts, those in the river eaten by fishes—all in such a putrefied condition that no one could be distinguished from another. As soon as General Clark, then at the Falls of the Ohio, who was ever our ready friend, and merits the love and gratitude of all his countrymen, understood the circumstances of this unfortunate action, he ordered an expedition, with all possible haste, to pursue the savages, which was so expeditiously effected, that we overtook them within two miles of their towns, and probably might have obtained a great victory, had not two of their number met us about two hundred poles before we come up. These returned quick as lightening to their camp with the alarming news of a mighty army in view. The savages fled in the utmost disorder—evacuated their towns and reluctantly left their territory to our mercy. We immediately took possession of Old Chillicothe without opposition, being deserted by its inhabitants. We continued our pursuit through five towns on the [stated] Miami Rivers—Old Chillicothe—Pecaway—New Chillicothe—Will's Towns—and Chillicothe, burnt them all to ashes, entirely destroyed their corn and other fruits—and everywhere spread a scene of desolation in the country. In this expedition we took seven prisoners and five scalps, with the loss of only four men, two of whom were accidentally killed by our own army. This campaign in some measure damped the spirits of the Indians and made them sensible of our superiority. Their connections were dissolved, their armies scattered, and a future invasion put entirely out of their power, yet they continued to practice mischief secretly upon the inhabitants in the exposed parts of the country. In October following, a party made an excursion into that district called the Crab Orchard—and one of them being advanced some distance before the others, boldly entered the house of a poor defenseless family, in which was only a Negro man, a woman and her children terrified with the apprehensions of immediate death. The savage, perceiving their defenseless situation, without offering violence to the family attempted to captivate the Negro, who, happily proved an overmatch for him, threw him on the ground, and in the struggle, the mother of the children drew an ax from a corner of the cottage and cut his head off while her little daughter shut the door. Other savages instantly appeared and applied their tomahawks to the door. An old rusty gun barrel without a lock lay in a corner, which the mother put through a small crevice, and the savages, perceiving it, fled. In the meantime, the alarm spread throughout the neighborhood—the armed men collected immediately and pursued the savages into the wilderness.

Thus Providence, by the means of this Negro, saved the whole of the poor family from destruction. From that time, until the happy return of peace between the United States and Great Britain, the Indians did us no mischief. Finding the great king beyond the water disappointed in his expectations, and conscious of the importance of the Long Knife, and their own wretchedness, some of the nations immediately desired peace to which, at present, they seem universally disposed, and are sending ambassadors to General Clark at the Falls of the Ohio with the minutes of their Councils a specimen of which, in the minutes of the Piankashaw Council, is subjoined.

To conclude, I can now say that I have verified the sayings of an old Indian who signed Colonel Henderson's deed. Taking me by the hand at the delivery thereof, brother, says he, we have given you a fine land, but I believe you will have much trouble in settling it. My footsteps have often been marked with blood and therefore I can truly subscribe to its original name. Two darling sons, and a brother, have I lost by savage hands, which have also taken from me forty valuable horses and abundance of cattle. Many dark and sleepless nights have I been a companion for owls, separated from the cheerful society of men, scorched by the summer's fun, and pinched by the winter's cold, an instrument ordained to settle the wilderness, but now the scene is changed. Peace crowns the sylvan shade. What thanks, what ardent and ceaseless thanks are due to that all-superintending Providence which has turned a cruel war into peace, brought order out of confusion, made the fierce savages placid, and turned away their hostile weapons from our country. May the same Almighty Goodness banish the accursed monster, war, from all lands, with her hated associates, rapine and insatiable ambition.

Let peace, descending from her native heaven, bid her olives spring amidst the joyful nations, and plenty, in league with commerce, scatter blessings from her copious hand. This account of my adventures will inform the reader of the most remarkable events of this country. I now live in peace and safety, enjoying the sweets of liberty, and the bounties of Providence, with my once fellow sufferers, in this delightful country, which I have seen purchased with a vast expense of blood and treasure, delighting in the prospect of its being, in a short time, one of the most opulent and powerful states on the continent of North America, which, with the love and gratitude of my countrymen, I esteem a sufficient reward for all my toil and dangers.

Epilogue

After the American Revolution ended Daniel Boone moved to Limestone, Kentucky. In 1786 he took part in a military expedition into the Ohio River area led by Benjamin Logan. He was elected to the Virginia State Assembly in 1787 as a representative from Bourbon County. During this time he also owned a tavern in Maysville, Kentucky and was employed as a surveyor, horse trader, and land speculator. Boone was successful at first in his many ventures but ultimately he became frustrated with his life and financial problems in Kentucky and moved upriver to Point Pleasant, Virginia. Boone's financial troubles continued in Virginia and he was forced to return to hunting and trapping wild animals to sustain a living. In 1795, Boone and his wife moved back to Nicholas County, Kentucky and though he tried, his woes continued rising. Finally, in 1799 Boone moved west to Missouri, which was then part of Spanish Louisiana. He was appointed as a military leader of the Femme Osage District, maintaining the position until 1804 when Missouri became part of the United States following the Louisiana Purchase in 1803.

Boone spent his final years in Missouri in the company of his children and grandchildren. He died quietly in September 1820 and was buried in a small cemetery near present-day Marthasville, Missouri. Supposedly in the mid-1830s his remains were disinterred and reburied in Frankfort, Kentucky. However, rumors persists to this day that the remains that were reburied in Kentucky were those of someone else and Boone still lies buried in the small cemetery where he was laid to rest back in 1820.

Boone's immortal legacy in American history continues to endure despite the passage of time. He has been honored with books, films, and television shows based on both factual and fictional aspects of his life and exploits which further enhanced his legacy for future generations. He will never be forgotten.

George Washington

Extracts from one of George Washington's diaries of which he kept while attending the Constitutional Convention of 1787

Originally from the *Philadelphia Times* which published the following excerpts from the manuscript copy of the "Diary of Washington" preserved in the Library of Congress—copied from the rough notes from which the diary in the State Department was written. Extracts from the latter have also been published by Jared Sparks in his bestselling biography *Life of George Washington*. Washington's original diary is a small volume about the size and appearance of a pocket memorandum book containing approximately 78 pages, of which 34 cover his interesting sojourn in Philadelphia in 1787.

1787. *Friday*, 11 *(May)*. Set out before breakfast and rode 12 miles to Skirrett's Tavern when we baited and proceeded to the ferry at Havre de Grace to dinner. The wind being high and the weather squally I did not cross the river—frequent showers through the day with mists and sunshine alternating. *Saturday*, 12. Crossed the river early in the morning and breakfasted at the ferry house at the east side—dined at the head of Elk and lodged at Wilmington—at the head of Elk Mr. (Francis) Corbin joined me and took a seat in my carriage to Wilmington. *Sunday*, 13. About nine o'clock Mr. Corbin and I set out, dined at Chester where I was met by Generals Mifflin, Knox and Varnum, Colonels Humphreys and Mentges and Majors Jackson and Nicholas—after dinner we proceeded for the city—at the ferry (Gray's) was met by the Troop of City Light Horse by whom and a large concourse I was escorted to Mr. House's—after passing the artillery officers (who saluted) at the entrance of the city. On my arrival a peal was rung—and Mr. Robert Morris and his lady again pressing me to lodge with them. I had my baggage moved and took up my quarters at their house—after paying my respects to the President of the State, Dr. Franklin. *Monday*, 14. This being the day appointed for the meeting of the Convention such members of it as were in town assembled at the State House, where it was found that two States only were represented, Virginia and Pennsylvania. Agreed to meet again tomorrow at 11 o'clock. Dined (in a family way) at Mr. Morris's and took tea there. *Tuesday*, 15. Repaired to the State House at the hour appointed. No more States represented, though there were members (but not sufficient to form a quorum) from two or three others, number Carolina and Delaware, as also Jersey. Governor Randolph, of Virginia, came in today. Dined with the Society of the Cincinnati. *Wednesday*, 16. Only two States represented. Agreed to meet at—o'clock. Doctor McClurg, of Virginia, came in. Dined at Doctor Franklin's. Drank tea and spent the evening with Mr. John Penn. *Thursday*, 17. Mr. (Charles) Pinkney, of South Carolina, coming in from New York, and Mr. Rutledge being here before, formed a representation from that State. Colonel Mason getting in this evening from Virginia, completed the whole number of this State in the delegation. *Friday*, 18. The State of New York was represented. Dined at a club at Gray's and drank tea at Mr. Morris's, after that went with Mrs. Morris and some other ladies to hear a lady read at the College Hall.

Saturday, 19. No more States represented. Agreed to meet at 1 o'clock on Monday. Dined at Mr. Ingersoll's and spent the evening at home, going to bed soon. *Sunday*, 20. Went into the country with Mr. and Mrs. Morris and dined at their place at the Hills—returned in the afternoon and drank tea at Mr. Powel's. *Monday*, 21.—Delaware State was represented. Dined and drank

Tea at Mr. Bingham's, splendor shown. *Tuesday*, 22. North Carolina represented. Dined and drank tea at Mr. Morris's.

Wednesday, 23. No more States represented. Rode to General Mifflin's to breakfast, after which, in company with him, Mr. Madison, Mr. Rutledge and others, crossed the Schuylkill above the Falls, called Mr. Peter's, Mr. Penn's and Mr. Hamilton's, and repaired at the hour of one to the State House. Dined at Mr. Chew's with the wedding guests. I drank tea there in a large circle of ladies. *Thursday*, 24. No more States represented. Dined and drank tea at Mr. Ross's—one of my Postillion boys (Paris) being ill sent for Doctor Jones to him. *Friday*, 25. Another delegate comes in from the State of New Jersey. Made a quorum. And seven States being now represented the body was organized and I was called to the Chair by a unanimous vote. Major Jackson was appointed Secretary and a Committee consisting of Mr. Wythe, Mr. Hamilton and Mr. Charles Pinkney chosen to prepare rules and regulations by which the convention should be governed. To give time for this it adjourned till Monday, 10 o'clock. Returned many visits in the forenoon and dined at Thomas Willings. Spent the evening at my quarters. *Saturday*, 26. Returned all my visits this forenoon where I could get an account of the lodges of those to whom I was indebted for theirs. Dined at a club at the City Tavern, and spent the evening at my quarters writing letters. *Sunday*, 27. Went to the Romish Church to a High Mass. Dined, drank tea and spent the evening at my lodgings. *Monday*, 28. Met in Convention at 10 o'clock. Two States more—Massachusetts and Connecticut being represented, made nine more on the floor—proceeded to the establishment of rules for the government of the Convention and adjourned about 2 o'clock. Dined at home. Drank tea in a large circle at Mr. Francis's.

Tuesday, 29. Dined at home and went to Mr. Juhan's benefit concert at the City Tavern. The same number of States met in the Convention as yesterday. *Wednesday*, 30. Convention as yesterday. Dined with Mr. (John) Vaughan, drank tea and spent the evening at Mr. and Mrs. John Lawrence's. *Thursday*, 31. Convention representation increased by coming in of the State of

Georgia, occasioned by the arrival of Major Pierce and Mr. Houston. Dined at Mr. Francis's and drank tea with Mrs. Meredith. *Friday*, June 1. Convention as yesterday. Dined with Mr. John Penn and spent the evening at Bush Hill at a very elegant entertainment given to a numerous company by Mr. Hamilton, the owner of it. *Saturday*, 2. Major Jenifer, coming in with powers from the State of Maryland authorizing one member to represent it, added another State, now eleven, to the convention. Dined at club at the City Tavern and spent the evening at my quarters.

Sunday, 3. Dined at Mr. Clymer's and drank tea there. *Monday*, 4. Convention as on Saturday. Dined with General Mifflin, reviewed the Light Infantry Cavalry and part of the Artillery of the city and drank tea with Mrs. Cadwalader. *Tuesday*, 5. Dined at Mr. Morris's with a large Company and spent the evening there. *Wednesday*, 6. Dined at the President's with a large Company and drank tea there, after which came home and wrote letters for France. *Thursday*, 7. Dined at a club at the Indian Queen—drank tea and spent the evening there. *Friday*, 8. Dined, drank tea and spent the evening at home. *Saturday*, 9. Dined at the club at the City Tavern, drank tea, and sat till 10 o'clock at Mr. Powel's. *Sunday*, 10. Breakfasted by agreement at Mr. Powel's, and, in company with him, rode to see the Botanical Garden of Mr. Bartram, which, though stored with many curious trees, shrubs and flowers, was neither large nor laid out in much taste. From hence we rode to the farm of one Jones to see the effect of the Plaster of Paris. This appeared obvious—from hence visited Mr. Powel's farm, after which I went to Mr. Morris's country seat to dinner by appointment, and returned to the city about dark.

Monday, 11. Dined, drank tea and spent the evening (in my own room) at Mr. Morris's. *Tuesday*, 12. Dined at Mr. Morris's and drunk tea there. Went afterwards to the concert at the City Tavern. *Wednesday*, 13. Dined at Mr. Clymer's and drank tea there—spent the evening at Mr. Bingham's. *Thursday*, 14. Dined at Major Moore's and spent the evening at my own lodgings. *Friday*, 15.—Dined at Mr. Powel's and drank tea there. *Saturday*, 16. Dined at the club at the City Tavern and spent the evening at my own lodgings. *Sunday*, 17. Went to church, heard Bishop (William) White preach, and see him ordain two gentlemen into the order of Deacons. After which rode eight miles into the country, dined with Mr. John Ross, and returned to town again about dusk. *Monday*, 18. Dined at Quarterly meeting of the Sons of St. Patrick at the City Tavern, and drank tea at Dr. Shippen's with the party of Mrs. Livingston. *Tuesday*, 19. Dined in a family way at Mr. Morris's and spent the evening there in a large party. *Wednesday*, 20. Dined at Mr. Meredith's and drank tea there. *Thursday*, 21 Dined at Mr. Prager and spent the evening in my own room. *Friday*, 22. Dined in a family way at Mr. Morris's and drank tea at Mr. Francis Hopkinson's. *Saturday*, 23. Dined at Doctor (Benjamin) Rush's and drank tea at Mr. Morris's.

Sunday, 24. Dined at Mr. Morris's and spent the evening at Mr. Meredith's in drinking tea only. *Monday*, 25. Dined at Mr. Morris's. Drunk tea there and spent the evening in my own room. *Tuesday*, 26th. Took a family dinner with Governor Randolph and made one of a party to drink tea at Gray's Ferry. *Wednesday*, 27th. Dined at Mr. Morris's. Drunk tea there and spent the evening in my own room. *Thursday*, 28th. Dined at Mr. Morris's in a large company. Drank tea there and spent the evening in my own room. *Friday*, 29. Dined at Mr. Morris's and spent the evening at home. *Saturday*, 30. Dined at a club of gentlemen and ladies at the Cool Spring, Springsbury, and spent the evening at home. *July* (Sunday) 1. Dined and spent the evening at home. *Monday*, 2. Dined with some of the members of Convention at the Indian Queen. Drank tea at Mr. Bingham's and walked afterwards in the State House Yard. Sat for Mr. (Robert Edge) Pine. *Tuesday*, 3. Sat for Mr. Peale this morning, dined at Mr. Morris's, drank tea at Mr. Powel's and went with him to the Agricultural Society at Carpenters Hall. *Wednesday*, 4th. Visited Dr. Aratory. Heard at the Calvinist Church an oration on the Anniversary of the Independence. Dined afterwards with this State Society of Cincinnati and drank tea at Mr. Powel's. *Thursday*, 5. Dined at Mr. Morris's, drank tea and spent the evening there. *Friday*, 6. Sat for Mr. Peale to draw my picture in the morning, dined at the City Tavern with some gentlemen of the convention and spent the evening at home. *Saturday*, 7th. Dined at the Cold Spring with the club, returned in the evening and drank tea at Mr. Meredith's. *Sunday*, 8th. About 12 o'clock rode to Dr. Logan's, near Germantown, where I dined, returned in the evening and drank tea at Mr. Morris's. *Monday*, 9. Sat in the morning for Mr. Peale. Dined at Mr. Morris's and drank tea at Dr. Redman's. *Tuesday*, 10. Dined at Mr. Morris's—drank tea at Mr. Bingham's and went to the play. *Wednesday*, 11th. Dined at Mr. Morris's and spent the evening at home. *Thursday*, 12th. Dined at Mr. Morris's and drank tea with Mrs. Livingston. *Friday*, 13th. Dined at Mr. Morris's, drank tea there and spent the evening.

Saturday, 14th. Dined at the Cold Spring Club and went to the play in the afternoon. *Sunday*, 15. Dined at Mr. Morris's and remained there all afternoon. *Monday*, 16. Dined at Mr. Morris's and drank tea at Mr. Powel's. *Tuesday*, 17. Dined at Mr. House's and made an excursion with a party to Gray's Ferry to tea. *Wednesday*, 18. Dined at Mr. Milligan's and drank tea at Mr. Meredith's. *Thursday*, 19. Dined at Mr. John Penn's (the younger), drank tea and spent the evening at home. *Friday*, 20. Dined at home and drank tea at Mr. Clymer's. *Saturday*, 21. Dined at the Cold Spring Club and went to the play in the afternoon. *Sunday*, 22nd. Left town by 5 o'clock, breakfasted at General Mifflin's, rode up to the Spring Mills and returned to General Mifflin's to dinner, after which came to the city. *Monday*, 23. Dined at Mr. Morris's and drank tea at Lansdowne, the country seat of Mr. John Penn, returned in the evening. *Tuesday*, 24. Dined at Mr. Morris's and drank tea at Doctor Rush's. *Wednesday*, 25. Dined at Mr. Morris's, drank tea and spent the evening at home. *Thursday*, 26. Dined at Mr. Morris's, drank tea there. I stayed within all the afternoon. *Friday*, 27. Dined at Mr. Morris's drank tea at Mr. Powel's. *Saturday*, 28th. Dined at the Cold Spring Club, and after drank tea there—returned to Mr. Morris's and spent the evening there. *Sunday*, 29th. Dined and spent the whole day at Mr. Morris's. *Monday*, 30. In company with Mr. Governor Morris went into the neighborhood of the Valley Forge—to a Widow

Moore's—a fishing—at whose house we lodged. *Tuesday*, 31. Before breakfast I rode to the Valley Forge and over the whole cantonment and works of the American Army in the winter of 1777-1778, and on my return to the Widow Moore's found Mr. and Mrs. Robert Morris. Spent the day there, fishing and etc.—and lodged at the same place. *Wednesday*, August 1st. Returned at 11 o'clock with the above company to Philadelphia. *Thursday*, 2. Dined at Mr. Morris's, drank tea and spent the evening there.

Friday, 3rd. Went up to Trenton on a fishing party with Mr. and Mrs. Robert Morris, and Mr. and Mrs. Governor Morris. Dined and lodged at Colonel Sam Ogden's. In the evening fished. *Saturday*, 4th. In the morning between breakfast and dinner, fished. Dined at General (Philemon) Dickinson's and returned in the evening to Colonel Ogden's. *Sunday*, 5th. Dined at Colonel Ogden's and about 4 o'clock set out for Philadelphia. Halted an hour at Bristol and reached the city before 9 o'clock. *Monday*, 6. Again met in convention agreeably to adjournment and read the report of the (committee). Dined at Mr. Morris's and drank tea at Mr. Meredith's. *Tuesday*, 7. Dined at Mr. Morris's and drank tea nowhere. Spent the evening at home. *Wednesday*, 8th. Dined at the City Tavern and remained there till near 10 o'clock.

Thursday, 9th. Dined at Mr. (John) Swanwick's and spent the evening in my own room, reading letters and accounts from home. *Friday*, 10th. Dined and drank tea at Mr. Bingham's—spent the evening at home. *Saturday*, 11th.—Dined at the Cold Spring Club, and after tea returned and spent the evening at home. *Sunday*, 12. Dined at Bush Hill with Mr. William Hamilton, spent the evening at home writing. *Monday*, 13th. Dined at home and drank tea with Mr. Bache at the President's. *Tuesday*, 14th. Dined and drank tea at home. *Wednesday*, 15. Did the same. *Thursday*, 16. Dined at Mr. Pollock's and spent the evening at my own room. *Friday*, 17. Dined and drank tea at Mr. Powel's. *Saturday*, 18. Dined at Chief Justice McKean's and spent the evening at home. *Sunday*, 19. In company with Mr. Powel rode up to the White Marsh—dined at Germantown—drank tea at Mr. Peters and returned home in the evening. *Monday*, 20. Dined and drank tea at home. *Tuesday*, 21. Did the same. *Wednesday*, 22. Dined at the Hills, Mr. Morris's, and visited at Mr. Powel's in the evening. *Thursday*, 23rd. Dined at home and drank tea there. *Friday* 24. Dined at home. *Saturday*, 25. Dined at the Club and spent the evening at home. *Sunday*, 26. Rode into the country 8 or 10 miles and dined with Mr. Morris at the Hills and spent the evening writing letters. *Monday*, 27. Dined at Mr. Morris's and drank tea at Mr. Powel's. *Tuesday*, 28th. Dined at home and drank tea there. *Wednesday*, 29. Did the same. *Thursday*, 30th. Did the same. *Friday*, 31st. Dined at home and in company with others went into the country and drank tea with Mr. Penn. *Saturday*, September 1. Dined at home and drank tea there. *Sunday*, 2nd. Rode to Mr. Bartram's and other places in the country and dined and drank tea at Mr. Gray's. *Monday*, 3. Dined and drank tea at home. *Tuesday*, 4th. Dined and did the same after visiting a machine at Dr. Franklin's for smoothing clothes instead of ironing of them.

Wednesday, 5. Dined at Mr. House's and drank tea at Mr. Bingham's. *Thursday*, 6th. Dined at Doctor Hutchinson's and spent the afternoon and evening at home. *Friday*, 7. Dined and spent the afternoon at home (except whilst riding a few miles). *Saturday*, 8. Dined at the Cold Spring Club and spent the afternoon at home. *Sunday*, 9. Dined at home, after paying a visit to Mr. Gardogne (Minister from Spain), who had come from New York on a visit to me. *Monday*, 10th. Dined at home and drank tea there. *Tuesday*, 11th. Dined at home in a large company and drank tea and spent the evening there. *Wednesday*, 12th. Dined at the President's and drank tea at Mr. Pine's. *Thursday*, 13. Dined at the Vice President's, Charles Biddle's, and drank tea at Mr. Powel's. *Friday*, 14. Dined at the City Tavern at an entertainment given on my account by the City Troop of Light Horse. Spent the evening at Mr. Meridith's. *Saturday*, 15. Finished the business of the Convention all to signing the proceedings, to do which the House set till 6 o'clock. Spent the evening at my lodgings. *Sunday*, 16. Wrote many letters in the forenoon, dined with Mr. and (Mrs.) Morris at the Hills and returned to town in the evening. *Monday*, 17. Met in Convention and signed the proceedings, all except Governor Randolph, Colonel Mason and Mr. Gerry. Dined all together at the City Tavern and returned to my lodgings.

Tuesday, 18. Finished what private business I had to do this forenoon. Dined at 1 o'clock at Mr. Morris's, and set off afterwards in company with Mr. (John) Blair, who took a seat in my chariot with me on my return home—reached Chester, where we lodged. *Wednesday*, 19. Prevented by rain, much of which fell in the night, from setting off early, baited at Wilmington, dined at Christiana Bridge and lodged at head of Elk, at the bridge, near which I narrowly escaped an ugly accident to my chariot and horses. One fell through and another, with the chariot, was on the point of following, but by exertion was saved.

Thursday, 20. Set off after an early breakfast, crossed the Susquehanna and dined in Havre de Grace and lodged at Skirrett's Tavern. *Friday*, 21st. Breakfasted in Baltimore. Dined at the Widow Ball's, formerly Spurrier's and lodged at Major Snowden's. *Saturday*, 22nd. Breakfasted at Bladensburg. Passed through Georgetown. Dined at Alexandria and reached home by sunset, after being absent 4 months and 14 days.

Tobias Lear

Excerpt from the personal memoir *Last Words of General Washington*. Originally published in 1892 as a special edition.

The following account about the last illness and death of George Washington was noted by his personal secretary Tobias Lear on the Sunday following his death, which took place on Saturday evening, December 14, 1799.

On Thursday December 12 the General rode out to his farms about ten o'clock, and did not return home till past 3 o'clock. Soon after he went out, the weather became very bad, rain, hail and snow falling alternately, with a cold wind. When he came in I carried some letters to him, to frank, intending to send them to the post office in the evening. He franked the letters, but said the weather was too bad to send a servant up to the office that evening. I observed to him that I was afraid he had got wet, he said no, his great coat had kept him dry—but his neck appeared to be wet, and the snow was hanging on his hair. He came to dinner without changing his dress. In the evening he appeared as well as usual. A heavy fall of snow took place on Friday, which prevented the General from riding out as usual. He had taken cold (undoubtedly from being so much exposed the day before) and complained of having a sore throat—he had a hoarseness, which increased in the evening, but he made light of it, as he would never take anything to carry off a cold, always observing, "let it go as it came." In the evening the papers having come from the post office, he sat in the room, with Mrs. Washington and myself, reading them, till about nine o'clock, and, when he met with anything which he thought diverting or interesting, he would read it aloud. He desired me to read to him the debates of the Virginia Assembly, on the election of a senator and Governor—which I did. On his retiring to bed, he appeared to be in perfect health, excepting the cold before mentioned, which he considered as trifling, and had been remarkably cheerful all the evening. About 2 or 3 o'clock on Saturday morning he awoke Mrs. Washington and told her he was very unwell, and had had an ague. She observed that he could scarcely speak, and breathed with difficulty—and would have got up to call a servant, but he would not permit her lest she should take cold. As soon as the day appeared, the woman (Caroline) went into the room to make a fire—and he desired that Mr. Rawlins, one of the overseers who was used to bleeding the people, might be sent for to bleed him before the doctor could arrive—and the woman (Caroline) came to my room requesting I might go to the General, who was very ill. I got up put on my clothes as quick as possible, and went to his chamber. Mrs. Washington was then up, and related to me his being taken ill about 2 or 3 o'clock, as before stated.

I found him breathing with difficulty and hardly able to utter a word intelligibly. I went out instantly—and wrote a line to Dr. Craik, which sent off by my servant, ordering him to go with all the swiftness his horse could carry him—and immediately returned to the General's chamber, where I found him in the same situation I had left him. A mixture of molasses, vinegar and butter was prepared, to try its effect in the throat—but he could not swallow a drop, whenever he attempted it he appeared to be distressed, convulsed, and almost suffocated. Mr. Rawlins came in soon after sunrise—and prepared to bleed him. When the arm was ready—the General, observing that Rawlins appeared to be agitated, said, as well as he could speak, "*don't be afraid*" and after the incision was made, he observed, "*the orifice is not large enough.*" However, the blood ran pretty freely. Mrs. Washington, not knowing whether bleeding was proper or not in the General's situation, begged that much might not be taken from him, lest it should be injurious, and desired me to stop it—but when I was about to untie the string, the General put up his hand to prevent it—and as soon as he could speak—he said "*more.*"

Mrs. Washington being still uneasy lest too much blood should be taken, it was stopped after about half a pint was taken from him. Finding that no relief was obtained from bleeding, and that nothing would go down the throat, I proposed bathing the throat externally with sal-volatile, which was done, and in the operation, which was with the hand, and in the gentlest manner, he observed *'tis very sore*. A piece of flannel was then put round his neck. His feet were also soaked in warm water. This, however, gave no relief. In the meantime, before Doctor Craik arrived, Mrs. Washington requested me to send for Doctor Brown of Port Tobacco, whom Doctor Craik had recommended to be called, if any case should ever occur that was seriously alarming.

I dispatched a messenger (Cyrus) to Dr. Brown immediately (about nine o'clock) Doctor Craik came in soon after, and upon examining the General he put a blister of cantharis on the throat and took more blood from him, and had some vinegar and hot water put into a teapot, for the General to draw in the steam from the nozzle—which he did, as well as he was able. He also ordered sage tea and vinegar to be mixed for a gargle.

This the General used as often as desired—but when he held back his head to let it run down, it put him into great distress and almost produced suffocation. When the mixture came out of his mouth some phlegm followed it, and he would attempt to cough, which the Doctor encouraged him to do as much as he could—but without effect—he could only make the attempt. About eleven o'clock Dr. Dick was sent for. Dr. Craik bled the General again about this time. No effect, however, was produced by it, and he continued in the same state, unable to swallow anything. Doctor Dick came in about 3 o'clock and Dr. Brown arrived soon after. Upon Dr. Dick's seeing the General and consulting a few minutes with Dr. Craik, he was bled again, the blood ran slowly appeared very thick, and did not produce any symptoms of fainting. Doctor Brown came into the chamber room after, and upon feeling the General's pulse and etc. the physicians went out together. Dr. Craik soon after returned.

The General could now swallow a little (about 4 o'clock) calomel and tartar were administered—but without any effect. About half past 4 o'clock, he desired me to ask Mrs. Washington to come to his bedside when he requested her to go down into his room and take from his desk two wills which she would find there, and bring them to him, which she did. Upon looking at them he gave her (one) which he observed was useless, as it was superseded by the other, and desired her to burn it, which she did, and then took the other and put it away. After this was done, I returned again to his bedside and took his hand. He said to me "*I find I am going, my breath cannot continue long, I believed, from the first attack it would be fatal, do you arrange and record all my late military letters and papers—arrange my accounts and settle my books, as you know more about them than anyone else, and let Mr. Rawlins finish recording my other letters, which he has begun.*" He asked "*when Mr. Lewis Washington would return?*" I told him I believed about the 20th of the month. He made no reply to it.

The physicians again came in (between 5 and 6 o'clock) and when they came to his bedside, Dr. Craik asked him if he could sit up in the bed. He held out his hand to me and was raised up, when he said to the physicians. "*I feel myself going, you had better not take any more trouble about me, but let me go off quietly—I cannot last long.*" They found what had been done was without effect—he laid down again and they retired excepting Dr. Craik. He then said to him, "*Doctor, I die hard, but I am not afraid to go. I believed from my first attack that I would not survive it, my breath cannot last long.*" The doctor pressed his hand but could not utter a word. He retired from the bedside and sat by the fire absorbed in grief. About 8 o'clock the physicians again came into the room, and applied blisters to his legs—but went out without a ray of hope. From this time he appeared to breathe with less difficulty than he had done—but was very restless, constantly changing his position to endeavor to get ease. I aided him all in my power, and was gratified in believing he felt it—for he would look upon me with his eyes speaking gratitude, but unable to utter a word without great distress. About ten o'clock he made several attempts to speak to me before he could effect it—at length, he said, "*I am just going, have me decently buried, and do not let my body be put into the vault in less than two days after I am dead.*" I bowed assent. He looked at me again, and said "*Do you understand me*" I replied Yes, Sir, "*Tis well*" said he. About ten minutes before he expired his breathing became much easier—he lay quietly—he withdrew his hand from mine and felt his own pulse—I spoke to Dr. Craik who sat by the fire—he came to the bedside. The General's hand fell from his wrist. I took it in mine and laid it upon my breast. Dr. Craik put his hand over his eyes and he expired without a struggle or a sigh. While we were fixed in grief Mrs. Washington asked, with a firm and collected voice "*Is he gone*" I could not speak, but held up my hand as a signal that he was. "Tis well" said she in a plain voice "All is now over. I have no more trials to pass through. I shall soon follow him."

Henry Whiteley

Excerpt from *Three Months in Jamaica in 1832—Comprising a Residence of Seven Weeks on a Sugar Plantation*. Written by Henry Whiteley and published in 1833 by J. Hatchard and Son. This book led to the abolition of slavery in all British Colonies through the Slavery Abolition Act of 1833.

The reasons that have induced me, after mature reflection, to lay before the public the following account of what I witnessed in Jamaica, during my late visit, are briefly these. 1st. I feel it due to my own character, unimportant as is my station in society, to detail, for the information of many friends who have kindly interested themselves in my welfare, the circumstances that led to my return home so unexpectedly, and after so short a residence. 2ndly. I feel it due to my fellow men—to my countrymen in England, and to their fellow subjects in Jamaica—to state, without reserve and without exaggeration, the facts which there fell under my observation. Lastly, I feel it to be a religious duty—a duty to God as well as to man (since Providence, by means so unforeseen, and at so eventful a juncture, has placed me in circumstances that render my humble testimony of some immediate value), to give my plain and deliberate testimony respecting the character of the system which I found in operation in that colony. In performing this task, I am aware that I shall inevitably give some offense, and awaken some hostility, but, constrained as I am by considerations which I dare not disregard, and avoiding, as I shall carefully do, all disclosures but such as are requisite to authenticate the facts and develop the system, I will not flinch from whatever responsibility the performance of my duty involves, however painful in some instances it may be to others as well as to myself. I arrived in Jamaica on the 3rd of September, 1832. I was sent out by a respectable West India House in London, under the patronage of a relative of mine, who is a partner in that house, being furnished with a recommendation to their acting attorney in the island, with a view to be employed either in a store, or as a bookkeeper upon a plantation.

Previously to my arrival in Jamaica I had no clear conception of the nature of Colonial Slavery and my anticipations in regard to the treatment and condition of the slaves were favorable rather than otherwise. It so happened, that, excepting what I had seen in newspapers, I had never read a single publication against Colonial Slavery, and had never either attended a public meeting, or heard a lecture delivered on the subject. I was, in fact, one of those individuals who believe that there is more *real* slavery in England than in any of her colonies. Many a time I had blamed such gentlemen as Mr. Buxton, Dr. Lushington, and others, for making so much ado in Parliament about Colonial Slavery, and neglecting (as I conceived) the slavery of the poor factory children at home, with whose condition I was well-acquainted, having been all my life resident in a manufacturing district, and concerned, with some of my relatives, in the blanket business, at Heckmondwike, near Leeds. What tended to confirm me much in these views was the perusal of the last Order in Council for the Amelioration of Slavery which I understood to have been sent out for adoption in all our slave colonies. A copy of this document had been sent by a member of parliament to the Central Committee at Leeds on the Factory System, of which I was a member, in order to enable us to judge whether the condition of the West India slaves or that of the factory children was preferable, and the conclusion which I came to upon its perusal, and under the persuasion that it had been generally adopted, was this—that, all things considered, the condition of the Negro slave was much preferable to that of the factory child. And with these impressions I landed at St. Ann's Bay, in Jamaica. The day that I landed I was informed, by a clerk of the manager's that a horse would be sent down from New Ground estate for me next morning, and that I would have to remain on that estate till I heard from the manager, or attorney of the proprietors, who was then at his own property, about sixteen miles from the Bay. The same day I dined at St. Ann's Bay, on board the vessel I arrived in, in company with several colonists, among whom was Mr. Hamilton Brown, representative for the parish of St. Ann, in the Colonial Assembly. Some reference having been made to the new Order in Council I was rather startled to hear that gentleman swear by his Maker that that Order should never be adopted in Jamaica, nor would the planters of Jamaica, he said, permit the interference of the Home Government with their slaves in any shape. A great deal was said by him and others present about the happiness and comfort enjoyed by the slaves, and of the many advantages possessed by them of which the poor in England were destitute. Among other circumstances mentioned in proof of this, Mr. Robinson, a wharfinger, stated that a slave in that town had sent out printed cards to invite a party of his Negro acquaintance to a supper party. One of these cards was handed to Mr. Hamilton Brown, who said he would present it to the Governor, as a proof of the comfortable condition of the slave population. This, and other circumstances then mentioned, tended to conform the notions I had brought from England respecting slavery in Jamaica, and, although I was somewhat shocked and staggered by seeing the same day the Methodist chapel at St. Ann's Bay lying in ruins, as it had been destroyed by the whites six months before, and by learning that the Missionaries were no longer permitted to preach in that parish, I nevertheless left the place next morning with my favorable impressions respecting the condition of the slaves not materially abated. These impressions, however, I was not permitted long to indulge. I proceeded on horseback to New Ground estate the next day. On my way thither I saw much majestic and beautiful scenery, and enjoyed the prospect exceedingly, until I came in sight of a gang of Negroes at work.

Most of them were females and they were superintended by a driver, with the cart whip in his hand. Just as I rode past, the driver cracked his whip and cried out "Work! Work!" They were manuring the canes, and carrying the manure in baskets on their heads. It appeared to me disgustingly dirty work—for the moisture from the manure was dripping through the baskets, and running down the bodies of the Negroes. This sight annoyed me considerably, and raised some doubts as to the preferable condition of West India slaves to factory children. The enchanting scenery and beautiful humming birds no longer amused me, and the thundering crack of the cart whip, sounding in my ears as I rode along, excited feelings of a very unpleasing description.

On reaching the estate I was received in the most friendly manner by the overseer, and entertained with West Indian hospitality. This gentleman, after some inquiries as to the state of things in England, began to enlarge on the comfortable condition of the slaves, and, pointing to some Negro coopers who were working in the yard, asked if I could perceive any difference between the condition of these slaves and that of English laborers. I owned I could not, they seemed to work with great regularity and apparent good humor. Immediately afterwards the overseer called out, in a very authoritative tone, "blow shell." A large conch shell was then blown by one of the domestic slaves, and in a few minutes four Negro drivers made their appearance in front of the house, accompanied by six common Negroes. The drivers had each a long staff in his hand, and a large cart whip coiled round his shoulders. They appeared to be very stout athletic men. They stood before the hall door, and the overseer put on his hat and went out to them, while I sat at the open window and observed the scene which followed—having been informed that the other six Negroes were to be punished. When the overseer went out, the four drivers gave him an account, on notched tallies, of their half day's work, and received fresh orders. The overseer then asked a few questions of the drivers respecting the offenses of the six slaves brought up for punishment.

No question was asked of the culprits themselves, nor was any explanation waited for. Sentence was instantly pronounced, and instantly carried into execution. The first was a man of about thirty-five years of age. He was what is called a pen keeper, or cattle herder, and his offense was having suffered a mule to go astray. At the command of the overseer he proceeded to strip off part of his clothes, and laid himself flat on his belly, his back and buttocks being uncovered. One of the drivers then commenced flogging him with the cart whip. This whip is about ten feet long, with a short stout handle, and is an instrument of terrible power. It is whirled by the operator round his head, and then brought down with a rapid motion of the arm upon the recumbent victim, causing the blood to spring at every stroke. When I saw this spectacle, now for the first time exhibited before my eyes, with all its revolting accompaniments, and saw the degraded and mangled victim writhing and groaning under the infliction, I felt horror struck. I trembled, and turned sick—but being determined to see the whole to an end, I kept my station at the window.

The sufferer, writhing like a wounded worm, every time the lash cut across his body cried out "Lord! Lord! Lord!" When he had received about twenty lashes, the driver stopped to pull up the poor man's shirt (or rather smock frock), which had worked down upon his galled posteriors. The sufferer then cried, "Think me no man? Think me no man?" By that exclamation I understood him to say "Think you I have not the feelings of a man?" The flogging was instantly recommenced and continued, the Negro continuing to cry "Lord! Lord! Lord!" till thirty-nine lashes had been inflicted. When the man rose up from the ground, I perceived the blood oozing out from the lacerated and tumefied parts where he had been flogged, and he appeared greatly exhausted. But he was instantly ordered off to his usual occupation. The next was a young man apparently about eighteen or nineteen years of age. He was forced to uncover himself and lie down in the same mode as the former, and was held down by the hands and feet by four slaves, one of whom was a young man who was himself to be flogged next. This latter was a mulatto—the offspring, as I understood, of some European formerly on the estate by a Negro woman, and consequently born to slavery. These two youths were flogged exactly in the mode already described, and writhed and groaned under the lash, as if enduring great agony. The mulatto bled most, and appeared to suffer most acutely. They received each thirty-nine lashes.

Their offense was some deficiency in the performance of the task prescribed to them. They were both ordered to join their gang as usual in the afternoon at cane cutting. Two young women of about the same age were, one after the other, then laid down and held by four men, their back parts most indecently uncovered, and thirty-nine lashes of the bloodstained whip inflicted upon each poor creature's posteriors. Their exclamation likewise was "Lord! Lord! Lord!" They seemed also to suffer acutely, and were apparently a good deal lacerated.

Another woman (the sixth offender) was also laid down and uncovered for the lash, but at the intercession of one of the drivers she was reprieved. The offense of these three women was similar to that of the two young men—some defalcation in the amount of labor. The overseer stood by and witnessed the whole of this cruel operation, with as much seeming indifference as if he had been paying them their wages. I was meanwhile perfectly unmanned by mingled horror and pity. Yet I have no reason to believe that the *natural* feelings of this young man (whose age did not exceed twenty-four years) were less humane or sensitive than my own. But such is the callousness which constant familiarity with scenes of cruelty engenders. He had been a bookkeeper for four years previously, on another estate belonging to the same proprietors, and had been appointed overseer on this estate only a few months before. His reception of me when I arrived was so kind, frank, and cordial, that I could not have believed him, had I not seen it with my own eyes, to be *capable* of inflicting such cruelty on a fellow creature.

As soon as this scene was over, the overseer came into the hall, and asked me to drink some rum and water with him. I told him I was sick, and could taste nothing—that I was in fact overwhelmed with horror at the scene I had just witnessed. He said it was not a pleasant duty certainly, but it was an indispensable one—and that I would soon get used, as others did, to such spectacles. I asked if he found it necessary to inflict such punishments frequently. He replied it was uncertain, "I may not," he said, "have to do it again this month, or I may have to do it tomorrow." This, my first full view of West India slavery, occurred on the 4th of September, 1832, between twelve and two o'clock, being the day after my landing in the island, and within an hour after my arrival on the plantation. I resided on New Ground estate, from the time of my arrival in the beginning of September, and exclusive of some occasional absences, altogether fully seven weeks, and, during that period, I witnessed with my own eyes the *regular* flogging of upwards of twenty Negroes. I heard also of many other Negroes being flogged by order of the overseer and bookkeepers in the field, while I resided on the plantation, besides the cases which came under my own personal observation. Neither do I include in this account the slighter floggings inflicted by the drivers in superintending the working gangs—which I shall notice afterwards. The following are additional cases of which I have a distinct recollection. But I have retained the precise date of only one of these cases (the 12th) from having found it necessary to destroy almost all my papers, in consequence of the threats of the Colonial Unionists. *1st.* A slave employed in the boiling house. He was a very stout Negro, and uncommonly well-dressed for a slave. He was laid down on the ground, held by two men, and flogged on the naked breech in the mode I have described, receiving 39 lashes. I was afterwards assured by one of the bookkeepers that this Negro had really committed no offense, but that the overseer had him punished to *spite* a bookkeeper under whose charge this slave was at the time, and with whom he had a difference, and, as he could not flog the bookkeeper, he flogged the slave. Such at least was the account I received from a third party, another bookkeeper. I could scarcely have given credit to such an allegation, had I not heard of similar cases on other plantations, on authority I had no cause to doubt. 2nd & 3rd. Two young women. This punishment took place one evening on the barbecue, where pimento is dried.

Mr. McLean, the overseer, and I, were sitting in the window seat of his hall, and I was just remarking to him that I observed the drivers took great pride in being able to crack their whips loud and well. While we were thus conversing, the gang of young slaves, employed in plucking pimento, came in with their basket loads. The head bookkeeper as usual proceeded to examine the baskets, to ascertain that each slave had duly performed the task allotted. The baskets of two poor girls were pronounced deficient—and the bookkeeper immediately ordered them to be flogged. The overseer did not interfere, nor ask a single question, the matter not being deemed of sufficient importance to require his interference, though this took place within a few yards of the open window where we were sitting.

One of the girls was instantly laid down, her back parts uncovered in the usual brutal and indecent manner, and the driver commenced flogging—every stroke upon her flesh giving a loud crack, and the wretched creature at the same time calling out in agony, "Lord! Lord! Lord!" "That," said the overseer, turning to me, with a chuckling laugh, "that is the best cracking, by G—d!" The other female was then flogged also on the bare posteriors, but not quite so severely. They received, as usual, each 39 lashes. 4th & 5th. On another occasion I saw two girls from 10 to 13 years of age, flogged by order of the overseer.

They belonged to the second gang, employed in cane weeding, and were accused of having been idle that morning. Two other girls of the same age were brought up to hold them down. They got each 39. 6th & 7th. After this I saw two young men flogged (very severely) in the cooper's yard. I did not learn their offense. 8th. On another occasion, a man in the road leading from New Ground to Golden Spring. We met this man while riding out, and for some offense which I did not learn (for by that time I had found my inquiries on such points had become offensive), the overseer called a driver from the field and ordered him 39 on the spot. *9th & 10th.* Two young men before breakfast for having slept too long. They were mule drivers, and it being then crop time, they had been two days and a night previously at work without sleep. As the overseer and I were going out at daybreak (the sun was not yet up), we found them only putting the harness on their mules. They ought, according to the regulations then prescribed on the plantation, to have been out half an hour sooner—and for this offense they received a very severe flogging. *11th.* A girl who had been missing for some days having absconded from the plantation for fear of punishment.

I shall mention only other two cases which particularly excited my sympathy, for, after a few weeks, although my moral abhorrence of slavery continued to increase, my sensibility to the sight of physical suffering was so greatly abated, that a common flogging no longer affected me to the very painful degree that I at first experienced. *12th.* The first of these two cases was that of a married woman, the mother of several children. She was brought up to the overseer's door one morning, and one of the drivers who came with her accused her of having stolen a fowl. Some feathers, said to have been found in her hut, were exhibited as evidence of her guilt. The overseer asked her if she would pay for the fowl. She said something in reply which I did not clearly understand. The question was repeated, and a similar reply again given. The overseer then said, "Put her down." On this the woman set up a shriek, and rent the air with her cries of terror.

Her countenance grew quite ghastly, and her lips became pale and livid. I was close to her and particularly noticed her remarkable aspect and expression of countenance. The overseer swore fearfully—and repeated his order "Put her down!" The woman then craved permission to tie some covering round her nakedness, which she was allowed to do. She was then extended on the ground, and held down by two Negroes. Her gown and shift were literally torn from her back, and, thus brutally exposed, she was subjected to the cart whip. The punishment inflicted on this poor creature was inhumanly severe. She was a woman somewhat plump in her person, and the whip being wielded with great vigor, every stroke cut deep into the flesh. She writhed and twisted her body violently under the infliction—moaning loudly, but uttering no exclamation in words, except once when she cried out, entreating that her nakedness (her parts of shame) might not be indecently exposed—appearing to suffer, from matronly modesty, even more acutely on account of her indecent exposure than the cruel laceration of her body. But the overseer only noticed her appeal by a brutal reply (too gross to be repeated), and the flogging continued. Disgusted as I was, I witnessed the whole to a close. I numbered the lashes, stroke by stroke, and counted *fifty*—thus exceeding by eleven the number allowed by the Colonial Law to be inflicted at the arbitrary will of the master or manager. This was the only occasion on which I saw the legal number of 39 lashes exceeded, but I never knew the overseer or head bookkeeper give less than 39. This poor victim was shockingly lacerated. When permitted to rise, she again shrieked violently. The overseer swore roughly, and threatened, if she was not quiet, to put her down again. He then ordered her to be taken to the hot house or hospital, and put in the stocks. She was to be confined in the stocks for several nights, while she worked in the yard during the day at light work. She was too severely mangled to be able to go to the field for some days. This flogging took place on the 27th of September. *13th.* The flogging of an old man about 60 years of age, is the last case I shall mention.

He was the third driver upon the estate—there being five altogether, whose sole employment was literally *driving*, or coercing by the whip, the Negro population to labor. With this old man I had, had some conversation, and felt particularly interested in him, for his silvery locks and something in his aspect reminded me powerfully of my aged father, whom I had left in England. He had been upon the estate a great number of years. He told me that not one of the Negroes belonging to the gang he wrought in when he first came to New Ground was now alive. He came up to the overseer's door at shell blow one day, and gave in, as is the practice, on a tally or bit of notched stick, his account of the half day's work of the gang he superintended. The overseer was dissatisfied—said it was insufficient—and ordered him to get a flogging. The old man said "Well, Busha, me could have done no better, had you been standing by." Then, groaning deeply, he laid down his staff and whip, unloosed his clothes, and lay quietly down to be flogged without being held. One of the other drivers, who had been called forward, appeared very reluctant to perform the office, but, on the overseer swearing a rough oath or two, he proceeded to inflict the usual punishment of 39 lashes. The old man, looking up in the overseer's face imploringly, cried out after every stroke for several minutes "Busha! Busha! Busha!" but seeing no signs of relenting, he ceased to call on him, expressing his feelings only by groans. I was deeply affected by the sight, and felt at the moment that these groans were an awful appeal to the judgment seat of *him* who heareth the cry of the oppressed. When the punishment was over, and the poor man arose, the other drivers looked at each other and shook their heads, but uttered not a word. They dared not. In conversing with the overseer about these floggings, I had more than once expressed the pain and horror I felt at seeing that Negro slavery was accompanied by so much suffering. The overseer endeavored to persuade me, contrary to the evidence of my own senses, that the punishments were not severe, and assured me that there were, moreover, Negroes who had never been flogged in their lives. I afterwards questioned the head bookkeeper, Mr. Burrows, on this point, and asked him if he could point out a single working Negro on the estate, male or female, single or married, who had not been flogged? After some reflection he replied, that he could not specify a single one who had not been punished with the cart whip. Now there were 277 slaves on that estate, of whom a very small proportion were children, and yet a man who had been among them for only two years did not know of one (with the exception of mere children) who had not been once or oftener subjected to this cruel, degrading, and revolting punishment.

After these conversations I made every exertion to ascertain this fact, by making inquiries among the slaves themselves, as opportunities occurred. The general reply to such interrogations was "Ah! Massa, me been flog many a time by Busha." On putting the question to an aged Negro who had formerly been employed to take care of the sheep, but was now in the stable, he said he had been flogged many a time.

"And what were you flogged for?" I inquired. "When sheep go stray—when sheep sick—when sheep die—then" said he "Busha put me down and flog me till me bleed." "And how many lashes" I asked "did Busha ever give you?" "Ah! Massa" said the poor old man "when me down na ground, and dey flog me till me bleed, me someting else to do den for count de lashes." This same man, as he was saddling my horse on the day I finally left the estate, made a remark that struck me. "Now, Massa" said he "you see how poor Negro be 'pressed (oppressed). We no mind de work—but dey 'press us too, too bad." I asked another Negro, a married man and the father of a family, if either he or his wife had ever been flogged. He replied, that both he and his wife had been flogged frequently—and further remarked, that it was very disheartening that after trying "to be good Negro" they could not escape the lash anymore than the worst slaves on the estate.

This man was a Baptist—a very religious and exemplary man. He had been a member of the Baptist chapel at St. Ann's Bay, which I saw lying in ruins. He could read a little, and I gave him a hymn book. This last mentioned slave was a carpenter.

I, therefore asked the head carpenter (a Scotchman named Walden) if he had ever flogged this man. He replied that he had, and added, that he was obliged to flog all the slaves under his charge. He never took them out with him into the wood, he said, without the cart whip, so that if any of them did not please him he might put him down and give him a flogging.

I asked others similar questions, and received, in every instance, answers to the same effect—all proving the truth of the head bookkeeper's statement that he knew not a single working slave on the estate who had not been flogged. I may here mention that on meeting with a slave of the name of Johnstone belonging to the neighboring estate of Green Park, I asked him if he had ever been flogged. He replied "Yes, Massa, me been flog, and been work in chains three months and three days." On inquiring further, I found this man's offense was going to the Methodist chapel (Mr. Whitehouse's) and that for this offense he had been cruelly flogged by order of his owner, Mr. Hurlock (not by the *overseer*), and worked in chains for three months. During my residence at New Ground, the St. Ann's workhouse gang (of convict slaves) was employed in digging cane holes on the plantation. I had thus frequent opportunities of seeing and conversing with them. I shall never forget the impression I received from the first near view of these wretched people.

The son of the captain, or superintendent of the workhouse (a person named Drake), accompanied me to the field the first day I went out to see this gang, and, as we went along, he remarked that I should probably be somewhat shocked by their appearance, but ought to bear in mind that these Negroes were convicted malefactors—rebels, thieves, and felons. On approaching the spot I witnessed indeed a most affecting and appalling spectacle. The gang, consisting of forty-five Negroes, male and female, were all chained by the necks in couples—and in one instance I observed a man and a woman chained together.

Two stout drivers were standing over them, each armed both with a cart whip and a cat-o-nine tails. Nearly the whole gang were working without any covering on the upper part of their bodies—and on going up to them with a view to closer inspection, I found that their backs, from the shoulders to the buttocks, were scarred and lacerated in all directions, by the frequent application of the cat and the cart whip, which the drivers used at discretion, independently of severer floggings by order of the superintendent. I could not find a single one who did not bear on his body evident marks of this savage discipline.

Some were marked with large weals and with what in Yorkshire we should call *wrethes* or ridges of flesh healed over. Others were crossed with long scabbed scars across the buttocks on others, again, the gashes were raw and recent. Altogether it was the most horrid sight that ever my eyes beheld. One of them had on a coarse shirt or smock frock, which was actually dyed red with his blood. The drivers struck some of them severely while I was present for falling behind the rank in their work. I asked one of the drivers what were the offenses for which these people had been condemned. He replied that some of them were convicts from Trelawney parish, who had been concerned in the late rebellion—others were thieves and runaways, and, pointing out three individuals (two men and a woman), he added that these had been taken up while martial law was in force—*for praying*.

I asked if I might be permitted to speak to these three persons, and, meeting with no objection, I went forward and conversed with them. One of them, whose name was Rogers, in reply to my inquiries, informed me that he had been condemned to the workhouse gang for meeting with other Negroes for prayer. The other man, whose name I have forgot, told me that this was the second time that he had been sent to work in chains solely for this offense—namely, joining with some of his friends and relatives in social prayer to his Maker and Redeemer. In order to assure myself further of the truth of this extraordinary fact, I made inquiry respecting it of some of the most intelligent Negroes on New Ground estate, to whom the particulars connected with these people's condemnation were known, and received such full corroboration of their statement as left me no doubt whatever of its truth. Indeed I soon found good reason to believe that on many estates there are few offenses for which the unhappy slaves are punished with more certainty or severity than *praying*. Drake, the superintendent of this workhouse gang, came frequently to New Ground, while they were employed there, to see that they did sufficient work (for it was paid for by the piece) and one day he was invited by the overseer to dine with us. After dinner, while he and I were standing at the door, he proceeded to abuse the friends of Negro emancipation in England in very violent terms, and added, that if ever I uttered a word unfriendly to them (the slaveholders), he would have great pleasure in cutting my head off. Then, extending his arm, and pointing to his miserable gang, who were at work, full in view, at no great distance, he uttered a tremendous oath, and said "Oh! If I had but Buxton and Lushington chained by the necks in yonder gang I would *cure* them—that would I, by G—d! We would be all right," he added, "if these devils would but let us alone." This man, Drake, as I was told by the overseer, has a salary of £500 currency. I may here notice a few other particulars illustrative of the Jamaica plantation system, which fell under my observation. On New Ground estate there were about fifteen or sixteen religious Negroes who became personally known to me, and I heard that there were others. Those that I knew were Baptists and Wesleyans. After they found they might have confidence in me, they often expressed their deep regret for the banishment of the missionaries. While I was there they durst not be found praying together. If they had, they would have been sure of a flogging. One of the proprietors in England (my relative) had told me that I might preach to the slaves on the estate, and attend to their religious instruction—but I soon found that this would not be permitted by their own Colonial agents. Indeed the attorney, at our very first interview, expressly prohibited me so much as to mention religion to the Negroes. On Sunday there was no religious observance whatever on the estate, nor did I see or hear of any religious observance on any estate in that parish.

The whites usually occupy Sunday in visits to their brother overseers and bookkeepers on other estates, or if at home, in playing at draughts and quoits. The Negroes were all at work on their provision grounds, or in carrying their provisions to market, except the cooper's gang, who were at work for the estate, but for wages on that day, as the overseer assured me. The Negroes receive only a few salt herrings from the estate, and must necessarily employ the Sundays in cultivating their provision grounds. The law allows them only twenty-six week days in the year for this necessary work. In week days the Negroes always went to their work before daylight in the morning, on an average about five o'clock or a quarter past five. They left off after dusk or from a quarter to half-past six in the evening. They had half an hour for breakfast, and sometimes an hour for dinner, but generally not a full hour. During crop, which was proceeding while I was there, they worked in spells the whole of every alternate night, that is to say, the spell that commenced on Monday morning got no sleep till Tuesday night, working all day in the field and all night in the boiling house. The sufferings of the slaves from this hard and continuous labor, and from the continual floggings of the drivers to exact it, are severe beyond description. When they are digging cane holes, they generally work all in a row—and it frequently happens that the strong Negroes outstrip the weaker ones. Then it is that the drivers (who stand *in front* of the gang in holeing, but *behind* in cane cutting) march up to those who have fallen back in their work, and flog them on to further exertion—the drivers being themselves liable to be flogged, if the prescribed work is not duly executed by their gang. I have seen the drivers put down slaves in the field, and inflict at their own discretion, from six to twelve lashes with the cart whip. I have seen them order females to stand at a convenient distance, and flog them as long as they saw fit.

    I have frequently seen the boatswain (as the driver at the boiling house is called) flog old and young, male and female, in this manner. One night I saw this driver flog a female slave very severely, and one blow which struck her in the face caused her to scream out violently. Upon inquiry I found that this woman had a child in the hot house (or hospital), and she had ventured to leave her work a little earlier than usual to see her sick child. For this she received the punishment. On another occasion, I saw this same boatswain put down a very handsome brown girl, and give her ten lashes. The overseer was with me at the time, and looked on, without making any remark. Another time I saw the head driver, a very powerful man, give a tremendous cut with the cart whip to a female about fifty years of age, who was cutting canes with the great gang. The overseer and one of the bookkeepers were standing by with me, but neither took the least notice.

In fact, these floggings were taking place incessantly upon the working Negroes—insomuch that I came to this conclusion after some observation—that the slaves suffered more in the aggregate from the *driving* in the field than from the severer regular punishments inflicted by order of the overseer and bookkeepers. The drivers invariably flog Negroes severely who happen to be too late in coming out in the morning—and it frequently happens that when they oversleep their time the Negroes for fear of punishment run away for days or weeks from the estate. When they do return, as they generally do after a short space, it is with the certainty of encountering a tremendous flogging from the overseer, and being condemned to sleep every night in the stocks for weeks running. I have frequently seen six or seven of these runaways turned out of the stocks in a morning, taken to the field to cut canes, and then brought back at night to be again locked into the stocks. The fear of punishment, I was told, was the ordinary cause of their becoming runaways.

The tyrannical severity of the system may be aptly illustrated by another little incident which I shall here mention. One Sunday afternoon, while I was sitting, as usual, with the overseer at the open window of the hall, an old Negro woman, apparently upwards of sixty years of age, came forward, and begged leave to tell her story to "Busha." She proceeded to state that she was now old and stiff, that she had some infirmity in her knees, which she bared to exhibit to him that she was no longer able to stand the field labor and under these circumstances she pleaded to be allowed to "sit down"—that is—to be released from the regular labor of the estate. The overseer refused her suit, ordered her two or three times to be gone, and said "she talked English too well." At length, on the old woman still continuing her importunity, he lost patience, called one of the domestic slaves and ordered him to put the supplicant in the stocks. To the stocks accordingly she was instantly taken, and confined in them every night for a week continuing to work as usual in the field by day. At length on the following Sunday, she was begged off by the head driver, and came to return thanks, in my presence, to the overseer for her release. And thus was quashed her supplication for mitigation of hard labor, and other supplicants intimidated from appearing. On conversing with Mr. McLean, (as I frequently did when I first went to New Ground) respecting the extreme severity of the system pursued on that estate, he assured me that he was far from being a harder taskmaster than other overseers on sugar plantations and to convince me of this he told me of "severities" (or rather atrocities) exercised on other estates in the same parish, far beyond any which I witnessed on New Ground. I also heard of extraordinary instances of cruelty from others and I was told, by a resident in St. Andrew's parish, that the floggings there were more severe than in St. Ann's—switches of the prickly ebony being frequently used after the cart whip. But I shall not attempt to detail what I learned only by hearsay, although on the evidence of persons implicated in supporting the system.

I can only vouch, of course, for what I myself witnessed and that most assuredly I have rather softened than exaggerated. The open and avowed licentiousness of the plantation whites disgusted me almost as much as the cruelty of the system. At New Ground, the overseer, bookkeepers, and head carpenter, all lived in the habitual practice of gross and unblushing profligacy.

The tremendous *moral* tyranny that may be, and unquestionably often is, exercised in the uncontrolled indulgence of this brutalizing vice, is as obvious as it is appalling.

One of the bookkeepers voluntarily mentioned to me, that he had had twelve "Negro wives" within six months. I saw another of the whites on this estate give his "housekeeper" (concubine), a cruel beating with a supplejack while she was in a state of pregnancy, and for a very trifling fault.

For refusing to degrade myself by complying with "the custom of the country" as it was lightly termed, in this point, I was looked upon, as I soon perceived, with mingled contempt and suspicion by the plantation whites generally.

I shall now mention the circumstances which led to my abandonment of the views I had in going out to Jamaica, and obliged me to return to England, after so short a residence.

After I had been about a week on New Ground estate, I had an interview at St. Ann's Bay with the attorney or agent of the proprietors, to whose patronage I had been recommended by my relative in England. I told him that from what I had seen of a planter's life I felt myself to be but ill-adapted for that profession and that I had resolved to abandon all thoughts of it, but, as I had neither friend nor acquaintance save himself in that part of the island, I should feel much indebted to him if he would allow me to remain, as a resident merely, on the estate until I could hear from a correspondent in Kingston, to whom I had written, requesting him to make every possible exertion to procure me employment in a store, or any other creditable occupation, by which I might earn a livelihood unconnected with the plantation system. The attorney asked the name of the gentleman to whom I had written. I told him it was Mr. Pennock, the Wesleyan missionary, and informed him that I was a member of that Society myself, and had occasionally officiated as a local preacher before I left England. The attorney seemed a good deal disconcerted by this information. He assured me that Mr. Pennock could do nothing to assist me, and added, that such was the feeling of the inhabitants of Jamaica against the sectarians, that he himself, though he was the man of the greatest influence in that parish, would be exposed to great odium—perhaps peril—if the planters knew that he was patronizing a person of my character. "They would think nothing" he said, pointing to the sea "of throwing me in *there* for that, and for no other offense." As, however, I had been sent out to him by the proprietors, he added, that he would do the best he could to promote my interests. Meanwhile he advised me to remain on the estate, where, he said, as I disliked the system, I should have nothing to do with it—but charged me to let no person know that I was a Methodist, and, (as I have already mentioned) he strictly prohibited me from attempting to instruct the Negroes, or to say a single word to them about religion.

In other respects he appeared friendly, and promised to give me a letter to Mr. Whitehorn, an attorney at Kingston, a relative of his, with a view to find me some other occupation.

About a week after this, I was informed by a neighboring bookkeeper that it had been discovered by the address of my letter to Mr. Pennock, that I was in correspondence with the sectarians, and that some gentlemen at St. Ann's Bay had formed a plan to tar and feather me, if they could find a convenient opportunity. This information I communicated by letter to the attorney, who resided on a property of his own, about twenty miles distant from New Ground. He immediately sent for me to come to him, warning me not to travel by the bay, for fear of the Colonial Unionists, but to come round by the mountain road.

I went accordingly, and remained a night with him. I then proceeded to Kingston in search of employment, and saw Mr. Pennock, and other persons who were very desirous to promote my views, but meeting with no success, I was obliged to return to New Ground. I subsequently made another journey to Kingston, but with no better result. At another interview which I soon afterwards had with the attorney, I told him I thought it very hard, that after having been at so much expense in coming out to Jamaica, I could obtain no situation in the island merely because I was a Methodist. He then spoke of another charge he had in view for me, and mentioned also, that Mr. Hamilton Brown was desirous of giving me employment, but that he was so much intimidated by the threats that were held out against all who favored Sectarians, that he durst not venture to do it.

He further assured me, that unless I would agree to enroll myself as a member of the Colonial Church Union, and renounce "even the very appearance of sectarianism" he saw no likelihood of my being enabled to obtain or hold any situation in the colony, adding emphatically, that unless I did this, he could not guarantee anything in regard to me—no, not even life itself.

On this occasion I expressed my surprise that the planters should be so *outrageously* partial to Churchmen in opposition to the Sectarians, when they could not be ignorant that many eminent ministers and members of the Church of England were laboring for the abolition of slavery with not less zeal than the Wesleyans or Baptists. The attorney replied significantly, (and his words made a deep impression on me) "It is an opinion amongst us, but one which we do not wish to acknowledge or to be known, that *slavery and knowledge are incompatible*." These were this gentleman's own words—a man of whom I would not willingly speak unkindly, for I was always hospitably received, and otherwise kindly treated by him but as respects his unscrupulous support of the Colonial system, I leave the reader to judge for himself. On this and other occasions I thought it my duty to acquaint the attorney with my observations and my feelings, in regard to the cruel floggings and severe treatment generally, which I had witnessed at New Ground. He admitted the facts, but said that plantation work could not be carried on without the cart whip. He moreover labored hard to convince me that the flogging did not injure the health of the Negroes. I also told him of the exceeding immorality and licentiousness which I had witnessed, mentioning, in substance, the facts previously detailed. He replied that, that was a thing which they (the attorneys) must "wink at." He said he had but two married overseers under him upon the several properties he managed, and he intended never to have another, for (he remarked) the overseers, bookkeepers, and head carpenters, generally took for their mistresses the sisters or daughters of the drivers or carpenters, by which means, if any plot was hatching amongst the slaves, some intimation of it was almost certain to be conveyed by these channels to the whites upon the plantation. And for the sake of such a wretched security, this gentleman, in the true spirit of the system (though in other respects apparently a benevolent and honorable man) was content to "wink at" the wickedness. Soon after this, a person of my acquaintance came up from St. Ann's Bay, and advised me to leave New Ground estate without delay, because the members of the Colonial Church Union down at the Bay were determined to do me some mischief. I felt somewhat alarmed on receiving this intimation, and expressed my apprehensions to the overseer. He replied, that there was no occasion for me to leave the estate—that I need not be at all afraid, for (as he vehemently swore) he would sooner lose his own life than deliver me up to my enemies. How far Mr. McLean was sincere in his assurances and professions I shall not pretend positively to determine. I subsequently thought I saw good cause to believe him not averse to any scheme that would lead to my removal *quietly* from New Ground estate—of nothing worse, as regards myself, have I the least reason to suspect him. But, at the period I now advert to, I did not entertain even the suspicion I have now expressed, and, moreover, I was at a great loss what course to adopt, for if I left the estate, I knew not well where else to betake myself.

About a fortnight after my return from my last visit to the attorney, a deputation from St. Ann's Colonial Church Union waited upon me. This took place on one of the militia muster days. I observed that day that a number of overseers and bookkeepers called at New Ground estate, as they returned from muster, and I noticed a great deal of whispering among them.

Just at dusk two persons, under the character of a deputation from the Colonial Church Union made their appearance and demanded an interview with me. The overseer introduced them—a Mr. Dicken and a Mr. Brown. The former I had previously met with, but to my salutation he now made no response. Mr. Brown was spokesman, and commenced by informing me that they came as a deputation from more than a hundred gentlemen at St. Ann's Bay, to state to me.

1st. That they had heard I had been leading the minds of the slaves astray by holding forth doctrines of a tendency to make them discontented with their present condition. *2ndly*. That I was a Methodist, and that my relative who had sent me to Jamaica was a damned Methodist. And, *3rdly*. That they had a barrel of tar down at the Bay to tar and feather me, as I well deserved, and that they "would do so, by G—d." In reply, I acknowledged that I was undoubtedly a Methodist, but added, mildly, that I was altogether unconscious of any act, since I arrived in the island, whereby I could have given any reasonable offense to the planters or any other class of men—and I begged them to specify my offenses. Mr. Brown than stated, that in the first place, I had written a letter to the Reverend Thomas

Pennock, Wesleyan Missionary, *2ndly*. That in a letter I had written to an attorney, I had said "The Lord reward you for the kindnesses you have shown me, and grant you in health and wealth long to live." *3rdly*. That I had said to a slave who had opened a gate to me at a certain place "The Lord bless you." *4thly*. That I had asked the drivers of the workhouse gang questions respecting the offenses of the Negroes of that gang.

5thly. That I had made private remarks about the way in which I had seen Mr. McLean, the overseer, treat the slaves. (Here Dicken, who was an overseer at Windsor, a neighboring plantation, told me he had two Negroes at that moment in the stocks, and added, with a brutal oath, if I would come over in the morning he would let me see them properly flogged.) *6thly*. That I had preached to a hundred and fifty slaves at one time. To all these charges I pleaded guilty, except the last, which was without foundation—without even a shadow of truth—though, if it had been true, it would have been difficult for me to admit its criminality. Dicken then drew his hand across my throat, and swore by his Maker that he would be the first man to cut it if I should dare to talk to the slaves in the same way again. He then pulled out a pistol, which he cocked, and held out (but did not point it at my person), saying, that if he was to fire it off, there would be twenty men in the house in one minute, ready to do whatever they chose with me. Mr. McLean, the overseer, here spoke up, and said, with considerable vehemence, that before he would see me abused he would rather have a ball through his own breast. I then told them that there was no occasion for violence, that I was quite willing, under the circumstances in which I found myself, to leave the island by the very first conveyance, and should be glad if they and their friends would only permit me to do so quietly. They promised to report this reply to their Society, the Colonial Church Union, and so departed. It was agreed that I should sail in the ship *Huskisson* and that I might remain on the estate till that vessel was ready—but having been seen conversing with Mr. Watkins, a Wesleyan, and a brother of the member of the Colonial Assembly of that name, the attorney was informed of this (no other fault was alleged), and he sent word to the overseer to enforce my departure *immediately*. I was hurried off accordingly, and, in my way from St. Ann's to Annotto Bay, I saw the attorney once more. He then told me that it was necessary, for both his sake and mine, that I should leave the country and apologized for his hurrying my departure by stating that he had recently received many violent letters on my account from the Colonial Unionists, threatening to pull his house about his ears, as other houses had been pulled about the ears of the owners, on similar grounds elsewhere. I proceeded from St. Ann's to Annotto Bay to await the sailing of the vessel, and, while thus detained, I had a pretty severe attack of the country fever, which confined me for ten days. On the 8th of December I sailed from Jamaica, having been just three months and six days on the island. I leave the facts thus plainly related, as they fell under my observation during this short residence, to the reader's calm reflection. They will sufficiently display the character of Negro slavery, as it now exists in Jamaica, without any comment of mine. But as I have mentioned that I left England with a persuasion that the general condition of the West India slaves was, on the whole, much preferable to that of the children in our factories, it is proper to state the conviction with which I have returned—which is this. The condition of the factory children is certainly very deplorable, and calls loudly for amelioration—and I shall most cordially rejoice to see the friends of Negro Emancipation cooperating with the friends of Factory Regulation in carrying the Ten Hours Bill speedily through Parliament.

But between the cases of the factory child and the plantation slave there can be no just comparison.

The former is very bad—the latter is *infinitely worse*.

Abraham Lincoln

Excerpt from the *Autobiography of Abraham Lincoln* which was first published in 1905 in a limited edition by the Francis D. Tandy Company.
It was originally published in 1894 as part of the *Complete Works of Abraham Lincoln* which was edited by John G. Nicolay and John Hay.

Autobiographical sketch written for Jesse W. Fell Springfield, December 20, 1859

My dear Sir—Herewith is a little sketch, as you requested. There is not much of it, for the reason, I suppose, that there is not much of me. If anything be made out of it, I wish it to be modest, and not to go beyond the material.
If it were thought necessary to incorporate anything from any of my speeches I suppose there would be no objection. Of course it must not appear to have been written by myself. Yours very truly.

    I was born February 12, 1809, in Hardin County, Kentucky. My parents were both born in Virginia, of undistinguished families—second families, perhaps I should say. My mother, who died in my tenth year, was of a family of the name of Hanks, some of whom now reside in Adams and others in Macon County, Illinois. My paternal grandfather, Abraham Lincoln, emigrated from Rockingham County, Virginia, to Kentucky about 1781 or 1782, where a year or two later he was killed by the Indians, not in battle, but by stealth, when he was laboring to open a farm in the forest. His ancestors, who were Quakers, went to Virginia from Berks County, Pennsylvania. An effort to identify them with the New England family of the same name ended in nothing more definite than a similarity of Christian names in both families, such as Enoch, Levi, Mordecai, Solomon, Abraham, and the like.

My father, at the death of his father, was but six years of age, and he grew up literally without education. He removed from Kentucky to what is now Spencer County, Indiana, in my eighth year. We reached our new home about the time the State came into the Union. It was a wild region, with many bears and other wild animals still in the woods. There I grew up.

There were some schools, so called, but no qualification was ever required of a teacher beyond "reading, writing, and deciphering" to the rule of three. If a straggler supposed to understand Latin happened to sojourn in the neighborhood, he was looked upon as a wizard. There was absolutely nothing to excite ambition for education. Of course, when I came of age I did not know much. Still, somehow, I could read, write, and cipher to the rule of three, but that was all. I have not been to school since. The little advance I now have upon this store of education, I have picked up from time to time under the pressure of necessity. I was raised to farm work, which I continued till I was twenty-two.

At twenty-one, I came to Illinois, Macon County. Then I got to New Salem, at that time in Sangamon, now in Menard County, where I remained a year as a sort of clerk in a store. Then came the Black Hawk War—and I was elected a captain of volunteers, a success which gave me more pleasure than any I have had since. I went the campaign, was elated, ran for the legislature the same year (1832), and was beaten—the only time I ever have been beaten by the people. The next and three succeeding biennial elections I was elected to the legislature. I was not a candidate afterwards. During this legislative period I had studied law, and removed to Springfield to practice it. In 1846 I was once elected to the lower House of Congress. I was not a candidate for reelection. From 1849 to 1854, both inclusive, I practiced law more assiduously than ever before. Always a Whig in politics—and generally on the Whig electoral tickets, making active canvasses. I was losing interest in politics when the repeal of the Missouri Compromise aroused me again. What I have done since then is pretty well-known. If any personal description of me is thought desirable, it may be said I am, in height, six feet four inches, nearly, lean in flesh, weighing on an average one hundred and eighty pounds, dark complexion, with coarse black hair and gray eyes. No other marks or brands recollected. Yours Truly.

Autobiographical Memorandum
Given to the artist Thomas Hicks—June 14, 1860

I was born February 12, 1809, in then Hardin County, Kentucky, at a point within the now county of LaRue, a mile, or a mile and a half, from where Hodgen's Mill now is. My parents being dead, and my own memory not serving, I know no means of identifying the precise locality. It was on Nolin Creek.

A short autobiography—written in June 1860—at the request of a friend to use in preparing a campaign biography in the election of that year.
It is written in third person (though written by Abraham Lincoln) about his background and childhood as well as his adult years.

Abraham Lincoln was born February 12, 1809, then in Hardin, now in the more recently formed county of LaRue, Kentucky. His father, Thomas, and grandfather, Abraham, were born in Rockingham County, Virginia—whither their ancestors had come from Berks County, Pennsylvania. His lineage has been traced no farther back than this. The family was originally Quakers, though in later times they have fallen away from the peculiar habits of that people. The grandfather, Abraham, had four brothers—Isaac, Jacob, John, and Thomas. So far as known, the descendants of Jacob and John are still in Virginia. Isaac went to a place near where Virginia, North Carolina, and Tennessee join, and his descendants are in that region. Thomas came to Kentucky, and after many years died there, whence his descendants went to Missouri. Abraham, grandfather of the subject of this sketch, came to Kentucky, and was killed by Indians about the year 1786. He left a widow, three sons, and two daughters. The eldest son, Mordecai, remained in Kentucky till late in life, when he removed to Hancock County, Illinois, where soon after he died, and where several of his descendants still remain. The second son, Josiah, removed at an early day to a place on Blue River, now within Hancock County, Indiana, but no recent information of him or his family has been obtained.

The eldest sister, Mary, married Ralph Crume, and some of her descendants are now known to be in Breckinridge County, Kentucky. The second sister, Nancy, married William Brumfield, and her family are not known to have left Kentucky, but there is no recent information from them. Thomas, the youngest son, and father of the present subject, by the early death of his father and very narrow circumstances of his mother, even in childhood was a wandering laboring boy and grew up literally without education. He never did more in the way of writing than to bunglingly write his own name. Before he was grown he passed one year as a hired hand with his Uncle Isaac on Watauga, a branch of the Holston River. Getting back into Kentucky, and having reached his twenty-eighth year, he married Nancy Hanks—mother of the present subject—in the year 1806. She also was born in Virginia and relatives of hers of the name of Hanks, and of other names, now reside in Coles, in Macon, and in Adams counties, Illinois, and also in Iowa. The present subject has no brother or sister of the whole or half blood. He had a sister, older than himself, who was grown and married, but died many years ago, leaving no child, also a brother, younger than himself, who died in infancy.

Before leaving Kentucky, he and his sister were sent, for short periods, to ABC schools, the first kept by Zachariah Riney, and the second by Caleb Hazel Jr. At this time his father resided on Knob Creek, on the road from Bardstown, Kentucky, to

Nashville, Tennessee, at a point three or three and a half miles south or southwest of Atherton's Ferry, on the Rolling Fork.

From this place he removed to what is now Spencer County, Indiana, in the autumn of 1816, Abraham then being in his eighth year. This removal was partly on account of slavery, but chiefly on account of the difficulty in land titles in Kentucky. He settled in an unbroken forest, and the clearing away of surplus wood was the great task ahead. Abraham, though very young, was large for his age, and had an ax put into his hands at once, and from that till within his twenty-third year he was almost constantly handling that most useful instrument—less, of course, in plowing and harvesting seasons. At this place Abraham took an early start as a hunter, which was never much improved afterwards. A few days before the completion of his eighth year, in the absence of his father, a flock of wild turkeys approached the new log cabin, and Abraham with a rifle gun, standing inside, shot through a crack and killed one of them. He has never since pulled a trigger on any larger game. In the autumn of 1818 his mother died—and a year afterwards his father married Mrs. Sally Johnston, at Elizabethtown, Kentucky, a widow with three children of her first marriage. She proved a good and kind mother to Abraham, and is still living in Coles County, Illinois. There were no children of this second marriage. His father's residence continued at the same place in Indiana till 1830. While here Abraham went to ABC schools by Littles—kept successively by Andrew Crawford, William Sweeney, and Azel W. Dorsey.

He does not remember any other. The family of Mr. Dorsey now resides in Schuyler County, Illinois. Abraham now thinks that the aggregate of all his schooling did not amount to one year. He was never in a college or academy as a student, and never inside of a college or academy building till since he had a law license. What he has in the way of education he has picked up. After he was twenty-three and had separated from his father, he studied English grammar—imperfectly, of course, but so as to speak and write as well as he now does. He studied and nearly mastered the six books of Euclid since he was a member of

Congress. He regrets his want of education, and does what he can to supply the want. In his tenth year he was kicked by a horse, and apparently killed for a time. When he was nineteen, still residing in Indiana, he made his first trip upon a flatboat to New Orleans. He was a hired hand merely, and he and a son of the owner, without other assistance, made the trip. The nature of part of the "cargo load" as it was called, made it necessary for them to linger and trade along the sugar coast—and one night they were attacked by seven Negroes with intent to kill and rob them. They were hurt some in the melee, but succeeded in driving the Negroes from the boat, and then "cut cable, weighed anchor" and left. March 1, 1830, Abraham having just completed his twenty-first year, his father and family, with the families of the two daughters and sons-in-law of his stepmother, left the old homestead in Indiana and came to Illinois. Their mode of conveyance was wagons drawn by ox-teams, and Abraham drove one of the teams. They reached the county of Macon, and stopped there sometime within the same month of March.

His father and family settled a new place on the north side of the Sangamon River, at the junction of the timber land and prairie, about ten miles westerly from Decatur. Here they built a log cabin, into which they removed, and made sufficient of rails to fence ten acres of ground, fenced and broke the ground, and raised a crop of sown corn upon it the same year.

These are, or are supposed to be, the rails about which so much is being said just now, though these are far from being the first or only rails ever made by Abraham. The sons-in-law were temporarily settled in other places in the county. In the autumn all hands were greatly afflicted with ague and fever, to which they had not been used, and by which they were greatly discouraged, so much so that they determined on leaving the county. They remained, however, through the succeeding winter, which was the winter of the very celebrated "deep snow" of Illinois.

During that winter Abraham, together with his stepmother's son, John D. Johnston, and John Hanks, yet residing in Macon County, hired themselves, to Denton Offutt to take a flatboat from Beardstown, Illinois, to New Orleans, and for that purpose were to join him—Offutt—at Springfield, Illinois, so soon as the snow should go off. When it did go off, which was about the first of March, 1831, the county was so flooded as to make traveling by land impracticable—to obviate which difficulty they purchased a large canoe, and came down the Sangamon River in it. This is the time and the manner of Abraham's first entrance into Sangamon County. They found Offutt at Springfield, but learned from him that he had failed in getting a boat at Beardstown. This led to their hiring themselves to him for twelve dollars per month each, and getting the timber out of the trees and building a boat at Old Sangamon town on the Sangamon River, seven miles northwest of Springfield, which boat they took to New Orleans, substantially upon the old contract.

During this boat enterprise acquaintance with Offutt, who was previously an entire stranger, he conceived a liking for Abraham, and believing he could turn him to account, he contracted with him to act as clerk for him, on his return from New Orleans, in charge of a store and mill at New Salem, then in Sangamon, now in Menard County. Hanks had not gone to New Orleans, but having a family, and being likely to be detained from home longer than at first expected, had turned back from St. Louis. He is the same John Hanks who now engineers the "rail enterprise" at Decatur, and is a first cousin to Abraham's mother. Abraham's father, with his own family and others mentioned, had, in pursuance of their intention, removed from Macon to Coles County. John D. Johnston, the stepmother's son, went to them, and Abraham stopped indefinitely and for the first time, as it were, by himself at New Salem, before mentioned.

This was in July, 1831. Here he rapidly made acquaintances and friends. In less than a year Offutt's business was failing—had almost failed—when the Black Hawk War of 1832 broke out. Abraham joined a volunteer company, and, to his own surprise, was elected captain of it. He says he has not since had any success in life which gave him so much satisfaction.

He went to the campaign, served near three months, met the ordinary hardships of such an expedition, but was in no battle. He now owns, in Iowa, the land upon which his own warrants for the service were located. Returning from the campaign, and encouraged by his great popularity among his immediate neighbors, he the same year ran for the legislature, and was beaten—his own precinct, however, casting its votes 277 for and 7 against him—and that, too, while he was an avowed Clay man, and the precinct the autumn afterwards giving a majority of 115 to General Jackson over Mr. Clay. This was the only time Abraham was ever beaten on a direct vote of the people.

He was now without means and out of business, but was anxious to remain with his friends who had treated him with so much generosity, especially as he had nothing elsewhere to go to. He studied what he should do—thought of learning the blacksmith trade—thought of trying to study law—rather thought he could not succeed at that without a better education.

Before long, strangely enough, a man offered to sell, and did sell, to Abraham and another as poor as himself, an old stock of goods, upon credit. They opened as merchants, and he says that was *the* store. Of course they did nothing but get deeper and deeper in debt. He was appointed postmaster at New Salem—the office being too insignificant to make his politics an objection. The store winked out. The surveyor of Sangamon offered to depute to Abraham that portion of his work which was within his part of the County. He accepted, procured a compass and chain, studied Flint and Gibson a little, and went at it. This procured bread, and kept soul and body together. The election of 1834 came, and he was then elected to the legislature by the highest vote cast for any candidate. Major John T. Stuart, then in full practice of the law, was also elected. During the canvass, in a private conversation he encouraged Abraham to study law.

After the election he borrowed books of Stuart, took them home with him, and went at it in good earnest. He studied with nobody. He still mixed in the surveying to pay board and clothing bills. When the legislature met, the law books were dropped, but were taken up again at the end of the session. He was reelected in 1836, 1838, and 1840. In the autumn of 1836 he obtained a law license, and on April 15, 1837, removed to Springfield, and commenced the practice—his old friend Stuart taking him into partnership. March 3, 1837, by a protest entered upon the *Illinois House Journal* of that date, at pages 817 and 818, Abraham, with Dan Stone, another representative of Sangamon, briefly defined his position on the slavery question, and so far as it goes, it was then the same that it is now. The protest is as follows below.

Resolutions upon the subject of domestic slavery having passed both branches of the General Assembly at its present session, the undersigned hereby protest against the passage of the same. They believe that the institution of slavery is founded on both injustice and bad policy, but that the promulgation of abolition doctrines tends rather to increase than abate its evils. They believe that the Congress of the United States has no power under the Constitution to interfere with the institution of slavery in the different States. They believe that the Congress of the United States has the power, under the Constitution, to abolish slavery in the District of Columbia, but that the power ought not to be exercised unless at the request of the people of the District. The difference between these opinions and those contained in the above resolutions is their reason for entering this protest.

Dan Stone and Abraham Lincoln
Representatives from the County of Sangamon

In 1838 and 1840, Mr. Lincoln's party voted for him as Speaker, but being in the minority he was not elected. After 1840 he declined a reelection to the legislature. He was on the Harrison electoral ticket in 1840—and on that of Clay in 1844—and spent much time and labor in both those canvasses. In November, 1842, he was married to Mary, daughter of Robert S. Todd, of Lexington, Kentucky. They have three living children, all sons, one born in 1843, one in 1850, and one in 1853. They lost one, who was born in 1846. In 1846 he was elected to the lower House of Congress, and served one term only, commencing in December, 1847, and ending with the inauguration of General Taylor, in March, 1849. All the battles of the Mexican American War had been fought before Mr. Lincoln took his seat in Congress, but the American army was still in Mexico, and the treaty of peace was not fully and formally ratified till the June afterwards. Much has been said of his course in Congress in regard to this war. A careful examination of the *Journal* and *Congressional Globe* shows that he voted for all the supply measures that came up, and for all the measures in any way favorable to the officers, soldiers, and their families, who conducted the war through—with the exception that some of these measures passed without yeas and nays, leaving no record as to how particular men voted. The *Journal* and *Globe* also show him voting that the war was unnecessarily and unconstitutionally begun by the President of the United States. This is the language of Mr. Ashmun's amendment, for which Mr. Lincoln and nearly or quite all other Whigs of the House of Representatives voted. Mr. Lincoln's reasons for the opinion expressed by this vote were briefly that the President had sent General Taylor into an inhabited part of the country belonging to Mexico, and not to the United States, and thereby had provoked the first act of hostility, in fact the commencement of the war, that the place, being the country bordering on the east bank of the Rio Grande, was inhabited by native Mexicans born there under the Mexican Government, and had never submitted to, nor been conquered by, Texas or the United States, nor transferred to either by treaty—that although Texas claimed the Rio Grande as her boundary, Mexico had never recognized it, and neither Texas nor the United States had ever enforced it, that there was a broad desert between that and the country over which Texas had actual control, that the country where hostilities commenced, having once belonged to Mexico, must remain so until it was somehow legally transferred, which had never been done.

Mr. Lincoln thought the act of sending an armed force among the Mexicans was unnecessary, inasmuch as Mexico was in no way molesting or menacing the United States or the people thereof—and that it was unconstitutional, because the power of levying war is vested in Congress, and not in the President.

He thought the principal motive for the act was to divert public attention from the surrender of "Fifty-Four, Forty, or Fight" to Great Britain, on the Oregon boundary question. Mr. Lincoln was not a candidate for reelection. This was determined upon and declared before he went to Washington, in accordance with an understanding among Whig friends, by which Colonel Hardin and Colonel Baker had each previously served a single term in this same district. In 1848, during his term in Congress, he advocated General Taylor's nomination for the presidency, in opposition to all others, and also took an active part for his election after his nomination, speaking a few times in Maryland, near Washington, several times in Massachusetts, and canvassing quite fully his own district in Illinois, which was followed by a majority in the district of over fifteen hundred for General Taylor.

Upon his return from Congress he went to the practice of the law with greater earnestness than ever before. In 1852 he was upon the Scott electoral ticket, and did something in the way of canvassing, but owing to the hopelessness of the cause in Illinois he did less than in previous presidential canvasses.

In 1854 his profession had almost superseded the thought of politics in his mind, when the repeal of the Missouri Compromise aroused him as he had never been before. In the autumn of that year he took the stump with no broader practical aim or object, than to secure, if possible, the reelection of Honorable Richard Yates to Congress. His speeches at once attracted a more marked attention than they had ever before done. As the canvass proceeded he was drawn to different parts of the State outside of Mr. Yates's district. He did not abandon the law, but gave his attention by turns to that and politics.

The State Agricultural Fair was at Springfield that year and Douglas was announced to speak there. In the canvass of 1856 Mr. Lincoln made over fifty speeches, no one of which, so far as he remembers, was put in print. One of them was made at

Galena, but Mr. Lincoln has no recollection of any part of it being printed—nor does he remember whether in that speech he said anything about a Supreme Court decision. He may have spoken upon that subject, and some of the newspapers may have reported him as saying what is now ascribed to him—but he thinks he could not have expressed himself as represented.

House Divided Against Itself
Speech at Springfield, June 16, 1858

Speech was delivered at Springfield, Illinois, at the close of the Republican State Convention by which Convention Abraham Lincoln was officially named as a candidate for United States Republican Senator.
Stephen Douglas was not present. By this time Lincoln had gained a reputation and was quite popular.

Mr. President and Gentlemen of the Convention if we could first know where we are, and whither we are tending, we could better judge what to do, and how to do it. We are now far into the fifth year since a policy was initiated with the avowed object and confident promise of putting an end to slavery agitation. Under the operation of that policy, that agitation has not only, not ceased, but has constantly augmented. In my opinion, it will not cease until a crisis shall have been reached and passed. "A house divided against itself cannot stand." I believe this Government cannot endure permanently half slave and half free.

I do not expect the Union to be dissolved, I do not expect the house to fall—but I do expect it will cease to be divided. It will become all one thing, or all the other. Either the opponents of slavery will arrest the further spread of it, and place it where the public mind shall rest in the belief that it is the course of ultimate extinction—or its advocates will push it forward till it shall become alike lawful in all the States, old as well as new, North as well as South. Have we no tendency to the latter condition?

Let anyone who doubts carefully contemplate that now almost complete legal combination—piece of machinery, so to speak—compounded of the Nebraska doctrine and the Dred

Scott decision. Let him consider, not only what work the machinery is adapted to do, and how well-adapted—but also let him study the history of its construction, and trace if he can, or rather fail, if he can, to trace the evidences of design and concert of action among its chief architects from the beginning.

The new year of 1854 found slavery excluded from more than half the States by State constitutions and from most of the national territory by congressional prohibition. Four days later commenced the struggle which ended in repealing that congressional prohibition. This opened all the national territory to slavery, and was the first point gained. But, so far, Congress *only* had acted—and an endorsement by the people, real or apparent, was indispensable, to save the point already gained and give chance for more. This necessity had not been overlooked, but had been provided for, as well as might be, in the notable argument of "squatter sovereignty" otherwise called "sacred right of self-government" which latter phrase, through expressive of the only rightful basis of any government, was so perverted in this attempted use of it as to amount to just this—that if any *one* man choose to enslave *another*, no *third* man shall be allowed to object. That argument was incorporated into the Nebraska bill itself, in the language which follows—*It being the true intent and meaning of this Act not to legislate slavery into any Territory or State, nor to exclude it therefrom, but to leave the people thereof perfectly free to form and regulate their domestic institutions in their own way, subject only to the Constitution of the United States.* Then opened the roar of loose declamation in favor of "squatter sovereignty" and "sacred right of self-government." "But" said opposition members "let us amend the bill so as to expressly declare that the people of the Territory may exclude slavery." "Not we" said the friends of the measure, and down they voted the amendment. While the Nebraska bill was passing through Congress, a *law case*, involving the question of a Negro's freedom, by reason of his owner having voluntarily taken him first into a Free State, and then into a Territory covered by the congressional prohibition, and held him as a slave for a long time in each, was passing through the United States Circuit Court for the District of Missouri—and both Nebraska bill and lawsuit were brought to a decision in the same month of May, 1854.

The Negro's name was "Dred Scott" which name now designates the decision finally made in the case. Before the then next Presidential election, the law case came to, and was argued in the Supreme Court of the United States, but the decision of it was deferred until after the election. Still, before the election, Senator Trumbull, on the floor of the Senate, requested the leading advocate of the Nebraska bill to state *his opinion* whether the people of a Territory can constitutionally exclude slavery from their limits, and the latter answered "that is a question for the Supreme Court." The election came. Mr. Buchanan was elected, and the endorsement, such as it was, secured. That was the second point gained. The endorsement, however, fell short of a clear popular majority by nearly four hundred thousand votes, and so, perhaps, was not overwhelmingly reliable and satisfactory. The outgoing President, in his last annual message, as impressively as possible echoed back upon the people the weight and authority of the endorsement. The Supreme Court met again—did not announce their decision, but ordered a reargument. The presidential inauguration came, and still no decision of the court—but the incoming President, in his inaugural address, fervently exhorted the people to abide by the forthcoming decision, whatever it might be. Then, in a few days, came the decision. The reputed author of the Nebraska bill finds an early occasion to make a speech at this capital indorsing the Dred Scott decision, and vehemently denouncing all opposition to it. The new President, too, seizes the early occasion of the Silliman letter to endorse and strongly construe that decision, and to express his astonishment that any different view had ever been entertained. At length a squabble springs up between the President and the author of the Nebraska bill on the mere question of *fact*—whether the Lecompton Constitution was or was not in any just sense made by the people of Kansas—and in that quarrel the latter declares that all he wants is a fair vote for the people, and that he cares not whether slavery be voted *down* or voted *up*. I do not understand his declaration, that he cares not whether slavery be voted down or voted up, to be intended by him other than as an apt definition of the policy he would impress upon the public mind—the principle for which he declares he has suffered so much, and is ready to suffer to the end. And well may he cling to that principle. If he has any parental feeling, well may he cling to it. That principle is the only shred left of his original Nebraska doctrine. Under the Dred Scott decision "squatter sovereignty" squatted out of existence, tumbled down like temporary scaffolding, like the mold at the foundry, served through one blast, and fell back into loose sand, helped to carry an election, and then was kicked to the winds. His late joint struggle with the Republicans, against the Lecompton Constitution, involves nothing of the original Nebraska doctrine.

That struggle was made on a point—the right of a people to make their own constitution—upon which he and the Republicans have never differed. The several points of the Dred Scott decision, in connection with Senator Douglas's "care not" policy, constitute the piece of machinery, in its present state of advancement. This was the third point gained. The working points of that machinery are, first, that no Negro slave, imported as such from Africa, and no descendant of such slave, can ever be a citizen of any State, in the sense of that term as used in the Constitution of the United States. This point is made in order to deprive the Negro. In every possible event, of the benefit of that provision of the United States Constitution which declares that "the citizens of each State shall be entitled to all the privileges and immunities of citizens in the several States." Secondly, that, "subject to the Constitution of the United States" neither Congress nor a Territorial Legislature can exclude slavery from any United States territory. This point is made in order that individual men may fill up the territories with slaves, without danger of losing them as property, and thus enhance the chances of permanency to the institution through all the future.

Thirdly, That whether the holding a Negro in actual slavery in a Free State, makes him free, as against the holder, the United States courts will not decide, but will leave to be decided by the courts of any Slave State the Negro may be forced into by the master. This point is made, not to be pressed immediately, but, if acquiesced in for a while, and apparently endorsed by the people at an election, then to sustain the logical conclusion that what Dred Scott's master might lawfully do with Dred Scott in the Free State of Illinois, every other master might lawfully do with any other one, or one thousand slaves, in Illinois, or in any other Free State. Auxiliary to all this, and working hand-in-hand with it, the Nebraska doctrine, or what is left of it, is to educate and mold public opinion, at least Northern public opinion, not to care whether slavery is voted down or voted up. This shows exactly where we now are—and partially, also, whither we are tending. It will throw additional light on the latter to go back and run the mind over the string of historical facts already stated.

Several things will now appear less dark and mysterious than they did when they were transpiring. The people were to be left "perfectly free" "subject only to the Constitution." What the Constitution had to do with it, outsiders could not then see. Plainly enough now, it was an exactly fitted niche, for the Dred Scott decision to afterwards come in, and declare the perfect freedom of the people to be just no freedom at all. Why was the amendment, expressly declaring the right of the people, voted down? Plainly enough now, the adoption of it would have spoiled the niche for the Dred Scott decision. Why was the court decision held up? Why even a senator's individual opinion withheld till after the presidential election? Plainly enough now, the speaking out then would have damaged the "perfectly free" argument upon which the election was to be carried. Why the outgoing President's felicitation on the endorsement? Why the delay of a reargument? Why the incoming President's advance exhortation in favor of the decision? These things look like the cautious patting and petting of a spirited horse preparatory to mounting him, when it is dreaded that he may give the rider a fall.

And why the hasty after-endorsement of the decision by the President and others? We cannot absolutely know that all these exact adaptations are the result of preconcert. But when we see a lot of framed timbers, different portions of which we know have been gotten out at different times and places and by different workmen—Stephen, Franklin, Roger, and James, for instance—and when we see these timbers joined together, and see they exactly make the frame of a house or a mill, all the tenons and mortises exactly fitting, and all the lengths and proportions of the different pieces exactly adapted to their respective places, and not a piece too many or too few, not omitting even scaffolding—or, if a single piece be lacking, we see the place in the frame exactly fitted and prepared yet to bring such piece in—in such case, we find it impossible not to believe that Stephen and Franklin and Roger and James all understood one another from the beginning, and all worked upon a common plan or draught drawn up before the first blow was struck.

It should not be overlooked that, by the Nebraska bill, the people of a *State* as well as Territory were to be left "perfectly free" "subject only to the Constitution." Why mention a State? They were legislating for Territories, and not for or about States. Certainly the people of a State are and ought to be subject to the Constitution of the United States—but why is mention of this lugged into this merely territorial law? Why are the people of a Territory and the people of a State therein lumped together, and their relation to the Constitution therein treated as being precisely the same? While the opinion of the court by Chief Justice Taney, in the Dred Scott case, and the separate opinions of all concurring judges, expressly declare that the Constitution of the United States neither permits Congress nor a territorial Legislature to exclude slavery from any United States Territory, they all omit to declare whether or not the same Constitution permits a State, or the people of a State, to exclude it.

Possibly, this is a mere omission, but who can be quite sure, if McLean or Curtis had sought to get into the opinion a declaration of unlimited power in the people of a State to exclude slavery from their limits, just as Chase and Mace sought to get such declaration, in behalf of the people of a Territory, into the Nebraska bill—I ask, who can be quite sure that it would not have been voted down in one case as it had been in the other?

The nearest approach to the point of declaring the power of a State over slavery is made by Judge Nelson. He approaches it more than once, using the precise idea, and almost the language, too, of the Nebraska act. On one occasion, his exact language is "except in cases where the power is restrained by the Constitution of the United States, the law of the State is supreme over the subject of slavery within its jurisdiction." In what cases the power of the States is so restrained by the United States Constitution is left an open question, precisely as the same question, as to the restraint on the power of the Territories, was left open in the Nebraska act. Put this and that together, and we have another nice little niche, which we may, ere long, see filled with another Supreme Court decision, declaring that the Constitution of the United States does not permit a *State* to exclude slavery from its limits. And this may especially be expected if the doctrine of "care not whether slavery be voted down or voted up" shall gain upon the public mind sufficiently to give promise that such a decision can be maintained when made. Such a decision is all that slavery now lacks of being alike lawful in all the States. Welcome, or unwelcome, such decision is probably coming, and will soon be upon us, unless the power of the present political dynasty shall be met and overthrown. We shall lie down pleasantly dreaming that the people of Missouri are on the verge of making their State free, and we shall awake to the reality instead that the Supreme Court has made Illinois a Slave State. To meet and overthrow the power of that dynasty is the work now before all those who would prevent that consummation. That is what we have to do. How can we best do it? There are those who denounce us openly to their own friends, and yet whisper us softly that Senator Douglas is the aptest instrument there is with which to affect that object. They wish us to *infer* all, from the fact that he now has a little quarrel with the present head of the dynasty, and that he has regularly voted with us on a single point, upon which he and we have never differed. They remind us that he is a great man, and that the largest of us are very small ones. Let this be granted. But "a living dog is better than a dead lion." Judge Douglas, if not a dead lion, for this work is at least a caged and toothless one. How can he oppose the advances of slavery? He don't care anything about it. His avowed mission is impressing the "public heart" to *care nothing about* it. A leading Douglas Democratic newspaper thinks Douglas's superior talent will be needed to resist the revival of the African slave trade. Does Douglas believe an effort to revive that trade is approaching? He has not said so. Does he really think so?

But if it is, how can he resist it? For years he has labored to prove it a sacred right of white men to take Negro slaves into the new Territories. Can he possibly show that it is less a sacred right to buy them where they can be bought cheapest?

And unquestionably they can be bought cheaper in Africa than in Virginia. He has done all in his power to reduce the whole question of slavery to one of a mere right of property—and, as such, how can he oppose the foreign slave trade?

How can he refuse that trade In that "property" shall be "perfectly free" unless he does it as a protection to the home production? And as the home producers will probably not ask the protection, he will be wholly without a ground of opposition.

Senator Douglas holds, we know, that a man may rightfully be wiser today than he was yesterday—that he may rightfully change when he finds himself wrong. But can we, for that reason, run ahead, and infer that he will make any particular change of which he himself has given no intimation?

Can we safely base our action upon any such vague inference? Now, as ever, I wish not to misrepresent Judge Douglas's position, question his motives, or do aught that can be personally offensive to him. Whenever, if ever, he and we can come together on principle, so that our great cause may have assistance from his great ability, I hope to have interposed no adventitious obstacle. But clearly he is not now with us, he does not pretend to be—he does not promise ever to be. Our cause, then, must be entrusted to, and conducted by, its own undoubted friends—those whose hands are free, whose hearts are in the work, who *do care* for the result. Two years ago the Republicans of the nation mustered over thirteen hundred thousand strong. We did this under the single impulse of resistance to a common danger, with every external circumstance against us. Of strange, discordant, and even hostile elements, we gathered from the four winds, and formed and fought the battle through, under the constant hot fire of a disciplined, proud, and pampered enemy.

Did we brave all then, to falter now—now, when that same enemy is wavering, dissevered, and belligerent?

The result is not doubtful. We shall not fail—if we stand firm, we *shall not fail*. Wise counsels may accelerate, or mistakes delay it, but, sooner or later, the victory is sure to come.

Martha Morgan

Excerpt from *A Trip Across the Plains in the Year 1849 with Notes of a Voyage to California by Way of Panama*. Published in 1864 in a limited edition.

[1849 diary]

Left St. Joseph for California via Salt Lake, May 24th, 1849. *May 25th*—Passed Savannah, Nodaway River, Little Sarkey River and Big Sarkey River. *June 1st*—Passed Linden, county seat of Atchison. Sunday, *June 3rd*—Crossed the Nishnabotany. *June 7th*—Passed Kanesville, and encountered a tremendous thunder shower. *June 8th*—Arrived at Upper Ferry Bayou, and stopped there till the 1st of July. *July 2nd*—Crossed the Missouri River. *July 4th*—Encamped in Indian Territory—Omahas Indians—near Mormon Winter Quarters, a city built of logs by Mormons, containing some seven or eight hundred houses, or rather hovels, all of which, at present, are deserted. *July 6th*—Left Mormon Winter Quarters, and arrived at Elkhorn River on the evening of the 7th, 27 miles from Missouri. The Elkhorn River is from four to six rods in width, with about four feet of water—a dirty stream, and empties into Platte River. *July 10th*—Crossed Elkhorn River in six hours and forty minutes, with sixty-five wagons and encamped on the west side. *July 11th*—Traveled twelve miles and encamped on the bank of the Platte River—at the Liberty Pole here we found some bodies of dead Indians, apparently killed in battle. The Plain we passed over is beautiful. *July 12th*—Nothing particular—we traveled thirteen miles over a beautiful Plain. The day was very warm, and passed the First Fifty. *July 13th*—We traveled ten miles, crossed a branch called the Shell, and encamped by an excellent spring—this was the first good water we found after leaving Winter Quarters. *July 14th*—Traveled twelve miles, had a bad road, crossed two sloughs, saw one deer, the first we saw on the Plains, and encamped on the banks of the Platte. *Sunday, July 15th*—Traveled ten miles and a half, had good roads, and encamped on Loup Pork—beautiful camping ground. The Loup Fork empties into the Platte River, the bank and bed of this river is composed of white sand, this section of the country is claimed by the Pawnee Indians.

July 16th—Traveled nine and a half miles, corralled, and that night had a stampede in the coral, broke two wagons, killed one sheep, and broke the horns off several head of cattle. *July 17th*—Mended the wagons and moved a short distance, made a strong coral, and that night had another stampede, nothing killed, one cow crippled. *July 18th*—In the morning, after the cattle were all yoked, and most of them chained together, we had another stampede, which was truly awful to behold, cattle rushed from the coral, chained together, from 2 to 8, 4 and 5 yoke, and were literally piled up in heaps, some with broken legs, some with horns broken off, but none killed, two men badly and two slightly hurt. Through the course of the day, we had some six or eight stampedes, and it was with extreme difficulty that we got them quieted, we then separated them into squads of ten, during this operation I think I saw some of the tracks of the "big elephant." *July 19th*—Traveled eighteen miles, and encamped on Loup Fork near Pawnee village. The Pawnee country is beautiful.

July 20th—Removed from near Pawnee town and encamped six miles from Loup Fork fording, some twelve miles travel, crossed Cedar Creek, which is from 4 to 5 rods wide, and from 2 to 3 feet deep. *July 21st*—The past night was noted for a remarkably severe shower of rain, we commenced our march at daylight in the morning, and traveled six miles to the Loup Ferry, in a heavy rain, and encamped, through the day a draft of thirty men, from the One Hundred, was made, to examine the fording. They reported unfavorably. At this place we found a letter left by Mr. Egan, captain of a company that passed this place, on the 29th of June last, stating the death of 4 men, two from cholera, one from drowning, and one killed by the Indians. *July 22nd*—We lay in camp all day, waiting for Alred's Fifty, to pass over the Loup Fork River. *July 23rd*—We crossed the river, had very good luck, and encamped one mile distant. The bed of this river is quicksand, and the borders are liable to change materially in half an hour. The water was, at the time of crossing, about twenty inches deep. *July 25th*—We took up our line of march in the morning, traveled twelve miles through a different country from the east of the river, the Plains were round hills of sand, and the road was sandy and hard to travel on, grass thin and short, water scarce, and no wood at all. This day I saw the first antelope, it was killed by the ten ahead of us. *July 26th*—Traveled ten miles, saw one antelope, crossed one mile of wet bottom and deep mud, and encamped within five miles of Platte River, in a heavy rain, had no wood. *July 27th*—Traveled eight miles. Mr. Gray broke his wagon tongue in the morning, which hindered us, we encamped on Wood River. This river is from twelve to eighteen feet wide, eighteen inches water and excellent camping ground. Here we found thirty-seven head of cattle, evidently lost by some emigrants ahead of us, the most of them were work cattle. The real cause of their being found astray from their owners is shrouded with the mantle of invisibility. It may be, however, they were stampeded by the Indians or buffaloes. From this on, we expect to see sights—hear old women dream and young men prophecy. This morning we had to repair Hatch's wagon wheel and, consequently, started at a very late hour. *July 28th*—In the morning we made some division of above-mentioned cattle and with a protracted start, traveled fifteen miles, and encamped on Platte River. Opposite Grand Island, passed two graves, one designated by the name of Moses Hale, from Wisconsin—died of cholera. Wood River runs parallel, partly, with Platte River, widening from one to ten miles, in traveling fifteen miles west, and it is the most beautiful country I ever saw. Here I saw the first prairie dogs, they resemble the dog, but they partake more of the nature of the rabbit, they are about as large as a small groundhog, and live in little villages, containing from one half to one acre of territory. Their holes are very thick, they live on grass, and they are good to eat. *Sunday, July 29th*—Traveled twelve miles and encamped on the prairie, had bad roads, and passed the grave of Captain Gully and one of his men, who died of cholera, he was captain of the hundred that started four weeks previous to us. This day we found forty head more of cattle. *July 30th*—Traveled eighteen miles, and encamped near Dry Creek, at the head of Grand Island. We passed Fort Kearny this forenoon, which lies about six miles south, on Grand Island. The country remains handsome, and the prairie dogs are as thick as grasshoppers. We are now two hundred and twenty miles from Missouri, or Mormon Winter Quarters. This was the first night we used buffalo chips to cook with. *July 31st*—Traveled fifteen miles and encamped. Plenty of grass and water, but no wood. The evenings and mornings are quite cool, and the days are rather cool for this season of the year. *August 1st*—Traveled twelve miles, and encamped near the Platte River. Started rather late on account of a broken axletree. *August 2nd*—Traveled eighteen miles, this day, for the first time, we were gratified with the sight of the buffalo, I suppose we saw one thousand, our company killed two and one deer, I made two shots without effect. *August 3rd*—Lay in camp, and hunted buffalo, caught none, but wounded several. Here we found a grave, death out of the Hawk Eye Company, Iowa—named Haggard. *August 4th*—Traveled 13 miles, and our company killed and brought in one buffalo and one calf, and killed several more. This day we found the road very bad, and the owners came for the cattle we had found. They belonged to Captain Owens Company of gold diggers, from New York and Wisconsin, they lost them during a severe storm, which lasted two days and one night. *Sunday, August 5th*—Traveled twelve miles over tremendous bad roads of sand and mud, and encamped near Skunk Creek. This day we received intelligence from G. A. Smith that England had sent sixty thousand troops to California, and as many more to Mexico, and that France and England were in difficulty, also of the death of James K. Polk and General Gaines. Here we met five wagons of gold diggers, on their return home, on the south side of the river, they had lost some of their men and got discouraged. *August 6th*—Traveled thirteen miles over bad roads, for the last three or four days the country has not been so handsome, the prairies are low and wet, with occasional sand hills. We pass a very large spring of excellent water, a great luxury to me, as it was the first draught of good water I had enjoyed for four weeks. We also passed the junction of the South Fork of Platte River—kept up by the North Branch and encamped on the bank of the river—had no wood—and were compelled to boil our mush pot with buffalo chips.

August 7th—Lay in camp. S. Snider killed one buffalo and one antelope. Here we gave up the lost cattle. We have been traveling amongst the Sioux Indians since we left Grand Island. Their country extends from Independence Rock. The Crow Indians occupy the country lying between the South Fork and Francis River. *August 8th*—Traveled fourteen miles, had good roads in the forepart of the day, and encamped on the bank, across the river. We saw buffaloes in droves, and at night some of them tried to cross over to our camp. I should have mentioned that on the 7th we had a dance. *August 9th*—Traveled seventeen miles, and encamped on the river. In the forepart of the day we had good roads, but in the latter part sandy and hilly. Crossed Bluff Creek, six rods wide, eighteen inches water, sandy bottom and good crossing. This day we passed Captain Alred's Fifty, resting their cattle. They had killed two buffalo, plenty of buffalo now in sight. *August 10*—Traveled twelve miles over hard hills and sandy roads, passed several streams of good water, and encamped under the bluff, plenty of buffalo in sight all day.

August 11th—Traveled seventeen miles over good roads and passed Cedar Bluff. *Sunday, August 12th*—Lay in camp, killed four ducks, in the afternoon we had a religious meeting, the first we enjoyed since we started. *August 13th*—Traveled fourteen miles, one mile and a half being high sandy bluff, in consequence of which we had to double teams—the bottom land has grown much narrower, and the bluffs more rocky. The river here will average three-fourths of a mile in width, but I think the water would all run in a stream twenty rods wide and four feet deep. The bluffs on the south side are partially covered with small cedar. We passed the grave of a gold digger, from Iowa. *August 14th*—Traveled sixteen miles, passed Ash Hollow, on the south side of the river, and the Lonely Tree on the north side, this is the only tree on the north side of the river, for the distance of two hundred miles—from this it takes its name. It is cottonwood, and stands about halfway between the road and the river. We passed the grave of a gold digger, from Adams County, Illinois—died of cholera. *August 15th*—Traveled fourteen miles, good roads. Received request from Captain Taylor to stop till he came up. This evening, Mr. Perkins came on and informed us that they had, had a stampede in the wagons—about fifty, they broke some and injured several persons. We furnished them with two new axles, and a blacksmith to repair damages, encamped on the bank of the river. *August 16th*—Lay in camp all day, nothing worthy of notice transpired. *August 17th*—Still in camp, at evening, Perkins and Moore's teams came up, and also Alred's Fifty, and informed us that one woman had died of the wounds she received in the stampedes. *August 18th*—In the morning we had a meeting of the One Hundred, called by Captain Taylor. The Mormons quarreled like fiends, and I think besmeared about three-fourths of an acre of ground but Perkins's Ten went ahead, in the evening we met brother Babbit, from Salt Lake, we traveled ten miles.

August 19th—In the morning we heard some letters read, from the valley, quite interesting and cheering, and I believe we all traveled on with much lighter hearts than we commenced our journey. We traveled eighteen miles and encamped on the bank of the river, had good roads and good feed. *August 20th*—In the morning we saw twenty-nine government wagons pass down the south side of the river, they were from Fort Laramie, bound for the States, they had with them some unfortunate gold diggers, one crazy man, and several crippled by being in a stampede. We traveled twenty miles and encamped on the river, opposite Chimney Rock. This rock is quite notorious, and can be seen forty or fifty miles with the naked eye. This rock, together with the bluffs, up to the Scotts Bluffs, are very interesting, and many of them appear more like the work of art than of nature.

August 21st—Traveled nineteen miles and encamped on the river, opposite Scotts Bluff. These bluffs appear like so many fortifications, they are from one to three hundred feet high.

August 22nd—Traveled fifteen miles, nothing particular transpired. It was, however, a very warm day and one ox gave out. *August 23rd*—Traveled fourteen miles, weather excessively warm. *August 24th*—In the morning, we received a visit from three Indians, the first we had seen since we left Missouri, a distance of five hundred miles, through an Indian territory, they were Sioux and ostensibly very friendly, we traveled five miles, and found an Indian camp with some French traders with them. Sioux is a new trading post, fifteen miles east of Fort Laramie, they received us with friendship, we stopped some four hours and traded with them, giving flour, meal, powder, lead and cloths, for buffalo robes and moccasins. In the evening we traveled six miles, over a heavy, sandy road, and encamped on the river in the night. *August 25th*—Lay in camp, set wagon tire and made general repairs, in the afternoon the wind blew a hurricane, and the sand rose in clouds and drifted like snow. *Sunday, August 26th*—Lay in camp until three o'clock and finished repairs, then traveled five miles and encamped on the river, four miles below Fort Laramie, we received a visit from some teamsters across the river, going to the Fort, Gray broke his wagon. *August 27th*—We crossed the north branch of the river, at Fort Laramie. Here stands an old Fort, called Fort John, built by the Western Fur Company, it is nearly torn down. Laramie Fort is built one mile up. Laramie River a beautiful place for a town. Here, the roads from Independence, Fort Leavenworth, Saint Joseph, Council Bluff and Arkansas River come together. From this place we began to see the destruction of both life and property, in the first eight miles we saw five graves, made within the last two months. Here begins what is called the Black Hills, they are high bluffs, covered with pitch pine, the river at this place is easily forded, in common stages of water. *August 28th*—Traveled eighteen miles, the day was very windy and dusty, the road tolerably good, though we had to encounter some high and rocky mountains. We took the river road, saw the head of a mountain sheep—its horns were very large. *August 29th*—In the morning killed a buffalo, he came to the camp, it then commenced raining and ended in snow, lasting until noon. In the afternoon, we traveled ten miles over mountains high as the clouds, saw, northwest of us, a mountain white with snow, this is the first we ever saw in August. We came down on the Platte River bottom, and encamped at the mouth of a ravine—here we saw fresh signs of plenty of elk and bear—here Captain Taylor pushed us hard, the country here is mountainous and never can be inhabited—but a small amount of vegetation grows here. *August 30th*—Traveled twenty miles and encamped on the river alone, for the first time since we left George, Charley and Taylor shot at and wounded a buffalo, driven across the road by some hunters, the roads were tolerably good, the country is poor, with thin sandy soil, producing but little, except in patches on the river, we had frost every night since the 27th.

August 31st—Traveled eighteen miles, came into the road that leads over the hills, a little north of Laramie Peak, here we commenced going downhill, until we came to LaBonte River. Mr. Gray broke his wagon while here, Captain Samuel Snider and myself had a little quarrel, we are now on the Crow Indian Territory. *September 1st*—Left Samuel Snider and joined George Snider's team and traveled eighteen and one-fourth miles—and encamped on a small stream. Found no grass. Here we covered the dead body of a buffalo with sand, to keep ourselves from being stunk out of camp. *September 2nd*—Traveled eight miles and encamped on the Seboyn River, at 12 o'clock. In the afternoon, Mr. Barnet and myself made a hunting excursion, but found no game. In the evening, Mr. Campbell and two others returned from George A. Smith's camp, with the express from Salt Lake, and drew on our party for horses and provisions. *September 3rd*—Traveled twelve miles and encamped on the river, where we had a beautiful camping ground, and good feed. Here we found the remains of a number of wagons, which had been cut up, burnt and destroyed, together with the remnants of various other camping materials. *September 4th*—Traveled fifteen miles, had good roads, but very windy and dusty. Encamped on the river. Passed one good wagon. The wagons above alluded to were left by gold diggers. In the evening the Express returned, and stopped with us overnight. Had a religious meeting in the evening. *September 5th*—Returned back and met Captain Alred's Fifty. Our party stayed with Captain Taylor overnight.

September 6th—Came back, forded Platte River, knee deep, overtook the wagons in a dry place, without wood or water. In the evening, joined with some others to go to the river for water for supper. We traveled about five miles to the river, and encamped over night, and returned in the morning with the water for breakfast. This is a dry, sandy, barren country, hilly and mountainous, and grows little else than wild sage.

September 7th—Stopped on the Plains until Captain Thomas came up. We stopped overnight, and then traveled seventeen miles over hills and hot sand, and encamped three miles west of Willow Springs. At these Springs we found the remains of some ten or twelve wagons, which clearly evinced a vast destruction of property. *Sunday, September 9th*—Traveled, sixteen and a half miles over some very sandy roads. Here we passed the Saleratus Heads, presumed to be one hundred acres, as white as snow. It was a windy day, and the saleratus would drift like snow before the wind. We gathered all we wanted, went on, and encamped near Independence Rock. This Rock is notorious for size and is a great curiosity. I presume the names of more than three thousand people are recorded on it. Here we struck the Sweetwater River—a pretty, gravelly stream, which abounds with fine trout. It empties into Platte River.

September 10th—Traveled five miles to the Devil's Gate. This is an opening through the mountain, for the Sweetwater River to pass. The channel is one hundred feet wide, and the rock, each side, is four hundred feet high, perpendicular. In the afternoon, Mr. Shaw and myself made a hunting excursion, saw many antelope, but killed none. *September 11th*—Lay in camp all day. Had a hunt, made two shots at a buffalo, but did not kill him. Saw between fifty and one hundred antelope, killed one antelope and twenty wolves. At this place I found a log chain, eighteen feet long. *September 12th*—Traveled eleven miles, over sandy roads. Had a shot at an antelope, missed him, but killed some rattlesnakes, and encamped on the river Sweetwater.

September 13th and 14th—Traveled fourteen and fifteen miles, nothing but a continual scene of rocky mountains, sandy barren plains, destruction of cattle, wagons, and other property. Here the rattlesnake has taken up his abode. This is a section of country usually coursed by herds of buffalo, but we found none, supposed to have been driven back by the Indians. *September 15th*—Traveled sixteen miles over good roads, and encamped on the river, went on a hunting excursion, saw hundreds of antelope but killed none. At night, old Zabriskie and his wife had a tremendous fight. *September 16th*—Traveled eight miles, and encamped on the river, met the teams from the valley, going to meet George Smith. They numbered twenty-one wagons.

September 17th—Traveled five miles, and encamped on Sweet River. Mr. Brown killed one antelope in the morning, and I killed a duck, and found a log chain. *September 18th*—Traveled ten miles, left the Sweetwater to the left, passing over high mountains and rocky roads, and encamped with Captain Egbert, on a branch of the Sweetwater. Had poor feed and little wood. *September 19th*—Traveled seven miles, and encamped on the Sweetwater, at the upper fording last place of crossing. No feed far cattle. *September 20th*—Traveled twelve and a half miles, going through the South Pass of the Rocky Mountains, and encamped at the Pacific Springs. This was the first water we came across that empties into the Pacific Ocean. It is a nice little run, large enough to run a mill. Hero we found some feed—the first good feed in several days travel. This morning we found two of our cattle dead, and the balance of them looking as if they had nothing in them. *September 21st*—The past night we were unusually troubled with wolves, we had to drive them off several times. In the morning we found another dead ox. This day we traveled twenty-four miles, without feed or water, and encamped on Little Sandy, two hours after dark. *September 22nd*—In the morning another cow dead, traveled twelve miles, and encamped on Big Sandy. The general appearance of the country, thus far west of the Pass, more level, but remains sandy and barren.

Little or no grass to be found, except on the streams. For the last ten days we have been traveling in sight of a mountain of snow. We were, at one time, within ten miles of it, yet the weather was so warm that we experienced no inconvenience in traveling in our shirt sleeves. We have been in the Oregon Territory since we came through the Pass, and in the Snake Indian country, now two hundred miles from Salt Lake.

September 23rd—Traveled seventeen miles, passed a government train of thirty wagons, loaded with corn, and bound for Bear River, under the command of Captain Reed, and encamped on Big Sandy. *September 24th*—Traveled twelve miles, and encamped on Green River. This is a beautiful river, from ten to twelve rods wide, and from two to three feet deep sand, gravel and round stone bottom. Good camping ground, plenty of wood, water and grass. *September 25th*—Lay in camp, rested our cattle and ourselves. Went on a hunting excursion, and killed eight ducks. Pacific Spring empties into Little Sandy, Little Sandy into Big Sandy, Big Sandy into Green River, and Green River into the Colorado River. *September 26th*—Traveled eight miles, and encamped on Green River. The weather is warm and pleasant.

The roads good, and grass more plentiful. From this place—Green River—we took our departure *"for the West."*

September 27th—Traveled fifteen miles, and encamped on Black's Fork, poor feed. *September 28th*—In the morning found Old Zabriskie's cow dead, and Joe Okany found an ox.

We traveled five and a half miles, and encamped on Black's Fork. Found good grass. Here Captain George Hancock got the big lead, went on, and left all the company behind. *September 29th*—Traveled fifteen miles, and encamped on Black's Fork. This day I quit Old Zabriskie to make a hunting excursion through the Valley. We overtook Captain George Snider. He had killed an antelope. *September 30th*—Traveled fifteen miles, and encamped on Black's Fork, one mile from Fort Bridger. The nights here were very cold, but the middle of the days quite warm and pleasant. We discovered another mountain of snow to the south of us. *October 1st*—We lay in camp all day.

In the morning, with some others, I visited the Fort, found Captain [Jim] Bridger in good spirits, a frank, open-hearted mountaineer. He is a Virginian by birth, has lived in the mountains for the last twenty-eight years, has visited the States but twice, and sixteen years of this time he assures us that he never tasted bread. He has a squaw, or several of them, for his wife. We then went to an Indian camp, one mile off here we found six or eight Frenchmen, who have lived with the Indians many years, following hunting and trading. Through the day we exchanged corn, flour, and other rations, for dressed skins, ready-made antelope and elk pants and moccasins. Here we overtook a government train, out of provisions. One of our men sold them five hundred pounds of flour, for seventy-five dollars.

Flour frequently sells here for twenty-five dollars per one hundred pounds. *October 2nd*—Traveled fifteen miles, and encamped at Soda Springs, found poor water, little food, cold, windy day. John Chany lost an ox on the road. *October 3rd*—In the morning, we found ourselves shoe deep in the snow, snowed all day. Mr. Hawk and myself went on alone, traveled ten miles and encamped on Bear River. This river is about three rods wide and one foot deep, in a common stage of water. It runs north then west, then south and empties into Salt Lake. *October 4th*—Lay in camp all day. In the afternoon Captain George came up, here we left Mr. Hammon. *October 5th*—Traveled-fifteen miles, and encamped on the head of Echo Creek. Had good feed and water, but little wood. In the evening, we met some teams from the valley. We encamped one mile a head of the rest.

October 6th—Traveled fifteen miles, and encamped on Echo Creek. Had plenty of wood, water, and feed.

The country, since we left Fort Bridger, begins to assume a more productive appearance. Bear River Valley is a rich soil, and increases in richness as we travel west. *October 7th*—Traveled fifteen miles, and encamped on Weber River. This river is three or four rods wide, two feet deep, runs northwest, and empties into Salt Lake. Found plenty of bear signs, but saw none. *October 8th*—Lay in camp, waiting for Captain Taylor to come up, but they did not come. *October 9th*—Mr. Reeves found a bull that the wolves were about to kill, and old Mr. Brown came from the valley, to meet his children. In the morning, we found one ox mired and one missing, which detained all but Mr. Hawk and myself. We traveled twelve miles, and encamped on Carrion Creek, had bad roads. We encamped with Captain Corbet's train. *October 10th*—Encamped on Carrion Creek, at the foot of the four-mile Hill. Here Captain Hancock came up with us. Had very bad roads. *October 11th*—Crossed over the last mountain, and encamped at the foot of the Canyon, leading to the valley.

October 12th—The long-looked for time arrived. We landed in the valley of the Salt Lake. [End of 1849 diary.]

[1850 diary]

April 22nd, 1850—Left Great Salt Lake City, traveled ten miles, and encamped on North Mill Canyon, on the road to California, in company with J. N. Spalding and William Prouse.

April 23rd—Took in pork at Neil's, traveled eighteen miles and encamped on a fine run of water. Had good food here.

Green, Long, and Martin came up, and encamped with us. *April 24th*—Lay in camp all day. *April 25th*—Traveled seventeen miles and crossed Weber River, and encamped on the Ogden where the bridge was taken up. Roads sandy and muddy. *April 26th*—In the morning, Mr. Long fell from the Ogden Bridge, and was drowned. His body was not found. The bridge was repaired, and we crossed over in the afternoon, and encamped at Mr. Chase's. *April 27th*—Bought some potatoes and butter, and traveled sixteen miles. Some part of the way the road was very muddy, passed some hot springs, overtook some wagons, and encamped on a beautiful run of water. Several Indians encamped here. *Sunday, April 28th*—Traveled eight miles, and encamped on Box Elder. Good roads, good food, and plenty of wood.

    Here we overtook Barnes, Perkins, Smith, and others, also, a grizzly bear, but did not kill him. *April 29th*—Stayed in camp all day, on Box Elder. *April 30th*—Traveled twenty miles, and encamped on Bear River, at the Ferry. Good roads, but little wood. *May 1st*—Crossed over Bear River, good ferry. The river at this place is about twenty rods wide. We then traveled three miles and came to the Malad. This stream is about fifteen feet wide, nine feet deep, and the bottom is about twenty rods across, and in crossing, takes the wheels of a wagon out of sight in mud and water, decidedly the worst place I ever saw to cross with a team. We traveled seven miles, and encamped at the point of the mountain. Here we joined Captain Ork's company, and Barnes, Perkins, Smith, and myself traveled with him. *May 2nd*—Lay in camp all day. *May 3rd*—We took up our line of march, traveled eighteen miles, and encamped in Salt Spring Valley. Our course from the city was north, eighty-four miles, to Bear River, from thence west, or north of west. The water at this place was warm and impregnated with salt. Some Indians came into camp to trade dressed skins, for powder and lead. *May 4th*—Traveled thirteen miles, and encamped at Basin Spring. Good water, hilly roads. From 9 o'clock in the morning to sunset, a man is comfortable in shirt and pants, but the nights are as cold as January in the States. *Sunday, May 5th*—Traveled fifteen miles, and encamped on Deep Creek, in a valley, some twenty-five miles across. This valley lies northwest from Salt Lake, and the mountains are covered with snow at this time, roads good, weather fine, but poor feed for the cattle. *May 6th*—Traveled eighteen miles, over a good road, across the valley, and encamped at the foot of the mountain, by a spring, in the Cedars. Here, we have the last view of Salt Lake. This valley is principally covered with large brush. *May 7th*—Traveled thirteen miles, over hilly and rocky roads, and encamped at the head of a large valley, on a good run of water that came from the mountain, wood and water eight miles east of the little mounds where the Indians killed three men last fall. *May 8th*—Traveled twelve miles, over good roads, and encamped on Raft Creek, found the stream too high to cross. Here Messieurs Foot and Barnard overtook us. We had some difficulty in our course and six wagons and men left us and went on. At night, it rained hard, and lasted till late in the morning. We at last, yoked up, and took the back track for one mile, and then turned to the right, around a small mountain. Had a good road. Struck the old road above the second crossing, then came on and crossed at the third crossing, followed up Raft Creek and encamped, making two miles travel. *May 10th*—In the morning, we started by daylight, came to City Rock, eight miles, then turned out and took breakfast. Here the Salt Lake Road comes into the Emigrant Road, by way of Fort Hall, to California. Six miles just took us across the second valley. Here we had to leave the road several times, to pass around snow banks.

May 11th—In the morning, we commenced climbing the mountains, the assent was gradual, but the descent almost up and down, from the summit. We had a splendid view of Goose Creek Valley, which is quite a valley, filled with little mountains. It is quite romantic in appearance. This valley, like the rest, produces little else than sagebrush, some grass near the Rock. Goose Creek rises in the mountains, and is supposed to sink in some valley, like all other rivers that rise in the mountains.

The direction of this stream is northwest, traveled up this stream nine miles, and encamped, making in all, nineteen miles. *Sunday, May 12th*—Continued up Goose Creek a southwest course, twelve miles, then struck up Canyon Creek, followed up three miles and encamped. The last three were very stony and rough roads, plenty of cedar and good water. *May 13th*—In the morning the roads were rough, but, in the latter part of the day, very good. We traveled ten miles, and encamped on Sage Run, poor wood and poor water. *May 14th*—The first two miles were rather rough. We passed a large spring on the west side of the road, then struck a narrow valley, followed it twelve miles, then turned to the right, traveled over a small mountain, struck another valley, followed it six miles to a large spring, and encamped—making, in all, twenty-three miles. The general appearance of the country is much the same as that we have passed—mountains not quite so high, and cedar more plenty.

May 15—Traveled seven miles, came to Warm Spring Creek. This creek forms three rivers, at the crossing, and is very deep, here a number of Indians came to its, apparently rather fearful at first, but, finding us friendly, came into camp and exchanged dressed skins for powder, balls and etc.

May 16th—Traveled ten miles up a branch of Warm Spring Creek to a river in the mountain. Here we found good grass, took a *"nooning"* and proceeded on over the mountains, found good roads, and feed growing better, traveled six miles in the afternoon, and encamped in the valley—making, in all, sixteen miles. This mountain divides the waters of Goose Creek and Marys River. The waters of the first run northeast, and of the second southwest. *May 17th*—Followed down Crane Creek, southwest, to a pass in the mountain. The mountain, on the south side of the pass, is high, and covered with snow. We passed through the mountain and encamped—making, in all, eighteen miles. This brought us to Marys River, east branch.

May 18th—In the morning traveled ten miles, came to the east branch of Marys River, two sloughs, deep, and had to cross them. Six miles farther brought up to the main branch of Marys River, where we encamped. The first company had just crossed the river. *May 19th*—We crossed the river in a boat arranged for the purpose, by unloading our wagons and hauling them over by hand. The river being over the banks, we had three deep sloughs to cross, before we got to the west side of the valley. I carried such things across them as would not be injured by wetting, wading in mud and water to my arm pits, worked hard all day, and gained one mile. This river is two rods wide, and, at this time ten feet deep, but in the fall, affords little or no water.

May 20th—Lay in camp, rested, washed, and dried such things as got wet. *May 21st*—Traveled twenty miles down Marys River, and encamped, had good roads. *May 22nd*—Two miles after we started, we came to the west branch of Saleratus Creek, we had to boat over our goods, and swim our cattle with the wagons, we had much difficulty in crossing, had a fight in the company, traveled three miles further and encamped, it commenced raining in the evening and rained all night, in the morning we observed that the mountains around had a new coat of snow, it was quite cold. *May 24th*—Traveled twenty-two miles, had good roads, this brought us to a narrow pass, barely room enough for the river, in high water. *May 25th*—In common stages of water this road runs through the pass, but at present is full of water, so we took a narrow passage into the mountains, had one hard hill and then a gradual rise, very crooked but smooth road.

When on the tops of the mountains we could see the river both ways, about ten miles over this road we came to Willow Creek—followed this down two miles and crossed with much difficulty, traveled three miles further and encamped on Basin Creek, thirty-six feet wide, eight feet deep and has to be ferried. *May 26th*—In the morning, (Sunday) we commenced ferrying, and by one o'clock were all over, we then took up to Spring Creek Canyon, a new road, eight miles, struck the old road two miles ahead and encamped, had plenty of sage grass and water. *May 27th*—Traveled twenty miles, over mountains and down Rincon's rough roads, and encamped, once more, on Marys River.

May 28th—Traveled fifteen miles west, over a valley, to Bluff Creek, and encamped, some had ferried over, when we found good fording eighty rods above. This creek is thirty-six feet wide, seven feet deep, but in dry weather is nearly dry. *May 29th*—Traveled twenty-two miles, crossed the points of some mountains to avoid the overflow of the river, found it very sidelong, rocky and difficult to pass, and encamped on the slough. *May 30th*—Traveled eighteen miles of a new road, somewhat sandy, and encamped on the river at Matrimonial Bend. Here William Prouse and Roberts got married.

May 31st—Traveled twenty miles northeast, and encamped on the river. *June 1st*—Traveled twenty-five miles, roads mostly good, and encamped at the bend of the river, opposite the White Sandy Bluff, good feed, but no wood.

June 2nd—Traveled sixteen miles over a heavy, sandy road, in a southwest direction. *June 3rd*—Traveled fourteen miles, over a heavy, sandy road, and encamped on a bottom near the river, where the road runs across the point of a mountain westward, when it comes to the river again. *June 4th*—Traveled twenty-two miles over good roads, passed the Oregon Road at a large bend of the river. This road leaves the river here and runs northwest, went down the river three miles and encamped, had no feed but sagebrush. *June 5th*—Traveled twenty miles, without feed or water on the road until we encamped on the river. Here we overtook Captain Demont's company. *June 6th*—Compelled to travel twenty-five miles to the sloughs, one watering place on the road, but no feed. Soon after we encamped we found our cattle nearly all sick, water salty, good roads Here we saw some of the Pawnee Indians, they appeared friendly.

June 7th—In the morning our cattle were better, lay in camp and rested, here the river begins to spread into sloughs. *June 8th*—Lay in camp and rested. *Sunday, June 9th*—Traveled twenty-five miles, and encamped on the edge of the desert, three miles below Humboldt Lake, or the main Sink of Marys River, fine grass, but water salty. The most of the country, during this day's travel, was nearly entirely clear of vegetation of any kind, the mountains, also, are as clear of it as the roof of a house. The lake is about twenty miles across, we passed it on the west side. *June 10th*—This morning we entered the desert, traveled thirty miles and encamped at half-past nine o'clock in the evening. *June 11th*—In the morning, at four o'clock, we started—came to

Salmon Trout River, ten miles, without water, our course through the desert was south. This river rises in the mountains—runs east to the desert, then bears southeast, and is said to form a lake. This river is four rods wide, six feet deep, and has some timber on its banks, the balance of the day we rested. *June 12th*—Traveled eight miles and encamped on the river, poor feed and poor wood, roads sandy, hilly and rough. *June 13th*—Traveled twelve miles and encamped on the river, roads sandy, hilly and rough, poor feed. *June 14th*—Traveled twenty miles, reached a mountain over a rough, heavy road, and encamped on the river, good feed and good wood. *June 15th*—Traveled eighteen miles, roads sandy, hilly and stony and encamped on the river. About seven miles back from this place, William Prouse discovered gold in a Canyon that came in from the north. *Sunday, June 16th*—Lay in camp, some men went back to examine the gold and reported favorably. Four Indians came into camp, apparently more fierce than any we had seen on the route. *June 17th*—Traveled seven miles, Mrs. Sparks got hurt, and we encamped on a branch bottom, good feed and good roads. *June 18th*—Lay in camp.

June 19th—Traveled twenty-two miles—went down the west side of the valley, near the foot of the mountain, this valley commences at the river and runs north, thirty miles long and ten miles wide, beautiful valley, grass in abundance, the mountain covered with pine timber. *June 20th*—Lay in camp, waiting for the snow to thaw off the mountain. Six men came from the other side of the mountain, prospecting for gold. *June 21st*—Lay in camp, five men from our camp went back to examine the mine we had found. *June 22nd*—Lay in camp. *Sunday, June 23rd*—Lay in camp. *June 24th*—Lay in camp. *June 25th*—Oliver Norton and myself came to mouth of the Canyon, eight miles, and encamped. *June 26th*—Came up the Canyon seven miles, and encamped in the first little valley, crossed the river three times, swam the cattle by putting a lariat on to keep them from being carried away by the current. Five miles of this road is the worst I ever saw—rocks and stones beyond description—mountains on each side, thousands of feet high, almost perpendicular. *June*

27th—Traveled six miles and came over the first mountain, snow from 1 to 20 feet deep, we had to drive almost straight up over snow banks and big rocks. *June 28th*—Traveled four miles over a very rough road and encamped at the Mountain Lake.

Sunday, June 29th—Traveled eight miles and encamped on the top of the second mountain. *June 30th*—Traveled eighteen miles over mountains of snow and encamped on the mountain, had to melt snow for use. *June 1st*—Traveled sixteen miles, this carried us through the snow. The last five days we traveled through or over snow, from one to one hundred feet deep.

July 2nd—Traveled fifteen miles, roads hilly and rough. These mountains are covered with white pine, yellow pine, pitch pine, fir, red and live oak, woods very tall. *July 3rd*—Traveled twelve miles, this brought us into the diggings in Pleasant Valley.

July 4th—Lay in Pleasant Valley, and enjoyed ourselves as well as we could, after a long journey. [End of 1850 diary.]

[1854 diary]

New York, *Thursday, 1st day, 5th January, 1854*. At two o'clock, on Thursday afternoon, we started off in the steamship *Ohio*, Captain Fox, and proceeded down the bay of New York in charge of a pilot. When fairly outside we discharged our pilot, and sent back with him one man who had lost his ticket and four others who were stowed away, hoping to get to the land of gold by working their passage. Weather is clear and cold, sun shining brightly. Quite a number felt no inclination to eat supper, and retired early to their berths. *Friday, 2nd day, 6th January*. Very little breakfast eaten, rather foggy and thick weather, fog cleared away before noon, and then the weather was very fine, saw a large shoal of porpoises. I watched their gambols for some time, nothing of any importance occurred all day. *Saturday, 3rd day, 7th January*. Morning broke cold, cloudy and very disagreeable rained in the afternoon—saw a sail in the distance—did not speak, however. *Sunday, 4th day, 8th January*. Rainy all morning, and at intervals all day, ship rocking badly, no comfort on board, numbers sick, thunder and lightning, with rain, all the afternoon. *Monday, 5th day, 9th January.* Morning broke fine, sun shining and sky beautiful and clear, saw a vessel in the distance, rainy and rather squally toward night. *Tuesday, 6th day, 10th January.* Morning broke fine again, and sun quite warm. Overcoats not needed, land in sight, west, saw a sail, in afternoon slight gust of rain, weather quite hot at night. *Wednesday, 7th day, 11th January.* Sky beautiful and clear, sun very hot, awnings over the decks, weather feels very much like July or August weather in the States. Evening very cool and pleasant. *Thursday, 8th day, 12th January.* The weather is becoming very hot indeed. I expect we feel it more in consequence of coming from a colder climate, expect to arrive in Kingston, Jamaica, tonight, ship's crew cleaning and scouring up everything that can be cleaned, in the afternoon some of the machinery gave way, causing a delay of about an hour or so, we then started on our way as brisk as ever, judging from appearances, a great many stayed up all night, watching for Kingston, about three o'clock, the Captain thought it prudent to lay to and signal a pilot, which signal was answered, about five o'clock, by a boat coming alongside, and a voice asked if we wanted a pilot. We, of course, answered yes, and he came aboard, and the first thing he asked for was a piece of bread and meat. He was the most singular looking mortal I ever saw, being as black as a dark night, and dressed with numerous colors, and his head tied up in a large handkerchief of many colors.

Friday, 9th day, 13th January. Early in the morning, we are going into the harbor of Kingston, long lines of mountains on our right, and ahead, little huts are to be seen from here.

At eight o'clock we passed the British man-of-war stationed here, and exchanged signals, and stopped to allow the doctor and another person to come aboard, half-past eight at the wharf, and then commenced a scene which beggars all description, fruit in plenty, oranges fifty cents per hundred, fresh from the trees, Negroes in profusion. The houses are all built with innumerable windows, to afford a free circulation of air.

The island of Jamaica has gone down very much since the slaves have had their freedom. The manner in which we coaled up here is quite singular, this is done by Negro women, who carry large tubs of coal on their heads, and follow each other in long rows, singing and making a most terrible noise and confusion. *Saturday, 10th day, 14th January.* This morning we set sail for Aspinwall, about nine o'clock. The weather is fine, three o'clock, land all out of sight, once more on the broad ocean. *Sunday, 11th day, 15th January.* Fine morning, weather much the same as yesterday, nothing of importance occurred all day. *Monday, 12th day, 16th January.* Fine day and wind blowing fresh from the west. About two o'clock the cry of fire spread throughout the ship, causing a thrill of horror to pass through the body of every passenger, we soon found, however, that it was only a slight burning in the galley, and had it speedily extinguished.

Tuesday, 13th day, 17th January. Arrived in Aspinwall about seven o'clock, went on shore and took our tickets for the [Panama] Railroad, and about nine o'clock we went off, in fine style, for Cruces. We stopped on the river Chagres, and went up in boats to Cruces, where we arrived about four o'clock, and immediately took supper, as we were very hungry, and then looked about the town. This is a miserable place, all the houses nearly being thatched with straw, and the natives extort all they can from travelers. We soon retired, and found we had to sleep in a room with about seventy-five other beds in it, however, we managed to sleep a little, and got up early next morning and took our breakfasts, when we started off for Panama, and such a road I never saw in my life, sometimes we almost touched the cliffs with our knees as we hung over the mules, at others we were perched on the summit of a high precipice, we got to Panama, however, without any difficulty, and took board at the American Hotel, and such board! Tough meat, no butter, old rye, coffee, and no milk, I was glad we were not going to stop long in the place. Panama is an old style Spanish town, with cathedrals that look as if they might have been built in the year one. *Thursday, 15th day, 19th January.* Got our tickets and had to pay a tax of $2.00 for hospital fees. We had to be lifted from the shore to the boats, as there are no wharves here, some of the ladies were very much opposed to being carried in this manner, they had to do it, however, and consequently submitted. We got on board, and sailed about six o'clock, once more on the ocean. *Friday, 16th day, 20th January.* Sea smooth and sun shining brightly, nothing of importance doing, very hot. *Saturday, 17th day, 21st January.* Same old tune, card playing, nothing of importance. *Sunday, 18th day, 22nd January.* Morning broke with a very high sea, and very disagreeable all day, had Church service in evening. *Monday, 19th day, 23rd January.* Morning fine, got up rather late, nothing but the old routine all day, nothing to break the monotony. *Tuesday, 20th day, 24th January.* The morning broke with rough weather, wind blowing and sea running very high, a number of times the decks were washed by the sea coming clean over them.

Wednesday, 21st day, 25th January. Morning broke fine in a calm, no wind of any account. We are now (twelve o'clock) one hundred and thirty-eight miles from Acapulco, Mexico. *Thursday, 22nd day, 26th January.* We arrived in Acapulco early this morning, numbers went on shore, the town looks much like all the towns we have seen on our route, mountains surround it on three sides. Nine o'clock we fired a gun, for all boats to return from shore, at twelve o'clock we are standing along the coast, going as fast as we can, from Acapulco to San Francisco. *Friday, 23rd day, 27th January.* Morning fine, same old tune, nothing to do, traveled in the last twenty-four hours, up to twelve o'clock today, two hundred and thirty miles. *Saturday, 24th day, 28th January.* Nothing worth mentioning, distance two hundred and five miles. *Sunday, 25th day, 29th January.* Weather fine, had service this morning, distance two hundred and twenty miles. *Monday, 26th day, 30th January.* Nothing of importance occurred all day, except, a little excitement in consequence of musty bread being given to the forward passengers, distance two hundred and eighteen miles. *Tuesday, 27th day, 31st January.* Weather fine, spoke the whale ship *Marlow*, of New Bedford, twenty months out, distance two hundred and twelve miles. *Wednesday, 28th* day, 1st February*. Weather fine, no rain as yet, distance two hundred and twenty-two miles. *Thursday, 29th day, 2nd February*. Weather foggy and looks like rain, cool weather, overcoats in requisition, distance two hundred and twenty miles. *Friday, 30th day, 3rd February*. Weather still foggy, half-past one, so near shore that we could see the green sides of the mountains, distance two hundred and forty-two miles. We expect to arrive in San Francisco, sometime tonight, or tomorrow morning early.

Friday, April 14th. Occupied the house of Mr. J. Renfro at twenty-five dollars per month. [End of 1854 diary.]

Note—It seems clear by the writing in this journal that the writer seemed to have a specific image about society and held views that probably made her a bit of an outcast with those who knew her during her travels west. From the way this journal is written it also appears she was not shy about expressing her views either—no matter how unpopular they might have been to others—and was a chronic complainer as well who held racist beliefs despite supposedly being a Christian woman. However, it can probably be assumed she didn't like it when she was confronted for comments she may have said publicly that offended others and of which an apology was expected but never offered.

James Akin Jr.

Excerpt from the journal of teenager James Akin Jr. Originally published by the University of Oklahoma Press Bulletin in a limited edition in 1919. Other versions appear online also. An unabridged edition of the journal was published in 1989 with additional genealogy material.

Journal of James Akin Jr.

Tuesday, April 15, 1852 First day—crossed Fish Creek three-fourths of a mile—roads good—plenty of water and wood. *Friday 16* Rains till noon—started—came to Salem—left Salem at 3 o'clock. Traveled 6 miles—plenty of wood—not much water. *Saturday 17* Start pretty soon—rains nearly all day—roads very muddy—traveled 15 miles—plenty of water and wood.

Sunday 18, 1852 Start at 9 o'clock—roads very bad. Pass Birmingham and Winchester. Camp at Libertyville. Corn 55 cents per bushel—hay 50 per centum weight—good place to camp.

Monday 19 Roads better—travel 15 miles—passed through agency. Camp in a good place—plenty of wood—not much water. *Tuesday 20th* Roads very good—travel 16 miles—passed Altumira—pretty cold day—camp in good place—plenty of wood and water—overtook Caleb Richey. *Wednesday April 21, 1852* Bad roads—travel 16 miles—cold weather—passed Eddyville about noon—bad place to camp—plenty wood and water. *Thursday 22* Travel 15 miles—fine weather—crossed the Des Moines River in the evening—good place to camp on the bank of the river.

Friday 23 Travel 3 miles and then stopped and stayed the balance of the day—cool, dandy weather—oats 40 cents a dozen—corn 50 cents per bushel—good place to camp. *Saturday April 24, 1852* Traveled 12 miles—roads hilly and rough—cloudy weather—passed Knoxville—crossed White Breast Creek and camped on the bank—bought hay. *Sunday 25, 1852* Layed by all day—cloudy weather—herded all the cattle all day—good place to camp—plenty of wood and water. *Monday 26th 1852* Traveled 12 miles—cool weather—passed Pleasantville crossed South River and camped on the bank of the river—good place to camp.

Tuesday 27th Traveled 16 miles—very good prairie road. Palmyra-Indianola camp in the prairie—good place to camp. Plenty of water not much wood. *Wednesday 28th* Traveled 16 miles—very good roads—crossed Big Creek and camped on the bank of the same creek—good place to camp. Plenty wood and water. *Thursday April 29th 1852* Traveled 7 miles. Warm day and good roads—crossed Middle River and camped on the north side 2½ miles of Winterset—good place to camp stop at noon.

Friday 30th 1852 Start at 9 o'clock—travel 3 miles and pass Winterset—roads very good—windy cold day—stop and camp 1 mile west of Winterset—camp in a deep hollow—good place to camp—47 wagons on the same ground. *Saturday 1st 1852* Started early—traveled 20 miles—very good roads—camped in the prairie. Plenty water—carry wood 3-4 mile—herded the cattle till 9 o'clock. *Sunday 2nd* Very cold windy morning—start about noon and travel 8 miles. Camp in the prairie and hauled wood with us—not much grass—plenty water—rains at night.

Monday May 3rd 1852 Start early—travel 15 miles—cool weather—camp in the prairie—good place to camp—plenty wood and water—more grass than common—muddy branch.

Tuesday May 4th 1852 Start early. Travel 18 miles—pretty day—plenty of grass—plenty of water. Camp in the prairie. Drive the cattle a half mile to grass. *Wednesday 5th* Start early—travel

15 miles—good roads—warm day—rains at night—camp in the prairie—plenty of water and grass. Good place to camp—no timber. *Thursday May 6th 1852* Travel 16 miles—good roads but muddy. Rained part of the day—camp in a beautiful place on the bank of the creek—grass plenty. *Friday 7th May 1852* Started early and travel 2½ miles to the creek and wait 4 hours to cross and the boat sunk—good roads in the prairie—camp in the prairie—plenty water and grass—no wood.

Saturday 8th 1852 Travel 15 miles—good roads—camp in Kanesville—bad place to camp—plenty wood and water but no grass—beautiful day—great many camped around.

Sunday May 9th 1852 Travel 3 miles and camp on the banks of the Missouri River—beautiful day—good place to camp—plenty wood water and grass. *Monday 10th May 1852* Camped in the same place—corn 20 cents per bushel—new boat started. Fine day—many Indians around tents. *Tuesday 11th May 1852* Beautiful day. Ferry boat sunk—2 or 3 drowned—herded the cattle—plenty of grass—flour 16 dollars per pound.

Wednesday May 12 1852 Camped in the same place—rains in the evening—a man killed by the wagon running over him. Teams coming in all the time. *Thursday 13th May 1852* Camped in the same place—beautiful day—a great many teams on the ground—not much grass—river raised a little. *Friday 14 May 1852* Camped in the same place—boat bought flour at 16 dollars per barrel—beautiful day—pack up the wagons.

Saturday 15th May 1852 Start early and travel 14 miles up the river to another ferry—warm day—camp in 2 miles of the ferry—good place to camp—plenty wood—water and grass—rains at night. *Sunday 16th 1852* Camp in the same place—cold windy day—good place to camp—plenty wood—and water—and grass. Great many teams pass. *Monday 17th May 1852* Start early and go to the river—boat could not get to cross—camp here and drive the cattle back about 2 miles to grass. *Tuesday 18th May 1852* Commence crossing in the morning and cross nearly all day—very windy—cross till midnight—get all the cattle cross except 10 yoke. *Wednesday 19th 1852* Ferry the other 2 teams early in the morning. Start and travel 12 miles—herded the cattle twice. Camp in a good place. *Thursday 20th May 1852* Travel 15 miles. Crossed Elkhorn River. Wagons 2 dollars a-piece—camp in a good place. *Friday May 21st 1852* Start early travel 10 miles—rains nearly all day. Camp at 2 o'clock get scared at nothing and went back a mile for company—camp on Platte River. *Saturday 22nd* Travel 16 miles—warm weather—travel up Platte River bottom. Camp and then leave on account of smallpox—drive on to good place to camp. *Sunday 23rd* Traveled 15 miles up Platte River bottom—bad roads—seen 30 Indians with their ponies loaded with buffalo skins—good place to camp. *Monday May 24th 1852* Traveled 18 miles to Loup Fork. Ferry then went up the river 6 miles in a very good place—plenty wood—water and grass.

Tuesday 25th May 1852 Start early—travel 13 miles up Loup Fork to the ferry—cross Beaver River—camp near Loup Fork—bad place to camp. *Wednesday May 26th 1852* Travel 10 miles—bad roads. Warm day—crossed Loup Fork in the evening. Deep fording with quicksand bottom—good place to camp. *Thursday 27th May 1852* Layed by all day—pretty good grass. Water and wood plenty. Camp near Loup Fork—good place to camp—no Indians about—come to the Sioux Indians.

Friday 28th Start early—travel 18 miles—come to the buffalo range—sandy roads—camp in the prairie—plenty of grass—no wood—water scarce. *Saturday May 29 1852* Start early—travel 18 miles—prairie roads—some bad places to cross. Saw the first antelope—camp—no wood. *Sunday May 30th 1852* Travel 16 miles—very good roads. Passed no timber—crossed one small creek—camp near Wood River—plenty of wood and grass. Not much water. *Monday 31st May 1852* Travel 15 miles—very good roads—travel in ½ mile of Platte River all day—camp in a good place—drive cattle to Platte River to water. *Tuesday June 1st 1852* Start early—travel 17 miles. Very good roads—water the cattle at noon in Platte—camp in good place—plenty water and grass—no wood. *Wednesday June 2nd 1852* Travel 20 miles—very hot calm day—roads very dusty. Crossed Elum and Buffalo Creeks—camp—not much grass—drive them two miles to water—rainy and muddy night—Grand Island. *Thursday June 3rd 1852* Travel 18 miles—muddy roads—cool day. Came to Platte River again—saw 5 graves—camp near Platte—no wood—some buffalo chips—came to alkali. *Friday June 4th 1852* Travel 16 miles—good roads—saw 5 buffalo in the morning. Passed 1 grave—camped near Platte—good place to camp.

Saturday June 5th 1852 Travel 16 miles—good roads but sandy—crossed over a low sandy bluff extending to the river. Rain and wind in evening—camp in a good place near Platte. *Sunday June 6th 1852* Travel 20 miles. Sandy roads—crossed Skunk Creek—three died with the cholera along the road—camp on Canyon Creek—no timber. *Monday June 7th 1852* Travel 14 miles—crossed Canyon Creek—passed the last timber for 200 miles—took a buffalo hunt and wounded one. Camp in a good place near the river—buffalo chips. *June 8th Tuesday 1852* Laid by all day—13 of the boys went hunting and killed one antelope. Good grass and buffalo chips—a great many wagons passing all the time. *Wednesday June 9th 1852* Travel 19 miles—road ascends the bluff—very sandy roads—cross North Bluff Forks and Bluff Creek—camp in a good place—plenty of grass and chips—water scarce. *Thursday June 10th 1852* Travel 25 miles—cool day and sandy roads—Platte River—high springs along the road—camp in a good place—plenty of grass—water and chips. *June 11th Friday 1852* Travel 18 miles over very sandy bluffs—very warm day. Camp in a bad place—no grass—not much water—great many campers in sight. *Saturday June 12th 1852* Travel 12 miles till noon then stop and stay the balance of the day—camp in a good place—a good spring and plenty of grass—lone tree.

Sunday June 13 1852 Start early and travel 16 miles—good roads and warm day—rains in the evening—good place to camp. Plenty grass and water. *Monday June 14th 1852* Travel 14 miles. Sandy road—cool day—came in sight of Chimney Rock—bad storm in the evening—good place to camp—water grass and chips. *Tuesday June 15th 1852* Laid by all day on account of sickness—not much grass—Caleb Richey and his company overtook us—plenty water—not much chips. *Wednesday June*

16th 1852 Louise Richey, wife of Stuart Richey died at two o'clock in the morning. Started at noon and traveled 15 miles—good roads—pleasant weather—camp on Platte—not much grass.

Thursday 17th 1852 Travel 18 miles—very good roads. Passed Chimney Rock—drive the cattle 2 miles to the river to water at noon—camp near Platte—plenty of grass. *Friday June 18th 1852* Traveled 16 miles—excellent roads and warm day. Passed Scotts Bluffs—camp near the creek—good spring—burnt up one old wagon. *Saturday 19th 1852* Traveled 16 miles—good roads and grass—camp close to Platte River—good place to camp—plenty water and chips. *Sunday 20th 1852* Travel 16 miles—sandy and dusty roads—drive the cattle into the river at noon to water. Camp near the river—plenty grass and water.

Monday June 21st 1852 Travel 5 miles—camp within 1½ miles of Platte River. Considerable sickness in company—good place to camp. *Tuesday June 22nd 1852* Travel 20 miles over the Black Hills—found no water till 2 o'clock—camp in good place. Plenty of pine and cedar wood but no water. *Wednesday 23rd 1852* Travel 12 miles—very hilly bad roads—pine and cedar bluffs—cloudy, rainy weather. Elva Ingram, daughter of James and wife died—camp in good place—plenty wood no water. *Thursday 24th June 1852* Travel 15 miles—good roads but hilly. Very cold rainy day—some sickness in company—camp in a good place—plenty wood and grass—not much water.

Friday 25 June 1852 Travel 18 miles—good roads. Road returns to the river—warm weather. Camp near Platte. Plenty wood and water—not much grass. *Saturday June 26 1852* Travel 16 miles—bad country. Platte River very small—not much grass any place—camp near the river—not much wood.

Sunday June 27th Travel 17 miles. Level sandy roads. Warm day—passed no timber—camp near the river—drive the cattle 2 miles to grass—not much wood. *Monday June 28th 1852* Travel 18 miles—sandy roads—met 6 men and 16 horses packing through from California—passed considerable timber camp near the river—plenty grass. *Tuesday June 29th 1852* Travel 18 miles. Sandy road and windy day—get to the upper ferry—camp near the river—drive—good place to camp—plenty wood and water. Drive the cattle 3 miles to grass. *Wednesday June 30th 1852* Left the upper ferry on Platte and travel 18 miles without water—good roads—camp near a spring—good grass—the cattle got scattered very badly. *Thursday July 1st 1852* Travel 12 miles—good roads but dusty. Camp near Platte River—passed no timber—not much grass. Drive the cattle three miles to grass. *Friday July 2nd 1852* Travel 18 miles—sandy road and dusty—passed Independence Rock. Crossed Sweetwater—passed Devil's Gate—camped near Sweetwater—not much grass. *Saturday July 3rd 1852* Travel 18 miles up Sweetwater—this river is about 40 feet wide. Rattlesnake Mountains on the north side—Snake Indians camp. Not much grass. *Sunday July 4th 1852* Laid by all day to let the cattle rest—cold and windy day and night—not much grass. Plenty sagebrush for use—many teams pass us—wrote a letter. *Monday July 5th 1852* Travel 17 miles—sandy roads—windy cold day—crossed Sweetwater 4 times—bad to cross—camp near the river on the south side—some grass and sagebrush. *Tuesday July 6th 1852* Laid by all day—good grass—sagebrush—great many Indians come and camp in 2 miles of us—trade some with us.

Wednesday July 7th 1852 Travel 17 miles without water. Indians go with us—Joseph Mace overtook us—not much grass near Indian camp 1 mile above us. *Thursday July 8 1852* Travel 15 miles. Drive the cattle 2½ miles to grass in the morning—rough roads. Indians plenty—camp in two miles of the river—good grass on the river. *Friday July 9th 1852* Travel 15 miles—rough rocky roads. Crossed north fork of Sweetwater—passed some snow. Camp on south fork of Sweetwater—water good—grass at camp. *Saturday July 10th 1852* Travel 13 miles—good roads—crossed Sweetwater the last time—passed over the summit of the Rocky Mountains. Camp at Pacific Springs—pleasant day.

Sunday July 11th 1852 Travel 20 miles—very good roads. Camp on Little Sandy—drive cattle 2 miles to grass—poor place to camp—plenty wood. *Monday July 12th 1852* Start about noon and travel 6 miles to big camp 1½ miles above the ford—drive the cattle 6 miles to grass—good place to camp. *Tuesday July 13th*

1852 Camp in the same place and let the cattle rest—no more water for 40 miles ahead. *Wednesday July 14th 1852* Start at 10 o'clock and travel till night—stop for supper—travel till midnight—stop an hour—travel till daylight—grass plenty. *Thursday July 15th 1852* Travel till noon and reach Green River. Green River quite low. Camp one mile below the ford—take the cattle onto an island and let them stay without guarding.

Friday 16th 1852 Lay by all day—not much grass—warm weather—Green River low—plenty wood and water. *Saturday July 17th 1852* Forded Green River—good ford but swift current 2 foot deep—travel 10 miles to Bear Creek—good place to camp—plenty grass water and wood. *Sunday July 18th 1852* Lay by all day.

Good grass near camp—sold one ox and bought a cow and an ox—Gilliam left the company—some rain and hail up the creek. *Monday July 19th 1852* Travel 20 miles—very hilly roads and broken country—windy day. Camp on a small creek—good grass—plenty wood and water—rains at night. *Tuesday 20th 1852* Travel 12 miles—very hilly—bad roads—pass some quaking aspens and some graves—camp on Hams Fork of Bear River. Very good grass, wood and water. *Wednesday July 21st 1852* Travel 18 miles—rough hilly roads—pass over the summit of the Bear River Mountains—camp near a good spring—good grass. *Thursday July 22nd 1852* Travel 14 miles—good roads on Bear River—very dusty—camp on Bear River—very good grass on the island. Plenty wood—mosquitoes very bad. *Friday July 23rd 1852* Travel 16 miles. Very bad roads—cross Thomas Fork on the bridge—paid $1.00 per wagon—camp on Bear River—good grass—mosquitoes bad—overtook Caleb Richey. *Saturday July 24th 1852* Travel 10 miles—very good roads but dusty—crossed several small creeks. Camp near a good spring—plenty good grass and water. *Sunday July 25th 1852* Travel 10 miles—stop at 10 o'clock and stay till night—very good grass—plenty wood and water—good place to camp. *Monday July 26th 1852* Travel 16 miles—very dusty roads but good—passed Soda and Steamboat Springs camp on Bear River—very bad watering cattle—grass plenty. *Tuesday 27th 1852* Left Bear River—travel 18 miles—very good dusty roads—passed the forks of Oregon and California roads—plenty water—good place to camp. *Wednesday July 28th* Travel 7 miles—stop at 11 o'clock—stay on account of sickness. Portneuf Indians plenty. Camp on deep creek—good grass. *Thursday July 29th 1852* Travel 18 miles—rough roads—passed plenty of springs—camp on a small creek—very good grass. Plenty of wood, water, and serviceberries. *Friday July 30th 1852* Travel 17 miles—very rough and dusty roads—showers in the evening—camp on the creek. Plenty grass—wood and water—no wagons in sight today. *Saturday July 31st 1852* Laid by all day. Good grass—Miranda Jane Richey, daughter of Caleb and Alice Richey died—rained some in the evening—wood and water plenty. *Sunday August 1st 1852* Travel 16 miles—sandy and muddy roads—considerable rain. Passed Fort Hall—camped on a fork of Snake River—plenty of water—wood scarce. *Monday August 2nd 1852* Take an Indian cutoff and travel 10 miles to the other road—travel 7 miles farther—crossed Snake River camp. Grass plenty. *Tuesday August 3rd* Travel 18 miles—very rough roads. Passed the American Falls of Snake River—camp on Bench Creek—grass very scarce—wood plenty. *Wednesday 4 August 1852* Travel 12 miles—stop at 10 o'clock and give the cattle grass—rained considerable—camp on river at the forks of the Oregon and California Roads—good grass. *Thursday August 5th 1852* Travel 15 miles without water. Very rocky rough roads. Camp on Marsh Creek—drive cattle two miles to grass. *Friday August 6th 1852* Travel 15 miles—good roads—passed a great many dead cattle—camp on Goose Creek. Good grass—plenty wood and water. *Saturday August 7th 1852* Travel 25 miles—the last 13 without water—very rough dusty roads—camp an hour after dark on dry creek—water scarce—grass plenty. *Sunday August 8th 1852* Laid by all day—very good grass. Great many camped around—water very scarce—great many dead cattle on this creek. *Monday August 9th 1852* Traveled 8 miles—camp at 2 o'clock—very good roads but dusty—camp on 2nd Rock Creek—very good grass—water plenty. *Tuesday August 10th 1852* Travel 12 miles—very rough and dusty roads—grass scarce—camp on 2nd Rock Creek—some grass—water and wood plenty—mother sick in the evening—this is James Akin's wife that is sick. *Wednesday August 11th 1852* Travel 16 miles—start very early—very bad watering place at noon in Snake River—stop at 4 o'clock and take the cattle to grass—start at dark and travel 8 miles to water. *Thursday August 12th 1852* Travel 3 miles—stop and camp on banks of Snake River. Lay by the balance of the day—good grass three miles off—wood and water plenty. *Friday August 13th 1852* Lay by all day—good grass—wood and water plenty. *Saturday 14 August* Start and travel 12 miles to Salmon Falls—water plenty—Indians fishing. *Sunday 15th August* Lay by till sundown—start and travel till 2 o'clock—stop and sleep till daylight. *Monday August 16th 1852* Travel till breakfast—stop on good grass—start and leave the road and go to the river—very bad place to water—lay by till night—start and travel till 1 o'clock. *Tuesday August 17th 1852* Start at daylight and travel 6 miles to the crossing of Snake River lay by the balance of the day. Emigrants going down the river in wagon beds. *Wednesday 18th August 1852* Lay by all day in same place—very bad place to camp—preparing to cross the river. *Thursday August 19th* Try all day to get the cattle across the river and could not.

Friday August 20th Tow the cattle across the river between the wagon beds. Ferry them over in the evening. James Nicholson starts in a wagon bed. *Saturday August 21st 1852* All cross the river except two and gone after them—cool weather.

Sunday August 22nd Mother taken worse in the morning and died about 9 o'clock in the evening. We are about 30 miles below Salmon River Falls on the north side of the Snake River. Eliza Akin is the wife of James Akin. *Monday 23rd August 1852* Mother was buried about 10 o'clock in the morning about 200 yards above the crossing of the river. Traveled eight miles to a spring. *Tuesday August 24th* Lay by till noon. Moses Rhodes died in the morning. Traveled 11 miles good roads—camp on dry creek—water scarce—grass plenty. *Wednesday August 25 1852* Travel 15 miles—good roads but hilly—plenty grass all the time. Wood and water plenty—passed boiling hot springs—camp on beautiful creek. *Thursday August 26th* Travel 14 miles—very rocky creek—camp at Charlotte Creek. No water for the cattle—grass and wood plenty. *Friday August 27th 1852* Travel 15 miles—hilly roads but good—plenty of grass all the time—camp on White Horse Creek—wood and water plenty. *Saturday August 28* Travel 20 miles without water—good roads and cool day—camp on Boise River—this is a beautiful river—wood and grass plenty.

Sunday August 29th 1852 Travel 12 miles down Salmon River. Good grass all the time—camp at 2 o'clock—good grass, wood, and water—hares plenty—got some fish from the Indians. *Monday August 30th* Travel 18 miles down Salmon River—good roads—cool day—camp on Salmon River. Good grass, wood, and water. *Tuesday August 31st 1852* Travel 15 miles down Salmon River—cross the river—good grass—wood and water plenty.

Wednesday September 1st 1852 Travel 8 miles to Fort Boise. Crossed Snake River in the evening—pay $2.50 per wagon—good grass on the north side of the river. *Thursday September 2nd* Travel 15 miles to a large creek. Good grass. Camp at 10 o'clock in the night—very dusty roads. *Friday 3rd September 1852* Travel 2½ miles down the river to a spring—good grass and water—wood scarce. *Saturday September 4th* Start at 2 o'clock AM. Traveled 12 miles to Sulphur Springs by 8 o'clock PM. Traveled 12 miles further to Birch Creek—not much grass—water and wood plenty. *Sunday 5 September 1852* Travel 10 miles to Burnt River—camp at 1 o'clock—not much grass. Herded the cattle on Willows—wood plenty. *Monday September 6th* Travel 10 miles. Stop at noon and stay the balance of the day. Windy and cold nights—considerable sickness in the company. Willow wood and water plenty. *Tuesday September 7th 1852* Travel 18 miles. Leave Burnt River—very rough hilly roads—camp on a branch of Burnt River—no grass—wood and water plenty. *Wednesday September 8* Travel 11 miles—rough roads—camp at noon on Burnt River—grass, wood, and water plenty. *Thursday September 9th 1852* Lay by all day on account of sickness. Company all left except Uncle Stuart and Caleb Richey—not much grass—wood and water plenty. Eliza Ann Richey daughter of Stuart Richey died at 9 o'clock PM. *Friday September 10th* Start at noon and travel 9 miles—good roads camp on small creek—not much grass—wood and water plenty. *Saturday September 11th 1852* Travel 23 miles—very dusty roads—camp on dry branch. Not much water—camp at 9 o'clock—grass pretty good.

Sunday September 12th Travel 16 miles—very good roads—fine showers in the afternoon—camp on a branch of Powder River—grass wood and water plenty. *Monday September 13th 1852* Travel 12 miles—good roads and cool day—nooned at Powder River—camp on a small creek—good grass, wood, and water. *Tuesday September 14th* Travel 16 miles to the west side of Grand Round—bought some beef at 20 cents per pound. Excellent grass and water—pine wood. *Wednesday September 15th 1852* Lay by all day—great many camped here on account of sickness and to recruit their teams—plenty of Cayuse Indians with vegetables to sell. Abe Gilliam died. *Thursday September 16th* Lost 9 of our cattle—hunt for them all day and found them just at sunset—considerable sickness in company. *Friday September 17th 1852* Travel 15 miles—crossed the Blue Mountains and Grand Round River—roughest roads we have ever had—travel through pine timber all day—camp. *Saturday September 18th* Travel 13 miles through thick timber and rough roads without water—camp on a creek—plenty water and wood—some grass—tie the cattle at night. *Sunday September 19th 1852* Start at 10 o'clock—travel 5 miles through the timber—roads better—camp in the timber. Same grass—not much water. *Monday September 20th* Travel 10 miles—good roads to Umatilla River—passed a Cayuse village. Camp on the river—grass scarce—the Cayuse was holding a war dance when we passed them—they was in war costume. *Tuesday September 21st 1852* Travel 12 miles—down the river good roads—rained in the morning—camp on the river—no grass. Wood and water plenty. *Wednesday September 22nd* Lay by till noon—travel 11 miles dry—camp—plenty grass—no wood or water. *Thursday September 23rd* Travel 7 miles to Umatilla camp at noon. Lay by the balance of the day—plenty wood and grass.

Friday September 24 Travel 12 miles to Umatilla River and agency to Butter Creek—camp on creek—good grass—wood and water. *Saturday September 25th 1852* Lay by all day—plenty of Umatilla Indians about the camp all night—plenty grass—wood and water. *Sunday September 26th* Start at noon—travel 10 miles dry—camp—no wood or water—grass plenty. *Monday September 27th 1852* Travel 12 miles to Wells Springs—water scarce and not good—travel 6 miles further—dry camp not much grass. *Tuesday September 28th* Start at 3 o'clock AM. Travel 9 miles to Willow Creek—water scarce not much grass—wood plenty. *Wednesday September 29th* Start at noon—travel 12 miles—hilly roads very windy day—camp—no wood, water, or grass. *Thursday September 30th 1852* Start at daylight traveled 18 miles—good roads—camp on John Day River—plenty wood and water. *Friday October 1st* Travel 12 miles—crossed John Day River—camp 6 miles from river—no water or wood—good grass—good roads.

Saturday October 2nd Start at midnight—travel 12 miles by sunrise—get breakfast—traveled 5 miles further to Columbia River—camp on the Deschutes River. *Sunday October 3rd* Crossed Deschutes River before breakfast—start at noon and travel 6 miles—camp on a creek—not much wood—plenty water and grass. *Monday October 4th 1852* Traveled 10 miles down Columbia River—passed the Dalles. Flour wood. Plenty water and grass—camp in two miles of the Dalles. *Tuesday October 5th* Travel 10 miles down Columbia River—pass the Dalles—flour 35 cents per pound—camp in Columbia River bottom—wood and water and grass plenty. *Wednesday October 6th* Traveled 2 miles—camped and go to preparing to raft down the river—haul some pine logs to the river—grass plenty. *Thursday October 7th* Cut logs and cork wagon beds all day—very windy evening and night—plenty of wood, water, and grass—boats, canoes, running up and down the river. *Friday October 8th 1852* Very windy—cold day—haul logs all day—no boats—running cattle—doing very well. *Saturday October 9th* Still preparing our raft to go down the river—blustering cool weather. *Sunday October 10th* James Nicholson and John T. Stewart and John Akin start with the cattle on the pack trail. *Monday October 11th 1852* Calm day—take our raft to pieces—put it together again. *Tuesday October 12th* Start down the river about 10 o'clock—travel 6 miles—wind upstream. *Wednesday October 13th* Travel 5 miles—high winds up the river. Camp in a big willow thicket—plenty of wood.

Thursday October 14th 1852 Travel 5 miles—all leave the raft and go down the river in an Indian canoe except Uncle Stuart and W. A. Coulter. F*riday October 15th* Reached the cascades about 2 o'clock in the evening—everyone sick. Stayed until my father and Coulter came with the raft and the cattle—came and then we went to the lower cascades and camped there until the steamboat came from Portland—*this is my remembrance.*

After their adventurous journey ended in the middle of October of 1852 Stuart Richey took the surviving Akin children to live with him and his family in Pleasant Valley just outside of Portland since their mother was dead and their father died upon his arrival in Oregon. James Akin Jr. died in 1880 at 47.

Frances Sawyer

Excerpts from notes of a journal kept by Frances Horr Lamar Sawyer in a perilous journey across the Plains from May 9 to August 17, 1852. Compiled for the readers of *Breckenridge News* in Cloverport, Kentucky. Sawyer's story was originally published in six installments in 1894.

We left Louisville, Kentucky, on the 25th day of April, 1852 passengers on the steamer, *Pike Number 9* bound for St. Louis.

Mr. Sawyer bought his wagon and two mules and some of the supplies, which we would need on our long and tedious journey across the western Plains, in Louisville. He had bought two more mules, and the steamer stopped at his father's farm in Hancock County, Kentucky, to take these animals aboard.

At St. Louis we changed onto a small Missouri River steamboat, and came up that river to St. Joseph. Here it was necessary to lay in the remainder of our supplies, so Mr. Sawyer bought a single horse carriage for my use and one more mule.

There are four persons in our company—Mr. Sawyer and myself and two young men, Burk Hall and Benjamin Sampson, from Hancock County, Kentucky. Mr. Sampson is my cousin. He is a consumptive, and is going out hoping that the trip may benefit his health. These gentlemen pay my husband for the expense of their trip, and he furnishes everything except one mule bought by

Burk Hall. This is not the first trip for Mr. Sawyer. He was in the great California rush of 1849, and went over with a large pack train. In this train was one wagon loaded with medicine, to be used in case of sickness. He drove this wagon all the way himself, and was thus the first man who ever drove a wagon over the Sierra Nevada Mountains. He knows just what we will need on this trip and has made his purchases accordingly.

Two days after our arrival in St. Joseph all the preparations for our long overland journey were completed, and we came out and camped six miles from the city.

May 9. We left camp this morning, and soon found that our road was as hard to travel as the proverbial one that leads to Jordan. The mud was so deep and tough that our team of four mules mired down and stuck tight on two different occasions, and we were greatly delayed in having to stop and get them out. Our progress was very slow. We passed through Savannah, a small village, and went into camp one mile and a half beyond that place. We intend to travel in Missouri until we reach old Fort Kearny, where we expect to cross the Missouri River. Grass for our mules is very short here tonight. Distance traveled today, eight miles. *May 10*. We started out this morning with renewed courage, hoping that we might not be visited by similar trials and difficulties to those of yesterday, but our hopes and desires went to nought. Our mules mired again before we went far, and our progress was much impeded. We find some very bad branches, brooks, and ravines to cross. It seems that the farmers in this section take no interest in improving their roads, and this makes it so disagreeable for emigrants. It commenced raining this evening, and everything is very gloomy and unpleasant.

We pitch our camp by a flowing creek of good water where the grass is very plentiful. Distance traveled today, twelve miles. *May 11*. We came to the Nodaway, a small river, before noon today, crossed the stream, and are in camp on its bank. We were informed at the ferry that there was no more grass for a distance of twelve miles, and as it is plentiful here we want our mules to get a good feed and be well-rested before we start over the long barren stretch. Distance traveled, ten miles. *May 12.* We got along without much difficulty today, as our roads are improving somewhat. Our way lay over a beautiful prairie.

My mule and carriage go along so nicely and comfortably. She never stops for mud holes. She is the best animal we have. Mr. Sawyer bought her of Dr. Scott, of Cloverport, and she is named for the Doctor's daughter, Jennie. We have but little grass tonight. Distance traveled, twenty miles. *May 13.* Ben Sampson was so unfortunate this morning as to meet with a painful accident. In crossing a deep hollow he got his foot caught between the doubletree and wagon box and the member was severely sprained. He has suffered greatly all day. We have had several showers of rain this afternoon, but I keep dry and comfortable. I sleep in my carriage every night on a feather bed, and am not exposed in any way in bad weather. The boys sleep either in the wagon or in the tent. Distance traveled, twenty miles. *May 14.* We arrived within one mile of old Fort Kearny this evening, and Mr. Sawyer sent to the ferry to register his name. To our discomforture we learned that there were a great many before us waiting to cross, and it will probably be several days before our turn will come. Our road has been over a prairie today and it was very good. We passed through Linden, another small village, and crossed several large creeks on bridges, and ferried one. Ben's foot is better, though he is not yet able to walk. We have pitched our camp on the edge of the prairie, in a grove of timber. Distance traveled, twenty-two miles. *May 15.* One of our mules got away last night and Mr. Sawyer has had a chase for it today. He had to go back six miles before he caught her. She is so wild and hard to break to work. We sent to the ferry today to learn when we could cross, and were informed that we could not possibly get over before tomorrow or the next day. Mr. Sawyer dislikes having to wait here so long. He is anxious to be traveling all the time, and I prefer it myself. We have had more rain today, and the indications are that it will continue tonight. The grass is not good here. *May 16.* Sabbath day. I have been in my carriage all day, for it is very disagreeable out. The wind commenced blowing at a high rate last night and it has continued to blow a perfect gale ever since. Mr. Sawyer got up in the night and pulled the carriage, with me in it out into the prairie for fear that timber would fall on us. The men do all the cooking in bad weather, though I never have to do anything but make up the bread. *May 17*. We are still in camp, waiting and watching for our time to come to cross the Missouri, but it seems to be very uncertain when that will be. Mr. Sawyer went out hunting this morning and killed a deer. This was very acceptable to all of us, as fresh meat is quite a treat on a trip like this. *May 18*. The wind is blowing very hard today and the waves are rolling so high in the river that the ferry cannot run. This camp is growing monotonous and we are all so anxious to get away and continue our journey. Up to this time 906 wagons have crossed the river here this year.

May 19. We drove up to the ferry this afternoon thinking that probably we might get over. However, we soon learned that we would have to content ourselves until morning. The old Fort is on the opposite side of the river, but there is not much of it left to be seen. The ferryman has a log cabin here and keeps some groceries and whiskey to sell at high prices. *May 20*. After having been delayed a week, we succeeded in getting safe across the river this morning. And here we make another start on our long journey, hoping that we will not again be delayed for so long a time. We are now in the Indian country, and we suspect that it will not be many days before we see some of these wild natives.

We are in camp tonight with a small company of emigrants, among whom are several ladies. These, like myself, were all engaged in helping to cook supper, and I have no doubt but that they all enjoyed it heartily, as I did. There is an abundance of grass. Distance traveled, sixteen miles. *May 21*. Mr. Sawyer was taken sick last night with a hard chill and he has a high fever today. I feel very uneasy about him and sincerely hope that he will not have a hard spell of sickness, for on the Plains is a bad place to be sick. We have a good supply of all kinds of medicine with us, but doctors are very hard to find.

It began to rain last night and it has continued to pour down nearly all this day. We did not leave camp until nearly 3 o'clock this afternoon. Distance traveled, eight miles. *May 22.* Mr. Sawyer is some better today, and he hopes to soon be well again. We picked some nice prairie peas today but they cannot be considered as much of a luxury, as they are only good for making pickles. The roads are very good now, and we go along with ease, making good time. Distance traveled, twenty-six miles. *May 23.* Sabbath. We camped this afternoon at 2 o'clock, to rest the remainder of the day. We have been traveling, for several days, in company with an old gentleman and his family. He had with him his wife, two sons, daughter, and daughter's husband.

The daughter is dressed in bloomer costume pants, short skirt and red-top boots. I think it is a very appropriate dress for a trip like this. So many ladies wear it, that I almost wish that I was so attired myself. The old lady wears a short skirt and pantalets. She is fifty years old. Her health was not good when she started, but it is improving now. Distance traveled, sixteen miles. *May 24.* Today has been a very warm one, but nothing startling has occurred to break the monotony of the trip. The roads however continue good and we are making rapid strides toward the Far West. Mr. Sawyer guards his mules of nights now for fear that the Indians may steal them. Distance traveled, thirty miles.

May 25. We came to the Platte River today. It is a wide and shallow stream, and its water is warm and muddy. There is some timber on its banks and on the islands. Some Indians are in camp near us tonight, and they came over to our camp, begging for something to eat. They are not very pleasant looking guests, though they seem to be friendly and peaceable. Distance traveled, twenty-five miles. *May 26.* A large party of Pawnee Indians passed us this morning going on to their hunting grounds after buffalo, and this afternoon we met them returning. They had met a party of Sioux, and the result was a battle took place.

The Sioux had whipped them, killing and scalping two of the party and wounding several others. The Pawnees were very angry and badly frightened. Some were armed with bows and some with guns. I met some ladies that saw the fight, and they said that they were scared almost to death themselves.

The Pawnees had made a poor fight. There were only thirteen Sioux and they whipped sixty or seventy Pawnees. When we came to where the battle had been fought, Mr. Sawyer and I drove off the road a short distance to see one of the Indians who had been killed. It was the most horrible sight I ever saw.

Four or five arrows were sticking in his body and his scalp was gone, leaving his head bare, bloody and ghastly. I am sorry I went out to look at him. I have had the blues ever since.

We are in camp with a large company of emigrants tonight, and have out a strong guard. So we women are safe and secure from danger, and may rest in peace and comfort, if we don't dream of dead Indians. The grass is good here, but mosquitoes are very bad. Distance traveled, twenty-two miles.

May 27. Morpheus cozily wrapped us all in his arms last night, and the pleasant dreams of our far away Kentucky were not disturbed by the Indians either dead or alive. I have plucked some beautiful prairie flowers today. The prairie is very pretty, dressed in its May bright colors, and the atmosphere is sweet with its fragrance. The flowers somewhat resemble the bloom of the sweet pea. Distance traveled, twenty-five miles. *May 28.* Nothing of startling importance happened today, the same old monotony—endless prairies. Distance traveled, thirty miles. *May 29.* We arrived at New Fort Kearny at 2 o'clock this afternoon and went into camp near it. We wrote some letters home and mailed them at the Fort. The Fort is a neat little place, kept in the best of order, and the best of order is kept in it. There are several ladies here with their husbands who are officers. They keep an account of the number of emigrants who pass this place, and a soldier came out this afternoon to get our names to register. Distance traveled today, fifteen miles. *May 30.* Sabbath. We passed the Fort this morning and kept the bank of the Platte River until we arrived at a point ten miles above, where we forded the stream.

The Platte is a mile wide at this point, and our wagons pulled very hard in the quicksand. Mr. Sawyer went over in the carriage with me. The water was so deep that our mule had to swim in some places. I was greatly frightened and held on tightly to my husband. When we got over Mr. Sawyer took the mule out of the carriage and went back on her to help the boys over with the wagon. The mules stopped once and the wagon settled down so that oxen had to be procured to help start it again.

 At last they got over safe, and as the wagon box had been propped up, everything kept dry, though in this we were more fortunate than many others who were crossing today. Many had their effects greatly damaged by water. We went into camp on the bank of the river where we had crossed. *May 31.* We have traveled all day in heat and dust. It is quite warm and dusty now, and the grass is not good. Distance traveled, twenty-eight miles. *June 1.* We heard of three very sudden deaths this morning and the disease is supposed to be cholera. The emigrants in traveling over the Plains dig shallow wells to procure cold water.

 This water is strongly impregnated with alkali, and, it is thought, that by drinking this, these unfortunate people have been taken severely sick and died. We are making good time now. Distance traveled, twenty-eight miles. *June 2.* We are now in the buffalo regions, and the only fuel we have is buffalo chips. These make a good, hot fire. We are in camp near the Shawnee Springs. The water is very fine, cold as ice and clear as crystal. We enjoy this treat very much, after having been compelled to use the unwholesome water contained in the shallow wells of the Plains for several days past. The grass is also very good here. Distance traveled, twenty-five miles. *June 3.* We had a hard rain and thunderstorm last night and it is cool and pleasant today. We camp by a creek of good, clear water tonight. This is to our liking as the water of the Platte is so warm that we avoid its use whenever it is possible to do so. Distance traveled, twenty-five miles. *June 4.* Today we passed a great many new-made graves and we hear of many cases of the cholera. We hear of so much sickness that we are becoming fearful for our own safety. Distance traveled, twenty miles. *June 5.* One of the men in the camp of the old gentleman who is traveling with us was taken sick with cholera last night and it is thought that he will die. We have not left camp today, though the doctors say that it is much better to be traveling. *June 6.* Sabbath day. The sick man is some better, but other members of the company have similar symptoms. The disease is very bad among the emigrants, being more prevalent among the ox teams than the others.

There was more rain last night, and it is still cooler today. It is hoped that this will check the disease somewhat. Distance traveled, twenty-two miles. *June 7.* It rained again last night and is still cool and windy. Mr. Sawyer has slight symptoms of cholera this evening, but hopes to get it checked before it becomes serious. Distance traveled, twenty-five miles. *June 8.* Mr. Sawyer is better today. We met some Mormons from Salt Lake, and they told us there was no sickness ahead of us. This gives us brighter hopes and encourages us greatly. We passed Castle Ruins today. They are large stones on the top of a hill, and they resemble old ruins very much, though it was the hand of nature that placed them there. Distance traveled, twenty-five miles.

June 9. It is now one month since we left St. Joseph, and we have traveled a little more than 500 miles, making an average of about seventeen miles a day. We still have a long, rugged and weary road before us that will take us many weeks to go over. The health of the emigrants is so much better that we don't hear of any deaths now. We passed Chimney Rock and Courthouse Rock today. They were both on the opposite side of the Platte from us, but we could see them very distinctly. Distance traveled, thirty-one miles. *June 10.* We "nooned" today opposite the Scotts Bluffs. These bluffs were named for a man by the name of Scott, who perished under them for the want of food. The story of his death is a pitiful one. The view of the bluffs was grand and beautiful from our position. A Mr. Fox and his son, of Louisville, Kentucky caught up with us today, and they will travel with us a while. Mr. Sawyer had a slight acquaintance with him in Louisville. Distance traveled, twenty-four miles. *June 11.* We are in sight of Laramie Peak now, though it will be several days before we are opposite it. We have driven fast today and passed a great many ox teams, though the dust is so heavy that it almost blinds us. Distance traveled, thirty miles. *June 12.* We arrived opposite Fort Laramie in time to camp for the night. The Fort is on the south side of the Platte. We will lay over here tomorrow as Mr. Sawyer wishes to get a mule shod and make some purchases of a few things that we need. They keep supplies here, but sell at high prices. *June 13.* Sabbath day, and my birthday, too, just twenty-one. I have been in bed most all day, taking a good rest and trying to sleep. Mr. Sawyer got one shoe put on his mule and the others tightened. Cost him five dollars. We had to leave camp late this afternoon and come out where we could get grass for the mules. Distance traveled, six miles. *June 14.* We are now in the Black Hills. The scenery is very beautiful. Pines and cedars are scattered over the hills and beautiful flowers are abundant.

I gather tulips and larkspurs and many other lovely kinds that I cannot name. Distance traveled, twenty-two miles.

June 15. We passed an Indian camp today. A Frenchman living there keeps a trading post in a wagon. He has a squaw for a wife who has borne him several children. These seem playful and happy. Distance traveled, twenty-five miles. *June 16.* Nothing has occurred or been seen worthy of not today. Same old weary road to travel. Distance traveled, thirty miles. *June 17.* We have a heavy sand road to travel now. It is very hard on the mules.

Mr. Sawyer killed a fine antelope this morning, whose fragrant flesh was quite a luxury for us. Grass is not good here and mosquitoes are very bad. Distance traveled, twenty-three miles. *June 18.* We heard today that a murdered man had been found in a deep hollow a short distance from the road. The men who found him had seen him before and knew him. They think that he was murdered for his money, as he was known to have a considerable amount, and it is thought that his murderers are in the company with which he was traveling. He had a wife and one child. Great must be their sorrow to be thus so cruelly deprived of a dear friend and protector, and left alone in this wild and friendless country. Some men have gone in pursuit of the murderers. Just ahead of us a wagon ran over a little boy and broke both his legs. Distance traveled, twenty miles. *June 19*. We heard of another murdered man today. In this case, as in yesterday's, the man was murdered by a man in his own company, but the proof in this instance was positive, and the murderer was hung to a tree by the indignant emigrants.

We passed opposite the ferry on the North Fork of the Platte. Numbers of emigrants were there waiting to get over, but we were saved the trouble and expense of ferrying now by having forded the main Platte several days ago. We camped at the Willow Spring, where the water is cold and good. Distance traveled, thirty-one miles. *June 20*. Sabbath day. We left the Platte for good today. Passed the famous Independence Rock, and went into camp one mile from it, near the first crossing of Sweetwater River. This rock is a great curiosity, standing, as it does, here on the level plain, single and alone, hundreds of miles from any companion. It is a huge granite pile, 600 feet long, 200 feet wide and 75 feet high. It should have been named Emigrant's Register, as it contains thousands of names on its smooth surface, some being carved, some being placed there with paint, and others with tar. The Sweetwater runs along within a few hundred yards of the rock. We have had a long and tiresome march today without much water or grass for our mules.

The grass is not good tonight, and the only fuel we have is wild sage. Distance traveled, twenty-two miles. *June 21*. We have laid by today as we found good grass for the mules not more than a mile from camp. Dr. Barkwell, from Troy, Indiana, caught up with us today. We would not have known of his presence, had not one of our boys seen him when he was watering his oxen near us, and called to him. He Informed us that his youngest child had died on the Plains, which I was very sorry to hear.

The trials and troubles of this long, wearisome trip are enough to bear without having our hearts torn by the loss of dear ones. We went to the big rock this afternoon and placed our names on it. A rain caught us while there, and we had to shelter under the projecting shelves of the rock. We can see a burning volcano on the mountains near us tonight *June 22*. We forded

Sweetwater River this morning and passed near the Devil's Gate. This is a pass where the river has washed a channel through the mountains. While we were nooning today there came up the hardest hailstorm that it had ever been my lot to witness.

The stones came down thick and fast, and they were as large as walnuts, none smaller than large bullets. The wind blew so hard and furiously that all the animals within our hearing stampeded. All hands had a hard time getting them together again. Some escaped entirely, but we had the good fortune to recover all of ours. Some of our men got bruised heads and hands by the heavy hailstones striking them. I was badly frightened, and thought the wind would surely blow us away. We are still at our nooning place. Distance traveled, ten miles. *June 23.* We have concluded to go to California instead of Oregon, as was our first intention. I am greatly pleased by this change of intentions, as I had much rather go to California. My brother, Benjamin Lamar, is there, and to see him is a greater inducement for me than the whole of Oregon can offer. Distance traveled, twenty-two miles. *June 24.* We are in sight of the Rocky Mountains now, and we can see the glistening snow on the tops of the high peaks.

We camp with Dr. Barkwell, wife and little daughter tonight. I am so glad to meet them, and I enjoy their company so much, as they are the only persons that I have met on the broad Plains that I ever knew before. Forded Sweetwater River twice today. Distance traveled, twenty-seven miles. *June 25.* We passed a trading post today. The keeper is a Frenchman. Mr. Sawyer exchanged his wagon for a lighter one, as ours was too heavy for four mules to pull over the mountains. The wagon he got in the trade is not as good as the one we had, but when you trade for anything on this trip, you usually give double value for what you get in return. He also exchanged the wild mule that he bought at St. Joseph, for an Indian pony. The pony is not half as valuable as the mule, but we never could break the mule to work or ride well. We are ascending the Rocky Mountains, but the ascent is so gradual that one would hardly know that he is going up a mountain. We pass plenty of snow and had all the ice water that we could use. Distance traveled, fifteen miles. *June 26.* Passed through the South Pass today, and commenced descending the mountains on the western side. We soon came to the Pacific Springs and went into camp a few miles from them.

Mr. Sawyer started out from the springs to hunt a good place to pitch our camp, and we got lost from him. We got on a wrong road and did not get back to the emigrants road until ten o'clock at night. I was so worried about him, and for fear that he could not find us otherwise, I got all the men near us to fire off their guns and pistols. He heard the firing and came directly to us. Distance traveled, twenty-eight miles. *June 27.* We crossed Dry Sandy Creek this morning. There are some pools of brackish water in it, though it is not fit to use. We came to the forks of the road, the left being the road to Salt Lake and the other the Fort Hall route. We took the Salt Lake Road, though we do not know yet whether we will go by there or take some of the cutoffs.

We are all anxious to see the Mormon city, but that route is 90 miles longer than the other, and we don't much like to travel that far out of our way just to see it. We forded the Little Sandy. Distance traveled, twenty miles. *June 28.* We forded the Big Sandy today and camp twelve miles from Green River on a beautiful meadow. The grass is so good that our mules are feasting tonight. Distance traveled, twenty-five miles. *June 29.* Soon came to Green River and got ferried over it and camped one mile from the ferry. There is a trading post at the ferry and some Indians are in camp around it. We have taken the McKinney Cutoff, as we thought it better to take all the advantages of the trip we could, than to satisfy our desire to see Salt Lake.

I saw some beautiful bloom of cactus today. They were of many different colors. Distance traveled, thirteen miles. *June 30.* Mr. Sawyer went off the road this morning on his pony and killed two sage hens. We ate them for dinner, and they were delicious. He was in sight of us all the time, though I drove along for several miles before he got back to the road. I drive a great deal now, as I am very fond of handling the lines. Our road has not all been good today. We passed one good spring of water and went in camp near another one on the top of a Shoshone hill. Distance traveled, thirty miles. *July 1*. We traveled, over some very steep mountains today, and again came into the main road.

We are now in the Bear River Mountains. Passed through a pine grove and a quaking aspen grove. Tonight we visited an adjoining camp to see a lady and her little daughter, who had been turned over in a carriage today while coming down a steep mountain side. When the husband and father got to them he thought that they were killed, but now it is thought that they are only painfully and not seriously hurt. We saw some very beautiful landscapes today. The principal stream crossed was Hams Fork of Bear River. Distance traveled, thirty miles. *July 2*. Came to the main Bear River today, and forded Smiths Fork. It was a very rocky and dangerous ford. We went into camp on the bank of the river and thought we would fish some, but the mosquitoes were so thick, so brave and so resolute that all our time was occupied in fighting them off. I never saw the like of mosquitoes in all my life before, and we thought that they would surely eat us up.

The grass is good here, but our mules could not eat any until 3 o'clock or after, when the mosquitoes left us. Distance traveled, thirty miles. *July 3*. Crossed Thomas Fork of Bear River on a toll bridge. Cost us one dollar per wagon. There is a ford eight miles out of our way, but it is not very good, so we concluded to toll. We went over some very steep mountains today too. Ben Sampson is real sick this afternoon, with high fever and a headache. He has taken cold, but the mountain air is so bracing that I think he will soon feel better. He has stood the trip so well this far that I have hopes of his health being greatly benefited. The mosquitoes are nearly as bad tonight as they were last night. Distance traveled, thirty miles. *July 4*. Sabbath day. We arrived at the noted Soda Springs this afternoon. Stopped and went out to see them. I made some soda drinks and cream tartar with the water, and they were very nice and cool.

I brought some to Ben and he enjoyed it very much. Said it made him feel much better. The Soda Springs is one of the natural curiosities of our country that is worth seeing. The water is so beautiful foaming up out of the crevices of the rock. It is quite cool here this evening and it snowed on the mountain and rained in the valley where we were. We camped three miles beyond the Soda Springs under a mountain. We have plenty of good pine wood and lots of grass. I traded a string of beads to an Indian boy for some fish, and we ate them for supper. Distance traveled, twenty seven miles. *July 5*. Lying by today to celebrate the Fourth, as we had to travel yesterday. We went fishing this morning, then came back and cooked a good dinner. We had canned vegetables, fish rice cakes and other little dishes.

We see lots of Indians now, and some are at our camp most all the time. They usually want to trade fish for fish hooks and something to eat. We found ice on the water in camp this morning, so you can see how cold it sometimes is here on the glorious Fourth. We were glad to get the ice water to drink.

July 6. We took Sublette Cutoff six miles from Soda Springs. We have been told that it is ninety miles shorter than the Fort Hall route, but we had some very bad roads today. Distance traveled, twenty miles. *July 7*. Mr. Sawyer traded our Indian pony for a two-year-old colt today. The colt is not worth much, but we were glad to get that much for the pony as it was nearly given out. So, you see that we lost money on that plaguy wild mule that we bought at St. Joseph. Traveled over two large mountains and camped in a valley. Distance traveled, seventeen miles.

July 8. Went over two more mountains today, and pitched our camp on Gravel Creek about 1 o'clock PM. It is twenty-five miles to the next water, so we concluded to remain here until morning and take a fresh start for the long, dry march. We went fishing this afternoon, but did not get a nibble, so we had to give it up as a bad job. Distance traveled, fifteen miles. *July 9*. It is very warm and dusty today, but the nights are always cool and pleasant in the country. We are out of the mosquitoes for the present, and I hope we will not catch up with anymore of them soon. We went over two more large mountains again today, and one of them was very hard to descend. These mountains are very tiresome to travel over, as we walk up most all of them, and I never ride down one. Distance traveled, twenty-five miles. *July 10.* We commenced descending one of the Bear River Mountains this morning and we are not out of it yet tonight. Most of our road lay in a ravine, with frequent small branches to cross. We camp on one of these branches, where we have splendid bluegrass for our mules. Distance traveled, twenty-one miles.

July 11. Sabbath day. We are lying by today, as there is such good grazing here for our animals. We have been traveling slow for the last week, and we will continue to take our time until we get to Marys River. We want to get our mules in good condition for that river valley. As there is so much alkali water and grass in it we will have to make quick time over it. After that comes the Great Desert, so you see our road will soon be a difficult and weary one indeed. We picked some currants and gooseberries today and had some tarts for dinner.

July 12. We came on to the old Fort Hall Road today, and passed the carcasses of a great many dead cattle. We crossed several bad branches of Raft River, and had to make a bridge for one before we could get over. Distance traveled, twenty-four miles. *July 13.* Had a nice shower of rain today which, greatly to our liking, settled the dust, and it has cleared off cool and pleasant. We are in camp tonight at Steeple Rock. There are a great many names on the rocks. Distance traveled, eighteen miles. *July 14.* The Salt Lake Road meets us again, and all the California emigrants are now on this road. The Oregon emigrants have all turned off on the Oregon route. The Digger Indians stole thirteen mules and one ox, last night, from a company just ahead of us. We camp with some company every night now and keep a strong guard out all the time, for the Indians will steal the animals if they get half a chance. We traveled over the Goose Creek Mountains today and had a very steep one to descend. We are in camp on Goose Creek. Distance traveled, twenty-four miles.

July 15. Our four mule team got mired in a bad slough this morning, but we got them out without much trouble. We have had to make a long march today to get to water, and we find the grass very scarce. Camped in Thousand Springs Valley. Distance traveled thirty-five miles. *July 16.* The Digger Indians killed a white man a few days ago, at the place where we camped last night. We saw his grave, but did not know he had been killed by the Indians until today, when some emigrants informed my husband that such was the case. We camp in Hot Springs Valley tonight. Grass is good. Distance traveled, twenty-eight miles.

July 17. We came to the Hot Springs this morning, and stopped to see them. The water comes boiling, out of the earth, and it is so hot that I could not more than touch it without burning myself. We camp near Canyon Creek, where we found splendid grass—and clover. Distance traveled, twenty-three miles. *July 18.* Sabbath day. I have not been feeling well for several days. I have taken cold. My chest is sore and it pains me very much. I am taking medicine for it, and think that I will soon be better. We came to Marys River, or Humboldt as some call it, today. All the emigrants dread this river, but we found some grass, which is more than we expected, as Mr. Sawyer says that there was very little here when he came out in 1849. Distance traveled, thirty miles. *July 19.* The Digger Indians came to a camp near us last night and stole two horses. The man on guard went to sleep and let the Indians slip past him. These are the most thieving Indians on this route, and I will be glad when we are out of their range. We forded the North Fork of Marys River this afternoon. Distance traveled, twenty-nine miles.

July 20. A company of men went out yesterday in pursuit of those Indians who stole the horses. Neither the water or the weather is good on this river, and the dust is very bad. We forded the river four times today, within a distance of ten miles, to avoid going over the hills. Distance traveled, thirty miles.

July 21. We had a hard march of seventeen miles today over the hills without stopping except to water our mules at an excellent cold spring which we found in the hills, had to keep traveling until we came to grass. We forded to the north side of the river and went into camp. We will travel on this side for some distance row, as we were informed by some "packers" today that the best grass was on this side. Distance traveled, twenty-five miles. *July 22*. Mr. Sawyer killed another antelope today and we are feasting. Game of all kinds is very scarce this year on the road and I have been wishing for some fresh meat for some time.

My husband took some of the meat over to another camp near us and made the people a present of it. In return for his kindness the men came over to our camp with a bottle of old whiskey and treated our men. These men keep whiskey for sale and they retail it at two dollars a drink. That seems like a high price for liquor, but these men have to haul it from the States or from California, over the mountains, across the great desert and up this river for two hundred miles, so you see it is bound to be a costly drink. We had more mosquitoes tonight, more than we had ever caught up with before. We drove off the road to the river, intending to camp there, but the pesky insects were so bad that we were compelled to abandon the idea of camping.

I thought that they would surely eat us and the animals up before we could get back to the road. We traveled until ten o'clock at night before they left us. It turned cool at that time and we pitched our camp. Distance traveled, thirty-five miles.

July 23. The mosquitoes were so bad this morning that we had to leave camp at daylight without our breakfast. We traveled until the sun got too hot for them, then stopped and cooked our breakfast. They are not quite so bad tonight. Mr. Sawyer is not feeling well tonight. Distance traveled, twenty-five miles.

July 24. We have laid by this afternoon because Mr. Sawyer is too sick to travel. He has a high fever and a bad headache. His bones all ache and he thinks he has a touch of mountain fever. He is doctoring himself today and hopes to be better soon. This river is the worst place on the trip to be sick. The weather is bad, the water is not good and the mosquitoes annoy you to death of nights. Distance traveled, twelve miles.

July 25. Sabbath day. My husband is better today, though he don't feel too good yet. We had the good fortune to get a camp tonight where there are no mosquitoes. Distance traveled, twenty-three miles. *July 26*. They changed my carriage mule into the wagon today and put one of the wagon mules into the carriage. I did not admire the change, but submitted, and sure enough, bad luck came of it. While crossing a slough the mule I was driving mired down and before they could unharnass him, he began jumping and kicking and broke one of the shafts to the carriage. I was so sorry that I felt like crying, for I thought that we would have to leave my carriage behind. However, Mr. Sawyer went to work and mended it, so that now it is almost as stout as it ever was. Distance traveled, twenty-two miles.

July 27. We passed a trading post today and were informed that it was one hundred miles from there to the Sink of this river—and won't I be glad to see the end Sink out of sight.

I am getting a little tired of this wearisome trip and am very anxious to get through, but I intend to take it patiently as it comes, for I know that it will not be very long now until we reach California. My husband has a very bad sore mouth and throat and he suffered with them very much last night. Burk Hall is the only one of our party who has not been sick on the trip, nor have I ever seen him mad or out of humor and ready jokes always quiets the troubled waters. Distance traveled, twenty miles. *July 28.* We are not bothered much by mosquitoes of nights now. Mr. Sawyer shot some sage chickens this afternoon and we had them for supper. Mr. Sawyer ate heartily and says he thinks they will cure him. Distance traveled, twenty-three miles. *July 29.* We had a march of eighteen miles this morning without water or grass. Forded the river for the last time to the north side and we will travel on this side to the Sink. Distance traveled, twenty miles.

July 30. Our road is better on this side of the river than it was on the other. We had a nice shower of rain this afternoon, which is a very uncommon occurrence here at this season of the year. It settled the dust and was very refreshing. Distance traveled, twenty-two miles. *July 31.* Arrived at the noted Meadows this afternoon and will remain here until tomorrow. Then our men will cut enough grass to take the mules over the desert and we will have to take all the food and water we can from here. Distance traveled, seventeen miles.

August 1. Sabbath day. We went down into the Meadow this morning and the men cut some splendid grass, then went on down below the Sink of the Marys or Humboldt River and camped near Sulphur Springs, but the water is not good this year. Had plenty of mosquitoes last night. Distance traveled, twenty miles. *August 2.* We made a start across the great desert this morning a little after sunup and took, as Mr. Sawyer thought, the old Truckee route, but in about six miles we came to an alkali pond which it was impossible to cross. We then went over to the Carson route. This mistake tired our mules that much more than they ought to have been, but we traveled slowly, to save them all we could. We stopped at noon and fed them, then went on until sundown, when we stopped again and fed and cooked some supper with the remains of an old wagon as fuel. We stopped at a trading post in the afternoon and bought some water for the mules, paying seventy-five cents a gallon for it. The gentleman who keeps the post sent me a glass of port wine, and I drank it with good grace, for I was tired too. Distance traveled up to tonight, twenty-two miles. We started again at dark and traveled until midnight when our mules commenced failing fast. Stopped and fed them and bought six buckets more of water, paying one dollar a bucket for it. I thought for sure that we would not get our teams through, for the last twelve miles was a heavy sand road. Ben got in the carriage with me, while Mr. Sawyer and Burk Hall walked on each side of the four mule team, driving and whipping them up, but resting them often. Ben and I were in front and as I heard the whips popping and cracking, I sincerely pitied the poor beasts with all my heart. But when we came in sight of Carson River, my mule stuck up his head and started off in a fast walk, and the other mules followed suit. I was afraid my mule would run right into the river, as he was so hard-mouthed and resolute that Ben could hardly hold him. We arrived at Ragtown, on the Carson River sunrise this morning, August 3. Distance traveled, forty miles since dark yesterday evening. This desert and lower part of Marys River have been the worst sections of our trip and I am truly glad that we are over them safe. Though the desert is easier to cross this year than it has ever been before. There are seven or eight trading posts on it now, where refreshments and supplies of all kinds are kept for sale. There are also some trading posts here on Carson River. *August 3*. We went up the Carson River five miles from Ragtown and camped for the remainder of the day.

We bought some fresh beef, and have been feasting on beefsteak today. Grass is scarce. Distance traveled five miles.

August 4. We all slept well last night and didn't even have a guard out. None of us slept much the night before, as we were crossing the desert. However, I laid on my bed in the carriage and slept some in the forepart of the night and the boys did the same thing in the wagon, one at a time. But when the mules began to tire, we all became too anxious for a safe passage across the sandy waste to be visited by the angel of slumbers or the god of dreams. We had a weary march of fifteen miles today without water or grass, but we have splendid grass tonight. Distance traveled, fifteen miles. *August 5*. We had another hard march of ten miles over heavy sand this morning. This river, however, is a pretty little stream of clear, cold and good water. There are some cottonwood trees, willow and blackberry bushes growing on its banks, and good camping and nooning places are easily found. Distance traveled, twenty miles. *August 6*. I saw a lady where we nooned today, who had a fine son, three days old.

The arrival of the little stranger had made it necessary for his friends to go into camp for a week or more, and they had settled down to make themselves at home, quietly and patiently awaiting the time that they might resume their march. The lady was comfortably situated and in good spirits. I have heard of several children being born on the Plains, though it is not a very pleasant place for the little fellows to first see the light of day. Distance traveled, thirteen miles. *August 7*. Mr. Sawyer sold our four horse wagon and harness this morning for $25. He thought it was not worth taking over the Sierra Nevada Mountains, besides it would be very hard on the mules. The men have been getting ready all day for "packing." They will put some light things into my carriage and drive it as far as it will hold out. Mr. Sawyer will walk and drive over the bad places. I will ride a mule, and the boys will ride another. The remainder of our things will be packed on the backs of the other animals, and we will thus be converted into a pack train. We camp at Gold Canyon. There are fifty or sixty miners at work here, and there are three families living in log cabins. Distance traveled, three miles. *August 8.* Sabbath day. Mr. Sawyer went out prospecting this morning up the canyon. He obtained about twenty-five cents worth of gold dust, but he concluded that, that would not pay, so we left camp in the afternoon. I bought some turnips today, at ten cents each, and I was inclined to think that they were pretty dear vegetables. Distance traveled, ten miles. *August 9.* We came to Carson Valley today. It is a beautiful valley, and some emigrants are settling here. The Mormon station has been built one or two years.

It is a boardinghouse and house together, in a pretty location at the edge of the mountains, with tall pine trees all around it. There are some gardens here, and I bought some more turnips, at five cents each. We have at last arrived into civilization, though things are still very high. Mr. Sawyer got one shoe put on a mule at a blacksmith shop, and it cost him one dollar. Distance traveled, eighteen miles. *August 10.* We traveled up the Carson Valley today to the foot of Humboldt Canyon and went into camp. Distance traveled, nineteen miles.

August 11. Started into the mountains this morning through Humboldt Canyon. Crossed three toll bridges. Our road is very rough, rocky and difficult to travel over. Some stones, right round and as large as hogshead, lie right in the middle of the road. Our carriage broke down, and we have abandoned it.

One wheel got fastened between two rocks and broke all to pieces. We packed everything on to the mules and went on four miles further, where we are in camp on the bank of a beautiful mountain stream of pure, good water. Our men are making more pack saddles. Distance traveled, fourteen miles.

August 12. We traveled fast today and crossed the first summit of the Sierra Nevada Mountains before noon and stopped at a beautiful lake (Tahoe) to noon. I have had the toothache so bad today that I could not enjoy the beautiful landscapes and scenery. In the afternoon we crossed the second summit of the Sierra Nevada. It is 9,000 feet high and we went over snow six feet deep. We had to travel until ten o'clock at night before we could find a place level enough on which to pitch our camp.

After it got dark Mr. Sawyer walked in front and led the first mule and the others followed, with Ben and me in the rear. The road was difficult and nothing but rocks. I could not see the path in the dark, so I just gave my mule the rein and let it follow after the others. Distance traveled, twenty-five miles.

August 13. Our road has been better today. We met up with and have been traveling with another party of emigrants today. This party consists of two men, two ladies and several children. They, like us, have left their wagon behind and are "packing." We camp at Lake Springs, where there is good water and good grass. Distance traveled, nineteen miles.

August 14. I had the toothache so bad again today that I could take no interest in anything. We passed some very large and tall pine and spruce trees, and are in camp in heavy timber. Distance traveled, twenty-eight miles. *August 15*. We are over now to where there are some settlers. We stopped at an eating place, and the boys took the mules off the road to get water. One of them got mired and the packs got turned on the others.

We came to Placerville today about noon. On our arrival it was discovered that our dog had been left behind somewhere, and Mr. Sawyer had to go back twelve miles before he found him. We had a very dusty road today, and I tell you I am glad to be in California at last. This is quite a lively place. There are numbers of miners here, and gold mines are near the town, some families have settled here, too. I am stopping all night at a boardinghouse with a very nice lady. The boys are camping out in our tent, which we all have been sleeping in since we have been "packing" and the mules were taken to a hay yard. Distance traveled, twenty miles. *August 16*. This morning Ben Sampson and Burk Hall concluded that they would stop here and see the mines.

Ben is not stout enough to work in the mines, though his health has improved during the trip. However, he is ambitious and wants to dig gold. I hated to leave him very much, but I thought that he could do as well here as any place.

Mr. Sawyer and I left Placerville at 8 o'clock AM, intending to go to Sacramento City, and we are in camp near a ranch house on the prairie. Distance traveled, thirty miles.

August 17. We reached Sacramento City at noon today. I went in with the pack mules in a cloud of dust, Mr. Sawyer having to whip my mule up with the others. We have been out three months and eight days from St. Joseph. We are stopping at the American House and glad that we are, at last, at the end of our journey safe and well, though we are tired and need rest.

Epilogue written by Frances Horr Lamar Sawyer concluding her covered wagon story in the *Breckenridge News*.

Mr. Thomas Henry Sawyer made three trips in all to California. He went overland in 1849 and came back in the fall of 1850. He could not content himself to stay in Kentucky, however, and concluded to go back again. So in the spring of 1851 he, in company with my brother, Benjamin B. Lamar and George Bruner, all of Hancock County, went out by water, by the way of New Orleans and the Isthmus. He soon got homesick again and came back in the fall of 1851, thinking that he would either settle here in Kentucky or move with his wife to California. He chose the latter course, hence our overland trip in 1852. I thank the kind editors of the *Breckenridge News* for bearing with me thus lengthily, and I hope that the narrative of my tedious trip has not proved tedious to the many dear readers of our favorite paper. (March 1894)

James Richey

Originally published in 1908 in a limited edition. James Richey was one of the thousands of pioneers that left their homes in the middle of the nineteenth century searching for a better life in Western America. It is not clear if Richey himself wrote his account or dictated it to someone else.

RICHEY, CALIFORNIA, MARCH 15, 1908

Just fifty-four years ago today, in 1854, I left my home in Illinois for the trip across the Plains. After bidding all goodbye, brother Thomas took us, Alex and I, to Mr. Miller's, where Mr. Strahn had his outfit, but they had started. We overtook them at DeHague's. We then transferred our luggage to the ox team. Our company consisted of Miller Strahn, Tom Eberley, Bill Henry, John Flemmings, Alex Richey and James Richey from Illinois, and S. Steele, Mose Knox, Abe Earnest, and William Morse from Iowa. Arriving at the Mississippi River we experienced our first ferrying of cattle. After considerable trouble we got a load on the ferry boat, the *Flint Hills*. When it cast off for the other side the cattle were greatly excited and rushed from one side to the other, tipping the boat, and crowded four or five head into the river. On the upper side one went under the boat, coming up, followed the boat across making nearly as good time as we did. We then named her Mississippi. When other rivers were to ford she readily led the herd across. We stayed four miles west of Burlington the first night. The fifth day we arrived at Bloomfield, the home of Mr. Steele, had dinner, then took cattle to farm seven miles from town, stayed two weeks, here finishing our outfit for the trip.

On Monday morning broke our first campgrounds and left for the long trip to the "Golden State." Went south, passed a short distance into Missouri, then west to the Missouri River, up this river to St. Mary's, twelve miles below Omaha, where we camped for a few days waiting to be ferried across the river.

On the 28th of April, Hopper's train joined us here, where we had our first sight of Indians, two hundred or more of the Omaha tribe, all great beggars. Here commenced guard duty for the next three months. I was on duty the after part of the night.

It was a stormy night and the cattle very uneasy. We were each on guard one-half night every fifth night. On April 29 left the settlements and started out on the Plains and passed over some fine-looking country. Crossing the Elk Horn River, we ferried the wagons and let the cattle swim, then the Loupe Fork of the Platte River which we ferried, came to the Platte River at Grand Island, one hundred miles from Missouri. Here we saw the first Pawnee Indians, much finer looking than the Omahas and were very friendly. We now traveled up Platte River, having fine feed and good roads. Saw but few buffaloes, as but few had come north as yet. Here we had our first stampede. We had been in camp and had our supper. A heavy thunderstorm stampeded the cattle, they going with the storm, but the men stayed with them, getting them back to camp about two o'clock in the morning, had all of our cattle and the most of another train's. Following the Platte there was nothing of note for some time, regular daily duty. We separated company with Hopper, traveling by ourselves, three wagons and ten men. One day we came to the camp of a train that had part of their horses stolen and had to throw some of their wagons away. We took two of their men, also a wagon, cutting ours up and carrying it for wood, as there was none on our route. Following the Platte we had our first view of the Rocky Mountains. Laramie Peak, said to be two hundred miles away. We were in sight of it for four weeks. The next thing of interest was Chimney Rock, on south side of Platte, about twenty miles away, looked some like a chimney in the distance, height some 150 feet. Next was Courthouse Rock which resembled a large building. We arrived at Fort Laramie on May 25, being the first building after leaving Omaha. Here was our first chance for mailing letters. Strahn crossed the river at the Fort. After leaving Laramie we had our first mountain travel through the Black Hills. The view was fine but very rough roads.

On guard one night I saw what I thought was an Indian coming towards the cattle. After watching it a short time I made up my mind to find out, so I crawled on my hands and knees some one hundred yards and found my Indian was a little mule that had strayed from a camp some distance from us. We traveled up Platte River to the north, crossing where the road from the south crosses to the north and joined the road on which we were traveling from Fort Laramie, one hundred miles. Here we left the Platte and crossed to the Sweetwater, still on the Oregon Trail, table land country, very good roads. We met the Cheyenne tribe of Indians on their way down to hunt buffalo and fight the Pawnee. A trader said there were about five thousand men, women, and children. They had their belongings packed on horses and dogs, tent poles on the sides, the back ends dragging and baskets lashed to these with children in them. The morning before reaching Sweetwater we had a stampede of our horses. While we were yoking up they pulled their picket pins and were off. As they passed me I grabbed one of the ropes, it pulled me down but Strahn was near and held it. He threw a saddle on it and followed them, catching them at Sweetwater, some ten miles away. We arrived there about noon feeling very good that he had them. We followed this river to the south pass of the Rockies. Places of note on Sweetwater, Independence Rock, lying in the valley, covering about ten acres and one hundred feet high. Five miles from Independence Rock is Devil's Gate, where the river passes through a chasm of rock three hundred and fifty feet in depth. On the south side of the cliff overhanging the river, laying down I crawled out and looked down at the river. It looked like a small rivulet. After passing this point, the next was the Ice Fields, when digging down from one to two feet in the ground we found solid ice, said to be four miles wide. Following the river up to the last crossing, ten miles from the summit, which was our last camp on the east side of the Rockies. In the morning we had a heavy sleet and snowstorm, very cold. Cleared up by seven o'clock and had a fine day crossing the summit. About noon June 10th, stopped for dinner at Pacific Springs. The water flows to the Pacific Ocean from here through the Colorado River.

From here the road leads to the Little Sandy, a branch of Green River. Here the Salt Lake Road and the Oregon Road, form the Salt Lake Road. Bearing south, we kept the Oregon southwest, from Little Sandy we crossed to Big Sandy some twenty miles where we camped till the next day noon.

In the forenoon we were busy shoeing cattle and preparing for crossing the Green River Desert, fifty-four miles, with no water. This is a sagebrush country, with considerable bunch grass. We started at noon and traveled till near night, camped and had supper. About dark a heavy rainstorm came up so we had plenty of water for cattle as well as feed. It cleared up about midnight and we hitched up and put out for Green River, which we reached about nine o'clock the next morning. This is a fine looking stream, some two hundred yards wide, clear and deep, with a rapid current. They were well-prepared to handle the travel having fourteen ferry boats, charged $5 per wagon without any team. Our ferry bill was $30 which we paid in bacon at fifty cents per pound. We had a hard time getting our cattle to take the river. They would start, then when they struck the current they would downstream and back. We finally got them across about the middle of the afternoon. We went down the river some fourteen miles and camped here and had some trouble with a horse train. Strahn had put our horses on an island early that morning and during the day a horse train had put their horses on the same island where they forbid us putting our cattle on.

Strahn said there was plenty of feed for both but they said no, the first animal that we drive across they would shoot. Stepping to a wagon he took a shotgun down, also Mr. Hopper and several more of our men standing on the bank of the slough. Strahn told them his cattle were coming across and the first man that fired on them he would kill. He then ordered the cattle driven in which we did, but they backed down and got out of our way. We put on double guard but had no more trouble. The next morning he gave the captain of the train some good advice.

In the morning we left Green River traveling through a mountain country with plenty of water and good feed. At Forest Grove about midnight the cattle stampeded. They were lying quiet when they jumped to their feet and were off like a shot. We were up and after them in a hurry. They ran down the mountainside into a deep canyon, but when they tried to climb the other side, it being very steep, we soon got ahead of them and drove them back to camp where they soon quieted down for the night. The only accident to a wagon was mine which I upset coming down a mountain to Bear River, breaking the top off.

We followed down Bear River to Soda Springs, where there was a trading post, about sixty miles north of Salt Lake. A spring of very pleasant tasting water lies on the bank of the river. Steamboat Spring near a gushing spring through a hole about four inches in diameter, recedes out of sight then gushes several feet into the air, making a sound very much like a steamboat.

Our next point is the Humboldt. After leaving Soda Springs some six miles, we have the Oregon Trail which goes north. We took the Sublette Cutoff which goes southwest into the Goose Creek Mountains. When leaving the Oregon Trail we passed over a volcanic country covered with rock resembling broken black bottles and fissures where we dropped rocks to an unknown depth. Goose Greek Mountains are quite rough, but plenty of feed and water. Northwest Salt Lake then came to Raft River, a branch of Snake River, which we followed up for some distance. The morning we left the river we passed a train of wagons encamped. They had, had their horses stolen that morning. We followed up a small stream into Thousand Spring Valley. Here we found both hot and cold water. At the head of the valley we passed the divide between the Raft River and the Humboldt River, which we reached on July 3rd, crossed to the south side and traveled along the foot of the mountains, where we found fine feed and good streams of water. We traveled very slowly here to let the cattle recruit. Found a few Mormon settlers here. They said they were going back to Salt Lake.

    Crossed the south fork of the river then had a mountain range to cross, coming to the main Humboldt River, Gravelly Ford, about halfway down the river. From here the country to the Sink is sagebrush, with a meadow along the river. One day we suffered for water, leaving the river at sunrise we went through sagebrush and sand country until sundown, with no water to be had, both cattle and men were wild for water.

    Arriving at the river, the cattle rushed in and the boys grabbing tin cups, waded out past the cattle to clear water about waist deep. I think water never tasted better. There was a trading post here—they said we traveled forty miles that day. At the Sink we passed around the lake to the west side where we camped till noon the next day, when we took up our line of march to Truckee Desert. It is forty miles across. About sundown we stopped for supper, then resumed our travel, very good roads until we came to heavy sand, about ten miles across. Arrived at Truckee River about ten o'clock and stayed until morning. Traveled up the river to Big Meadows, turned to the right, took Beckwith Road, crossing the summit into the valley July 29. Just three months from Missouri River. Here they went into camp to stay three or four weeks. The next morning five of us shouldered our blankets and started for Downieville where we arrived on the third day.

Chief Joseph

Excerpt from the 1925 edition below was originally published in the *North American Review* (April 1879) and republished in the book *Northwestern Fights and Fighters* (1907) by noted historian Cyrus Townsend Brady. The 1925 special edition was reprinted with additional info and had a limited release.

Chief Joseph's Own Story
Told by him on his 1879 trip to Washington DC

My friends, I have been asked to show you my heart. I am glad to have a chance to do so. I want the white people to understand my people. Some of you think an Indian is like a wild animal. This is a great mistake. I will tell you all about our people and then you can judge whether an Indian is a man or not. I believe much trouble and blood would be saved if we opened our hearts more. I will tell you in my way how the Indian sees things. The white man has more words to tell you how they look to him, but it does not require many words to speak the truth. What I have to say will come from my heart, and I will speak with a straight tongue. Ah-cum-kin-i-ma-me-hut (the Great Spirit) is looking at me, and will hear me. My (official non-English) name is In-mut-too-yah-lat-lat (Thunder Traveling Over the Mountains). I am chief of the Wal-lam-wat-kin band of Chute-pa-lu, or Nez

Perces (nose-pierced Indians). I was born in eastern Oregon, thirty-eight winters ago. My father was chief before me. When a young man he was called Joseph by Mr. Spaulding, a missionary. He died a few years ago. There was no stain on his hands of the blood of a white man. He left a good name on the earth. He advised me well for my people. Our fathers gave us many laws, which they had learned from their fathers. These laws were good. They told us to treat all men as they treated us, that we should never be the first to break a bargain, that it was a disgrace to tell a lie, that we should speak only the truth, that it was a shame for one man to take from another his wife, or his property, without paying for it. We were taught to believe that the Great Spirit sees and hears everything, and that *he* never forgets, that hereafter *he* will give every man a spirit home according to his deserts, if he has been a good man, he will have a good home, if he has been a bad man, he will have a bad home. This I believe, and all my people believe the same. We did not know there were other people besides the Indians until about one hundred winters ago when some men with white faces came to our country.

They brought many things with them to trade for furs and skins. They brought tobacco, which was new to us. They brought guns with flint stones on them, which frightened our women and children. Our people could not talk with these white-faced men, but they used signs which all people understood. These men were Frenchmen, and they called our people "Nez Perces" because they wore rings in their noses for ornaments. Although very few of our people wear them now, we are still called by the same name. These French trappers said a great many things to our fathers, which have been planted in our hearts. Some were good for us, but some were bad. Our people were divided in opinion about these men. Some thought they taught more bad than good. An Indian respects a brave man, but he despises a coward. He loves a straight tongue, but he hates a forked tongue. The French trappers told us some truths and some lies. The first white men of your people who came to our country were named Lewis and Clark. They also brought many things that our people had never seen. They talked straight, and our people gave them a great feast, as a proof that their hearts were friendly. These men were very kind. They made presents to our chiefs and our people made presents to them. We had a great many horses of which we gave them what they needed, and they gave us guns and tobacco in return. All the Nez Perces made friends with Lewis and Clark, and agreed to let them pass through their country, and never to make war on white men. This promise the Nez Perces have never broken. No white man can accuse them of bad faith and speak with a straight tongue. It has always been the pride of the Nez Perces that they were the friends of the white men.

When my father was a young man there came to our country a white man (Reverend Mr. Spaulding) who talked spirit law. He won the affections of our people because he spoke good things to them. At first he did not say anything about white men wanting to settle on our lands. Nothing was said about that until about twenty winters ago when a number of white people came into our country and built houses and made farms. At first our people made no complaint. They thought there was room enough for all to live in peace, and they were learning many things from the white men that seemed to be good.

But we soon found that the white men were growing rich very fast, and were greedy to possess everything the Indian had. My father was the first to see through the schemes of the white men, and he warned his tribe to be careful about trading with them. He had a suspicion of men who seemed so anxious to make money. I was a boy then, but I remember well my father's caution. He had sharper eyes than the rest of our people.

Next there came a white officer (Governor Stevens) who invited all the Nez Perces to a treaty council. After the council was opened he made known his heart. He said there were a great many white people in the country, and many more would come, that he wanted the land marked out so that the Indians and white men could be separated. If they were to live in peace it was necessary, he said, that the Indians should have a country set apart for them, and in that country they must stay. My father who represented his band, refused to have anything to do with the council, because he wished to be a free man. He claimed that no man owned any part of the earth, and a man could not sell what was not his own. Mr. Spaulding took hold of my father's arm and said "Come and sign the treaty." My father pushed him away and said "Why do you ask me to sign away my country? It is your business to talk to us about spirit matters, and not to talk to us about parting with our land." Governor Stevens urged my father to sign his treaty, but he refused. "I will not sign your paper," he said, "you go where you please, so do I, you are not a child, I am no child, I can think for myself. No man can think for me. I have no other home than this. I will not give it up to any man. My people would have no home. Take away your paper. I will not touch it with my hand." My father left the council. Some of the chiefs of the other bands of the Nez Perces signed the treaty, and then Governor Stevens gave them presents of blankets.

My father cautioned his people to take no presents, for "after awhile," he said, "they will claim that you accepted pay for your country." Since that time four bands of Nez Perces have received annuities from the United States. My father was invited to many councils, and they tried hard to make him sign the treaty, but he was firm as the rock, and would not sign away his home. His refusal caused a difference among the Nez Perces.

Eight years later (1863) was the next treaty council. A chief called Lawyer, because he was a great talker, took the lead in this council, and sold nearly all of the Nez Perces country. My father was not there. He said to me "When you go into council with the white man, always remember your country. Do not give it away. The white man will cheat you out of your home. I have taken no pay from the United States. I have never sold our land."

In this treaty, Lawyer acted without authority from our band. He had no right to sell the Wallowa (winding water) country. That had always belonged to my father's own people, and the other bands had never disputed our right to it. No other Indians ever claimed Wallowa. In order to have all people understand how much land we owned, my father planted poles around it and said "Inside is the home of my people—the white man may take the land outside. Inside this boundary all our people were born. It circles around the graves of our fathers, and we will never give up these graves to any man." The United States claimed they had bought all the Nez Perces country outside the Lapwai Reservation from Lawyer and other chiefs but we continued to live on this land in peace until eight years ago when white men began to come inside the bounds my father had set. We warned them against this great wrong, but they would not leave our land, and some bad blood was raised.

The white man represented that we were going upon the warpath. They reported many things that were false. The United States Government again asked for a treaty council. My father had become blind and feeble. He could no longer speak for his people. It was then I took my father's place as chief.

In this council I made my first speech to white men. I said to the agent who held the council. "I did not want to come to this council, but I came hoping that we could save blood. The white man has no right to come here and take our country. We have never accepted presents from the Government. Neither Lawyer nor any other chief had authority to sell this land. It has always belonged to my people. It came unclouded to them from our fathers, and we will defend this land as long as a drop of Indian blood warms the hearts of our men." The agent said he had orders, from the Great White Chief at Washington, for us to go upon the Lapwai Reservation, and that if we obeyed he would help us in many ways. "You must move to the agency," he said. I answered him "I will not. I do not need your help, we have plenty, and we are contented and happy if the white man will let us alone. The reservation is too small for so many people with all their stock. You can keep your presents, we can go to your towns and pay for all we need, we have plenty of horses and cattle to sell, and we won't have any help from you, we are free now, we can go where we please. Our fathers were born here. Here they lived—here they died—here are their graves. We will never leave them." The agent went away, and we had peace for awhile. Soon after this my father sent for me. I saw he was dying. I took his hand in mine. He said "My son, my body is returning to my mother earth, and my spirit is going very soon to see the Great Spirit Chief. When I am gone, think of your country. You are the chief of these people. They look to you to guide them. Always remember that your father never sold his country. You must stop your ears whenever you are asked to sign a treaty selling your home. A few years more and white men will be all around you. They have their eyes on this land. My son, never forget my dying words. This country holds your father's body. Never sell the bones of your father and your mother." I pressed my father's hand and told him that I would protect his grave with my life. My father smiled and passed away to the spirit land. I buried him in that beautiful valley of winding waters. I love that land more than all the rest of the world. A man who would not love his father's grave is worse than a wild animal. For a short time we lived quietly. But this could not last. White men had found gold in the mountains around the land of the winding water. They stole a great many horses from us, and we could not get them back because we were Indians. The white men told lies for each other. They drove off a great many of our cattle. Some white men branded our young cattle so they could claim them.

  We had no friend who would plead our cause before the law councils. It seemed to me that some of the white men in Wallowa were doing these things on purpose to get up a war. They knew that we were not strong enough to fight them.

  I labored hard to avoid trouble and bloodshed. We gave up some of our country to the white men, thinking that then we could have peace. We were mistaken. The white man would not let us alone. We could have avenged our wrongs many times, but we did not. Whenever the Government has asked us to help them against other Indians, we have never refused. When the white men were few and we were strong we could have killed them off, but the Nez Perces wished to live at peace. If we have not done so, we have not been to blame. I believe that the old treaty has never been correctly reported. If we ever owned the land we own it still, for we never sold it. In the treaty councils the commissioners have claimed that our country had been sold to the Government. Suppose a white man should come to me and say, "Joseph, I like your horses, and I want to buy them." I say to him, "No, my horses suit me, I will not sell them." Then he goes to my neighbor, and says to him "Joseph has some good horses. I want to buy them, but he refuses to sell." My neighbor answers, "Pay me the money, and I will sell you Joseph's horses." The white man returns to me and says, "Joseph, I have bought your horses, and you must let me have them." If we sold our lands to the Government, this is the way they were bought. On account of the treaty made by the other bands of Nez Perces, the white men claimed my lands. We were troubled greatly by white men crowding over the line. Some of these were good men, and we lived on peaceful terms with them, but they were not all good.

Nearly every year the agent came over from Lapwai and ordered us onto the reservation. We always replied that we were satisfied to live in Wallowa. We were careful to refuse the presents or annuities which he offered. Through all the years since the white man came to Wallowa we have been threatened and taunted by them and the treaty Nez Perces. They have given us no rest. We have had a few good friends among white men, and they have always advised my people to bear these taunts without fighting. Our young men were quick-tempered, and I have had great trouble in keeping them from doing rash things. I have carried a heavy load on my back ever since I was a boy. I learned then that we were but few, while the white men were many, and that we could not hold our own with them. We were like deer. They were like grizzly bears. We had a small country. Their country was large. We were contented to let things remain as the Great Spirit Chief made them. They were not, and would change the rivers and mountains if they did not suit them.

Year after year we have been threatened, but no war was made upon my people until General Howard came to our country two years ago and told us that he was the white war chief of all that country. He said "I have a great many soldiers at my back. I am going to bring them up here, and then I will talk to you again. I will not let white men laugh at me the next time I come. The country belongs to the Government, and I intend to make you go upon the reservation." I remonstrated with him against bringing more soldiers to the Nez Perces country. He had one house full of troops all the time at Fort Lapwai. The next spring the agent at Umatilla Agency sent an Indian runner to tell me to meet General Howard at Walla Walla. I could not go myself, but I sent my brother and five other head men to meet him, and they had a long talk. General Howard said "You have talked straight, and it is all right. You can stay at Wallowa." He insisted that my brother and his company should go with him to Fort Lapwai.

When the party arrived there General Howard sent out runners and called all the Indians to a grand council. I was in that council. I said to General Howard "We are ready to listen." He answered that he would not talk then, but would hold a council next day, when he would talk plainly. I said to General Howard "I am ready to talk today. I have been in a great many councils, but I am no wiser. We are all sprung from a woman, although we are unlike in many things. We cannot be made over again. You are as you were made, and as you were made you can remain. We are just as we were made by the Great Spirit, and you cannot change us, then why should children of one mother and one father quarrel—why should one try to cheat the other? I do not believe that the Great Spirit Chief gave one kind of men the right to tell another kind of men what they must do." General Howard replied "You deny my authority, do you? You want to dictate to me, do you?" Then one of my chiefs—Too-hul-hul-sote—rose in the council and said to General Howard "The Great Spirit Chief made the world as it is, and as *he* wanted it, and *he* made a part of it for us to live upon. I do not see where you get authority to say that we shall not live where *he* placed us." General Howard lost his temper and said "Shut up! I don't want to hear anymore of such talk. The law says you shall go upon the reservation to live, and I want you to do so, but you persist in disobeying the law." (meaning the treaty). "If you do not move, I will take the matter into my own hand, and make you suffer for your disobedience." Too-hul-hul-sote answered "Who are you that you ask us to talk and then tell me I shan't talk? Are you the Great Spirit? Did you make the world? Did you make the sun? Did you make the rivers to run for us to drink? Did you make the grass to grow? Did you make all these things that you talk to us as though we were boys? If you did, then you have the right to talk as you do." General Howard replied "You are an impudent fellow, and I will put you in the guardhouse" and then ordered a soldier to arrest him.

Too-hul-hul-sote made no resistance. He asked General Howard "Is this your order? I don't care. I have expressed my heart to you. I have nothing to take back. I have spoken for my country. You can arrest me, but you cannot change me or make me take back what I have said." The soldiers came forward and seized my friend and took him to the guardhouse.

My men whispered among themselves whether they would let this thing be done. I counseled them to submit. I knew if we resisted that all the white men present, including General Howard, would be killed in a moment, and we would be blamed. If I had said nothing, General Howard would never have given an unjust order against my men. I saw the danger and while they dragged Too-hul-hul-sote to prison, I arose and said "I am going to talk now. I don't care whether you arrest me or not." I turned to my people and said "The arrest of Too-hul-hul-sote was wrong, but we will not resent the insult. We were invited to this council to express our hearts, and we have done so." Too-hul-hul-sote was prisoner for five days before he was released. The council broke up that day. On the next morning General Howard came to my lodge, and invited me to go with him and White Bird and Looking Glass, to look for land for my people. As we rode along we came to some good land that was already occupied by Indians and white people. General Howard pointing to this land, said "If you will come on to the reservation I will give you these lands and move these people off." I replied "No. It would be wrong to disturb these people. I have no right to take their home. I have never taken what did not belong to me. I will not now." We rode all day upon the reservation, and found no good land unoccupied. I have been informed by men who do not lie that General Howard sent a letter that night telling the soldiers at Walla Walla to go to Wallowa Valley, and drive us out upon our return home.

In the council next day General Howard informed us in a haughty spirit that he would give my people thirty days to go back home, collect all their stock, and move on to the reservation, saying "If you are not here in that time, I shall consider that you want to fight, and will send my soldiers to drive you on." I said "War can be avoided and it ought to be avoided. I want no war. My people have always been the friends of the white man. Why are you in such a hurry? I cannot get ready to move in thirty days. Our stock is scattered, and Snake River is very high. Let us wait until fall, then the river will be low. We want time to hunt our stock and gather our supplies for the winter."

General Howard replied "If you let the time run over one day, the soldiers will be there to drive you on to the reservation, and all your cattle and horses outside of the reservation at that time will fall into the hands of the white men." I knew I had never sold my country and that I had no land in Lapwai, but I did not want bloodshed. I did not want my people killed. I did not want anybody killed. Some of my people had been murdered by white men, and the white murderers were never punished for it. I told General Howard about this, and again said I wanted no war.

I wanted the people who lived upon the lands I was to occupy at Lapwai to have time to gather their harvest. I said in my heart that rather than have war I would give up my country. I would rather give up my father's grave. I would give up everything rather than have the blood of white men upon the hands of my people. General Howard refused to allow me more than thirty days to move my people and their stock. I am sure that he began to prepare for war at once. When I returned to Wallowa I found my people very much excited upon discovering that the soldiers were already in the Wallowa Valley. We held a council, and decided to move immediately to avoid bloodshed. Too-hul-hul-sote, who felt outraged by his imprisonment, talked for war, and made many of my young men willing to fight rather than be driven like dogs from the land where they were born. He declared that blood alone would wash out the disgrace General Howard had put upon him. It required a strong heart to stand up against such talk, but I urged my people to be quiet, and not to begin a war. We gathered all the stock we could find, and made an attempt to move. We left many of our horses and cattle in Wallowa, and we lost several hundred in crossing the river. All my people succeeded in getting across in safety. Many of the Nez Perces came together in Rocky Canyon to hold a grand council. I went with all my people. This council lasted ten days.

There was a great deal of war talk and a great deal of excitement. There was one young brave present whose father had been killed by a white man five years before. This man's blood was had against white men and he left the council calling for revenge. Again I counseled peace, and I thought the danger was past. We had not complied with General Howard's order because we could not, but we intended to do so as soon as possible. I was leaving the council to kill beef for my family when news came that the young man whose father had been killed had gone out with several hot-blooded young braves and killed four white men. He rode up to the council and shouted "Why do you sit here like women? The war has begun already."

I was deeply grieved. All the lodges were moved except my brother's and my own. I saw clearly that the war was upon us when I learned that my young men had been secretly buying ammunition. I heard then that Too-hul-hul-sote, who had been imprisoned by General Howard, had succeeded in organizing a war party. I knew that their acts would involve all my people. I saw that the war could not then be prevented. The time had passed. I counseled peace from the beginning. I knew that we were too weak to fight the United States. We had many grievances, but I knew that war would bring more. We had good white friends, who advised us against taking the war path. My friend and brother, Mr. Chapman, who has been with us since the surrender, told us just how the war would end. Mr. Chapman took sides against us and helped General Howard. I do not blame him for doing so. He tried hard to prevent bloodshed.

We hoped the white settlers would not join the soldiers. Before the war commenced we had discussed this matter all over, and many of my people were in favor of warning them that if they took no part against us they should not be molested in the event of war being begun by General Howard. This plan was voted down in the war council. There were bad men among my people who had quarreled with white men, and they talked of their wrongs until they roused all the bad hearts in the council.

Still I could not believe that they would begin the war. I know that my young men did a great wrong, but I ask, who was first to blame? They had been insulted a thousand times, their fathers and brothers had been killed, their mothers and wives had been disgraced, they had been driven to madness by the whiskey sold to them by the white men, they had been told by General Howard that all their horses and cattle which they had been unable to drive out of Wallowa were to fall into the hands of white men, and, added to all this, they were homeless and desperate. I would have given my own life if I could have undone the killing of white men by my people. I blame my young men and I blame the white men. I blame General Howard for not giving my people time to get their stock away from Wallowa.

I do not acknowledge that he had the right to order me to leave Wallowa at any time. I deny that either my father or myself ever sold that land. It is still our land. It may never again be our home, but my father sleeps there, and I love it as I love my mother. I left there, hoping to avoid bloodshed. If General Howard had given me plenty of time to gather up my stock, and treated Too-hul-hul-sote as a man should be treated, there would have been no war. My friends among white men have blamed me for the war. I am not to blame. When my young men began the killing, my heart was hurt. Although I did not justify them, I remembered all the insults I had endured, and my blood was on fire. Still I would have taken my people to the buffalo country without fighting, if possible. I could see no other way to avoid a war. We moved over to White Bird Creek, sixteen miles away and there encamped, intending to collect our stock before leaving, but the soldiers attacked us and the first battle was fought.

We numbered in that battle sixty men, and the soldiers a hundred. The fight lasted but a few minutes, when the soldiers retreated before us for twelve miles. They lost thirty-three killed, and had seven wounded. When an Indian fights, he only shoots to kill, but soldiers shoot at random. None of the soldiers were scalped. We do not believe in scalping, nor in killing wounded men. Soldiers do not kill many Indians unless they are wounded and left upon the battlefield. Then they kill Indians. Seven days after the first battle General Howard arrived in the Nez Perces country, bringing seven hundred more soldiers. It was now war in earnest. We crossed over Salmon River, hoping General Howard would follow. We were not disappointed. He did follow us, and we got between him and his supplies, and cut him off for three days. He sent out two companies to open the way.

We attacked them, killing one officer, two guides, and ten men. We withdrew, hoping the soldiers would follow, but they had got fighting enough for that day. They entrenched themselves, and next day we attacked them again.

The battle lasted all day, and was renewed next morning. We killed four and wounded seven or eight. About this time General Howard found out that we were in his rear. Five days later he attacked us with three hundred and fifty soldiers and settlers. We had two hundred and fifty warriors. The fight lasted twenty-seven hours. We lost four killed and several wounded. General Howard's loss was twenty-nine men killed and sixty wounded. The following day the soldiers charged upon us, and we retreated with our families and stock a few miles, leaving eighty lodges to fall into General Howard's hands. Finding that we were outnumbered, we retreated to Bitterroot Valley. Here another body of soldiers came upon us and demanded our surrender. We refused. They said "You cannot get by us." We answered "We are going by you without fighting if you will let us, but we are going by you anyhow." We then made a treaty with these soldiers. We agreed not to molest anyone and they agreed that we might pass through the Bitterroot country in peace. We bought provisions and traded stock with white men there. We understood that there was to be no war. We intended to go peaceably to the buffalo country, and leave the question of returning to our country to be settled afterward. With this understanding we traveled on for four days, and, thinking that the trouble was all over, we stopped and prepared tent poles to take with us. We started again, and at the end of two days we saw three white men passing our camp. Thinking that peace had been made, we did not molest them. We could have killed, or taken them prisoners, but we did not suspect them of being spies, which they were. That night the soldiers surrounded our camp. About daybreak one of my men went out to look after his horses. The soldiers saw him and shot him down like a coyote. I have since learned that these soldiers were not those we had left behind. They had come upon us from another direction. The new white war chief's name was Gibbon. He charged upon us while some of my people were still asleep. We had a hard fight. Some of my men crept around and attacked the soldiers from the rear. In this battle we lost nearly all our lodges, but we finally drove General Gibbon back. Finding that he was not able to capture us, he sent to his camp a few miles away for his big guns (cannons), but my men had captured them and all the ammunition. We damaged the big guns all we could, and carried away the powder and lead. In the fight with General Gibbon we lost fifty women and children and thirty fighting men. We remained long enough to bury our dead. The Nez Perces never make war on women and children, we could have killed a great many women and children while the war lasted, but we would feel ashamed to do so cowardly an act. We never scalp our enemies, but when General Howard came up and joined General Gibbon—their Indian scouts dug up our dead and scalped them. I have been told that General Howard did not order this great shame to be done. We retreated as rapidly as we could toward the buffalo country. After six days General Howard came close to us, and we went out and attacked him, and captured nearly all his horses and mules (about two hundred and fifty head). We then marched on to the Yellowstone Basin. On the way we captured one white man and two white women. We released them at the end of three days. They were treated kindly. The women were not insulted. Can the white soldiers tell me of one time when Indian women were taken prisoners, and held three days and then released without being insulted? Were the Nez Perces women who fell into the hands of General Howard's soldiers treated with as much respect? I deny that a Nez Perce was ever guilty of such a crime. A few days later we captured two more white men. One of them stole a horse and escaped. We gave the other a poor horse and told him that he was free. Nine days march brought us to the mouth of Clarks Fork of the Yellowstone. We did not know what had become of General Howard, but we supposed that he had sent for more horses and mules. He did not come up, but another new war chief (General Sturgis) attacked us. We held him in check while we moved all our women and children and stock out of danger, leaving a few men to cover our retreat. Several days passed, and we heard nothing of Generals Howard or Gibbon or Sturgis. We had repulsed each in turn, and began to feel secure when another army, under General Miles, struck us. This was the fourth army, each of which outnumbered our fighting force that we had encountered within sixty days. We had no knowledge of General Miles's army until a short time before he made a charge upon us, cutting our camp in two, and capturing nearly all of our horses. About seventy men, myself among them, were cut off.

My little daughter, twelve years of age, was with me. I gave her a rope, and told her to catch a horse and join the others who were cut off from the camp. I have not seen her since, but I have learned that she is alive and well. I thought of my wife and children, who were now surrounded by soldiers, and I resolved to go to them or die. With a prayer in my mouth to the Great Spirit Chief who rules above, I dashed unarmed through the line of soldiers. It seemed to me that there were guns on every side, before and behind me. My clothes were cut to pieces and my horse was wounded, but I was not hurt. As I reached the door of my lodge, my wife handed me my rifle, saying "Here's your gun. Fight!" The soldiers kept up a continuous fire. Six of my men were killed in one spot near me. Ten or twelve soldiers charged into our camp and got possession of two lodges, killing three Nez Perces and losing three of their men, who fell inside our lines.

I called my men to drive them back. We fought at close range, not more than twenty steps apart, and drove the soldiers back upon their main line, leaving their dead in our hands. We secured their arms and ammunition. We lost the first day and night, eighteen men and three women. General Miles lost twenty-six killed and forty wounded. The following day General Miles sent a messenger into my camp under protection of a white flag. I sent my friend Yellow Bull to meet him. Yellow Bull understood the messenger to say that General Miles wished me to consider the situation, that he did not want to kill my people unnecessarily. Yellow Bull understood this to be a demand for me to surrender and save blood. Upon reporting this message to me, Yellow Bull said he wondered whether General Miles was in earnest. I sent him back with my answer that I had not made up my mind, but would think about it and send word soon.

A little later he sent some Cheyenne scouts with another message. I went out to meet them. They said they believed that General Miles was sincere and really wanted peace. I walked onto General Miles's tent. He met me and we shook hands. He said, "Come, let us sit down by the fire and talk this matter over." I remained with him all night, next morning. Yellow Bull came over to see if I was alive, and why I did not return. General Miles would not let me leave the tent to see my friend alone. Yellow Bull said to me "They have got you in their power, and I am afraid they will never let you go again. I have an officer in our camp, and I will hold him until they let you go free." I said "I do not know what they mean to do with me, but if they kill me you must not kill the officer. It will do no good to avenge my death by killing him." Yellow Bull returned to my camp. I did not make any agreement that day with General Miles. The battle was renewed while I was with him. I was very anxious about my people. I knew that we were near Sitting Bull's camp in King George's land, and I thought maybe the Nez Perces who had escaped would return with assistance. No great damage was done to either party during the night. On the following morning I returned to my camp by agreement, meeting the officer who had been held a prisoner in my camp at the flag of truce. My people were divided about surrendering. We could have escaped from Bear Paw Mountain if we had left our wounded, old women, and children behind. We were unwilling to do this. We had never heard of a wounded Indian recovering while in the hands of white men. On the evening of the fourth day. General Howard came in with a small escort, together with my friend Chapman. We could talk now understandingly. General Miles said to me in plain words "If you will come out and give up your arms, I will spare your lives and send you back to the reservation." I do not know what passed between General Miles and General Howard. I could not bear to see my wounded men and women suffer any longer, we had lost enough already. General Miles had promised that we might return to our country with what stock we had left. I thought we could start again. I believed General Miles or I never would have surrendered. I have heard that he has been censured for making the promise to return us to Lapwai. He could not have made any other terms with me at that time. I would have held him in check until my friends came to my assistance, and then neither of the generals nor their soldiers would have ever left Bear Paw Mountain alive. On the fifth day I went to General Miles and gave up my gun, and said "From where the sun now stands I will fight no more." My people needed rest—we wanted peace.

    I was told we could go with General Miles to Tongue River and stay there until spring, when we would be sent back to our country. Finally it was decided that we were to be taken to Tongue River. We had nothing to say about it. After our arrival at Tongue River, General Miles received orders to take us to Bismarck. The reason given was that subsistence would be cheaper there. General Miles was opposed to this order. He said

"You must not blame me. I have endeavored to keep my word, but the chief who is over me has given the order, and I must obey it or resign. That would do you no good. Some other officer would carry out the order." I believe General Miles would have kept his word if he could have done so. I do not blame him for what we have suffered since the surrender. I do not know who is to blame. We gave up all our horses—over eleven hundred—and all our saddles—over one hundred—and we have not heard from them since. Somebody has got our horses. General Miles turned my people over to another soldier, and we were taken to Bismarck. Captain Johnson, who now had charge of us, received an order to take us to Fort Leavenworth. At Leavenworth we were placed in, on a low river bottom, with no water except river water to drink and cook with. We had always lived in a healthy country, where the mountains were high and the water was cold and clear. Many of our people sickened and died, and we buried them in this strange land. I cannot tell how much my heart suffered for my people while at Leavenworth. The Great Spirit Chief who rules above seemed to be looking some other way, and did not see what was being done to my people. During the hot days (July, 1878) we received notice that we were to be moved farther away from our own country. We were not asked if we were willing to go. We were ordered to get into the railroad cars. Three of my people died on the way to Baxter Springs. It was worse to die there than to die fighting in the mountains.

We were moved from Baxter Springs (Kansas) to the Indian Territory and set down without our lodges. We had but little medicine and we were nearly all sick. Seventy of my people have died since we moved there. We have had a great many visitors who have talked many ways. Some of the chiefs (General Fish and Colonel Stickney) from Washington came to see us, and selected land for us to live upon. We have not moved to that land, for it is not a good place to live. The Commissioner Chief (Ezra Ayres Hayt) came to see us. I told him, as I told everyone, that I expected General Miles's word would be carried out. He said it "could not be done, that white men now lived in my country and all the land was taken up, that, if I returned to Wallowa, I could not live in peace, that law papers were out against my young men who began the war, and that the Government could not protect my people." This talk fell like a heavy stone upon my heart.

I saw that I could not gain anything by talking to him. Other law chiefs (Congressional Committee) came to see us and said they would help me to get a healthy country. I did not know whom to believe. The white people have too many chiefs. They do not understand each other. They do not talk alike.

The Commissioner Chief (Mr. Hayt) invited me to go with him and hunt for a better home than we have now. I like the land we found (west of the Osage Reservation) better than any place I have seen in that country, but it is not a healthy land.

There are no mountains and rivers. The water is warm. It is not a good country for stock. I do not believe my people can live there. I am afraid they will all die. The Indians who occupy that country are dying off. I promised Chief Hayt to go there, and do the best I could until the Government got ready to make good General Miles's word. I was not satisfied, but I could not help myself. Then the Inspector Chief (General McNiel) came to my camp and we had a long talk. He said I ought to have a home in the mountain country north, and that he would write a letter to the Great Chief in Washington. Again the hope of seeing the mountains of Idaho and Oregon grew up in my heart. At last I was granted permission to come to Washington and bring my friend Yellow Bull and our interpreter with me. I am glad we came. I have shaken hands with a great many friends, but there are some things I want to know which no one seems able to explain.

I cannot understand how the Government sends a man out to fight us, as it did General Miles, and then breaks his word. Such a Government has something wrong about it. I cannot understand why so many chiefs are allowed to talk so many different ways, and promise so many different things. I have seen the Great Father Chief (the President), the next Great Chief (Secretary of the Interior), the Commissioner Chief (Hayt), the Law Chief (General Butler), and many other law chiefs

(Congressmen), and they all say they are my friends, and that I shall have justice, but while their mouths all talk right I do not understand why nothing is done for my people.

I have heard talk and talk, but nothing is done. Good words do not last long until they amount to something. Words do not pay for my dead people. They do not pay for my country, now overrun by white men. They do not protect my father's grave. They do not pay for my horses and cattle. Good words will not give me back my children. Good words will not make good the promise of your War Chief, General Miles. Good words will not give my people good health and stop them from dying.

Good words will not get my people a home where they can live in peace and take care of themselves. I am tired of talk that comes to nothing. It makes my heart sick when I remember all the good words and all the broken promises. There has been too much talking by men who had no right to talk.

Too many misrepresentations have been made, too many misunderstandings have come up between the white men about the Indians. If the white man wants to live in peace with the Indian he can live in peace. There need be no trouble.

Treat all men alike. Give them all the same law. Give them all an even chance to live and grow. All men were made by the same Great Spirit Chief. They are all brothers. The earth is the mother of all people, and all people should have equal rights upon it. You might as well expect the rivers to run backward as that any man who was born a free man should be contented penned up and denied liberty to go where he pleases. If you tie a horse to a stake, do you expect he will grow fat? If you pen an Indian up on a small spot of earth, and compel him to stay there, he will not be contented nor will he grow and prosper. I have asked some of the great white chiefs where they get their authority to say to the Indian that he shall stay in one place, while he sees white men going where they please. They cannot tell me. I only ask of the Government to be treated as all other men are treated.

If I cannot go to my own home, let me have a home in some country where my people will not die so fast. I would like to go to Bitterroot Valley. There my people would be healthy, where they are now they are dying. Three have died since I left my camp to come to Washington. When I think of our condition my heart is heavy. I see men of my race treated as outlaws and driven from country to country, or shot down like animals. I know that my race must change. We cannot hold our own with the white men as we are. We only ask an even chance to live as other men live. We ask to be recognized as men. We ask that the same law shall work alike on all men. If the Indian breaks the law, punish him by the law. If the white man breaks the law, punish him also.

Let me be a free man—free to travel, free to stop, free to work, free to trade, where I choose, free to choose my own teachers, free to follow the religion of my fathers, free to think and talk and act for myself—and I will obey every law, or submit to the penalty. Whenever the white man treats the Indian as they treat each other, then we shall have no more wars.

We shall be all alike—brothers of one father and one mother, with one sky above us and one country around us, and one government for all. Then the Great Spirit Chief who rules above will smile upon this land, and send rain to wash out the bloody spots made by brother's hands upon the face of the earth. For this time the Indian race are waiting and praying. I hope that no more groans of wounded men and women will ever go to the ear of the Great Spirit Chief above, and that all people may be one people. In-mut-too-yah-lat-lat has spoken for his people.

Young Joseph

Postscript

Though denied respect during his lifetime, Chief Joseph was later recognized by succeeding generations of Americans for leading such an extraordinary life. Today he is regarded among the greats who fought for civil rights through their actions or their writings. Greats such as Anne Frank, Mahatma Gandhi, Frederick Douglass, Princess Diana, Harriet Jacobs, Marvella Bayh, Nelson

Mandela, Rosa Parks, Eleanor Roosevelt, Harriet Tubman, Henry Whiteley and Martin Luther King Jr., just to name a few. And what about the voices of those who followed orders and tarnished their characters by not doing the right thing—just doing what others told them to do? Well, *they* have been forgotten. Does anyone today know who Oliver Otis Howard was without looking up his name on the Internet? I think not. Enough said.

Chief Joseph seemed to know that although his actions during his lifetime would mean nothing to those who met him and misunderstood his words—foresaw that future generations would know better. He seemed almost to have the unique ability to be able to see the future long before it occurred. But today his name is known to social and civic leaders everywhere and synonymous with having outstanding character. His simple comment "it does not require many words to speak the truth" was true in his time and true today. Adding endless words to a statement won't make it any more true than it was previous.

In a time when people who assume they have value seem to be searching for a reason to come up with excuses to explain away their flawed character—it should be easy to come up with the truth. Be yourself and people will like you. Try being someone else and no one will like you or what you have to say. In other words you'll be tolerated by those around you but not liked—and a person who no one likes is always going to be lonely.

Nancy Hunt

Originally published in 1916 from a manuscript copy provided by Nancy Hunt's son. Rockwell D. Hunt was a Professor at the University of Southern California as well as President of the Historical Society of Southern California. The manuscript for this book was created with the intention to preserve history but was written from memory according to her son.

  One of my sons has requested me to write the story of my early life. Whether he is in jest or in earnest I do not know, if in earnest, I know not why he thinks I could do such a thing. It must be either because I have given birth and raised to stalwart manhood seven sons, or because I was a pioneer in the great State of Illinois, and also in our sunny State, California. He must have some reason for it, perhaps it is this—just to know something of our family history. I myself have often wished I knew more of the history of my parents and ancestors, so I will do what I can to grant my son's request for this reason, if for no other. I must begin back with my ancestors. From a rare old book, *A History of the Pioneer Families of Missouri*, I have learned that Jacob Zumwalt emigrated from Germany to America during Colonial times and settled first in Pennsylvania, at the present site of Little York. Mr. Zumwalt was married twice. By his first wife he had two sons and two daughters, and by his second, five sons and one daughter. It is said that his son Jacob built the first hewed log house that was ever erected on the north side of the Missouri River in 1798, about one and a half miles northwest of O'Fallon Station, on the St. Louis, Kansas City and Northern Railway. I have not been able to trace the connection between the Missouri Zumwalts and my own parents, though all were no doubt related. The name of my great-great-grandfather was Adam Zumwalt.

His son, George Zumwalt, emigrated from Germany to America, and lived in Virginia, where my grandfather, Jacob Zumwalt, was born. The names of great-grandfather's children were Jacob, Elizabeth, Henry, Mary, Magdalene, Christina, Philip, Christian, and John. My grandfather (Jacob Zumwalt) also had nine children, whose names were Sarah, Mary, Joseph, Daniel, Jacob, Elizabeth, Eleanor, George, and John. The fifth of these, Jacob Zumwalt, was my father. Grandmother Zumwalt's maiden name was Nancy Ann Spurgeon. She was born in Pennsylvania, of parents who had come from England, and so was related to the Spurgeons of that country. My mother's maiden name was Susanna Smith. She was the daughter of Reuben Smith, whose children were Sally, John, Joel, Anna, Joseph, Phoebe, Reuben, Stephen, Mary Ann, Clarenda, Elizabeth, Susanna, and Cynthia. My great-grandparents, Oliver Smith and Sarah Herrick, who were born and married in England, came to America about 1770.

Sarah Herrick was a very large woman, taller than Reuben Smith, who was six feet six inches tall. Oliver Smith was a physician and surgeon, and was quite wealthy until the Indians took and destroyed his property. Grandmother Smith died January 17, 1834, and Grandfather Reuben Smith died September 25, 1840. My own parents were both born and raised in Ohio, as farmers. They received only a moderate education, as colleges and seminaries were then unknown in that part of the country.

They had no carriages to go riding in when they were young. A walk of five or six miles was not considered much, but horseback riding was very fashionable among old and young alike. To go to church on Sunday, or to market or to mill with bag of corn, wheat or buckwheat swung across the horse's back, or even to weddings, ten, twenty or more miles away—all these were the most common, everyday affairs. When my parents were married, father was twenty-two and mother nineteen. Father came twenty miles on horseback with his company of family relatives and friends. On arriving at mother's home, they all rode around the house three times for good cheer, according to the style of the day. On these long rides it was customary for the young men to carry the girls's collarettes in their high silk hats, so they would not get mussed up. The day after the wedding, they with their company, went to my father's home for the Infare. According to previous arrangement, they started after just one week to immigrate to Indiana. This was a wedding trip that some of our young folks wouldn't like very well nowadays—especially to go as my parents went, with their own team, taking in the wagon all they possessed, except their five horses and the cow named "Pink." I can remember hearing mother calling "Suke Pink" and the cow would come home from as far as she could hear the call, put of the thick woods. When they reached their journey's end, they settled in the beech and maple timber that was so thick they had to cut down trees and clear out a spot big enough on which to build their little log house of one room.

But since they were married in June and had started at once, the house was built before winter set in. Yet when they moved in, the only door was a quilt hung up, and the only curtain was another quilt at the little square window without glass.

Later the fireplace chimney was completed with split sticks chinked up with mud plaster. Father split some puncheons from the big hardwood trees and put down a floor big enough for the bed. By keeping diligently at work, they had soon made a door, bedstead, etc. A few hens were brought from a distant neighbor, mother borrowed a rooster and made a little chicken house from small trees she had cut down, so in a short time they had plenty of chickens. Father was a skillful hunter, so they fared well for meat, deer and other wild game being plentiful. They lived in happiness. In the spring they made enough maple sugar, syrup (or molasses, as we always called it) and vinegar to do for the year. And they also had a splendid garden, having been provided with seeds before leaving home. They had everything necessary that was good to eat, and live well. But on account of exposure and hard work, mother was troubled with rheumatism and both had chills and fever, so they concluded to go on to Illinois and try it there. The five horse team was hitched onto the great covered wagon, and old "Pink," with her tinkling bell and playful progeny was made ready for another journey. Father and mother had found two little girls in the timber of Indiana, my sister, Sarah, and I were born there, Hoosiers, and sometimes I feel glad, even proud, that I was born a sturdy, hardy Hoosier. I was then three years old, and Sarah was six weeks old—pretty young to be an emigrant to a new country, to be one of the pioneers. My parents and my uncle, Joseph Zumwalt, and his family, arrived in Will County, Illinois, at Troutman's Grove, near Joliet, in the spring of 1834, there to begin a pioneer life over again by starting a new home, and it had to be done very much as the first one had been. Here my school days began.

One of our neighbors who had come there about 1831 and was educated, was hired to teach the first school ever kept in that place. Scholars being scarce, the teacher got my parents to let me go, although a baby not four years old yet, but even now I can remember some things I did then. The teacher's name was Henry Watkins, he used to carry me home for dinner, for we lived near the little log schoolhouse. A row of wooden pins driven into the logs served for hooks for the boys coats and hats and the girls sunbonnets, hoods, and kiss-me-quicks. Our seats were slabs from the sawmill, with limbs of trees driven in for legs.

Our writing desks were rough boards about a foot and a half wide, made fast and sloping a little along the sides of the schoolroom. Our teacher who was a Baptist—read a chapter from the Bible every morning and prayed with every scholar—big or little—kneeling down. Oh, that our public schools could follow that good old-fashioned way now. The teacher set our copies for writing and made our pens of goose quills. We made our own ink out of oak bark. I never saw red ink in those days. We did not stay there long. Father thought best to move about five miles to the edge of Jackson's Grove, to be sheltered from the cold, bleak winds and storms. Then I had to walk more than a mile to school. I remember getting badly scared twice when alone—once when I saw a big snake lying across the path, and once when a mother pheasant came running after me to protect her brood of young.

About this time, stoves were coming into use, and father bought one for our home, it was an odd-looking concern.

One day the teacher brought home from Chicago a few matches. We thought it very strange that fire should come out of a little stick when he struck a match on the stove pipe. The girls never studied arithmetic in the school there, but did study grammar, the boys studied arithmetic, but no grammar. I was considered very good in *Kirkham's Grammar*. At times Mr. Watkins would let the entire school study out loud for five minutes, and then what a clattering and chattering we would have. During the wintertime we often had spelling schools in the evening, sometimes they would choose up and spell down several times the same evening. We also had singing school, which I attended after I became old enough, father usually went with us, which made it very pleasant. My father was uncommonly ingenious, he was able to make almost everything that we needed to use in the pioneer days of Indiana and Illinois.

He would go down by the Oplane River, cut down a cedar tree and rive out the staves. The wood next to the bark was white and the inside was red, he made his staves each half red and half white, so that it worked up very prettily into washtubs, kegs, buckets, keelers, and whatever we needed, taking young hickory trees and splitting them into strips for hoops to use on the utensils. Of larger hickories he made scrubbing brooms, by sawing a ring round the stick, then working the upper part down for the handle and splitting the other end into fine splints. He also used hickory splints for chair bottoms. He tanned the deer skin and made mittens, whip lashes and some gloves. He made and mended our shoes and boots, and did much of that for the neighbors. He did his own blacksmithing, and was a pretty good carpenter, too, making all his own axe handles, etc. He made very good, coarse combs and back combs from cow's horn.

After I was about ten years old, my mother was an invalid most of the time till we came to California, so Sarah and I had most of the housework to do. We were very early taught to work, not only in the house, but out of doors, too. When I was sixteen years old, mother sent to Indiana for feathers to make me a bed. I first became acquainted with Mr. Cotton, my first husband, at school, and at temperance meetings. He and his sister used to sing temperance songs, sometimes comic ones, which I thought were nice and appropriate. But when they lent me their book my father said, no, they were not religious songs, so I had to return the book right away. I do not know how old I was when I began the Christian warfare, I was too young to remember anything about it. My parents always went and took all of us children to the social and revival meetings—class, camp, quarterly, protracted, etc. I was a bashful, timid Christian, when I was young—so bashful that father threatened sending me away from home to live with a talkative milliner in Joliet. This very lady afterwards made my wedding dress and presented me with a beautiful headdress for my marriage. At seventeen and a half years I was married, no one seemed to think I was too young, nor my husband, Alexander Cotton, who was just past nineteen.

My parents made a large wedding for us. I was dressed in white nainsook, trimmed with lace. I wore pink and white ribbons and a long bow to my waist, the ribbon reaching almost to the bottom of the dress, with bows at my wrists and neck. My back hair was braided and put up around a horseshoe back comb, and in front I had three long curls hung from behind each ear. The wedding was at two o'clock, then came the dinner, such a repast as the fertile State of Illinois could afford, for the whole company of about seventy-five persons. We did not go off for a wedding trip in those days, but stayed at home, letting our parents and friends share in the festivities. We spent the evening sociably until near midnight, but about eleven, two of the girls went upstairs with me to my room, and then I went to bed.

After the girls had gone down, in came my husband, he drew me up from the back part of the bed, onto his arm, and just then the company came thronging at the door to catch a glimpse of us in bed. Then they left us, and soon were on the way to their homes. The next day, with some of our brothers and sisters, we went to Wilmington by invitation, to have our Infare at the home of a sister of my husband. Father had recently bought a farm of eighty acres, with ten acres of woodland and a sugar camp. He now said, "Children, go onto the place and see how much you can make, and have all you make." We went, and we worked, too. Father gave me a good young horse and two cows, besides hogs, sheep, chickens, and everything we had in the house. I fully believe there never was a happier couple, and oh, how we did work. We made maple sugar in the spring, picked wild strawberries in abundance, and in winter trapped all the prairie chickens and quail we wanted. We always found time to drive over to our old home about once a week, and to raise a few beautiful flowers in summer. We lived on this place only three years before we had enough saved up, with another "lift" from my father, to buy thirty acres of our own, in the edge of what was called Little Grove, then, but afterwards called Starr's Grove. There we had a beautiful place, with new house and fine creek of running water—everything, it seemed, to make us happy.

But this was not to last long. My husband began coughing, and rapidly grew worse and worse, until he went into the dread disease, consumption. Then our troubles began, and if we had not both learned to leave them with the great Burden Bearer, we would have been much worse off than we were. We had two darling little sons, Albert and Joel, but our dear little daughter, Irene, inherited her father's weakness, and died when but four months old. After strong and unmistakable symptoms, my father was taken with the California fever in the year 1849, when his brother (my uncle Zumwalt) crossed the Great Plains and came to California, bringing his wife and eleven children with him. Well, after that spring it seemed that all my father could do was to read every item of California news he could get and talk about the new wonderland—for mother would not be persuaded to undertake such a journey. But father kept reading and talking. One day he read that wheat and peaches were a sure crop every year, that greatly increased his desire to come. That desire, which was shared by all six of his sons and daughters, never waned nor grew cold. At last, early in 1854, the doctors told us the only chance there was for my husband to live was to come to California that year. Of course, I at once told my parents I was going to venture all and make the start with him for California, we began at once to make arrangements to come. Then my sister Sarah and her husband, James Shoemaker, decided they would come with us. And next, father's fever never having abated, mother consented to come, providing the old homestead could be kept unencumbered to return to in case we should not like California. All went to work with a will to get ready for the great journey. Father began buying oxen and having new wagons made, good and strong. Times were very lively with us all that winter, selling home effects and buying our outfit. We had to part with all of our old and dear keepsakes, mementoes of our childhood, for we could take only just what we would need on the way. My Uncle Joseph and family, who had gone to California in 1849, and returned to Illinois, were now ready for their second journey. Father's sister, Mrs. Nellie Troxel, and her family, with neighbors and friends, made up a party that started on with teams and livestock about the middle of March, even before the snow and ice had gone. But never mind that—they were on their way to the great new country. About the middle of April, the remainder of our party, having remained behind to finish the business affairs, started from Joliet by rail, and went to the terminus at Peoria. Then we took the steamboat down the Illinois River to the Mississippi, and down the great river as far as St. Louis. From St. Louis we proceeded up the Missouri to Kanesville. The Missouri River was then very low, and was full of mud, sandbars, snags, etc., so we had a hard time at the very outset of our journey. The steamboat was badly snagged, and it leaked so fast that it was necessary to unload everything and put it onto another boat. I had the quinsy and was seriously sick with it, and my husband, by taking cold, was very low and indeed near to death with his disease. But as soon as we were again on land, all began to feel better. The old boat never made another trip down the river, they left it at Kanesville to be used as a ferry boat.

Here we met my father and the members of the advance guard. After a few days preparation, we crossed the Missouri and our long, hard camping trip across the Great Plains was begun. We found all the ox drivers we needed, simply for their board along the way. There were in our train besides our immediate family, which included by brothers John, Joseph and Daniel, and my sisters, Sarah and Lizzie, and those of Uncle Joseph Zumwalt and Aunt Nellie Troxel, neighbors and friends occupying in all twenty-five wagons and teams, nearly all of them ox teams of five yoke for each wagon. When we camped at night we would drive our wagons so they would form a circle, and by putting the pole, or tongue, of each wagon upon the back axle-tree of the next, all around the circle, we had a pretty good corral.

But our large company could not remain together long, so much stock required more grass than could be found in one place near the road, for each family had besides the teams more or less loose stock, cows, calves, etc. Some members of the company would become impatient and wish to hurry along as fast as their teams could go, after a few days we would usually overtake them and crawl along past them, as they would be stopped by the roadside to rest their cattle. We always went along slowly but steadily, stopping half a day each week, whenever we possibly could, to do our washing. We always laid by over Sunday, I believe. Once we made a mistake, thinking it was Saturday, we were washing when some traders came along, from whom we learned it was Sunday. We quickly put away the washing for that day. That was the only time we completely lost track of the day of the week. Our wagons were big and strong, and had good, stout bows, covered with thick, white drilling, so there was a nice room in each wagon, as everything was clean and fresh and new.

Two strong iron hooks were fastened on the top of each side of our wagon box, and a pole (called a spring pole) laid in these hooks. Boards were laid across from pole to pole, thus making a spring bed that was very comfortable for my sick husband, after a good feather bed and plenty of covering were put in place. We had but one wagon of our own, with five yoke of oxen and two cows. Most of the emigrant wagons had the names of the owners, place where they were from and where they were bound, marked in large letters on the outside of the cover.

There were stations along the way at great intervals, these were called trading posts, and they kept supplies of provision, ammunition, etc., but the immigrants had to pay dearly for everything at these stations. The traders were glad to buy such dried fruits, jellies, jams, pickles, preserves, etc., as the emigrants had to spare. We called it a good day's drive if we went twenty miles and a big drive if we went twenty-five miles, but in the mountains, and where we had streams to cross, we worked hard many times and went only five miles. I think I must have walked half of the way to California. Many times I did not get into the wagon to ride all day. Oh, the roads we passed over were terrible. In some places in the mountains the men had to let the wagons down the deep pitches with chains, in other places it would take ten yoke of oxen, or more, to pull a wagon up the steep, slippery grades. But parts of our road were just beautiful, being level as a floor and bordered with carpets of green grass intermingled with flowers of every color. We often saw herds of buffalo at a distance, but they were wild enough to keep out of the way of emigrants. At their watering places we saw dead ones partly eaten by wolves or other wild beasts. We frequently had buffalo meat, as well as bear, elk, deer, antelope, and fish, ducks and other wild game. We always treated the Indians well and with respect, and they never molested us at any time. Day after day we heard stories of how the Indians had been treated badly by the emigrants, and how they were threatening to take the next train that came along to get revenge. Some emigrants did have trouble that year. We always gave them something to eat when they asked for it. I believe the Golden Rule helped us to get through safely. As soon as we went into camp, if any Indians were in hearing distance, they would come to see us. They climbed up and looked into our wagons with great curiosity, yes, and astonishment, too, when they saw the display of guns and ammunition we had. We always had these hanging rather artistically on the inside of the wagon cover, so they would be the first thing to attract the visitors attention, and they always looked sober at sight of them. At night we placed our weapons of defense by the sides of our beds in our tents. I claimed the ax for mine, and always saw that it was close to me, but I never had occasion to use it on an Indian. Sometimes it was trying to notice how the Indians would act with things we gave them.

For instance, on one occasion a big Indian and a pitiful little fellow begged food, and we gave each a plateful. The big fellow soon cleaned his plate and then took the little one's plate away from him, bringing a sorrowful look to the little face.

When we showed our astonishment, he said by way of explanation, placing his hand upon his stomach, then pointing to his companion "Me heap big, him little belly!" The little boy looked sorry, but did not cry—I surmise he was used to such treatment. One night in particular, more than any other, we expected to be killed or taken as captives. (Imagine for one moment what a feeling that is.) The Indians formed in line on both sides of our camp. It was very dark, but when they built fires on both sides, we knew they were in line. Then they set up their terrible war whoop, and kept it up until late into the night.

Greatly frightened, we made ready for an attack. But fortunately they did not molest us at all, except as we suffered in our minds from our fright. That night we kept ample guard, and what little sleep we did get, we took with our hands on our weapons. Early the next morning we moved on quietly as if nothing had happened. We had music in camp many an evening. Some of the company having brought their musical instruments, such as violins or guitars, and when not too tired we would sing hymns of praise. The young people had a good time and a great deal of fun. They were free from care, and could ride on horseback or in the wagons all they pleased, or could walk along the road together. We managed to sew enough to keep our clothes in order while the oxen were poking along where the road was level. Some worked at crocheting or knitting a little occasionally, just for pastime. We had nothing to read but our Bibles and a few hymn books. I did not notice the cold or heat very much on our trip. We had many hard, cold rain and hailstorms. I think the most severe were encountered while we were in the Rocky Mountains. Sometimes they would sluice us out of our tents, so we were compelled to hurry our beds and everything up into the wagons. I remember one night especially when I worked in the rain till I was drenched through and through, my feet *squished* in my shoes. In that condition I did not dare to get into bed with my poor, sick husband and my little children for fear of giving them cold, so I drew myself up into the front end of the wagon as far as I could, with my feet extending outside, and very soon I dropped off to sleep and slept soundly, being so tired out. Such exposure never hurt me in the least—we could live in almost any way out of doors, so hardened were we by that manner of life. And right here I want to recommend living out of doors for the invalid when the weather will at all permit, I believe it to be better than medicine. For about three weeks I was sick with what was called mountain fever. We were then traveling along the Humboldt River, where we could get no good water, although constantly in sight of plenty of snow. Oh, how good that snow looked to me. Surely, I thought, if anyone of the rest of our company were burning up with fever, as I was, and I was well, I would go and get some snow—it looked so near. And yet they said it must be a hundred miles from us. Distance was very deceiving. After the fever had, had its run, I recovered, with God's care—for little care did I have but his, before we came to the Sierra Nevada Mountains. While the young folk were having their good times, some of the mothers were giving birth to their babes—three babies were born in our company that summer. My cousin Emily Ibe (later Emily West of Dixon) gave birth to a son in

Utah, forty miles north of Great Salt Lake, one evening, and the next morning she traveled on until noon, when a stop was made, and another child was born—this time Susan Longmire was the mother made happy by the advent of little Ellen. The third birth occurred after we had separated from Uncle Joseph's family, the wife of my cousin Jacob Zumwalt gave birth to a daughter while traveling in the Sierra Nevada. To this baby they gave the name Alice Nevada. In every instance, after the birth, we traveled right along the next day, mothers and babes with the rest of us.

We had an unusual commotion one afternoon and night, near the fork of the Sweetwater River. My youngest sister, Lizzie, then twelve years old, was lost. She had started off in search of firewood and completely lost her bearings. Finally she found the road and walked back on it five miles, when she came to a camp of emigrants. Two of them brought her into our excited camp about eleven o'clock at night. My mother was nearly beside herself when they brought her in all safe and sound but very tired. Our train went north of Salt Lake and passed what was known as Sublette Cutoff, where Ogden now is. As most of our company wished to go through by Salt Lake, we were again divided, our own party having but one other family besides my father's—Mrs. Neff, a widow, with her three sons, Jim, Dan, and John, and a daughter named Sarah. Jim was married, having with him his wife and son. He was very sick through Nevada. At Carson we thought he would die, but he refused to take our medicine (calomel and quinine), saying he would die first. Coming so near to death's door, he finally concluded to take the medicine, so he got well in due time. He was a soft kind of man, with little *grit* or *vim* in him. Day after day we traveled along, slowly, very slowly.

The roads were almost impassable, the days were hot and the nights freezing cold. Near the summit of the Sierras we came to the snow, it was the month of August. It was here, in the midst of the great mountains that I met with the greatest trial and loss of my life, up to this time. It was the loss of my dear husband, the father of my two little boys. He died August 21st, 1854. He was a noble, good Christian man. Oh, the patience he showed all along the road. Never recovering sufficient strength to get out, he sat there in the wagon alone through those long months, except for a few weeks along the Sweetwater River. How proud he was then, and I, too. We thought he would get well. But when we came into the Sierras, he took fresh cold, from which he never recovered. The long, lingering disease had run its course and ended his short life, his brave spirit departed at Twin Lakes, a beautiful little valley on this side of the summit—so he died in California. We laid the body away in the best manner we possibly could, specially marking the grave so that emigrants passing that way for years afterwards would take particular notice of it, in this way we could hear from it sometimes. We could not linger there between the two majestic pines where my husband's body was tenderly laid to rest, there was no grass for the cattle. We must push on. That night we found grass, so decided to remain for a day or two for washing and other needful preparations, for we were now almost at our journey's end. Only two or three days more and we sighted the beautiful valley of the Cosumnes. We went on through to Sacramento, which had grown up around Sutter's Fort into a thriving city. Then we remained out on the American River (a branch of the Sacramento) for two weeks, while my father was looking about for a place to live. After looking over several different places, including the vicinity of Dixon—which he pronounced worthless for farming—he bought his farm on Deer Creek, near Daylor's Ranch, on the Cosumnes. It had a good, comfortable house, considering the early date. I remained with my parents, with my two little boys, but after a while, so many came to ask me to work for them, I concluded to hire out to work, although I had never worked away from home. For my work I never received less than $50 a month, and for a part of the time I received $75. Women were scarce in California in comparison to men, and it was hard to secure women's help. I would leave the children with mother, as she didn't have much work to do in those days. My wagon I had sold, a part of the money received for it being two fifty-dollar California slugs, one of them round and the other eight-sided. They were no rarity in those days, being quite plentiful as currency. My first acquaintance with Mr. Dennis Rockwell Hunt was made by riding with him for thirty miles on his grain wagon to the place where I went to work, a large country hotel called the Somerset House. He was then hauling barley to Coloma, and the landlord arranged with him to take me up.

As a matter of course, Mr. Hunt, being an old bachelor who had come to California four years earlier, would come into the parlor a little while on his arrival with every load to inquire how the young widow was getting along, bring some message from home, or take some word back to my folks. Each time I went to visit at home, I went with him on his grain or hay wagon.

I did not remain long at the Somerset House. One of the owners, whose wife was with him, sold out to the other, whose wife, was still in Boston, so if I were to remain I would be the only woman there and must take the place of landlady. Mr. Lindsey offered me $75 a month for all winter, and said I might keep little Albert and Joel with me, as well as do sewing and washing besides my wages. But no, I would not consent to stay. In a little while I began working for the El Dorado House on the Placerville Road, being engaged as cook for the house. Of course, teaming from the Hunt ranch paid better on the Placerville Road now, so I still had good opportunity of hearing from home often.

I remained at the Eldorado House until May, then Mr. Hunt thought I had better not work out anymore. So I did up a good lot of sewing for myself and children, feeling quite independent about my clothes, as I had earned the money to buy them myself. Mr. Hunt had a squatter's right to some land on a Spanish grant, only half a mile from my father's house.

He had built a small house of four rooms, but these were not finished then. So, we were married in my father's house, August 5th, 1855. I was dressed in white, with embroidered pink flowers. Thus, I began my married life in California.

It has brought many joys and many sorrows. And now my five stalwart sons, all native sons of California, the fruit of my second marriage, have grown to manhood's estate.

Frederick Walker

Selections from the diaries of a seafaring Pacific Ocean adventure memoir titled *Log of the Kaalokai* kept by Frederick Walker of Hawaii. This version has been edited from the original edition published in 1909.

In the early part of the year 1891, I was commissioned by the Survey Department of the then monarchy of the Hawaiian Islands, to survey the island of Lisianski. In pursuance therewith, I chartered the schooner *Kaalokai*, and on Saturday, May 23rd, of that year, we of the expedition sailed from Honolulu—not only in the interests of navigation, to acquire a perfect knowledge of the entire chain of islands and reefs lying to the west Northwest of the Hawaiian group proper, but to collect shark fins, and any other product, marine or otherwise of a commercial value.

It is (or was) the general custom, when notable departures from port take place, for the band to send them off with musical strains. On this occasion, however, as the band was absent, we had to start without it. A baseball game being on, the counter attraction proved too strong, and the usual crowd at the wharf was conspicuous by its absence, still, we had a few to witness our departure, Jimmy (of whom more hereafter) had his sisters, his cousins and his aunts there, he was the only one who furnished the fair sex. Just as we were about to cast off, Jimmy started in the kissing business, as he gave each about a dozen, it took some time to get through but at last he let go, and we let go and sailed away with a good breeze under the foresail and jib.

After a short run of two hours, we anchored off the entrance to Pearl Lochs to straighten things up—and indeed they wanted straightening, not excepting the crew.

May 24th. After rounding Barber's Point we stood well out towards the center of Kauai Channel, to avoid the calms which occasionally prevail on the southwest part of Oahu. On reaching the center, it fell calm, but soon a nasty sea got up, short but heavy. Towards evening it looked as though we were going to have a disagreeable time of it, and so we did, gusts of wind would come, with rain and more sea, then calm again, then a heavy squall would fetch us and send us beam into the sea. Our little craft, close reefed down, however, stood it well, at one moment our bowsprit would be pointing towards heaven and the next few seconds the jibboom would be investigating the depths of the sea. Having everything secure and hove to under the close-reefed foresail, we went below and blessed the composer of "Blow high ye winds." We were all as sick as cats. It rained all night on deck, and down below it reigned confusion, the boxes would knock about, a tin of tomatoes or some other festive article would get loose, and while in motion would give you a clip that would make you imitate Moses. But all things come to an end, and at 3 AM it cleared up. The wind came from the northeast, we made all sail and stood up the channel, and while traveling along merrily at the rate of five knots, our greatest speed, we forgot our woes.

Kauai Channel is a mean place, Bill says it is "all same hell." *On the 25th* we cleared the island of Kauai, said to be the "garden" island of the group—but, mark you, you must not mention it in the presence of a man who lives on Maui, he would pity your ignorance and look at you with contempt. I have not a ghost of an opinion on the subject myself, not having visited either, but it states so in the guide. Perhaps the guide lies—so a man from Maui told me. If the guide is edited by a person having a journalistic reputation like many that I know of, I will accept the

Maui man's statement without any mental reservation. I wish our craft would sail better! Here we have a good breeze, smooth sea, all sail set, and we do not make more than five knots. However, they say the faster you go the less fish you catch. If that proverb is reversible, we ought to have a deckful before night.

We have great trouble with the stove, I think we will have to make a new one. Captain Godfrey put that stove aboard, and while we damn the stove we bless Captain Godfrey, sometimes we suffer from mental aberration, I think they call it, and bless the stove and damn Captain Godfrey. *26th, 8 AM*—Sighted Bird Island, also called Nihoa, and at 1 PM was abreast of it. Sailed around it, but at only one point, as far as we could see, could a landing be affected, and even then the water should be smooth. The ocean swell rolls in heavy, there is a nice bit of sandy beach on the southern side, but at the time of our visit the green water rushed up too lively for a boat to land. It's all right if you are on a steamer where you can lay off and on. Sometime ago a crowd chartered a steamer and went there for a picnic. They had the time of their life, and are not done talking of it yet. We saw a few sharks, but as we were occupied sketching we allowed them to swim around and admire the graceful lines of our craft. As night drew on, we bore away. We have made a new stove, it is a daisy.

For the benefit of whoever requires such an article, I will give a brief description of it. Get a ten-gallon gasoline drum, cut one-third of the upper part off, cut a three-inch strip nearly half round the lower part of the drum, for the admission of air.

The upper third of the drum serves as a culinary utensil, and there you are. We now can fry fish, flapjacks. Or anything else, and for stews, chowders and such like, it is simply grand, no more pilikia now. *Thursday, 28th.* At daylight we sighted Necker Island, and at 10 AM were abreast of the island. Necker Island has been visited several times. On one occasion it was thoroughly explored and several curiosities in the shape of small idols were discovered. There are several places where small deposits of guano of good quality exist, but transportation is difficult. The best landing is on the west side, and then a steep climb to the summit. All species of aquatic birds are there. The frigate bird, or man-of-war hawk, with its natural feeder the tropic birds, tern, gannet, boatswain and several specimens of gull. All have an ocean home rarely visited by man. The weather was too squally to attempt a landing, but we maneuvered around it, and then proceeded to the southward. There is a fishing bank extending nearly sixty miles to the southward of the island.

We found twelve fathoms as the lowest sounding, the average being about thirty fathoms. Fish there is abundant, but the sharks are annoying. It is my idea that in times gone by, the island must have been known to the natives of Kauai, and that they had a fishing station there. It is an ideal place for catching fish, and drying them during the summer months, April till October. We did not stop long. At 9 PM we bore away for French Frigate shoals. *Friday 29th*. During the night we had squally weather and a nasty sea. No observation, as neither the sun by day nor moon and stars by night would put in an appearance, however, we made things as comfortable as possible, and took life easy. The wind shifted to southeast, then south then southwest, and blew hard from the northwest during the night, and this, too, in a region where the northeast trades are supposed to blow steady. I and several others hold steadfastly to the opinion that the days of good old steady trade winds are gone, gone alas, like our youth, too soon! We now have to say, the prevailing winds are easterly, and the navigator must take it at that. *Saturday 30th*. The day commenced beautiful and fine, we all felt so happy and cheerful, got our position by 10 AM and found we had been set to the southward thirty miles by the currents, whereas I had anticipated being ten miles to the northward, however, currents in the neighborhood of all the Islands throughout this chain are as mutable as a young girl's affections, so the Professor says. By noon we sighted the south end of the breakers and the islet at the same time. Stood in for anchorage and at 3 PM let go the anchor, exactly seven days from Honolulu. The sharks came around in hundreds to welcome us, which politeness we returned by inviting some twenty or thirty on board. They look quite interesting on deck. Jimmy is in ecstasies, Moses is happy, and Bill says, "Suppose go swim, catch hell." *June 2nd*, we got underway again and cruised about. We examined the islet, and steering from there northeast anchored again. We found between two of the islands a fine channel, with fifteen feet of water at low tide, into the lagoon. This lagoon constitutes a fine harbor, well-sheltered by the reefs from the eastward, and from the westward, northward and southward by the islets. A small vessel could heave down and repair here at any time, by having an anchor out and warps to the shore. This opening is northeast by east ½ east by compass, from the islet. Our time now is devoted to photographing and testing the soil of the different islets. We have quite a laboratory on board, but on no island can we locate guano of good quality. Fresh water we could not find, but at depths of eight feet we struck water of brackish quality. As heavy rains occur, with tanks that difficulty could be surmounted. We found also that the northwest horn of the crescent is rapidly extending, and in course of time will no doubt assume a circular form. After laying in a good stock of turtle and firewood, of which there is always an abundance, consisting of driftwood (there are several large logs over five feet in diameter nearly one hundred feet from the beach, they must have been washed op during a heavy storm many years ago) and with a fresh catch of fish we took our departure, having had a week of capital enjoyment. *Saturday, June 6th, 5 PM.* Lost sight of the islet, and are en route for Gardner Pinnacles. The weather is beautiful, sea smooth and wind light. During the night the chief officer reported a large school of sharks following the vessel. We offered them our proverbial hospitality, but they refused to accept of it. Choice pieces of red salmon and pork alternately were refused with disdain. I think they came in a body to see if we were really, really going for good. In an hour or two their minds were evidently made up, and they left us. Towards morning a beautiful specimen of the coryphene (mahi-mahi) commonly but erroneously called by sailors, the dolphin, came alongside.

We were unable to hook him, but the mate took the grains and buried the two prongs in him, to our disgust the prongs broke off, and he swam away. During the afternoon an immense swordfish came along, his sword was about five feet long, and his body about fourteen. He looked lovely as he followed in our wake. Unfortunately our artist could not get a snapshot at him, thus proving the value of a Kodak when on a cruise. We did not care about harpooning him, as he might have rammed us, which would have been a serious matter to both of us. After a brief visit of half an hour or so, he left. We have now got the vessel into apple pie order, and if it were not for the cockroaches our happiness would be unbounded. Our cockroaches are certainly very inquisitive, not an article of any description escapes their attention. They are of a sociable nature, and while you are asleep will walk over you, exhibiting no symptom of nervousness.

The forecastle, it seems, is their natural home. Their appetites are good. If they prefer one article of diet, to another, it's Moses's toenails, which they have eaten to the quick. We have a few barrels of dried mullet, the result of our fishing. The cockroaches are continually investigating those barrels, in a vain endeavor to get inside. This affords delightful amusement to Jimmy, who catches them and passes them over to the fish, who in turn investigate *them* with great gusto. *June 8th.* This morning there is sorrow depicted on the faces of Moses, Jimmy, and Bill. The reason thereof is—horrors—the poi has given out. To those who have not lived in the Hawaiian Islands, and do not know what poi is, I will explain. Poi is made from taro, a bulbous root, in the following manner, the taro root or tuber is washed and boiled, then peeled and pounded in a wooden vessel especially made for that purpose. During the pounding process, water is continually added till the whole assumes the consistency of billsticker's paste. Then it is poi. This business is now principally in the hands of Chinamen. They work laboriously at it, the perspiration pouring from their arms, face and body into the poi tub. This gives it the necessary flavor. To a stranger it looks disgusting and no inducement could he offered, that would make him get outside of a dishful. Poi when made at home, however, is one of the most nutritious articles of diet that can he found.

It is easily digested, and forms the staple food of the Hawaiian race. Poi and raw fish make them happy, with the addition of a bottle of gin, technically called square-face, they become hilarious, more gin, boisterous, and so on. Now that Moses, Jimmy and Bill have to eat hard tack and rice instead, they long for that which was but is not. The same feeling is experienced by those who go on a long voyage when the potatoes give out, then the backbone of the diet is gone. As we shall be absent some three months, we take the utmost care of our "spuds" picking and turning them every other day.

June 9th. This afternoon a coryphene came alongside, and to our great astonishment it turned out to be the same one the mate grained two days ago. Being an expert harpoonist, he quickly grained it, and there sure enough were the two prongs in his body. It is a question for the naturalist to decide, whether fishes suffer pain or not. From the rapidity of this fish's movements and general demeanor, I am inclined to think they do not. You can get a shark, cut his belly open and remove the contents, put him in the water again and the first thing he will do is to devour his own stomach. We had enough fish for all hands, with our prize. The flesh though dry is fair eating. At noon we sighted Gardner Pinnacles, and at 2:30 were up to it. *June 11th*. Light winds. Our time is now occupied in reading. We have a good stock of books, magazines and old papers. The wind is light and we make but little headway through the water. *June 12th*. On the afternoon of the twelfth, however, we had a change, the wind went to the southward, and it looked rainy. Towards night the wind increased, this is very annoying, as Maro Reef is very dangerous. The current during the last twenty-four hours set strongly to the southeast. As the weather grew worse, we bore away to the northward for ten hours, to avoid the dangerous reef which we were anxious to explore, Maro Reef, then stood on for Laysan Island. *June 13th*. Abreast of Maro Reef, thirty-five miles north. *June 16th*. What with baffling winds, we did not reach

Laysan Island till the morning of the sixteenth. It was a beautiful morning, wind northeast fresh breeze. As we approached we saw a boat shoot out from the north side of the island. In an hour Governor Freeth and his boat's crew were on board. We had some letters and papers for them. While we stood in for the anchorage, we unloosened our tongues and unburdened our brains of all the news we could think of. It is awfully jolly, those moments when you meet faces you know, so far from home. Former disagreements are forgotten and friendships renewed till we anchored on the northwest side of the island, and went ashore. *June 16th to June 20th.* Laysan Island was practically unknown, except to a very few, until 1890, when some samples of phosphate were brought from thence to Honolulu. An analysis was made, and proved satisfactory. A small steamer called the *Akamai* was sent to Laysan under charge of Mr. Freeth, and a thorough investigation made. On its return to Honolulu a company was formed under the auspices of the Pacific Guano and Fertilizer Company, and a settlement made.

    Mr. Freeth assumed charge under the high sounding title of Governor Freeth. He relinquished his position many years ago, and Hawaii nei mourns its loss. At the time of our visit the buildings were about all completed. A mule tramway was constructed to convey the phosphate to the wharf. A watchtower with a lantern served as a lighthouse during the loading months, April to the end of September. The winter months were utilized in filling the warehouse with phosphate. Loading at Laysan is somewhat dangerous, as a change of wind from the northeast to the westward, necessitates the ship to leave. Still, no vessel has ever been wrecked there, loss of anchors, however, is not an infrequent occurrence. After remaining on the island some three days, the weather being beautiful we took our departure, to return to the Maro Reef for further investigation. *June 20th.* Got underway and stood to the southward, and hauled on a wind, when about two miles from the island. No dangers were visible. *June 22nd.* Today we sighted the Maro Reef. It consists of a circle of coral boulders just awash—not an inviting place to be in bad weather. We were getting on nicely, when it suddenly came to blow. The current ran to the northwest about three knots an hour. Still, we hung around "in the interests of navigation."

As the sea got heavier, we lay to during the night, and at daylight we tackled it again. Our object was to discover an entrance, and if there existed an anchorage inside. All day we were plunging into the sea, but it was evident Providence did not want us to know much about the place. As we felt disinclined to dispute the wishes of Providence, we left and started for Laysan again. I think it is always bad weather at Maro Reef. In the winter months, when the heavy westerly seas which roll like mountains, set in, the "Maro Reef" must present a truly magnificent scene. If only it could be viewed from a balloon. On our way to Laysan, we opened a cask of shark meat, which we intended to present to the fertilizer works as a sample of high grade guano. We were about twenty miles from Laysan, and Freeth smelt it. The smell was so atrocious he thought he would have to abandon the island. That's what he said. It smelt as bad as dead rats, and nearly as bad as Limburger cheese. The cask and contents went overboard instantly. Towards evening we lay to for the night, and next morning stood on, at 7 AM we sighted the island, and at 11 AM anchored in about the same place as before. We found a schooner there, from Honolulu, and got the latest news. She was loaded with phosphate in a few days. So we got our letters and batch of Laysan canary birds to send by her. The evening previous to the sailing of the schooner, Governor Freeth gave us a complimentary dinner. When we had finished, we moved our chairs to the veranda, and sitting around a table well-stocked with liquid refreshments, commenced to spin yarns. The Governor lay back in his chair, lighted a cigar, and told us an Australian convict story. *June 27th*. Left Laysan and bore away for Lisianski Island. It was discovered by a captain of that name, in the Russian ship *Neva*, which discovered it too much. His ship struck one of the boulders that lay awash from a bearing from the south end of the island, east by south to southwest to west. No account of the damage he sustained is recorded. We had a fine trip and amused ourselves catching sharks. We have now quite a stock of shark fins, which fetch in Honolulu twenty-five cents per pound, but in Canton, China, would be worth double that amount. Shark fin soup is highly esteemed by the Chinese.

Bird's nest soup is still more appreciated, and in Peking sometimes fetches a fabulous price. It puzzles me, why the Americans with all their ingenuity, cannot make a marketable bird's nest. One would naturally imagine that men who can imitate a ham so effectually that people can eat five before they find out that they are made of wood, could easily fabricate a bird's nest and make a fortune thereby. Who knows but they are already doing it? *June 29th.* 8 AM sighted Lisianski Island, bearing southwest—distance five miles. Steered west true—and at 11 AM—island bearing south by west. Could see the bottom, sounded, twenty fathoms. Hauled in and stood west southwest. 9 AM bottom plainly visible, 18 fathoms. The boulders of coral have a lovely appearances the deepest blue, varied with pink, red, green, purple, in fact every color imaginable. We are now approaching the coral wall, in soundings of ten and twelve fathoms. 10 AM island north end southeast, stood southwest and at 10:30, being a mile from the reef, stood due south.

Shortly afterwards saw the opening clearly defined by the north and south rocks. The south end of the island now bears north 85 degrees east. Stood in, worked our way to anchorage, avoiding the numerous coral patches, anchored about half a mile from the shore. We had a hurried lunch, and proceeded on shore. Right around the island is a beautiful sandy beach about one hundred feet wide, above that the low scrub brush commences. Seals were sleeping on the beach, and the most appetizing mullet nearly three feet long, were in shoals everywhere. The island is a little paradise, or could be made one, at a moderate cost.

Ten to twelve feet is about the height of the island, but a hill about forty-five feet high running nearly the whole length of the island, is on the eastern side. There was formerly a lagoon, but it is now filled up. There is a small amount of good guano which could easily be removed. We estimated it at one thousand tons. There were no sea birds, as all had left. Plover, curlew and pewits were plentiful. After a peaceful stroll around the island we returned on board. Our supper was really fine, curlew potage and fried mullet. The mullet here are over thirty inches long and taste equal to those in Honolulu. After supper we caught enough fish of every description to fill a barrel, and a big barrel at that.

If there is an occupation that a native likes more than another, it is fishing. They will remain up all night or as long as the fish will bite. *June 30th.* So anxious were we to get on shore that we had breakfast at 6:30, and getting our instruments and paraphernalia into the boat, we went. Towards evening the island had quite a holiday appearance, with its numerous station staffs surmounted by a flag. While our party was busy triangulating the island, the rest were *shooting* mullet. A shoal of mullet would come up to the edge of the beach with their noses out of the water, a discharge of buckshot would knock over a dozen or so. Jumping into the water quickly is necessary, as young sharks with healthy appetites are around in great numbers, and it is simply a question who gets the mullet. Again, you have to be on your guard, for they are apt to imagine your bare legs are a species of mullet and take a vicious snap at them. It requires at least two people to fish in that style—one to look after the sharks, while the other secures what he shoots. We got a few seals. They are the ordinary hair seal. We secured some oil, but of a poor quality.

We dug for water, but it was slightly brackish. Perhaps if we had time to wait, say a week or two, it might improve. From our point of observation on the south end of the island, breakers were visible to the southward as far as our eyes could reach. On examining the extent of this dangerous ground, we found coral boulders level with the water, thirty miles south of the island and fifty miles east and west. To the north, no dangers were found.

July 5th. 5 AM got underway and carefully avoiding the numerous coral patches, passed out of the opening and stood for the Pearl and Hermes Reef. The bottom was visible on leaving for about a mile. After stowing the anchor and chains, we resumed our normal duties of sea life. In the saloon, reading, eating and sleeping, the crew overhauling the fish and fins, of which we have a good stock. After we had got the shark on board, we observed two sucker fish inside the upper part of his mouth. It was the largest shark we had caught, measured nineteen feet long, and weighed about fifteen hundred pounds. We got about thirty gallons of good oil, twenty pounds of fins, and his jaw we cleaned and polished. His tail ornaments the end of the jibboom.

Strange to say the suckers lived for four days, fastening themselves on the deck. They had no nutriment except what water they absorbed while the decks were being washed, which operation does not take many minutes. *July 6th.* During the morning watch after coffee while the decks were getting washed down several coryphene came along sporting about our craft. They look so beautiful, their bright colors, which vary with their movements, make a lovely picture which cannot be painted. *July 7th.* At daylight this morning we sighted the breakers on the south of the Pearl and Hermes Reef. We had but a light breeze, but as the current was setting fast to the northward, we arranged our long anchor rope on deck with a kedge. This is a maneuver not known generally to deep sea captains. Those in the China trade, especially opium schooners, are well-acquainted with the practice. I learned it there. A good four hundred fathom rope is put on board before leaving port. When a calm comes on, with a contrary current, should you have soundings even as deep as ninety fathoms, you let go your lightest kedge anchor, put out your rope till the vessel is brought to a standstill. When the current reverses and is in your favor, there is no trouble in hauling in the line, run your kedge up quickly, and drift away in the direction of your course. *July 8th.* This morning we started again. Skirting the reef, we counted eight islands, none of any considerable elevation. Finding as we thought the opening, we hauled in and beat up about a mile and a half, only to find we had struck the wrong passage. We anchored in the afternoon.

We could have taken the boat over the reef and got to one of the sand islands about three miles from us, but preferred waiting till next day. Pearl and Hermes Islands consist of about twelve islets, some densely covered with scrub, resembling the French Frigate Shoals. They were discovered, like a great many other islands have been, not so much by celebrated navigators as by the keels of ships. Two whalers were wrecked there in 1822, on the same night within ten hours of each other, and from the names of the whalers these islets take their name. Some of our most respected, wealthy residents are descendants of those who were on board the ill-fated vessels. *July 9th*. We got underway and ran out from our anchorage, and stood to the northward.

We found the entrance, but the weather looked threatening, heavy clouds gathered up to the westward. We had some heavy rain with variable winds, but at midnight it cleared up. The northeast wind came along fresh and we headed for Midway Islands, where, in 1888, my ship, the *Wandering Minstrel*, was wrecked while anchored in Welles Harbor, February 3rd. At midnight hove to and caught fifteen sharks, at daylight sighted Midway Islands. There was the old house, still standing.

Stood on to westward past the barrier reef, then hauled to the southward till the channel or passage was open, then hauled in and worked up to the anchorage, and anchored about the same place we did with the ill-fated *Wandering Minstrel*. *July 10th*. After dinner, or 1 PM, we went on shore. We felt a sickening feeling in our throats as we landed, and went up to the house. It was in bad repair. We looked for the well, but it was filled up, so we started to dig a new one. We brought four casks with us, so as to leave behind a good well for future visitors. My two sons (they were the mates) and I, then explored the deserted village. The mutton birds were occupying the houses, and their dismal cries, like the wail of a lost soul, made us very dismal indeed. *July 19th*. We got underway early in the morning. We cruised all around the reef, going as close as one thousand feet sometimes, but no dangers were visible, nothing but deep water on the west side. Soundings extend one mile from the entrance. The anchorage is studded with coral patches which are liable to cause the loss of an anchor. Having gone around the reef, we headed for home.

Frank Allen McCurdy and John Kirk McCurdy

Excerpt from the Spanish American War letters of the McCurdy brothers from the book *Two Rough Riders*. Originally published in 1902.

ON BOARD THE SS *YUCATAN*, GULF OF MEXICO. Wednesday, June 15, 1898. *Dear Father*—Thirty transports and war ships left Tampa Bay yesterday afternoon at four o'clock, and we are now on the way to Key West, where the mail will be taken off. We are going at about seven knots, as several of the boats are side wheelers, and unable to get up much speed. Two of the ships have pontoons in tow which will be used to land the batteries and horses. There is not much chance of our horses being shipped for some time, so we are drilled in the infantry tactics twice a day. Part of the Second Infantry (regulars) is on our boat, and their band plays twice a day, which helps to enliven things.

    The boat was too crowded, and two companies of the Second were taken off before we left Tampa Point, so that everyone now has plenty of room. There was a beautiful sunset last evening, and the thirty transports and battleships made a splendid picture. The general impression seems to be that we will land near Santiago de Cuba, but a great many think we are bound for Puerto Rico. Several of the men are seasick, but as there is a large supply of lemons and chewing gum on hand we hope to avert it. We each have a pair of running shoes in our locker at Franklin Field, and if you will give Lew my bunch of keys, he can get them. George Turner, the field manager, will show Lew where our locker is, but in case he is not there, I will enclose directions. Please remember me to Lovett. Your loving son, Allen. **ON BOARD THE SS *YUCATAN*, GULF OF MEXICO. Wednesday, June 15, 1898**. *My Dear Father*—Yesterday afternoon all the transports got underway and are now steaming for Key West where I will mail this letter. Allen and I are both well, and were both vaccinated day before yesterday, we thought it would be a good thing so had it done here on board. Sunday we went ashore and went to Tampa, where we told the express people to keep our boxes until we called for them, as it was impossible to get them then, being Sunday. We bought a few eatables and have them with us—a couple of boxes of pickles, sardines and lemons. The weather is fine and we are enjoying ourselves immensely and are both very well. The food is not so bad, and when one becomes used to it, it is quite good, and as our appetites are fine, most anything tastes good. A meal consists of a large tin cup of coffee, corned or roast beef (canned) and either beans or tomatoes, sometimes both and all the hardtack we want.

As we have made friends with several men on board we always get something else, and so fare very well. After we leave Key West there will not be any chance to write for a good while, so if you do not hear from us, it will be because there is no way for mail to go. I believe there is a post office to be located when we land, but it will be some time before the mail will be sent to the United States. When you see Lew, tell him we received his letter and thank him for the clippings, also I enclose one which he wished to be returned. The transports are steaming in a double line with the *USS Castine*, a gunboat, at the head of one, and the *USS Hornet*, a torpedo boat, heading the other, with several smaller boats, the *USS Helene* and *USS Annapolis*, on the flanks. We continue in this order until we reach Key West tonight and then we will be escorted by several large battleships. With this regiment and on this boat there are two rapid fire and one dynamite gun, with crews from the "Rough Riders." I will write again as soon as there is any chance of the mail going. Hoping you are as well as we are—with much love and many, many kisses. Your loving son, Kirk. **ON BOARD THE *SS YUCATAN*, OFF SANTIAGO. June 22, 1898.** *Dear Father*—We have been lying here for twenty-four hours, and there is a rumor current we will land at five o'clock, and as it is now four I will finish and mail this letter. As we steamed along the coast about fifty miles back, one of our torpedo boats ran into a harbor and reported it had just been captured by United States marines to be used as a coaling station. After one hundred hours fighting, without eating or sleeping, Spaniards had 150 killed, 200 wounded and 18 taken prisoners. Marines lost six killed, wounded not reported.

We have a shower every day, and for fifteen or twenty minutes the rain comes down in torrents, after which the sun comes out and the storm disappears as quickly as it came up. Today during our daily shower we witnessed a water spout towards the coast, and it certainly was a novel sight. We passed a sailing yacht the other day flying the Cuban flag, whereat there was much joy both aboard the Cuban boat and the transports. Morro Castle is plainly visible, and every once in awhile we can see a white puff from one of Sampson's big guns, which makes us think he is shelling the coast preparatory to our landing. Am writing this on the hurricane deck, which accounts for the unevenness of the writing. The wind is very strong, otherwise it would be very hot. We have been aboard now two weeks and one day, and landing will be a very welcome change. It is very hot below at night, so we "bunk" up here every night, although one of us has to remain here all the day, as "bunking" space on deck is scarce, and claims are continually being "jumped" as the cowboys express it. We will write as soon as a landing is made. With love and hoping to be with you soon. Your loving son, Allen.

OFF SANTIAGO. June 22, 1898. *My Dear Father*—We arrived here at Santiago last evening, and are now lying outside of the harbor. Sampson's fleet is blockading the harbor, and was firing when we came up. We expect to land tomorrow, after the fortifications have been reduced. Last night the *USS Bancroft* came alongside and told us there had been a fight at a port which we were passing about twenty-five miles from Santiago east, that after one hundred hours steady fighting the marines took the town, their loss being six, while the Spaniards lost 150 men, 200 wounded, and 18 prisoners. The Americans fought with great caution and our men were allowed to take no risks, also that our landing would only be made when there was comparatively no danger, and I suppose we will be landed last after the regulars. Allen and I are enjoying the best of health and have not been at all seasick, although we have been through several storms.

    Today during a thunderstorm a water spout passed about two miles to starboard, and was a fine sight. We are both enjoying ourselves immensely, and as we land in a very mountainous country there is little or no danger of our being sick, and if we do get sick we will be put aboard the *USS Olivette* and taken either to Tampa or Key West. The sanitary arrangements are good, everything cleaned every morning and disinfectant spread around. There is very little sickness in the morning, mostly colds and seasickness. No one expects the war to last more than a few months, so you must expect us back by fall. We will take the best possible care of ourselves, and I think we should both return all right. I hope that you are very well, and will not worry about us as we are all well and safe, and as we have good commanders I do not think we will be in much danger. With lots of love to my dear father and many, many kisses. Your loving son, Kirk. **NINE MILES FROM SANTIAGO. June 25, 1898.** *My Dear Father*—We landed at a small mining settlement Wednesday morning after the gunboats and *USS Indiana* had shelled the place for two hours and driven the Spaniards to the mountains, camped there overnight and marched ten miles Thursday evening to another coast town which the Spaniards left that morning after a fight with a Cuban regiment and our gunboats. Yesterday morning we made a forced march from five until seven o'clock when we ran into an ambush. The Spaniards were very strongly placed, but after two hours fighting of the hardest kind we routed them and are now camped on their stronghold. Our troop had the extreme left of our advance skirmish line and with "L" troop (the extreme right) bore the brunt of the work. In our fighting squad of ten men five were wounded (two mortally) and one killed, the man on my right was shot through the lungs and second man on my left was killed, so you can see how hot the fighting was.

   The Spaniards left two wagon loads of ammunition and all sorts of supplies and clothing. We lost everything, but after a long hunt yesterday afternoon and evening found all our things and are now comfortably fixed in our tent. Howard has not joined us, and we believe his troop is still at Tampa. We had our burial service this morning. They say the Spaniards left four hundred dead, but the exact number has not been determined as we are too busy gathering our own dead and wounded. Several regiments have gone ahead of us towards Santiago so our next fight will not be so severe with our regiment. We have only one envelope, so will you please mail the enclosed letters to the addresses on them? We expect Santiago to surrender soon, and will then be home in a few months. The marching is very hard work and we have dispensed with all unnecessary articles and cut our blankets to make our packs lighter. With love and hoping to be home soon. Your loving son, Allen. **NEAR SANTIAGO. June 25, 1898.** *My Dear Father*—Yesterday was my birthday, and I had a novel present. About seven o'clock after marching since five over mountains, we ran into about four or five thousand Spaniards strongly placed, with a rapid fire gun on a high mountain. Our troop is the second troop in advance, and when the fire opened we deployed as skirmishers to the left, and encountered the Spaniards in a blockhouse and an open field, with our advance covered by their rapid fire gun on the distant hill. We fought for two hours and a half and drove the Spaniards from their position, and are now encamped on their ground. The Spaniards left their provisions and killed, and retreated to Santiago. Allen and I escaped without a scratch, although five men in our squad were wounded and one killed within ten yards of us. In the two troops that were in the front, there were nine killed and sixty wounded. We have just had the funeral, and are now about nine miles from Santiago, and for awhile will take our position in the rear. In the first volley I had my hat knocked off, also my bugle and haversack. I will keep these things as they are curiosities. We are both well and having a good time. When you write will you please enclose some money, as we have none and need it, as rations are scarce, and we need money for food. Mail two letters with some in each, we will then be sure of one. I hope you are well and having a good summer. With much love and very many kisses. Your loving son, Kirk. **SANTIAGO NINE MILES. June 28, 1898.** *My Dear Father*—Day before yesterday (Sunday) we marched five miles, and are now encamped nine miles from Santiago. This is a fine location for a camp, water within a hundred yards and a good open field free from brush for our tents. The creek is about the size of Pike Creek (that runs through our farm) and is lined on both sides by fine shade trees. We are liable to camp here some time as the roads are only about three feet wide, and have to be widened in order to bring up the artillery and siege guns. Spies are captured every day, and the troops send out scouting parties continually. This is the garden spot of Cuba and a finer country I never saw. There are mountains all round us covered with coconut and mango trees, with a few pineapple and limes scattered here and there. Mango is a fruit about the size of a large pear, and when boiled in sugar makes a fine jelly. It is very good either raw or fried, and serves as a substitute for butter. The siege guns and artillery will do the brunt of the work at Santiago, and we expect to occupy the town before a month passes. Our daily shower is coming up, so I will close. We met Richard Harding Davis yesterday and had quite a talk with him. With love. Your loving son, Allen. *P. S.* Please save the accounts of Friday's engagement for us. Davis is writing a monthly account for *Scribner's* or *Harper's*, which also please keep. Please remail the enclosed letters. **June 28, 1898.** *Dearest Father*—As Allen has told you about our camp I will tell you about the food. Every day rations are issued consisting of a large slice of bacon and fat, two spoonfuls of sugar and the same of coffee, one-tenth of a pound can of tomatoes, and fifteen hardtack, which is plenty, so we are faring finely. We have become experienced cooks, and have several varieties of things—mango boiled in sugar, which is fine and like apple sauce, fried in sugar, it is like sweet potatoes, we also have hardtack fried in bacon grease which is about as good as anything toasted, we also soak about four hardtack in water until it is dough, add salt, then mix in coffee, fry in bacon grease, put a little sugar on top and enjoy it to its full extent, so you see we have all varieties to eat. We are both in fine health, and are having a good time, and as we have come through about as hot a fight as possible, there is now every chance of our coming home soon. I never thought we could do what we have done. Those marches were pretty tough and lots of strong men gave out. Our load was pretty heavy. We carry our pajamas, underclothes and other articles rolled in a heavy blanket which is rolled in a half tent and covered by a rubber blanket, this goes over our shoulders. We have a carbine, one hundred rounds of ammunition in a belt, a canteen, a haversack with three days rations (generally), and axe, pick or shovel, which is a pretty good load to carry four or five miles in the hot sun, but we both stand it well and feel all the better for it at night, when we sleep like rocks. We get up at four thirty, breakfast at five, dinner at noon, supper at five or six, and in bed by nine o'clock, we have a nice place to bathe and wash our clothes, and if we are only fixed like this always we will return in good health, although not quite so fat. I hope that you are very well and will take a good rest during the summer whenever you can, and when we come back we can all enjoy the farm more than ever. With lots of love to my dear father, and many kisses and wishes for his good health. I am your loving son, Kirk. **NEAR SANTIAGO. June 29, 1898.** *My Dear Father*—We wrote you yesterday, but forgot to mention about our shoes. Will you please send us each a pair of heavy russet shoes? Kirk wishes his half a size larger than the last pair he bought from Miles, but I would like mine the same size.

Do not send high boots, as they are too hot and heavy with our leggings over them. We have to wear leggings to protect ourselves from the heavy brush and thickets we travel through. Have leather strings put in, also several extra pair of strings and one toothbrush. The only way you can possibly get them here is by mail, so please put a pair in a box, as two pair in one box would be too heavy for mailing. There is a rumor here tonight of an armistice, and if that is so of course do not send the shoes.

Please do not send us the clothes you said you would order as we do not wish them until we reach the States. The size of the leggings is number one army leggings to match the cloth in the suit. The suit consists of trousers, leggings and blue army shirt. Kirk wishes trumpeter stripes on trousers two stripes about one-eighth inch apart, stripes one-quarter inch broad, and a yellow bugle on the blue shirt on each arm halfway between the elbow and shoulder. Please have the clothes made and keep for us. When we return we will probably stay at Tampa some time, and will get you to send them there. These are the same clothes we spoke to you about at Tampa. None of the men have coats, and if you have not already ordered them do not do so. With much love. Your loving son, Allen. **June 29, 1898.** *Dearest Father*—Unless there is a prospect of our immediate return, you had better send the shoes, as we will need them badly. If possible put a package of tea in each shoe, as it is quite a change from coffee, would be glad if you would send the shoes and undershirts (two apiece), no drawers, as we have them. Your loving son, Kirk. P. S. The leggings are cavalry leggings and reach about four inches below the knee. Kirk. **NEAR SANTIAGO. July 5, 1898.** *My Dear Father*—Since writing to you we have moved on to Santiago and have had three days fighting, and a two days truce has been declared which terminates at ten o'clock today. Our forces are working their way into Santiago although there have been quite a number killed and wounded, but the Spaniards killed are by far greater and our men are advancing steadily every day.

Allen and I are both unhurt, although our regiment has been to the front from the first, and I think Santiago will surrender in a day or so. Yesterday Sampson sunk four and captured one of the Spanish warships without losing a man, while the Spanish loss was large. After the fall of Santiago, I believe we go to Puerto Rico to finish the Spaniards there, and then we will be home again with you. I do hope you are taking care of yourself and will not get sick, for when we come home we want to find our dear father well, so that we can have a good rest with him at the farm. Allen will write to you soon and will tell you all the news. I hope you are not worrying about us, as we are both well and enjoying ourselves as much as possible. I would write more to you now but I have not the time, but will write a long letter to you from Santiago. Goodbye, dear papa, and remember about your health. Your own loving son, Kirk. *P. S.* We received a letter from Mr. Jamison today. Kirk. **OUTSKIRTS OF SANTIAGO, CUBA. July 7, 1898.** *My Dear Father*—We are lying on a hill in front of Santiago with the Spanish rifle pits two hundred yards in front on another hill. The town is in plain view, and is a very pretty place where we expect to have a good time, if they do not burn it before we get in. Last Thursday, June 30th, we broke camp and marched three miles to a blockhouse near a large hill.

There we camped overnight, and the next morning the battle opened at half past six. We were undercover of one of our batteries for fifteen minutes, and were then marched two miles and proceeded to take a strong position on a steep hill. After firing from the woods for an hour, we charged up the hill and the Spaniards retreated to another fortified hill three hundred yards towards Santiago. After firing on them for another half hour we charged the next hill, and the Spaniards again retreated to a hill further towards the town. This continued all day and was very hard work, several boys being sunstruck and exhausted by the heat. Our loss was heavy, but we escaped without a scratch except those made by the "Spanish needles" (a sort of cactus) and wire fences. We took a strong position at dusk and remained there that night digging trenches and rifle pits. Saturday the Spaniards opened fire at dawn hoping to drive us from our position, but we held the hill and are still here. Ever since

Saturday we have been digging pits and making bomb proofs. The Spaniards have had a flag of truce up for the last three days, and nobody knows when the battle will open. Hobson was exchanged yesterday, and we are all hoping the Spaniards will surrender today. They cannot retreat any further, and if we advance three hundred yards we will be in the town. I hope you are well. Please do not worry about us as we take the best of care, and hope to be home in time to eat Christmas dinner with you at the farm. The day the battle opened we piled our stuff in the road and left a guard over it. He was hit by a piece of a shell, and was taken to the hospital, and two days afterward when some of our troop went back, all our bundles had been opened, and most of our things stolen. We found two of Kirk's razors and a bundle of letters, which is all we have left except two University of Pennsylvania jerseys. We have since got hold of blankets and ponchos (rubber blankets), and are pretty comfortable. None of our boys have tents, but we could not put them up if we had them, so they are not missed much. Our chief surgeon received a letter from Dr. Adler and I had quite a talk with him yesterday.

Richard Harding Davis is with us, and is a very interesting man. He always has a large audience, and seems to enjoy talking to the boys. We are in the pits from six to ten hours a day, and there are many anxious eyes watching the flag of trace all day. I have to go on guard soon, so will close. With much love. Your loving son, Allen. **SANTIAGO, CUBA. July 8, 1898.** *My Dear Father*—The Spaniards have until tomorrow at noon to surrender, and the impression is they will give up without any more useless resistance. They asked for truce until tomorrow in order to confer with Blanco in Havana. It is said the Spanish volunteers have refused to go into their rifle pits, and the regulars are on the point of mutiny. Women and children have been coming through our lines for the last few days, and they say every house is filled with Spanish wounded and dead. We have been working very hard at night ever since we have been camped here, digging rifle pits and making those already dug more bulletproof. Last night we dug pits from ten until twelve, and then guarded a finished pit until four this morning, when we were relieved until four this afternoon. It is hard to keep awake as we are not allowed to say a word. In the daytime we can see the Spaniards changing guard, so you can imagine how close we are to their lines. The sky is black with buzzards and we send out searching parties every day to look for dead Spaniards, and bury them as quickly as possible in order to keep the camp healthy. One of our troop who was sent back on an errand found our University of Pennsylvania jerseys and flag and our letters and diary, so we consider ourselves lucky, as most of the boys lost everything they had. We owe our fraternity at the University some dues on the first of August, but have forgotten the exact amount. Will you please get Lovett to write to Warren P. Humphreys, Bryn Mawr, Pennsylvania, and he will either call at the office or write you the amount. We forgot about this until the other day. He has been in the office several times, and will explain to you how much we owe. I have not found an envelope in which to mail this, and expect to have quite a hunt, as they are very scarce, and those the boys have are stuck together and otherwise dilapidated. Please remail the enclosed letter to the address on the first page, and when you write again enclose a few envelopes and sheets of paper, as we have but three sheets left and cannot get any at present. With much love. Your loving son, Allen. **NEAR SANTIAGO. July 8, 1898.** *My Dearest Father*—Allen and I are both very well, and have come through this fight without a scratch. I hardly think there will be much more fighting, as there has been a truce since last Sunday, and there is a report of the foreign powers interfering, as the Spaniards have violated most all international laws by firing on and killing Red Cross men carrying stretchers, and have used explosive bullets, also have fired out of their own hospitals, and have fired from under the white flag. Everyone is hoping that the war will soon be over. At Siboney where our hospital is, there is quite a town, also a post office and commissary store. They have about twenty-five large tents, and about five houses where the wounded are cared for, and today I believe they are sending the sick and wounded back to the States. Our men are entrenched all around Santiago, and have the Spaniards completely hemmed in, so that there is no hope for them but to surrender. A good many have already surrendered, just simply marched in and laid down their arms. The other evening Hobson passed through Siboney on his way to our ships, and as I was in the town that night I had the opportunity of shaking hands with him. There is no fighting going on today, and the truce is extended day by day. I do not know why, as there are so many rumors that it is hard to believe any. We hope that you are very well, and are not working too hard nor worrying about us, for we are all right, and will soon be home again with you. Allen will write at the first opportunity, and sends his love to you, with much love for my dear father, and many, many kisses. Your loving son, Kirk. *P. S.* We will both write as soon as we reach another town. Goodbye, dear papa. I am sure we will soon be home again with you, and we will both enjoy all the more the pleasures you have gained for us. Hoping you are very well, with lots of love from your loving son, Kirk. **SANTIAGO DE CUBA. July 20, 1898.** *My Dear Father*—After writing you several days ago, we broke camp and recamped on another part of the entrenchments three miles to the right. Sunday, 17th, the Spaniards stacked their arms and the American flag was raised over Santiago. All the regiments were lined along the pits, and when the salute was fired, there was great cheering and enthusiasm. Your mail has gone astray, as we have not received a letter from you since leaving Tampa. Mr. Jamison has written us five or six letters, and we have heard from several other friends, also one from Lew. Monday we moved again and are now encamped five miles from Santiago, on the best camping ground we have had. There is a high hill close by, surmounted by a Spanish blockhouse. From the top of the hill we can get a fine view of Santiago and the entire harbor which is now filled with our transports and supply ships. We have lost two men from our troop and a great many are on their way to the States suffering from wounds and sickness, but we are feeling first rate and in good condition. Seventy men left Tampa with our troop—the other day at roll call thirty-eight reported for duty.

The non-combatants have been going into Santiago since Sunday and some of the people look hardly able to walk. The children are naked and about half the people are barefooted. There are a few respectable-looking people who have managed to keep their horses and carriages, but they all have a hungry look and seem glad the Spaniards have been defeated.

There is a rumor that we are going to the States soon, but you will probably know our destination before we do. One of the boys received some paper from home and gave us this sheet and envelope. With love. Your loving son, Allen. **July 20, 1898.** *My Dear Father*—We have been looking every day for a letter from you, but have not received any since leaving Tampa, although we have received several from Mr. Jamison and some girls, also one from Lew. Will you tell him to write again, as we cannot write to him on account of having no paper or pencil. We are camped now about ten miles from Santiago, in a very pretty camp.

It is reported that we are here for quarantine, and that we will either return to the States or Puerto Rico. The condition of the regiment is not good, yesterday there were one hundred and fifteen men on the sick report, which is not very good, as there are only about three hundred and fifty men in the regiment. Everyone in camp seems to think that the war is almost over, although it is very doubtful, but everyone would be glad to receive the news of Spain's surrender, as the life here has been very hard. Now we are getting a good rest, and both Allen and I are in fine health. When we were before Santiago the work in the trenches was pretty hard, every man having to stand six hours watch in the day or night and one night two-thirds of the troop were in the pit from 6:30 in the evening until 6:30 the next day, and all that time the rain came down in torrents, but after drying out and getting some sleep, we felt all right again, so I guess we are pretty healthy. When you write to Lew tell him we have received his letter and tell him to write again, you must have written to us, but we have heard nothing from you. I hope you are well and not working too hard. We both hope to be home soon, and hope to find you well. We are both in good health, and take good care of ourselves. With love to all and lots of love to you and many kisses. Your loving son, Kirk. **NEAR SANTIAGO, SANTIAGO DE CUBA, CUBA. July 24, 1898.** *My Own Dear Father*—We had quite a surprise today when we received your very welcome letter, as it is the first that we have received from you since landing, although we have written, once, twice, and sometimes more every week. The money was safe and we were really in need of it, as we had to borrow a dollar and a half, which we have paid. We are now about four miles from Santiago, and can buy many delicacies and some souvenirs also, but more important than all, clothes when we need them. For a day or so my shoes were pretty bad, but someone gave me a bag of tobacco, which I traded for a pair of shoes, the tobacco was worth twenty cents, and the shoes probably three dollars, as they are good and strong and durable, although not watertight.

During the fight, tobacco advanced to ten dollars for an ordinary twenty-cent bag, and other things accordingly, but now our fighting is over and we are getting a much-needed rest back in the mountains, and everyone is hoping to be back again in the States in the near future. There is a great deal of tropical fever, but it only lasts for a week or so, and then one is as well as ever. As yet no one in our regiment has had either smallpox or yellow fever, and we seem to be, as a whole, pretty healthy. Of course the sun knocks out the strongest, yet Allen and I are still well, and will continue so as long as possible. We have met Dr. Church, and he told us to come at once to him whenever we felt the slightest sickness, which we will certainly do. Our stomach bands have been worn night and day, and I guess that accounts for our good health. We have not as yet received our boxes, but will look for them, we received Lew's letter a day or so ago, and now that we have paper we will write to him at once, Mr. Jamison has been exceedingly good to us, as we have received at least two dozen letters from him—five today—and everyone is full of interest and good news, and are always welcomely received. If either one of us gets sick we will wire you from Santiago, which will be easy, as Lieutenant Keyes, now an adjutant, seems to take a personal interest in both of us. He is a fine fellow, and does everything he can for us. Do not wait long, dear papa, before writing to us, as we like to hear just how you are, and we do not know whether you are sick or well, if you do not write. Every letter will be as welcome as the one we waited over a month for. The mail is pretty sure to be delivered now, as it comes direct to Santiago. I forgot to tell you that Captain Luna was on the staff of Colonel Wood, who is Governor General of Santiago de Cuba. Sergeant Sherman was taken sick June 25th, and sent home, and we have not heard from him. I must close now, dear papa, hoping that you are well, and will not work hard during the hot months, and will take good care of yourself. With lots of love and kisses, from your loving son, Kirk. **NEAR SANTIAGO, CUBA. July 25, 1898**. *My Dear Father*—Yesterday was a most eventful day. We received a large amount of back mail, including your welcome letter and five letters from Mr. Jamison, besides letters from several friends.

Our chaplain was able to hold services for the first time since leaving Tampa and our regiment was supplied with fresh beef, the first we have tasted for over a month. As Kirk has told you, we have met Dr. Church, and he has given us several doses of quinine, which I think has been a great help in keeping us free from fever. Mr. Garrison we have not met, but will make his acquaintance today. Richard Harding Davis is with the regiment, and has given us several interesting talks. The official surrender was last Monday. On Sunday we broke camp and marched about five miles back in the country, where the ground is higher and water purer. We are now five miles from Santiago and several troopers are sent in every day for supplies. Our turn will come soon, and we will write you of the city. The stores are open, and we will be able to buy necessities. Tobacco has been very much in demand, and I saw a man pay five dollars for a small package. Last Sunday Kirk traded a small bag of "Durham" for a new pair of government shoes. General Wood is Governor General of the Province of Santiago de Cuba, and has his headquarters in Santiago. Captain Luna is on his staff as interpreter, and our troop is under Lieutenant Ferguson, of K troop, as Lieutenant

Keys is now adjutant, and Lieutenant Haskell, our second lieutenant, is in the hospital. He was shot during the first day's fight before Santiago. Sergeant Damie, of E troop, was promoted to second lieutenant of our troop, but he is in the hospital with malarial fever and as Sergeant Sherman is on his way home, we are without officers. MacIlhenny has been promoted to a sergeant, and the boys expect him to be made a lieutenant very soon, as he is popular, and understands tactics thoroughly. We have written you often, but as the mail service is poor, expect you have not received all our letters. The postmaster at Siboney died with a fever a few weeks ago and someone ordered the mail, both incoming and outgoing, burned. There has been a great deal of trouble about it, as it could have been disinfected and sent without any risk. Everything has been horribly mixed up, and our commissary has had all he could do keeping our regiment supplied with food. Things are running smoother since the boats have been able to unload at Santiago, and we hope to get mail oftener. Yesterday we were ordered to *floor* our tents, and parties composed of three or four men with a "non com" were sent out after bamboo. While going through the woods, the party we were in unexpectedly found a small clearing covered with corn, lima beans and cucumbers, and we found enough corn and beans to supply our mess. They certainly tasted good, as we have received no vegetables since leaving the transports, and hardtack and bacon become monotonous after a few weeks. There is a steep hill two hundred yards from camp, from the top of which we can get a splendid view of the entire city and harbor. It is a hard climb, but the view pays for the trouble. The Cubans have not been allowed to loot the town, and as a consequence threaten to make trouble. They have withdrawn to the hills and promise to make things lively if they are not allowed to do as they please.

    A cable office has been established in Santiago and we will cable you in case either of us is taken sick. Woodbury Kane, lieutenant of K troop, is today the most popular man in camp. His sister sent the regiment a large box of tobacco and several cases of canned peaches, and they were issued yesterday. We received a letter from Humphreys, one of the "frat" boys. He noticed on the bulletin board in College Hall, Kirk had been promoted to the sophomore class. Our fraternity debt is about paid off, and we move into our new house sometime next month. Only one regiment, the Ninth regulars, I think, have been stationed in the city. The others are on the foothills around the outskirts. The Ninth are quartered in the opera house and are used to police the town. The letter you enclosed us about our clothes mentioned "1st US Cavalry." We will go over there today—they are camped near us—and make arrangements to have the box sent over there in case it miscarries and is taken to their camp. A great many letters miscarry if not marked 1st *Volunteer* Cavalry, as the 1st Regular Cavalry is in our division. Please write often and do not work hard during the warm weather. Your loving son, Allen.

NEAR SANTIAGO, SANTIAGO DE CUBA, CUBA. July 26, 1898. *Dear Cousin*—We received your very newsy letter all right, and were very glad to hear from you, and hope you will not be offended at not hearing from us sooner, but things are always in confusion, that is until we came to this camp, where it is pretty comfortable. You have heard all about the scraps, so that it is no use writing about them, as I could not be able to write all I would like to tell you about Uncle Sam's hunting parties.

All I can say is that they are very interesting and exciting. It would do you good to be here and see the mules, there are hundreds of them—great big flop-eared lanky simples, which carry big packs of eatables, about a hundred in a flock, without any rider or bridle, but they all follow a mare with a bell around her neck, and go in single file, like geese. There are about five men to a hundred mules, and they travel in this order everywhere, even carrying ammunition into the battle, where a good many are killed, but they face the bullets like heroes.

Then there are four, six, eight and ten-mule teams which would delight you to drive, they are all driven with one rein and a lot of cussing, which I guess you could acquire with ease in this camp. Everyone is eagerly looking forward now to coming home, as our work on this end of the island is over. Gad, what a time we will have when we get home. And I think I can push the chainless all the faster for this spell off. How is your wheel? Don't stop riding, as we will begin riding again next summer. The weather here is very funny. The nights are fine and cool, but very dewy, and the breeze continues until about ten o'clock, then it begins to get beastly hot in the sun, but the shade is always pleasant.

About four o'clock it rains for an hour, and it knows how to rain in this country, too, then it clears and remains cool the rest of the day. I suppose you are having a glorious time at Atlantic, eating, drinking and swimming, how I wish we could enjoy it with you. Yet I would rather be here if there's any more scrapping to be done. You ought to see a battle. It would make you feel like about fifteen men all in one. The cannons are firing smoke to burn, men running, firing and yelling, and bugles blowing, and that charge you have read of up San Juan Hill was fine, the whole cheese went up with a whoop and drove the greasers out then we picked them off as they tried to come out of their rifle pits.

Of course they killed lots of our men, but we must have killed three of theirs to one of ours. They are not brave, and fight like the Indians you used to read of, hiding behind bushes, up in trees, crawling through grass and all that. Still, with all their fine work, we have defeated them, and taken their impregnable city, which they boasted of so much. By the way, this is Spanish paper and envelope I am writing on. Must close now, hoping you are well and having a good time. Write as often as you can, and address us, 1st United States Volunteer Cavalry, Troop F, Cuba, and they will come all right. Love to you and all. Your loving cousin, Kirk. **SANTIAGO DE CUBA, July 30, 1898.** *My Dear Father*—Your two letters, or rather one from you and one from Lovett, enclosing twenty dollars, received. I went into Santiago today as one of a detail on a commissary wagon and bought a few articles, such as handkerchiefs, shoestrings, writing paper, chocolate and condensed milk, and it will certainly be a pleasant change, as we have needed these articles a long time. There is a rumor current we will soon start for the States but it sounds too good to be true, although I do not see of what use we can be here after the Spanish prisoners have been sent home. The officers are a splendid looking set of men, but the privates are under grown and do not look as if they could put up much of a fight, which fact they demonstrated a few weeks ago. Were it not for our daily rain, we could be comparatively comfortable here, as it is, we are continually wet during the day, but manage to keep dry at night, as we have put a floor in our tent, and raised it a few inches off the ground. With much love. Your loving son, Allen.

NEAR SANTIAGO, CUBA. July 30, 1898. *My Dear Father*—We have received in all twenty dollars from you, and thank you very much, for it is very useful in getting articles of food and clothing, which are to be had in Santiago. We buy cocoa every day, and it is fine as a substitute for coffee, which we have grown tired of. There are many rumors tonight of our returning to the States. I hope it is true, as we are all tired of this land and climate, which is very disagreeable, for between the heat and the rain it keeps one in a perpetual drip, but it does not seem to hurt us, as we are in fine health, good appetites, and sleep like tops.

The food now is much better, we get bread and fresh beef, potatoes, tomatoes and onions. The other day Allen and I found a garden and had a good mess of corn and lima beans, and now we often buy corn and beans from the Cubans, and so we live pretty well. There is not much to write to you about, as we are only lying here in camp and doing nothing. Allen and I take long walks every day to keep in health. I hope you are well, and often take a trip down to the shore. Goodnight, with love and kisses, love to Lew. Your obedient son, Kirk. *P. S.* If you can, send us money once in awhile—it comes in very handy for extras. Kirk. **SANTIAGO DE CUBA, July 31, 1898.** *My Dear Father*—Nothing important has happened since our letters a few days ago, but as a great many letters miscarry, I will write you another, in case you should not receive our former ones. Shafter has issued a notice to the effect that as soon as the fever abates, our regiment will be transported to the States. There is a rumor today we will be sent to Hempstead Plains, Long Island, but some think we will be shipped to a camping ground on the Maine Coast. The fever is a malarial disease, and usually lasts about three or four days, so far we have escaped and hope to reach the States without being on the sick list. Mr. Jamison mentioned in one of his recent letters you were trying to get Kirk a commission. We still have some money left, as we only buy necessities. Shoes, stockings and blue top shirts were issued yesterday, and we expect our new uniforms and underwear in a few days. With love. Your loving son, Allen.

Excerpts of a Diary from the Cuban Campaign

The following is a brief record of the campaign in Cuba as made by Frank Allen McCurdy in his diary detailing his experiences adjusting to soldier life.

May 26th. Telegram from Colonel Roosevelt at 10 AM. Left on 4:41 PM train for Washington. Dinner with J. Russell Young. 10:43 train for New Orleans. *May 27th*. Atlanta, Georgia, 4 PM. Arrived at New Orleans 10:28. *May 29th*. Arrived San Antonio, Texas, 7:25 AM. Examined and sworn in, bought uniform, reported at stockyard at 1 PM assigned to Troop F, 2nd Squadron, Captain Luna. In stockyard all afternoon and night.

May 30th. Left for Tampa at 3:30 AM. On train all day. *May 31st*. Arrived at New Orleans. *June 1st*. Left New Orleans.

June 2nd. Train all day and stable guard all night. *June 3rd*. Arrived at Tampa and unloaded horses. *June 4th*. Camp. *June 5th*. Camp. *June 6th*. Camp. Slept on arms all night. *June 7th*. Paid off. Slept on R. R. tracks. *June 8th*, 4 AM. Left for Point Tampa in coal cars. Went aboard transport *Yucatan*, anchored in bay.

June 9th. Went back to dock. *June 10th*. In bay all night. *June 11th*. Anchored in bay. *June 12th*. Anchored in bay.

June 13th. Ran down bay three miles and anchored. *June 14th*. Started at 4 PM. with 30 transports and 4 warships. *June 15th*. At sea. *June 16th*. At sea, joined by more warships. *June 17th*. At sea, sighted land, lighthouse, and islands. *June 18th*. At sea. *June 19th*. At sea. *June 20th*. Off Cuba. *June 21st*. Off Santiago, steamed thirty miles up coast, laid off shore all balance of day. *June 22nd*. Landed at S. A. I. Company's wharf twelve o'clock, small settlement called Daiquiri, fleet shelled the place and Spaniards left, Cubans arrived. *June 23rd.* Siboney, three days rations, forced march of 10 miles. *June 24th.* Forced march. 5 AM, battle Las Guasimas, drove Spaniards from ambush. 7-9 AM, 60 men of regiment wounded and killed. 12 wounded, 1 killed, 2 mortally wounded in Troop F. Camped overnight in battleground. Assisted bringing in wounded and killed. *June 25th.* Buried killed, assisted carrying wounded to sea coast, light artillery, cavalry and infantry joined us. *June 26th.* Marched five miles and camped within nine miles of Santiago. On guard, assisted capturing spies, had long talk with R. Harding Davis. *June 27th.* Outpost duty, assisted capturing spies. *June 28th.* Outpost duty. *June 29th.* Camp duty. *June 30th.* Broke camp and moved three miles toward Santiago, stationed directly behind battery. *July 1st.* Battle opened 6:30 AM. Fighting all day. Dug pits all night. Beginning of San Juan fight. Our troops suffered severely. *July 2nd.* Firing commenced at daylight, held position all day, brother had sunstroke, assisted carrying him off field to hospital.

July 3rd. Spanish flag of truce raised 10 AM digging trenches all day. *July 4th.* In camp. *July 5th.* In camp. *July 6th.* In trenches, 4-10 PM. *July 7th.* In trenches, 4-10 AM. *July 8th.* Digging extra rifle pits. *July 9th.* In trenches all night. *July 10th.* Sunday, out of trenches 4 AM. 4:40 PM. Brother returned from hospital, commenced firing. Spaniards did not reply heavily. *July 11th.* Battle opened at 5 AM. Moved camp 1 PM. three miles. Rifle pits 8 PM. *July 12th.* 6:30 AM. Out of pits, heavy rain all night of 11th, in trenches midnight. *July 13th.* Hospital detail, rifle pits midnight. *July 14th.* Out of pits 6 AM. *July 15th.* Main guard 5:30 AM. to 6:45 PM. *July 16th.* Fatigue duty, digging well.

July 17th. American flag raised over Santiago at noon, rifle pits two hours. Spaniards stacked arms 11:45 AM. *July 18th.* Changed camp, occupied Spanish blockhouse on hill overlooking Santiago and harbor. *July 19th.* Digging road. *July 20th.* Brother in hospital. This is the first time we had fresh beef since June 6th. *July 23rd.* With brother in hospital. *July 25th.* Assisting putting floor in tent. *July 25th*, 26th, 27th, 28th. Guard duty.

July 29th. Went into Santiago with Damie. *July 30th.* Blue shirts and shoes issued. *July 31st.* Received two pairs stockings. *August 1st*, 2nd. Camp duty. *August 3rd.* Received two undershirts. *August 4th.* Orders to move. *August 5th & 6th.* Camp duty. *August 7th.* March three miles to R. R. trains to Santiago. Went aboard transport *Miami. August 8th.* Sailed for Montauk. *August 9th*, 10th, 11th. At sea. *August 12th.* Funeral at sea. *August 13th.* At sea. *August 14th.* Sighted land. *August 15th.* Landed at Montauk. *August 16th*, 17th, 18th. Detention camp.

August 19th. Ten days furlough. *August 21st.* Homesick with fever. *August 29th.* Brother returned to Montauk. *September 2nd.* Brother home from camp. *September 11th.* Returned to camp. *September 14th.* Mustered out at 5 PM.

Misc Notes

"There were several pairs of brothers with us—of the two Nortons—one was killed—of the two McCurdys—one was wounded." Colonel Roosevelt made this report, believing that Kirk McCurdy—having been carried from the field—was wounded, which was a mistake—as it was sunstroke which disabled him—although a bullet had passed through his hat.

The vivid description below of a few selected incidents in the personal lives of the McCurdy brothers following their triumphant return to civilian life after completing their service in the Spanish American War was taken from an excerpt of a story written by an anonymous Washington Correspondent of the *Philadelphia Star* prior to the publication of their war experiences.

A number of noteworthy incidents took place during the service of these two Rough Riders, which are most interesting and unusual. Parents and friends were very anxious to get news from Cuba, and to learn of the arrival of supplies which were constantly being forwarded. Mr. McCurdy was most constant in his devotion to his sons, and endeavored to communicate with almost everyone returning from the seat of war. The horrible experiences of the soldiers on the hospital ships going to

Montauk beggars description. After their arrival there, the McCurdy boys were granted a ten days furlough. Owing to their father's thoughtfulness, in sending them beautiful new uniforms of the best quality, they were enabled to start for New York in comfort. Upon taking the train, an old gentleman sitting opposite eyed them critically and ventured to say "What a pity you boys had no chance to see any service in this late war." Whereupon one of them replied "We were only volunteers, sir." The old gentleman inquired as to what regiment they were in. The reply came "First Cavalry." The stranger, being ignorant of the First Cavalry, asked of what it consisted, and who the officers were.

The boys modestly replied that the First Cavalry was known as the Rough Riders, under Theodore Roosevelt. The old gentleman was profuse in his apologies, and yet appeared to be so embarrassed that he excused himself and took another seat in the car, to the amusement of the crowd which surrounded them. An admirer who was standing near remarked to the old gentleman "You can never tell how far a frog can jump by his looks." Arriving at Long Island City the lads proceeded to indulge in the luxury of a "shine." Imagine their amazement when the bootblacks positively refused to receive any money from them.

They entered a restaurant and after testing, with remarkable avidity, all the goodies of which they had been so long deprived, they called for their bill, and were promptly informed that the proprietor could receive no recompense and would be honored and happy to further serve them with anything they might wish. That night they went to a theater. A long line of people were waiting in turn to purchase tickets, and they heard the man in front of them ask for a seat and was told there were none left. When the young Rough Riders presented themselves before the window they asked for standing room. "Why standing room?" asked the cashier. "You told the man ahead of us there were no seats." "So I did" said the ticket seller. "But you can't buy any seats, here's a box, with the compliments of the theater, and even that isn't good enough for you." On the occasion of the Naval Review in New York Harbor, the New York Yacht Club chartered a special steamer to meet the American warships. Mr. J. M. McCurdy, their father, being a member of that Club, his two sons and two other members of the Rough Riders were invited to witness the Review from the club boat. The boys wore their Rough Rider uniforms, and attracted so much attention, and were the recipients of so many congratulations and courtesies, that it was noted in the newspapers, and particularly in the *New York Herald*, which said they had received as many congratulations and were the objects of as much interest and attention as the man-of-war, which so proudly steamed up the Hudson. Another incident which was never published took place during the Anniversary exercises of the St. Paul School, when Governor Roosevelt went up from Albany to give out the prizes.

At the conclusion of one of his speeches, Governor Roosevelt was told that one of the students had two cousins with the Rough Riders, and he asked to meet him. Upon the student being introduced to him, he remarked that he remembered the McCurdy boys very well, and said "They were two boys who joined of their own free will, and went into the ranks willingly, and without asking for a commission." Upon several occasions, President Roosevelt has complimented the McCurdy boys, and particularly mentioned them in his book entitled the *Rough Riders*. I see "Teddy" Roosevelt is still culling the pick from our young fellows. Last week it was Howard Young, the son of Librarian John Russell Young, who, before his father went to Washington, attended school in this city, where he made many warm friends. This week it is two of Young's old classmates at Cheltenham, Allen and Kirk McCurdy. They determined to join the "Rough Riders" as soon as they heard of Young's enlistment.

They are the sons of my friend, John M. McCurdy, of the Union League. He tried to dissuade them but had to give in. Last week the two boys left their course as juniors in the University of Pennsylvania, and on Thursday evening started for San Antonio to join Roosevelt's troop. These three young men have been known among their Philadelphia friends as the "Inseparables" and I suppose they do not intend to allow anything like war to separate them. Colonel Roosevelt has acquired a trio who will do honor to the United States and to their regiment. My best wishes go with these youthful defenders of their country.

Excerpt of a story from the *Philadelphia Times*.

Privates F. Allen McCurdy and J. Kirk McCurdy are the only Pennsylvania boys who served with Roosevelt's Rough Riders.

They are sons of John M. McCurdy, and left their studies at the University to enter the volunteer cavalry. They joined the Rough Riders at San Antonio, Texas, a few days before going to Tampa, and were therefore fortunate not to be left in Florida with most of the later recruits. They are members of Troop F and were in the thickest of the fight at Las Guasimas. They escaped without a scratch, although out of their squad of ten men, five were wounded and one killed. This fight was on Kirk's twentieth birthday, and as a present from the Spanish, he cherishes the key escutcheon of the blockhouse, which was the enemy's stronghold there. They were also in the three days fight at Santiago, and escaped unharmed, save for scratches from wire fences.

After that and before their return to this country Kirk was in the hospital twice, the first time having malarial fever, and the second suffering from sunstroke. Both boys went to Cheltenham Academy, where Kirk was advanced to the rank of captain.

At the University both were members of the Mandolin and Guitar Club—while Allen was on the football team. Their only regret in their experience as soldiers was that they had to leave their horses in Tampa, for they did not ride at all in Cuba.

Harold Bride

Thrilling Story by *Titanic's* Surviving Wireless Man

Bride tells how he and Phillips worked and how he finished a Stoker who tried to steal Phillips's lifebelt—Ship sank to tune of "Autumn."

This statement was dictated by Mr. Bride to a reporter for *The New York Times* who visited him with Mr. Marconi in the wireless cabin of the *Carpathia* a few minutes after the steamship touched her pier.

Story written by Jim Speers as told by Harold Bride, the surviving junior wireless operator of the *Titanic*. It has been reprinted in various publications over the years and included in books about the *Titanic* tragedy.

In the first place, the public should not blame anybody because more wireless messages about the disaster to the *Titanic* did not reach shore from the *Carpathia*. I positively refused to send press dispatches because the bulk of personal messages with touching words of grief were so large. The wireless operators aboard the *Chester* got all they asked for. And they were wretched operators. They knew American Morse but not Continental Morse sufficiently to be worthwhile. They taxed our endurance to the limit. I had to cut them out at last, they were so insufferably slow, and go ahead with our messages of grief to relatives. We sent 119 personal messages today, and 50 yesterday. When I was dragged aboard the *Carpathia* I went to the hospital at first. I stayed there for ten hours. Then somebody brought word that the *Carpathia's* wireless operator was "getting queer" from the work. They asked me if I could go up and help. I could not walk. Both my feet were broken or something, I don't know what. I went up on crutches with somebody helping me. I took the key and I never left the wireless cabin after that. Our meals were brought to us. We kept the wireless working all the time. The navy operators were a great nuisance. I advise them all to learn the Continental Morse and learn to speed up in it if they ever expect to be worth their salt. The *Chester's* man thought he knew it, but he was as slow as Christmas coming. We worked all the time. Nothing went wrong. Sometimes the *Carpathia* man sent and sometimes I sent. There was a bed in the wireless cabin. I could sit on it and rest my feet while sending sometimes.

To begin at the beginning, I joined the *Titanic* at Belfast. I was born at Nunhead, England, 22 years ago, and joined the Marconi forces last July. I first worked on the *Haverford*, and then on the *Lusitania*. I joined the *Titanic* at Belfast.

Asleep When Crash Came

I didn't have much to do aboard the *Titanic* except to relieve Phillips from midnight until sometime in the morning, when he should be through sleeping. On the night of the accident, I was not sending, but was asleep. I was due to be up and relieve Phillips earlier than usual. And that reminds me—if it hadn't been for a lucky thing, we never could have sent any call for help. The lucky thing was that the wireless broke down early enough for us to fix it before the accident. We noticed something wrong on Sunday and Phillips and I worked seven hours to find it. We found a "secretary" burned out, at last, and repaired it just a few hours before the iceberg was struck. Phillips said to me as he took the night shift. "You turn in, boy, and get some sleep, and go up as soon as you can and give me a chance. I'm all done for with this work of making repairs." There were three rooms in the wireless cabin. One was a sleeping room, one a dynamo room, and one an operating room. I took off my clothes and went to sleep in bed. Then I was conscious of waking up and hearing Phillips sending to Cape Race. I read what he was sending.

It was traffic matter. I remembered how tired he was and I got out of bed without my clothes on to relieve him.

I didn't even feel the shock. I hardly knew it had happened after the Captain had come to us. There was no jolt whatever.

I was standing by Phillips telling him to go to bed when the Captain put his head in the cabin. "We've struck an iceberg" the Captain said "and I'm having an inspection made to tell what it has done for us. You better get ready to send out a call for assistance. But don't send it until I tell you." The Captain went away and in 10 minutes, I should estimate, he came back.

We could hear a terrible confusion outside, but there was not the least thing to indicate that there was any trouble. The wireless was working perfectly. "Send the call for assistance" ordered the Captain, barely putting his head in the door. "What call should I send?" Phillips asked. "The regulation international call for help. Just that." Then the Captain was gone.

Phillips began to send "CQD" He flashed away at it and we joked while he did so. All of us made light of the disaster.

Joked at Distress Call

We joked that way while he flashed signals for about five minutes. Then the Captain came back. "What are you sending?" he asked. "CQD" Phillips replied. The humor of the situation appealed to me. I cut in with a little remark that made us all laugh, including the Captain. "Send 'SOS' I said. It's the new call, and it may be your last chance to send it." Phillips with a laugh changed the signal to "SOS." The Captain told us we had been struck amidships, or just back of amidships. It was ten minutes, Phillips told me, after he had noticed the iceberg, that the slight jolt was the collision's only signal to us occurred. We thought we were a good distance away. We said lots of funny things to each other in the next few minutes. We picked up first the steamship *Frankfurt*. We gave her our position and said we had struck an iceberg and needed assistance. The *Frankfurt* operator went away to tell his Captain. He came back and we told him we were sinking by the head. By that time we could observe a distinct list forward. The *Carpathia* answered our signal. We told her our position and said we were sinking by the head. The operator went to tell the Captain, and in five minutes returned and told us that the Captain of the *Carpathia* was putting about and heading for us.

Great Scramble on Deck

Our Captain had left us at this time and Phillips told me to run and tell him what the *Carpathia* had answered. I did so, and I went through an awful mass of people to his cabin. The decks were full of scrambling men and women. I saw no fighting, but I heard tell of it. I came back and heard Phillips giving the *Carpathia* fuller directions. Phillips told me to put on my clothes. Until that moment I forgot that I was not dressed.

I went to my cabin and dressed. I brought an overcoat to Phillips. It was very cold. I slipped the overcoat upon him while he worked. Every few minutes Phillips would send me to the Captain with little messages. They were merely telling how the *Carpathia* was coming our way and gave her speed. I noticed as I came back from one trip that they were putting off women and children in lifeboats. I noticed that the list forward was increasing.

Phillips told me the wireless was growing weaker. The Captain came and told us our engine rooms were taking water and that the dynamos might not last much longer. We sent that word to the *Carpathia*. I went out on deck and looked around. The water was pretty close up to the boat deck. There was a great scramble aft and how poor Phillips worked through it I don't know. He was a brave man. I learned to love him that night and I suddenly felt for him a great reverence to see him standing there sticking to his work while everybody else was raging about. I will never live to forget the work of Phillips for the last awful fifteen minutes. I thought it was about time to look about and see if there was anything detached that would float.

I remembered that every member of the crew had a special lifebelt and ought to know where it was. I remembered mine was under my bunk. I went and got it. Then I thought how cold the water was. I remembered I had some boots and I put those on, and an extra jacket and I put that on.

I saw Phillips standing out there still sending away, giving the *Carpathia* details of just how we were doing. We picked up the *Olympic* and told her we were sinking by the head and were about all down. As Phillips was sending the message I strapped his lifebelt to his back. I had already put on his overcoat. I wondered if I could get him into his boots. He suggested with a sort of laugh that I look out and see if all the people were off in the boats, or if any boats were left, or how things were.

The Last Boat Left

I saw a collapsible boat near a funnel and went over to it. Twelve men were trying to boost it down to the boat deck. They were having an awful time. It was the last boat left. I looked at it longingly a few minutes. Then I gave them a hand, and over she went. They all started to scramble in on the boat deck, and I walked back to Phillips. I said the last raft had gone. Then came the Captain's voice "Men, you have done your full duty. You can do no more. Abandon your cabin. Now it's every man for himself. You look out for yourselves. I release you. That's the way of it at this kind of a time. Every man for himself." I looked out. The boat deck was awash. Phillips clung on sending and sending. He clung on for about ten minutes or maybe fifteen minutes after the Captain had released him. The water was then coming into our cabin. While he worked something happened I hate to tell about. I was back in my room getting Phillips's money for him, and as I looked out the door I saw a stoker, or somebody from below decks, leaning over Phillips from behind. He was too busy to notice what the man was doing. The man was slipping the lifebelt off Phillips's back. He was a big man, too. As you can see, I am very small. I don't know what it was I got hold of.

I remembered in a flash the way Phillips had clung—on how I had to fix that lifebelt in place because he was too busy to do it. I knew that man from below decks had his own lifebelt and should have known where to get it. I suddenly felt a passion not to let that man die a decent sailor's death. I wished he might have stretched rope or walked a plank. I did my duty.

I hope I finished him. I don't know. We left him on the cabin floor of the wireless room and he was not moving.

Band Plays in Ragtime

From aft came the tunes of the band. It was a ragtime tune, I don't know what. Then there was "Autumn." Phillips ran aft and that was the last I ever saw of him alive. I went to the place I had seen the collapsible boat on the boat deck, and to my surprise I saw the boat and the men still trying to push it off. I guess there wasn't a sailor in the crowd. They couldn't do it.

I went up to them and was just lending a hand when a large wave came awash of the deck. The big wave carried the boat off. I had hold of an oarlock and I went off with it.

The next I knew I was in the boat. But that was not all. I was in the boat and the boat was upside down and I was under it. And I remember realizing I was wet through, and that whatever happened I must not breathe, for I was underwater.

I knew I had to fight for it and I did. How I got out from under the boat I do not know, but I felt a breath of air at last.

There were men all around me—hundreds of them. The sea was dotted with them, all depending on their lifebelts. I felt I simply had to get away from the ship. She was a beautiful sight then. Smoke and sparks were rushing out of her funnel. There must have been an explosion, but we had heard none.

We only saw the big stream of sparks. The ship was gradually turning on her nose—just like a duck does that goes down for a dive. I had only one thing on my mind—to get away from the suction. The band was, still playing. I guess all of the band went down. They were playing "Autumn" then.

I swam with all my might. I suppose I was 150 feet away when the *Titanic*, on her nose, with her after quarter sticking straight up in the air, began to settle—slowly.

Pulled Into a Boat

When at last the waves washed over her rudder there wasn't the least bit of suction I could feel. She must have kept going just so slowly as she had been. I forgot to mention that, besides the *Olympic* and *Carpathia* we spoke to some German boat, I don't know which, and told them how we were. We also spoke to the *Baltic*. I remembered those things as I began to figure what ships would be coming toward us. I felt, after a little while, like sinking. I was very cold. I saw a boat of some kind near me and put all my strength into an effort to swim to it.

It was hard work. I was all done when a hand reached out from the boat and pulled me aboard. It was our same collapsible. The same crowd was on it. There was just room for me to roll on the edge. I lay there not caring what happened. Somebody sat on my legs. They were wedged in between slats and, were being wrenched. I had not the heart left to ask the man to move. It was a terrible sight all around—men swimming and sinking.

I lay where I was, letting the man wrench my feet out of shape. Others came near. Nobody gave them a hand. The bottom up boat already had more men than it would hold and it was sinking. At first the larger waves splashed over my clothing. Then they began to splash over my head and I had to breathe when I could. As we floated around on our capsized boat and I kept straining my eyes for a ship's lights, somebody said "Don't the rest of you think we ought to pray?" The man who made the suggestion asked what the religion of the others was. Each man called out his religion. One was a Catholic, one a Methodist, one a Presbyterian. It was decided the most appropriate prayer for all was the Lord's Prayer. We spoke it over in chorus with the man who first suggested that we pray as the leader. Some splendid people saved us. They had a right side up boat, and it was full to its capacity. Yet they came to us and loaded us all into it. I saw some lights off in the distance and knew a steamship was coming to our aid. I didn't care what happened I just lay and gasped when I could and felt the pain in my feet. At last the *Carpathia* was alongside and the people were being taken up a rope ladder. Our boat drew near and one by one the men were taken off of it.

One Dead on the Raft

One man was dead. I passed him and went to the ladder, although my feet pained terribly. The dead man was Phillips. He had died on the raft from exposure and cold, I guess. He had been all in from work before the wreck came. He stood his ground until the crisis had passed, and then he had collapsed, I guess.

But I hardly thought that then. I didn't think much of anything. I tried the rope ladder. My feet pained terribly, but I got to the top and felt hands reaching out to me. The next I knew a woman was leaning over me in a cabin and I felt her hand waving back my hair, and rubbing my face. I felt somebody at my feet and felt the warmth of a jolt of liquor. Somebody got me under the arms. Then I was hustled down below to the hospital. That was early in the day I guess. I lay in the hospital until near night and they told me the *Carpathia's* wireless man was getting "queer" and would I help. After that I never was out of the wireless room, so I don't know what happened among the passengers. I saw nothing of Mrs. Astor or any of them. I just worked wireless. The splutter never died down. I knew it soothed the hurt and felt like a tie to the world of friends and home.

How could I then take news queries? Sometimes I let a newspaper ask a question and get a long string of stuff asking for full particulars, about everything. Whenever I started to take such a message I thought of the poor people waiting for their messages to go—hoping for answer to them. I shut off the inquirers, and sent my personal messages. And I feel I did the right thing. If the *Chester* had, had a decent operator I could have worked with him longer but he got terribly on my nerves with his insufferable incompetence. I was still sending my personal messages when Mr. Marconi and the *Times* reporter arrived to ask that I prepare this statement. There were, maybe, 100 left.

    I would like to send them all, because I could rest easier if I knew all those messages had gone to the friends waiting for them. But an ambulance man is waiting with a stretcher, and I guess I have got to go with him. I hope my legs get better soon.

    The way the band kept playing was a noble thing. I heard it first while still we were working wireless, when there was a ragtime tune for us, and the last I saw of the band, when I was floating out in the sea with my lifebelt on, it was still on deck playing "Autumn." How they ever did it I cannot imagine.

    That and the way Phillips kept sending after the Captain told him his life was his own, and to look out for himself, are two things that stand out in my mind over all the rest.

Kate Evelyn Luard

Selections from the World War I memoir *Diary of a Nursing Sister on the Western Front 1914-1915*. Originally published anonymously in 1915, the author was officially credited as Kate Evelyn Luard several decades later. This version has been edited from the original edition.

Tuesday, 8 PM, August 18th. Orders just gone round that there are to be no lights after dark, so I am hasting to write this. We had a great send off in Sackville Street in our motor bus, and went on board about 2 PM. From then till 7 we watched the embarkation going on, on our own ship and another. We have a lot of Royal Engineers and Royal Field Artillery and Army Service Corps and a great many horses and pontoons and ambulance wagons, the horses were very difficult to embark, poor dears. It was an exciting scene all the time. I don't remember anything quite so thrilling as our start off from Ireland. All the 600 khaki men on board, and every one on every other ship, and all the crowds on the quay, and in boats and on lighthouses, waved and yelled. Then we and the officers and the men, severally, had the King's proclamation read out to us about doing our duty for our country, and God blessing us, and how the King is following our every movement. We are now going to snatch up a very scratch supper and turn in—only rugs and blankets. *Wednesday, August*

19th. We are having a lovely calm and sunny voyage—slowed down in the night for a fog. I had a berth by an open porthole and though rather cold with one blanket and a rug (dressing gown in my trunk) enjoyed it very much—cold sea bath in the morning.

We live on oatmeal biscuits and potted meat, with chocolate and tea and soup squares, some bread and butter sometimes, and cocoa at bedtime. There is a routine by bugle call on troopships, with a guard, police, and fatigues. The Tommies sleep on bales of forage in the after well deck and all over the place. We have one end of the 1st class cabin forrard, and the officers have the 2nd class aft for sleeping and meals, but there is a sociable blend on deck all day. Two medical officers here were both in South Africa at number 7 when I was and we have had great cracks on old times and all the people we knew. One is commanding a Field Ambulance and goes with the fighting line. There are 200 men for Field Ambulances on board. They don't carry Sisters, worse luck, only Padres. We had an impromptu service on deck this afternoon, I played the hymns—never been on a voyage yet without being let in for that. It was run by the three Church of England Padres and the Wesleyan hand in hand, the latter has been in the Nile Expedition of 1898 and all through South Africa. We had Mission Hymns roared by the Tommies, and then a Church of England Padre gave a short address—quite good. The Wesleyan did an extempore prayer, rather well, and a very nice huge Church of England man gave the blessing.

Now they are having a Tommies concert—a talented boy at the piano. At mid-day we passed a French cruiser, going the opposite way. They waved and yelled, and we waved and yelled. We are out of sight of English or French coast now. I believe we are to be in early tomorrow morning, and will have a long train journey probably, but nobody knows anything for certain except where we land—Havre. It seems so long since we heard anything about the war, but it is only since yesterday morning. (The concert is rather distracting, and the wind is getting up—one of the Tommies has an angelic black puppy on his lap, with a red cross on its collar, and there is a black cat about.) *Sunday, August*

23rd. The same dazzling blue sky, boiling sun, and sharp shadows that one seldom sees in England for long together, we've had it for days. We've had yesterday's London papers to read today, they quote in a rather literal translation from their Paris Correspondent word for word what we read in the Paris papers yesterday. I wonder what the English hospital people in Brussels are doing in the German occupation—pretty hard times for them, I expect. Two that I know are there doing civilian work and Lord Rothschild has got a lot of English nurses there. This morning I went to the great Requiem Mass at Notre Dame. It was packed to bursting with people standing, but we were immediately shown to good places. The Abbe preached a very fine war sermon, quite easy to understand. There was a great deal of weeping on all sides. When the service was finished the big organ suddenly struck up "God Save the King" it gave one such a thrill. And then a long procession of officers filed out—our generals with three rows of ribbons leading, and the French following. This is said to be our biggest base, and that we shall get some very good work. Of course, once we get the wounded in it doesn't make any difference where you are. *Wednesday, September 2nd.* We are leaving tomorrow, on a hospital ship, possibly for Nantes. We found some men invalided from the Front lying outside the station last night waiting for an ambulance, mostly reservists called up, they'd had a hot time, but were full of grit.

The men from Mons told us "it wasn't fighting—it was murder." They said the burning hot sun was one of the worst parts. They said "the officers were grand" many regiments seem to have hardly any officers left. They all say that the South African War was a picnic compared to this German artillery onslaught and their packed masses continually filling up. There is a darling little chapel on this floor, beautifully kept, just as the nuns left it, where one can say one's prayers. And there is also a lovely church, where they have Mass at 8 every morning. You can imagine how hard it has been to keep off grumbling at not getting any work all this time, it is one of the worst of fortunes of war. It seems as if most of the "dangerously" and many of the "seriously" wounded must have died pretty soon, or have not been picked up. The cases that do come down are most of them slight. Some of the worst must be in hospital at Rouen. *Saturday, September 5th.* Had a perfect voyage—getting in to Nantes tonight—after that no one knows. Shouldn't be surprised if we are sent home. *Wednesday, September 9th.* It is a month today since I left home, and seems like six and no work yet. Isn't it absolutely rotten? A big storm last night and the Bay of Biscay tumbling about like fun today—bright and sunny again now.

The French infants, boys and girls up to any age, are all dressed in navy knickers and jerseys and look so jolly. Matron has gone into Saint-Nazaire today to get all the whole boiling of our baggage out here to repack. Perhaps she'll bring some news or some letters, or, best of all, some orders. This is a lovely spot. I'm writing on our balcony at the Riffelalp, above the tops of the pines, and straight over the sea. Three Padres are stranded at Pornichet—two were troopers in the South African War, and they do duty for us. The window of the glass lounge where we have services blew in with a crash this morning, right on the top of them, and it took some time to sort things out, but eventually they went on, in the middle of the sentence they stopped at.

A French rag this morning had some cheering telegrams about the Allies—that left, center, and right were all more than holding their own, even if the enemy is rather near Paris. What about the Russians who came through England? We've heard of trains passing through Oxford with all the blinds down. *Sunday Evening, September 13th (La Baule and Nantes)* Orders at last. An Army Sister and I, and two Army Staff Nurses are to go to Le Mans, what for, remains to be seen, anyway, it will be work. It seems too good to be by any possibility true. We may be for Railway Station duty, feeding and dressings in trains or for a Stationary Hospital, or anything, or to join Number 5 General at Le Mans. *Monday, September 14th (Angers) (8 PM in the train)* We five got into the train at La Baule with kit bags and holdalls, with the farewells of Matron and our friends, at 9:30 this morning.

We are still in the same train, and shall not reach Le Mans till 11 PM. Then what? Perhaps Station Duty, perhaps Hospital. There is said to be any amount of work at Le Mans. We have an Royal Horse Artillery Battery on this train with guns, horses, five officers, and trucks full of shouting and yelling men all very fit, straight from home. One big officer said savagely, "the first man not carrying out orders will be sent down to the base" to one of his juniors, as the worst threat. The spirits of the men are irrepressible. The French people rush up wherever we stop (which is extremely often and long) and give them grapes and pears and cigarettes. We have had cider, coffee, fruit, chocolate, and biscuits and cheese at intervals. It is difficult to get anything, because no one, French or English, ever seems to know when the train is going on. We have been reading in the *Times* of September 3, 4, 5, and 7, all day, and re-reading last night's mail from home. What a marvelous spirit has been growing in all ranks of the Army (and Navy) these last dozen years, to show as it is doing now. And the technical perfection of all one saw at the Military Tournament this year must have meant a good deal—for this War. (We are still shunting madly in and out of Angers.) *Tuesday, September 15th.* The train managed to reach Le Mans at 1 AM this morning, and kindly shunted into a siding in the station till 6:30 AM, so we got out our blankets and had a bit of a sleep. At 7 a motor ambulance took us up to a Stationary Hospital, which is a rather grimy Bishop's Palace, pretty full and busy. The Sisters there gave us tea and biscuits, and we were then sorted out by the Senior Matron, and billeted singly. I'm in a nice little house with a garden with an old French lady who hasn't a word of English, and fell on my neck when she found I could understand her, and patter glibly and atrociously back. My little room has a big window over the garden, and will, I suppose, be my headquarters for the present in between train and station duty, which I believe is to be our lot. We go to a rather dim cafe for meals, and shall then learn what the duty is to be. It is yet a long time coming. We haven't had a meal since the day before yesterday, so I shall be glad when 12 o'clock comes. Now for a wash. *Saturday, September 19th.* It seems that we five sisters who came up last Monday are being kept to staff another Stationary Hospital farther up, when it is ready, at least that is what it looks like from sundry rumors—if so—good enough. We have been all day in caps and aprons at L'Eveche, marking linen and waiting for orders on the big staircase. I've also been over both hospitals.

The bad cases all seem to be dropped here, off the trains, there are some awful mouth, jaw, head, leg, and spine cases, who can't recover, or will only be crippled wrecks. You can't realize that it has all been done on purpose, and that none of them are accidents or surgical diseases. And they seem all to take it as a matter of course, the bad ones who are conscious don't speak, and the better ones are all jolly and smiling, and ready "to have another smack." One little room had two wounded German prisoners, with an armed guard. One who was shot through the spine died while I was there—his orderly and the Sister were with him. The other is a spy—nearly well—who has to be very carefully watched. They are all a long time between the field and the Hospital. One told me he was wounded on Tuesday—was one day in a hospital, and then traveling till today, Saturday. No wonder their wounds are full of straw and grass. (Haven't heard of anymore tetanus.) Most haven't had their clothes off, or washed, for three weeks, except face and hands. No war news today, except that the Germans are well-fortified and entrenched in their positions north of Rheims. *Sunday, September 20th.* Began with early service at the Jesuit School Hospital at 6:30 and the rest of the day one will never forget. The fighting for these concrete entrenched positions of the Germans behind Rheims has been so terrific since last Sunday that the number of casualties has been enormous. Three trains full of wounded, numbering altogether 1175 cases, have been dressed at the station today, we were sent down at 11 this morning. The train I was put to had 510 cases. You boarded a cattle truck, armed with a tray of dressings and a pail, the men were lying on straw, had been in trains for several days, most had only been dressed once, and many were gangrenous. If you found one urgently needed amputation or operation, or was likely to die, you called an medical officer to have him taken off the train for Hospital. No one grumbled or made any fuss. Then you joined the throng in the dressing station, and for hours doctors of all ranks, Sisters and orderlies, grappled with the stream of stretchers, and limping, staggering, bearded, dirty, fagged men, and ticketed them off for the motor ambulances to the hospitals, or back to the train, after dressing them. The platform was soon packed with stretchers with all the bad cases waiting patiently to be taken to hospital. We cut off the silk vest of a dirty, brigandish looking officer, nearly finished with a wound through his lung. The Black Watch and Camerons were almost unrecognizable in their rags. The staple dressing is tincture of iodine, you don't attempt anything but swabbing with Lysol and then gauze dipped in iodine. They were nearly all shrapnel shell wounds, more ghastly than anything I have ever seen or smelt—the Mauser wounds of the Boer War were pinpricks compared with them. There was also a huge train of French wounded being dressed on the other side of the station, including lots of weird, gaily-bedecked Zouaves. There was no real confusion about the whole day, owing to the good organizing of the Clearing Hospital people who run it. Every man was fed, and dressed and sorted.

They'll have a heavy time at the two hospitals tonight with the cases sent up from the trains. 9 PM—in charge of a train of 141 (with an medical officer and two orderlies) for Saint-Nazaire, we jump out at the stations and see to them, and the orderlies and the people on the stations feed them, we have the worst cases next to us. We may get there sometime tomorrow morning, and when they are taken off, we train back, arriving probably on Wednesday at Le Mans. The lot on this train are the best leavings of today's trains—a marvelously cheery lot, munching bread and jam and their small share of hot tea, and blankets have just been issued. We ourselves have a rug, and a ration of bread, tea, and jam, we had dinner on the station. When I think of your Red Cross practices on boy scouts, and the grim reality, it makes one wonder. And the biggest wonder of it all is the grit there is in them, and the price they are individually and unquestioningly paying for doing their bit in this War. *Tuesday, September 22nd.* Got back to Le Mans at 2 AM motor-ambulanced up to the hospital, where an orderly made lovely beds for us on stretchers, with brown blankets and pillows, in the theater, and labeled the door "Operation" in case anyone should disturb us. At 6 we went to our respective diggings for a wash and breakfast, and reported to Matron at 8. We have been two days and two nights in our clothes, food where, when, and what one could get, one wash only on a station platform at a tap which a sergeant kindly pressed for me while I washed one cleaning of teeth in the dark on the line between trucks. They have no water on trains or at stations, except on the engine, which makes tea in cans for you for the men when it stops. We are to rest today, to be ready for another train tonight if necessary. The line from the front to Rouen—where there are two General Hospitals—is cut, hence this appalling overcrowding at our base. When we got back this morning, nine of those we took off the trains on Sunday afternoon had died here, and one before he reached the hospital—three of tetanus. I haven't heard how many at the other hospital at the Jesuit school—tetanus there too.

    Some of the amputations die of septic absorption and shock, and you wouldn't wonder if you saw them. I went to the 9 o'clock Choral High Mass this morning at that glorious and beautiful Cathedral—all gorgeous old glass and white and gray stone, slender Gothic and fat Norman. It was very fine and comforting. The sick officers are frightfully pleased to see the *Times*, no matter how old. I've asked everyone to collect their halfpenny picture daily papers once a week for the men. *Thursday, September 24th, 3 PM.* Taking 480 sick and wounded down to Saint-Nazaire, with a junior staff nurse, one medical officer, and two orderlies. Just been feeding them all at Angers, it is a stupendous business. The train is miles long—not corridor or ambulance, they have straw to lie on the floors and stretchers.

    The medical officer has been two nights in the train already on his way down from the front (four miles from the guns), and we joined on to him with a lot of hospital cases sent down to the base. I've been collecting the worst ones into carriages near ours all the way down when we stop, but of course you miss a good many. Got my haversack lined with jaconet and filled with cut-dressings, very convenient, as you have both hands free. We continually stop at little stations, so you can get to a good many of them, and we get quite expert at clawing along the footboards, some of the men, with their eyes, noses, or jaws shattered, are so extraordinarily good and uncomplaining. Got hold of a spout feeder and some tubing at Angers for a boy in the Grenadier Guards, with a gaping hole through his mouth to his chin, who can't eat, and cannot otherwise drink. The French people bring coffee, fruit, and all sorts of things to them when we stop. We shall have to wait at Saint-Nazaire all day, and come back by night tomorrow. One swanky Ambulance Train carries four permanent Sisters to the front to fetch cases to Le Mans and the Base. They go to Villeneuve. They say the country is deserted, crops left to waste, houses empty, and when you get there no one smiles or speaks, but listens to the guns. The men seem to think the Germans have got our range, but we haven't found theirs. The number of casualties must be nearly into five figures this last battle alone, and when you think of the Russians, the Germans, the French, the Austrians, and the Belgians all like that, the whole convulsion seems more meaningless than ever for civilized nations. This is in scraps, owing to the calls of duty. The beggars simply swarm out of the train at every stop—if they can limp or pull up by one arm—to get the fruit and things from the French. *Wednesday, September 30th*. Have been doing the sick officers all day (or rather wounded). They are quite nice, but the lack of equipment makes twice the work. We are still having bright sunny days, but it is getting cold, and I shall be glad of warmer clothes. The food at the still filthy Inn in a dark outhouse through the backyard has improved a little. My Madame (in my billet) gives me coffee and bread and butter (of the best) at 7, and there is a ration tin of jam, and I have acquired a pot of honey.

On duty at 7:30 AM. At 12 or 1 we go to the Inn for *dejeuner*, meat of some sort, one vegetable, bread, butter, and cheese, and pears. Tea we provide ourselves when we can. At 7 or 8 we go to the Inn and have *potage* (which is warm water with a few stray onions or carrots in it) and tough cold meat, and sometimes a piece of pastry (for pudding), bread, butter, and cheese, and a very small cup of coffee, and little, rather hard pears. I am very well on it now since they changed the bread, though pretty tired. *Tuesday, October 6th.* I am now dividing my time between the top floor of Tommies and five Germans and the Officers Ward, where I relieve Sister for meals. There are some bad dressings in the top ward. The five Germans are quiet, fat, and amenable, glad to exchange a few remarks in their own language. I haven't had time to try and talk to them, but will if I can, two of them are very badly wounded. Some of the medical Tommies make the most of very small ailments, but the surgicals are wonderful boys. *Wednesday, October 7th.* I have been down to the station this evening, heard that Saint-Nazaire is being given up as a base, which means that no more ambulance trains will come through. The five Germans in my ward told me this morning that only the Reichstag and the Kaiser wanted the War, that Russia began it, so Deutschland *mussen*, that Deutschland couldn't win against Russia, France, England, Belgium, and Japan, and that there were no more men in Germany to replace the killed. They smiled peacefully at the prospect and said it was *ganz gut* to be going to England. They have fat, pink, ruminating, innocent, fair faces, and are very obedient. I made one of them scrub the floor, as the Orderly had a bad arm from inoculation, and he seemed to enjoy it. Only one is married. *Friday, October 9th.* My compound fractured femur man told me how he stopped his bullet. Some wounded Germans held up the white flag and he went to them to help them. When he was within seven yards, the man he was going to help shot him in the thigh. A Coldstream Guardsman with him then split the German's head open with the butt-end of his rifle. The wounded Tommie was eventually taken to the chateau of the "lidy what killed the Editor somewhere in this country." *Versailles, 7 AM, Sunday, October 11th.* At 3 AM at Chartres an officer of a Zouave Regiment, in blue and gold Zouave, blue sash, crimson bags like petticoats, and black puttees, and his smartly dressed sister, came into my carriage, both very nice and polite and friendly. He was 21, had fought in three campaigns, and been wounded twice, now convalescent after a wound in the foot a month ago—going to the depot to rejoin. Her husband also at the front, and another brother.

I changed at Versailles, and was given tea and a slight wash by the always hospitable station duty Sisters, who welcome you at every big station. The General Hospital here they belong to is a very fine hotel with lovely gardens, and they are very proud of it—close to the Palace. 10 AM, *Juvisy.* I am now in an empty 1st class saloon (where I can take a long walk) after a long wait, with *cafe au lait* and an omelet at Juvisy, and the *Times* of October 5th. There is a pleasing uncertainty about one's own share on Active Service. I haven't the slightest idea whether, when I get to Villeneuve in half an hour's time, I shall—(a) remain there awaiting orders either in a French billet, a railway carriage, or a tent, (b) be sent up to Braisne to join a train, or (c) be sent down to Havre to ditto. We had a man in a Stationary who got through the famous charge of the 9th Lancers unhurt, but came into hospital for an ingrown toenail. *Villeneuve, 5 PM.* Like a blithering idiot, I was so interested in the gunner's diary of his birthday "in my hole" that I passed Villeneuve Triage, and got out the station after! Had to wait 1½ hours for a train back, and got here eventually at 12. Collared four polite London Scottish to carry my baggage, and found the Sister in charge of train ambulance people. I wish I could describe this extraordinary place. It is the Swindon of France, a huge wilderness of railway lines, trains, and enormous hangars, now used as camps and hospitals. Sister is encamped in a shut-off corner of one of these sheds surrounded by London Scottish cooking and making tea in little groups, they swarm here. I sleep tonight in the same small bed in an empty cottage with a Sister I've never seen before. We meal at a Convent French Hospital. I delivered my "Very Urgent" envelope to the Railway Transport Officer for the Director of Supplies, and reported to a Major, and after lunch had an hour's sleep on the bed. There are rows of enterics on stretchers in khaki in this shed, waiting for motor ambulances to take them to Versailles General Hospital, being nursed here meanwhile. There are also British prisoners (defaulters) penned in, in another corner, and French troops at the other end. *Tuesday, October 13th.* At last I am on the train, and have just unpacked. There is an Army Sister and two Reserves, a Major, Officer in Charge, and two junior officers.

Don't know yet what messing arrangements are. We each have a bunk to ourselves, with a proper mattress, pillow, and blankets, a table and seat at one end, lots of racks and hooks, and a lovely little washing house leading out of the bunk, shared by the two Sisters on each side of it, each has a door into it. No one knows where we are going, we start this afternoon. 6 PM. Not off yet. We had lunch in a small dining car, we four Sisters at one table, Major and his two Civil Surgeons at another, and some French officials of the train at another. Meal cooked and served by the French—quite nice, no cloth, only one knife and fork. They are all very friendly and jolly. In between the actual dealing with the wounded, which is only too real, it all feels like a play or a dream, why should the whole of France, at any rate along the railways and places on them, be upside down, swarming with British soldiers, and all, French and English, working for and talking of the one thing? Everything and every house and every hotel, school, and college, being used for something different from what it was meant for, the billeting is universal. You hear a funny alternation of educated and uneducated English on all sides of you, and loud French gabbling of all sorts. By day you see aeroplanes and troop trains and artillery trains, and by night you see searchlights and hear the incessant wailing and squawking of the train whistles. On every platform and at every public doors or gates are the red and blue French soldiers with their long spiky bayonets, or our Tommies with the short broad bayonets that don't look half so deadly though I expect they are much worse. You either have to have a written passport up here, or you must know the "mot" if challenged by the French sentries. All this from Havre and Saint-Nazaire up to the Front. The train is one-third mile long, so three walks along its side gives you exercise for a mile. The ward beds are lovely, broad and soft, with lovely pillow cases and soft thick blankets, any amount of dressings and surgical equipment, and a big kitchen, steward's store, and three orderlies to each wagon. Shouldn't be surprised if we get "there" in the dark, and won't see the war country. Sometimes you are stopped by bridges being blown up in front of you, and little obstacles of that kind. *Wednesday, October 14th.* Still in the siding "waiting for orders" to move on. There's a lot of waiting being done in this war one way and another, as well as a lot of doing. What a splendid message the French Government has sent the Belgian Government on coming to Havre! Exciting for the people at Havre, they used to go mad when dusty motor cars with a few exhausted looking Belgians arrived in Havre. We seem to be going to Rouen and up from there. Villeneuve is going to be evacuated as a military post office center and other headquarters, and Abbeville to be the place—west of Amiens. I had an excellent night, no sheets (because of the difficulties of washing) my own rug next me, and lots of blankets, the view, with trucks on each side, is not inspiring, but will improve when we move, have only been allowed walks alongside the train today because it may move at any minute (although it has no engine as yet) and you may not leave the train without a pass from the Major. Military Officers and Sisters live on one wagon, all our little doors opening into the same corridor, where we have tea, it is a very easy family party. Our beds are all sofas in the daytime and quite public, unless we like to shut our doors. It is pouring today—first wet day for weeks. Orders just come that we move at 8:46 for Abbeville, and get orders for the Front from there. 6:30 PM. Another order just come that our destination is Braisne, not Abbeville.

They have always seen shells bursting at Braisne. I'm glad it's Braisne, as we shall get to the other part next journey, I expect. 8:45 PM. Started at last. *Thursday, October 15th, 10 AM.* Braisne. Got here about 8 o'clock. After daylight only evidence of the war I could see from my bed was long lines of French troops in the roads, and a few British camps, villages all look deserted.

Guns booming in the distance, sounds like heavy portmanteaux being dropped on the roof at regular intervals. Some London Scottish on the station say all the troops have gone from here except themselves and the Royal Army Medical Corps. There are some wounded to come on here. There is a Royal Engineers camp just opposite in a very wet wood, and quagmires of mud. They have built Kaffir kraals to sleep in—very sodden looking, they've just asked for some papers, we had a few. They build pontoons over the Aisne at night and camp here by day.

4 PM. We have only taken twelve cases on as yet, but are having quite an exciting afternoon. Shells are coming at intervals into the village. I've seen two burst in the houses, and one came right over our train. Two French soldiers on the line lay flat on their faces, one or two orderlies got under the train, one went on fishing in the pond close by, and the wounded Tommies got rather excited, and translated the different sounds of "them Jack Johnsons" and "them coal boxes" and "Calamity Kate" and of our guns and a machine gun popping. There is a troop train just behind us that they may be potting at, or some gunners in the village, or the Royal Engineers camp. There have been two aeroplanes over us this afternoon. You hear the shell coming a long way off, rather like a falsetto motor engine, and then it bursts (twice in the trees of this wood where we are standing). There is an endless line of French horse transport winding up the wood on the other side, and now some French cavalry.

The Railway Transport Officer is now having the train moved to a safer place. The troops have all gone except the 1st Division, who are waiting for the French to take their place, and then all the British will be on the Arras line, I believe, where we shall go next. (There's another close to the train.) They make such a fascinating purring noise coming, ending in a singing scream, you have to jump up and see. It is a yellowish-green sound. But you can't see it until it bursts. None of the twelve taken need any looking after at night besides what the orderly can do, so we shall go to bed. We had another shell over the train, which (not the train) exploded with a loud bang in the wood the other side, made one jump more than any yet, and that was in the "safer place" the Railway Transport Officer had the train moved to. *Sunday, October 18th, 9 PM.* Got underway at 6 AM, and are now about halfway between Paris and Rouen. Passed a train full of Indian troops. Put off the four wounded women at Paris, they have been a great addition to the work, but very sweet and brave, the orderlies couldn't do enough for them, they adored them, and were so indignant at their being wounded. Another man died today—shot through the pelvis. One of the enterics, a Skye man, thinks I'm his mother, told me tonight there was a German spy in his carriage, and that he had "50 dead Jocks to bury—and it wasn't the burying he didn't like but the feeling of it." He babbles continually of Germans, ammunition, guns, Jocks, and rations.

Sunday is not Sunday, of course, on a train, no Padre, no services, no nothing—not even anytime. The only thing to mark it today is one of the Civil Surgeons wearing his new boots. We shan't get any letters yet until we get to the new railhead. I'm hoping we shall get time at Rouen to see the Cathedral, do some shopping, have a bath and a shampoo, but probably shan't.

Monday, October 19th. Rouen, 9 PM. Got here late last night, and all the wounded were taken off straight away to the two general hospitals here. One has 1300 cases, and has kept two people operating day and night. A great many deaths from tetanus. Seen General French's 2nd dispatch (of September) today in *Daily Mail*. Had a regular debauch in cathedrals and baths today. This is the most glorious old city, two cathedrals of surpassing beauty, lovely old streets, broad river, hills, and lovely hot baths and hair shampooing. What with two cathedrals, a happy hour in a hot bath, a shampoo, and delicious tea in the town, we've had a happy day. The train stays here tonight and we are off tomorrow. *Tuesday, October 20th, 6 PM.* Just leaving Rouen for Boulogne. We've seen some of the Indians. The Canadians seem to be still on Salisbury Plain. No one knows what we're going to Boulogne empty for. We have been busy today getting the train ready, stocking dressings and etc. All the 500 blankets are sent in to be fumigated after each journey, and 500 others drawn instead. And well they may be, one of the difficulties is the lively condition of the men's shirts and trousers (with worse than fleas) when they come from the trenches in the same clothes they've worn for five weeks or more. You can't wonder we made tracks for a bath at Rouen. We've just taken on two Belgian officers who want a lift to Boulogne.

Thursday, October 22nd. Took on from convoys all night in pitch darkness—a very bad load this time, going to go septic, swelling under the bandages. There was a fractured spine and a malignant oedema, both dying, we put these two off today at Saint-Omer. We came straight away in the morning, and are now nearly back at Boulogne. *Monday, the 26th, 7 AM, Ypres.* We got here again about 10 PM last night in pouring wet, and expected another night like Friday night, but we for some reason remained short of the station, and when we found there was nothing doing, lay down in our clothes and slept, booted and spurred in mackintosh, aprons and etc. We were all so tired and done up yesterday, Medical Officers, Sisters, and Orderlies, that we were glad of the respite. There was a tremendous banging and flashing to the north about three o'clock, and this morning it was very noisy, and shaking the train. Some of it sounds quite close.

It is a noise you rather miss when it leaves off. One of the last lot of officers told us he had himself seen in a barn three women and some children, all dead, and all with no hands.

The noise this morning is like a continuous roll of thunder interrupted by loud bangs, and the popping of the French mitrailleuses, like our Maxims. This place is full of Belgian women and children refugees in a bad way from exhaustion. A long line of our horse ambulances is coming slowly in. Had a very interesting morning. Got leave to go into the town and see the Cathedral of St. Martin. None of the others would budge from the train, so I went alone, town chock full of French and Belgian troops, and unending streams of columns, also Belgian refugees, cars full of staff officers. The Cathedral is thirteenth century, glorious as usual. There are hundreds of German prisoners in the town in the Cloth Hall. It was a very war-ish feeling saying one's prayers in the Cathedral to the sound of the guns of one of the greatest battles in the world. A Medical Officer from the Clearing Hospital, with a haggard face, asked me if I could give him some eau-de-Cologne and Bovril for a wounded officer with a gangrenous leg—lying on the station. Sister and I took some down, also morphine, and fed them all—frightful cases on stretchers in the waiting room. They are for our train when we can get in. He told me he had never seen such awful wounds, or such numbers of them. They are being brought down in carts or anything. He said there are 1500 dead Germans piled up in a field five miles off. They say that German officers of ten days service are commanding. *Thursday, October 29th, Nieppe.* Woke up to the familiar bangs and rattles again—this time at a wee place about four miles from Armentieres. We are to take up 150 here and go back to Bailleul for 150 there. It is a lovely sunny morning, but very cold, the peasants are working in the fields as peacefully as at home.

A Royal Army Medical Corps lieutenant was killed by a shell three miles from here three days ago. We've just been giving out scarves and socks to some Field Ambulance men along the line. Just seen a British aeroplane send off a signal to our batteries—a long smoky snake in the sky, also a very big British aeroplane with a machine gun on her. A German aeroplane dropped a bomb into this field on Tuesday, meant for the Air Station here. This is the Headquarters of the 4th Division. *Friday, October 30th, Boulogne.* While we were at Nieppe, after passing Bailleul, a German aeroplane dropped a bomb on to Bailleul. After filling up at Nieppe we went back to Bailleul and took up 238 Indians, mostly with smashed left arms from a machine gun that caught them in the act of firing over a trench. They are nearly all 47th Sikhs, perfect lambs, they hold up their wounded hands and arms like babies for you to see, and insist on having them dressed whether they've just been done or not. They behave like gentlemen, and salaam after you've dressed them. They have masses of long, fine, dark hair under their turbans done up with yellow combs, glorious teeth, and melting dark eyes. One died. The younger boys have beautiful classic Italian faces, and the rest have fierce black beards curling over their ears. We carried 387 cases this time. *Later.* We got unloaded much more quickly today, and have been able to have a good rest this afternoon, as I went to bed at 3 AM and was up again by 8. It was not so heavy this time, as the Indians were mostly sitting up cases. Those of a different caste had to sleep on the floor of the corridors, as the others wouldn't have them in. One compartment of four lying down ones got restless with the pain of their arms, and I found them all sitting up rocking their arms and wailing. It is interesting to hear the individual men express their conviction that the British will never let the Germans through to Calais. They seem as keen as the Generals or the Government. That is why we have had such thousands of wounded in Boulogne in this one week. It is quite difficult to nurse the Germans, and impossible to love your enemies. We always have some on the train. One man of the Durham Light Infantry was bayoneted in three different places, after being badly wounded in the arm by a dumdum bullet. The man who bayoneted him died in the next bed to him in the Clearing Hospital yesterday morning. You feel that they have all been doing that and worse. We hear at firsthand from officers and men specified local instances of unprintable wickedness. *Tuesday, November 3rd, Bailleul, 8:30 AM.* Just going to load up, wish we'd gone to Ypres. Germans said to be advancing. *Wednesday, November 4th, Boulogne.* We had a lot of badly wounded Germans who had evidently been left many days, their condition was appalling, two died (one of tetanus), and one British. We have had a lot of the London Scottish, wounded in their first action. Reinforcements, French guns, British cavalry, are being hurried up the line, they all look splendid. *Boulogne, Thursday, November 12th, 8 PM.* Have been here all day. News from the Front handed down the line coincides with the *Daily Mail. Friday, 13th.* Still here—fourth day of rest. No one knows why, nearly all the trains are here. The news today is glorious. They say that the Germans did get through into Ypres and were bayoneted out again. *Friday, November 13th, Boulogne.* We have been all day in Park Lane Siding among the trains, in pouring wet and slush. I amused myself with a pot of white paint and a forceps and wool for a brush, painting the numbers on both ends of the coaches inside, all down the train, you can't see the chalk marks at night. This unprecedented four days rest and nights in bed is doing us all a power of good, we have books and mending and various occupations. *Tuesday, November 17th, 3 AM.* When we got our load down to Boulogne yesterday morning all the hospitals were full and the weather was too rough for the ships to come in and clear them, so we were ordered on to Havre, a very long journey. A German died before we got to Abbeville, where we put off two more very bad ones, and at Amiens we put off four more, who wouldn't have reached Havre. About midnight something broke on the train, and we were hung up for hours, and haven't yet got to Rouen, so we shall have them on the train all tomorrow too, and have all the dressings to do for the third time.

One of the night orderlies has been run in for being asleep on duty. He climbed into a top bunk (where a Frenchman was taken off at Amiens), and deliberately covered up and went to sleep. He was in charge of 28 patients. Another was left behind at Boulogne, absent without leave, thinking we should unload, and the train went off for Havre. He'll be run in too. Shows how you can't leave the train. That looks as if we were going to empty at Versailles instead of Havre. Lovely starlight night, but very cold. Everybody feels pleased and honored that Lord Roberts managed to die with us on Active Service at Headquarters, and who would choose a better ending to such a life? 7 AM. After all, we must be crawling round to Rouen for Havre, passed Beauvais.

Lovely sunrise over winter woods and frosted country. Our load is a heavy and anxious one—we shall be glad to land them safely somewhere. The amputations, fractures, and lung cases stand these long journeys very badly. *Wednesday, November 18th, 2 PM.* At last reached beautiful Rouen, through Saint-Just, Beauvais, and up to Sergueux, and down to Rouen. From Sergueux through Rouen to Havre is supposed to be the most beautiful train journey in France, which is saying a good deal. Put off some more bad cases here, a boy sergeant, aged 24, may save his eye and general blood poisoning if he gets irrigated quickly.

You can watch them going wrong, with two days and two nights on the train, and it seems such hard luck. And then if you don't write "Urgent" or "Immediate" on their bandages in blue pencil, they get overlooked in the rush into hospital when they are landed. So funny to be going back to old Havre, that hot torrid nightmare of Waiting-for-Orders in August. But, thank Heaven we don't stop there, but back to the guns again. 5 PM. We are getting on for Havre at last. This long journey from Belgium down to Havre has been a strange mixture. Glorious country with the flame and blue haze of late autumn on hills, towns, and valleys, bare beech woods with hot red carpets. Glorious British Army lying broken in the train—sleep (or the chance of it) three hours one night and four the next, with all the hours between (except meals) hard work putting the British Army together again, haven't taken off my puttees since Sunday. Seems funny, 400 people (of whom four are women and about sixty are sound) all whirling through France by special train. Why? Because of the swelled head of the all-highest. We had a boy with no wound, suffering from shock from shell bursts. When he came round, if you asked him his name he would look fixedly at you and say "Yes." If you asked him something else, with a great effort he said "Mother." 8 PM. Got to Havre. *Thursday, November 19th.* Spent the day in a wilderness of railway lines at Sotteville—sharp frost, walk up and down the lines all morning, horizon bounded by fog. This afternoon raw, wet, snowing, slush outside.

If it is so deadly cold on this unheated train, what do they do in the trenches with practically the same equipment they came out with in August? Can't last like that. Makes you feel like a pig to have a big coat, and hot meals, and dry feet. I've made a fine foot muff with a brown blanket, it is twelve thicknesses sewn together, have still got only summer underclothing. My winter things have been sent on from Havre, but the parcel has not yet reached me, hope the foot muff will ward off chilblains.

Got a *Daily Mail* of yesterday. We heard of the smashup of the Prussian Guard from the people who did it, and had some of the Prussian Guard on our train. Ypres is said to be full of German wounded who will very likely come to us. *Boulogne, Saturday, November 21st.* In the siding all yesterday and today. Train to be cut down from 650 tons to 450, so we are reconstructing and putting off wagons. It will reduce our number of patients, but we shall be able to do more for a smaller number, and the train will travel better and not waste time blocking up the stations and being left in sidings in consequence. The cold this week has been absolutely awful. The last train brought almost entirely cases of rheumatism. Their only hope at the Front must be hot meals, and I expect the Army Service Corps sees that they get them somehow. A troop train of a very rough type of Glasgow men, reinforcing the Highlanders, was alongside of us early yesterday morning, each truck had a roaring fire of Coke in a pail. They were in roaring spirits, it was icy cold. My winter things arrived from Havre yesterday, so I am better equipped against the cold.

Also, this morning an engine gave us an hour or two chauffage just at getting up time, which was a help. *Tuesday, November 24th.* Was up all Sunday night, unloaded early at Boulogne. Had a bath on a ship and went to bed. Stayed in siding all day. *Wednesday, November 25th.* Left Boulogne about 9:30. Last night at dinner our charming debonair French garcon was very drunk, and spilt the soup all over me. There was a great scene in French. The fat fatherly corporal (who has a face and expression exactly like the Florentine people in Ghirlandaio's Nativities, and who has the manners of a French aristocrat on his way to the guillotine) tried to control him, but it ended in a sort of fight, and poor Charles got the sack in the end, and has been sent back to Paris to join his regiment. He was awfully good to us Sisters—used to make us coffee in the night, and fill our hot bottles and give us hot bricks for our feet at meals. Just going on now to a place we've not been to before, called Chocques. The French have today given us an engine with the Red Cross on it and an extra man to attend to the chauffage, so we have been quite warm and lovely. We ply him at the stations with cigarettes and chocolate, and he now falls over himself in his anxiety to please us. The officers of the two Divisions which are having a rest have got 100 hours leave in turns. We all now spend hours mapping out how much we could get at home in 100 hours from Boulogne. *Thursday, November 26th.* We did a record yesterday. Loaded up with the Indians—full load—bad cases—quite a heavy day, back to Boulogne and unloaded by 9 PM, and off again at 11:30 PM. No waiting in the siding this time. Three hospital ships were waiting this side to cross by daylight. They can't cross now by night because of enemy torpedoes. So all the hospitals were full again, and trains were taking their loads on to Rouen and Havre. We should have had to if they hadn't been Indians.

We loaded up today at Bailleul, where we have been before—headquarters of 3rd and 4th Divisions. We had some time to wait there before loading up, so went into the town and saw the Cathedral—beautiful old tower, hideously restored inside, but very big and well-kept. The town was very interesting. Sentries up the streets every hundred yards or so, the usual square packed with transport, and the usual jostle of Tommies and staff officers and motorcars and lorries. We saw General French go through. The Surgeon General had been there yesterday, and five Sisters are to be sent up to each of the two clearing hospitals there. They should have an exciting time.

A bomb was dropped straight onto the hospital two days ago—killed one wounded man, blew both hands off one orderly, and wounded another. The airman was caught, and said he was very sorry he dropped it on the hospital, he meant it for Headquarters. We have a lot of cases of frostbite on the train.

One is as bad as in Scott's Expedition, may have to have his foot amputated. I'd never seen it before. They are nearly all slight medical cases, very few wounded, which makes a very light load from the point of view of work, but we shall have them on the train all night. One of us is doing all the train half the night, and another all the train the other half. The other two go to bed all night. I am one of these, as I have got a bit of a throat and have been sent to bed early. We've never had a light enough load for one to do the whole train before. The men say things are very quiet at the Front just now. Is it the weather or the Russian advance? Major got left behind at Hazebrouck, talking to the Railway Transport Officer, but scored off us by catching us up at Saint-Omer on an engine which he collared. *Monday, November 30th, Boulogne.* Yesterday a wounded Tommie on the train told me "the Jack Johnsons have all gone." Today's French communique says "the enemy's heavy artillery is little in evidence." There is a less strained feeling about everywhere—a most blessed lull. We were late getting our load off the train last night, and some were very bad. One of my Sikhs with pneumonia did not live to reach Boulogne. The Gurkhas are supposed by the orderlies to be Japanese. They are exactly like Japs, only brown instead of yellow. The orderlies make great friends with them all. One Hindu was singing "Bonnie Dundee" to them in a little gentle voice, very much out of tune. Their great disadvantage is that they are alive with "Jack Johnsons" (not the guns). They take off *all* their underclothes and throw them out of the window, and we have to keep supplying them with pajamas and shirts. They sit and stand about naked, scratching for dear life. It is fatal for the train, because all the cushioned seats are now infected, and so are we. I love them dearly, but it is a big price to pay.

Wednesday, December 2nd. We got to Chocques very late last night and are loading up this morning, but only a few here, we shall stop at Lillers and take more on. We went for our usual exploring walk through seas of mud. There are more big motor lorries here than I've seen anywhere. We wandered past a place where Indians were busy killing and skinning goats—a horrible sight—to one of these chateaux where the staff officers have their headquarters, it was a lovely house in a very clean park, there was a children's swing under the trees and we had some fine swings. *Later.* Officers have been on the train on both places begging for newspapers and books. We save up our *Punches* and *Daily Mails* and *Times* for them, and give them any seven pennies we have to spare. They say at least forty people read each book and they finish up in the trenches. His Majesty King George was up here yesterday afternoon in a motor and gave three Victoria Crosses. We have only taken on 83 at the two places.

There is so little doing anywhere—no guns have been heard for several days, and there is not much sickness. An officer asked for some mufflers for his Field Ambulance men, so I gave him the rest of the children's, the sailors on the armored train had the first half. He came back with some pears for us. They are so awfully grateful for the things we give them that they like to bring us something in exchange. Seven men off a passing truck fell over each other getting writing cases and chocolate today. They almost eat the writing cases with their joy. 9 PM. We filled up at Saint-Omer from the three hospitals there. A great many cases of frostbite were put on. They crawl on hands and knees, poor dears. Some left in hospital are very severe and have had to be amputated below the knee. Some of the toes drop off. I have one carriage of twenty-four Indians. A Sikh refused to sit in the same seat with a stout little major of the Gurkhas. I showed him a picture of Bobs, and he said at once, Robert Sahib. They love the *Daily Mirrors* with pictures of Indians. The Sikhs are rather whiney patients and very hard to please, but the little Gurkhas are absolute stoics, and the Bengal Lancers, who are Mohammedans, are splendid. *Sunday, December 6th.* A brilliant frosty day—on way up to Bailleul. We unloaded early at Boulogne yesterday, and waited at a good place halfway between Boulogne and Calais, a high down not far from the sea, with a splendid air. Some of the others went for a walk as we had no engine on, but I had been up since 2 AM, and have hatched another bad cold, and so retired for a sleep till tea time. Just got to Hazebrouck. Ten men and three women were killed and twenty wounded here this morning by a bomb. They are very keen on getting a good bag here, especially on the station, and for other reasons, as it is an important junction. 4 PM. We have been up to Boulogne and there were no patients for us, so we are to go back to the above bomb place to collect theirs. Boulogne was packed with pale, war-worn, dirty but cheerful French troops entraining for their Front.

They have been all through everything, and say they want to go on and get it finished. They carry fearful loads, including an extra pair of boots, a whole collection of frying pans and things and blankets, picks and etc., all on their backs. The British officers on the station came and grabbed our yesterday's *Daily Mails*, and asked for soap, so what you sent came in handy. They went into the town to buy grapes for us in return. This place is famous for grapes—huge monster purple ones—but the train went out before they came back. We had got some earlier, though.

9 PM. We are nearly back at Boulogne and haven't taken up any sick or wounded anywhere. One of the trains has taken Indians from Boulogne down to Marseilles—several days journey. *Monday, December 7th*. Pouring wet day. Still standing by, nothing doing anywhere. It is a blessed relief to know that, and the rest does no one any harm. Had a grand mail today. There is a heartbreaking account of my beautiful Ypres on page 8 of December 1st *Times*. There was a cavalry officer looking round the Cathedral with me that day the guns were banging. I often wonder where the Belgian woman is who showed me the way and wanted my South Africa ribbons as a souvenir. She showed me a huge old painting on the wall of the Cathedral of Ypres in an earlier war. I all but got left in Boulogne today. It was bad luck not seeing the King. We caught him up at St. Omer, and saw his train, and from there he motored in front of us to all our places. Where we went, they said "the King was here yesterday and gave Victoria Crosses." We haven't seen the "d—d good boy" either.

Saturday, December 12th. The French engine drivers are so erratic that if you're long enough on the line it's only a question of time when you get your smash up. Ours came last night when they were joining us up to go out again. They put an engine onto each end of one-half of the train (not the one our car is in), and then did a tug-of-war. That wasn't a success, so they did the concertina touch, and put three coaches out of action, including the kitchen. So we're stuck here now (Boulogne) until Heaven knows when. Fortunately no casualties. *Wednesday, December 16th*. We are on our way up again today, and by a different and much jollier way, to Saint-Omer, going south of Boulogne and across country, instead of up by Calais. We came back this way with patients from Ypres once. It is longer, but the country is like Hampshire Downs, instead of the everlasting flat swamps the other way. Of course it is raining. 6 PM. For once we waited long enough at Saint-Omer to go out and explore the beautiful ruined Abbey near the station. We went up the town—very clean compared with the towns farther up—swarming with gray touring cars and staff officers. Headquarters of every arm labeled on different houses, and a huge church the same date as the Abbey, with some good carving and glass in it. We kept an eye open for Sir John French and the prisoner of war, but didn't meet them.

Saw the English military church where Lord Roberts began his funeral service. For once it wasn't raining. *Thursday, December 17th.* Left Saint-Omer at 11 PM last night, and woke up this morning at Bailleul. Saw two aeroplanes being fired at—black smoke balls bursting in the air. Heard that Hartlepool and Scarborough have been shelled—just the bare fact—in last night's *Globe*. We're longing to get back for today's *Daily Mail*.

There has been a lot of fighting in our advance southeast of Ypres since Sunday. The Gordons made a great bayonet charge, but lost heavily in officers and men in half an hour, we have some on the train. The French also lost heavily, and lie unburied in hundreds, but the men say the Germans were still more badly "punished." They tell us that in the base hospitals they never get a clean wound, even the emergency amputations and trepanning and operations done in the Clearing Hospitals are septic, and no one who knew the conditions would wonder at it. We shall all forget what a septic work is by the time we get home. The anti-tetanus serum injection that every wounded man gets with his first dressing has done a great deal to keep the tetanus under, and the spreading gangrene is less fatal than it was. It is treated with incisions and injections of $H_2 O_2$ or, when necessary, amputation in case of limbs. You suspect it by the gray color of the face and by another sense, before you look at the dressing.

At Boulogne a man at the station greeted me, and it was my old theater orderly at Number 7 Pretoria. We were very pleased to see each other. I fitted him out with a pack of cards, postcards, acid drops, and a nice gray pair of socks. A wounded officer told us he was giving out the mail in his trench the night before last, and nearly every man had either a letter or a parcel. Just as he finished a shell came and killed his sergeant and corporal, if they hadn't had their heads out of the trench at that moment for the mail, neither of them would have been hit. The officer could hardly get through the story for the tears in his eyes. *Friday, December 18th, 10:30 AM.* We've had an all-night journey to Rouen, and have almost got there. One of my sitting-ups was 106° this morning, but it was only malaria, first typical one I have met since South Africa. A man who saw the King when he was here said "They wouldn't let him come near the trenches, if a shell had come and hit him I think the Army would've all gone mad, there'd be no keeping them in the trenches after that." This place before Rouen is Darnetal, a beautiful spiry town in a valley.

6 PM. We unloaded by 12, and had just had time to go out and get a bath at the best baths in France. Shipped a big cargo of J. J. this journey, but luckily made no personal captures. Got to sleep this afternoon, as I was on duty all yesterday and up to 2 AM this morning. Pouring cats and dogs as usual. No time to see the Cathedrals. We had this time a good many old seasoned experienced men of the Regular Army, who had been through all the four months (came out in August). They are very strong on the point of mixing Territorial Forces and Indians well in with men like themselves. One Company of Royal Engineers lost all its officers in one day in a charge. A Highland Light Infantry man gave a chuckling account of how they got to fighting the Prussian Guard with their fists at Wypers because they were at too close quarters to get in with their bayonets. They really enjoyed it, and the Germans didn't. *Sunday, 20th, 6 PM.* At last we are on our way back to Boulogne and mails, and the news of the War at home and abroad. At Rouen, or rather the desert four miles outside it, we only see the paper of the day before, and we miss

our mails, and have no work since unloading on Friday. This morning was almost a summer day, warm, still, clear and sunny. We went for a walk, and then got on with painting the red crosses on the train, which can only be done on fine days, of which we've had few. The men were paraded, and then sent route marching, which they much enjoyed. It was possible, as word was sent that the train was not going out until 1:30. It did, however, move at 12, which shows how little you can depend on it, even when a time is given. They had a mouth organ and sang all the way. *Xmas Eve, 1914.* And no fire and no chauffage, and cotton frocks, funny life, isn't it? And the men are crouching in a foot of water in the trenches and thinking of "home"—British, Germans, French, and Russians. We are just up at Chocques going to load up with Indians again. Had more journeys this week than for a long time, you just get time to get what sleep the engine driver and the cold will allow you on the way up. 8 PM. Just nearing Boulogne with another bad load, half-Indian, half-British, had it in daylight for the most part, thank goodness! Railhead today was one station further back than last time, as the Headquarters had to be evacuated after the Germans got through on Sunday. The two regiments, Coldstream Guards and Camerons, who drove them back, lost heavily and tell a tragic story. There are two men (only one is a boy) on the train who got wounded on Monday night (both compound fracture of the thigh) and were only taken out of the trench this morning, Thursday, to a Dressing Station and then straight on to our train. (We heard the guns this morning.) Why they are alive I don't know, but I'm afraid they won't live long, they are sunken and gray-faced and just strong enough to say "Anyway, I'm out of the trench now." They had drinks of water now and then in the field but no dressings, and lay in the slush.

Stretcher bearers are shot down immediately, with or without the wounded, by the German snipers. And this is Christmas, and the world is supposed to be civilized. They came in from the trenches today with blue faces and chattering teeth, and it was all one could do to get them warm and fed. By this evening they were most of them revived enough to enjoy Xmas cards, there were such a nice lot that they were able to choose them to send to Mother and My Young Lady and the Missis and the Children, and have one for themselves. The Indians each had one, and salaamed and said "God save you" and "I will pray to God for you" and "God win your enemies" and "God kill many Germans" and "The Indian men too cold, kill more Germans if not too cold." One with a South Africa (Victory Medal) ribbon spotted mine and said "Africa same like you." *Midnight*. Just unloaded, going to turn in, we are to go off again at 5 AM tomorrow, so there'll be no going to church. Mail in, but not parcels, there's a big block of parcels down at the base, and we may get them by Easter. With superhuman self-control I have not opened my mail tonight so as to have it tomorrow morning. *Xmas Day, 11 AM*. On way up again to Bethune, where we have not been before (about ten miles beyond where we were yesterday), a place I've always hoped to see. Sharp white frost, fog becoming denser as we get nearer Belgium. A howling mob of reinforcements stormed the train for smokes. We threw out every cigarette, pipe, pair of socks, mitts, hankies, pencils we had left, it was like feeding chickens, but of course we hadn't nearly enough. Everyone on the train has had a card from the King and Queen (King George V and Mary of Teck) in a special envelope with the Royal Arms in red on it. And this is the message (in writing hand) "*With our best wishes for Christmas, 1914. May God protect you and bring you home safe.*" That is something to keep, isn't it? An officer has just told us that those men haven't had a cigarette since they left Southampton, hard luck. I wish we'd had enough for them. It is the smokes and the rum ration that has helped the British Army to stick it more than anything after the conviction that they've each one got that the Germans have got to be "done in" in the end. A Sergeant of the Coast Guard told me a cheering thing yesterday. He said he had a draft of young soldiers of only four months service in this week's business. "Talk of old soldiers" he said "you'd have thought these had, had years of it. When they were ordered to advance there was no stopping them." After all we are not going to Bethune but to Merville again. This is a very slow journey up, with long indefinite stops, we all got bad headaches by lunchtime from the intense cold and a short night following a heavy day. At lunch we had hot bricks for our feet, and hot food inside, which improved matters and I think by the time we get the patients on there will be chauffage. The orderlies are to have their Xmas dinner tomorrow, but I believe ours is to be tonight, if the patients are settled up in time.

Do not think from these details that we are at all miserable, we say "For King and Country" at intervals, and have many jokes over it all, and there is the never-failing game of going over what we'll all do and avoid doing after the War.

7 PM. Loaded up at Merville and now on the way back, not many badly wounded but a great many minor medicals, crocked up, nothing much to be done for them. We may have to fill up at Hazebrouck, which will interrupt the very festive Xmas dinner the French Staff are getting ready for us. It takes a man, French or British, to take decorating really seriously. The orderlies have done wonders with theirs. This lot of patients had Xmas dinner in their Clearing Hospitals today—and the King's Xmas card—and they will get Princess Mary's present. Here they finished Xmas cards and had oranges and bananas, and hot chicken broth directly they got in. 12 *Midnight*. Still on the road. We had a very festive Xmas dinner, going to the wards which were in charge of nursing orderlies between the courses. We had many toasts in French and English. The King, the President, Absent Friends, Soldiers and Sailors, and I had the *Blesses* and the *Malades*. We got up and clinked glasses with the French staff at every toast, and finally the little chef came in and sang to us in a very sweet musical tenor. Our great anxiety is to get as many orderlies and non-commissioned officers as possible through the day without being run in for drunk, but it is an uphill job, I don't know where they get it. We are wondering what the chances are of getting to bed tonight. 4 *AM*. Very late getting in to Boulogne, not unloading till morning. Just going to turn in now until breakfast time. End of Xmas Day. *Saturday, December 26th*. Saw my lambs off the train before breakfast. One man in the Royal

Warwickshire Regiment had twelve years service, a wife and two children, but "when Kitchener wanted more men" he rejoined. This week he got an explosive bullet through his arm, smashing it up to rags above the elbow. He told me he got a man "to tie the torn muscles up" and then started to crawl out, dragging his arm behind him. After some hours he came upon one of his own officers wounded, who said "Good God, sonny, you'll be bleeding to death if we don't get you out of this, catch hold of me and the Chaplain." "So he cuddled me, and I cuddled the Chaplain, and we got as far as the doctor." At the Clearing Hospital his arm was taken off through the shoulder joint, but I'm afraid it is too late. He is now a pallid wreck, dying of gangrene. But he would discuss the War, and when it would end, and ask when he'd be strong enough to sit up and write to that officer, and apologized for wanting drinks so often. He is one of the most top-class gallant gentlemen it's ever been my jolly good luck to meet. And there are hundreds of them. We had Princess Mary's nice brass box this morning. The Volunteer Aid Detachment here brought a present to every man on the train this morning, and to the orderlies.

They had 25,000 to distribute, cigarette cases, writing cases, books, pouches, and etc. The men were frightfully pleased, it was so unexpected. The processions of hobbling, doubled-up, silent, muddy, sitting-up cases who pour out of the trains want something to cheer them up, as well as the lying-downs. It is hard to believe they are the fighting men, now they've handed their rifles and bandoliers in. (It is snowing fast.) We have to go and drink the men's health at their spread at 1 o'clock. Then I hope a spell of sleep. We have chauffage on today to thaw the froidage, the pipes are frozen. *6 PM.* We all processed to the Orderlies Mess truck and the Officer in charge made a speech, and the Quartermaster Sergeant dished out drinks for us to toast with, and we had the King and all of ourselves with great enthusiasm. Mr. T. had to propose "the Sisters" and after a few trembling, solemn words about "we all know the good work they do" he suddenly giggled hopelessly, and it ended in a healthy splodge all round. Orders just come to be at Saint-Omer by 10 PM. If that means loading up further on about 1 AM. I think we shall all die! Too noisy here to sleep this afternoon. And the men are just now so merry with Tipperary and dressing up, that they will surely drop the patients off the stretchers, but we'll hope for the best. *Tuesday, December 29th.* We've had a quite useful day off today. Still at Sotteville-les-Rouen, had a walk this morning, also got through arrears of mending and letter writing. They played another football match this afternoon, and did much better than last time, but still got beaten. *Wednesday, December 30th.* Still at Sotteville-les-Rouen. One of our coaches is off being repaired here, and goodness knows how long we shall be stuck.

Had a walk this morning along the line. The train puffed past me on its way to Rouen for water. I tried to make the engine driver stop by spreading myself out in front of the engine, but he "shooed" me out of the way, and after some deliberation I seized a brass rail and leapt on to the footboard about halfway down the train, it wasn't at all difficult after all. We had Seymour Hicks's lot tacked on behind us, they are doing performances for the Hospitals and rest camps in Rouen today, but unfortunately we are too far out to go in. *January 3rd 1915.* A sergeant we took down to Havre yesterday told me of his battalion's very heavy losses. He said out of the 1400 of all ranks he came out with, there are now only 5 sergeants, 1 officer, and 72 men left. He said the young officers won't take cover "they get too excited and won't listen to people who've had a little experience."

One would keep putting his head out of the trench because he hadn't seen a German. "I kept telling of him" said the sergeant "but of course he got hit!" *Thursday, January 7th.* We moved out of Boulogne about 4 AM, and reached Merville (with many long waits) at 2 PM. Loaded up there, and filled up at Hazebrouck on way back. Many cases of influenza with high temperatures, also rheumatisms and bad feet, very few wounded. When they got the khaki hankies they said, "Khaki? That's extra." 9:30 PM. We have 318 on board this time, including four enterics, four diphtherias, and eighteen convalescent scarlets (who caught it from their billet). A quiet-looking little man has a very fine new German officer's helmet and sword. "He gave it to me" he said. "I had shot him through the lung. I did the wound up as best I could and tried to save him, but he died. He was coming for me with his sword." Seems funny to first shoot a man and then try to mop it up. The Germans don't, they finish you off. An officer on the train told me how another officer and twenty-five men were told off to go and take a new trench which had been dug in the night. Instead of the few they expected they found it packed with Germans, all asleep. "It's not a pretty story" he said "but you can't go first and tell them you're coming when you are outnumbered three to one." They had to bayonet every one of those sleeping Germans, and killed everyone without losing a man. All my half of the train had khaki hankies and sweets, they simply loved them. They are all, except the infectious cases, just out of the trenches, and such things make them absurdly happy, you would hardly believe it. I am keeping the writing cases and bull's eyes for the next lot. There were just enough mufflers to muffle the chilly necks of those who hadn't already got them. The wet has outwetted itself all day—it must be a record flood everywhere. We shall not unload tonight, so I had better think about turning in, as I have the third watch at 4 AM. I found some lovely eau-de-Cologne and shampoo powders from among the mufflers, and a pet aluminum candlestick. Such things give a Sister an absurd pleasure, you'd hardly believe it.

Friday, January 8th. Still pouring. We unloaded by 9 AM, got our mail in. My Wardmaster was so drunk tonight that the Quartermaster Sergeant had to send for the Officer in Charge. And he had just got his corporal's stripe. He was a particular ally of mine and was in South Africa. We are in that foulest of all homes for lost trains today, the Petit Vitesse siding out of Boulogne station, with the filth of all the ages around, about, and below us. You have to shut your window to keep out the smell of burning garbage and other horrors. It is nearly three months since I sat in a chair, except at meals, and that is only a flap-down seat, or saw a fire, except the pails of Coke the Tommies have on the lines. I expect we shall be off again tonight somewhere.

Monday morning, January 11th, Rouen. The approach to Rouen at six o'clock on a pitch dark, wet, and starlight morning, with the lights twinkling on the hills and on the river, and in the old wet streets, is a beautiful sight. My mad boy has been very quiet all night. *Thursday, January 14th.* We picked up a load in the dark and wet, with some very badly wounded, who kept us busy from 6 PM to 4 AM without stopping. Some were caked with mud exactly to their necks. One told me he got hit trying to dig out three of his section who were half buried by an exploded coal box. When he got hit, they were left, and eventually got finished by our own guns. Another lot of eleven were buried likewise, and are there still, but were all killed instantaneously. One man with part of his stomach blown away and his right thigh smashed was trying to get a corporal of his regiment in, but the corporal died when he got there, and he got it as well. He was smiling and thanking all night, and saying how comfortable he was.

Another we had to put off at Saint-Omer on the off chance of saving his life. He was made happy by two tangerine oranges. Many of the sitting ups have no voice, and they cough all night. We unloaded this morning, got a sleep this afternoon, and are now, 5 PM, on our way up again. The Clearing Hospitals are overflowing as of old, and like the Field Ambulances have more than they can cope with. We have to redress the septic things with H_2O_2 which keeps them going till they can be specially treated at the base. Some of the enterics are very bad, train journeys are not ideal treatment for enteric hemorrhage, but it has to be done. Two of my orderlies are very good with them, and take great care of their mouths, and know how to feed them.

It is a great anxiety when a great hulking General Duty Orderly has to take his turn on night duty with the badly wounded. It is time the sun shone somewhere—but it will surely, later on. *Sunday, January 17th.* We didn't unload at Boulogne last night, and are still (11 AM) taking them on to Etretat, a lovely place on the coast, about ten miles north of Havre. The hospital there is my old General Hospital, that I mobilized with, so it will be very jolly to see them all again. We are going through most lovely country on a clear sunny morning, and none of the patients are causing any anxiety, so it is an extremely pleasant journey, and we shall have a good rest on the way back. 3 PM. Just as I was beginning to forget there were such things as trenches and shrapnel and snipers, they told me a horrible story of two Camerons who got stuck in the mud and sucked down to their shoulders. They took an hour and a half getting one out, and just as they said to the other "all right, Jock, we'll have you out in a minute" he threw back his head and laughed, and in doing so got sucked right under, and is there still. They said there was no sort of possibility of getting him out, it was like a quicksand.

    One told me—not as such a very sensational fact—that he went for eleven weeks without taking off his clothes, *or a wash*, and then he had a hot bath and a change of everything. He remarked that he had to scrape himself with a knife. We have been traveling all day, and shan't get to Etretat until about 7 PM. It is a mercy we got our bad cases off at Boulogne—pneumonias, enterics, and some badly wounded, including the officer dressed in bandages all over. He was such a nice boy. When he was put into clean pajamas, and had a clean hanky with eau-de-Cologne, he said "by Jove, it's worth getting hit for this, after the smells of dead horses, dead men, and dead everything." He said no one could get into Messines, where there is only one house left standing, because of the unburied dead lying about. He couldn't move his arms, but he loved being fed with pigs of tangerine orange, and, like so many, he was chiefly concerned with "giving so much trouble." He looked awfully ill, but seldom stopped smiling. Of such is the Kingdom of Heaven. *Later. On way to Havre*. These are all bound for home and have been in hospital some time. They are clean, shaved, clothed, fed, and convalescent. Most of the lying downs are recovering from severe wounds of weeks back. It is quite new even to see them at that stage, instead of the condition we usually get them in.

    Some are the same ones we brought down from Bethune three weeks ago. One man was in a dugout going about twenty feet back from the trench, with sixteen others, taking cover from our howitzers and also from the enemy's. The cultivated ground is so soft with the wet that it easily gives and the bursting of one of our shells close by drove the roof in and buried these seventeen—four were killed and eleven injured by it, but only two were gotten out alive, and they were abandoned as dead. However, a rescue party of six faced the enemy shells above ground and tried to get them out. In doing this, two were killed and two wounded. The other two went on with it. My man and another man were pinned down by beams—the other had his face clear, but mine hadn't, though he could hear the picks above him. He gave up all hopes of getting out, but the other man when rescued said he thought this one was still alive, and then got him out unconscious. When he came to he was in hospital in a chapel, and it took him a long time to realize he was alive. "They generally take you into chapel before they bury you" he said "but I told them they done it the wrong way round with me. That was the worst mess ever I got into in this war" he finished up. *Wednesday, January 20th, Sotteville.* The others have all been out, but I've been a bit lazy and stayed in, washed my hair and mended my clothes. This place is looking awfully pretty today, because all the fields are flooded between us and the long line of high hills about a mile away, and it looks like a huge lake with the trees reflected in it. No orders to move, as usual. Ambulance trains travel as "specials" in a "marche" which means a gap in the timetable. We do not get final orders of where our destination is till we get to Hazebrouck or Saint-Omer. We have been six days without mail now, and have taken loads to Etretat and to Havre. *Thursday, January 21st.* We were not a whole day at Sotteville for once, moved out early this morning and are still traveling, 9 PM, between Abbeville and Boulogne. It has been especially slow journey, and, alas we didn't go by Amiens, the only time we might have, by daylight. Beauvais has a fine Cathedral from the outside. I believe we are to go straight on from Boulogne, so we may not get our six days mail, alas. *Friday, January 22nd.* We didn't get in to Boulogne until midnight, too late to get mails, and left early this morning. At Calais it was discovered that the kitchen had been left behind, in shunting a store wagon, so we have been hung up all day waiting for it at Saint-Omer. Went for a walk. It is a most interesting place to walk about in, swarming with every kind of war material, and the gray towers of the two Cathedrals looked lovely in a blue sky. Such a dazzling day, we were able to get on with painting the train, which is breaking out into the most marvelous labeling, the orderlies competing with each other. But when at 6 PM it seemed the day would never end, and in the kitchen was the mail bag—joy of joys. We have just got to Bailleul, 10:30 PM a few guns banging. We are wondering if we shall clear the hospitals tonight or wait until morning, depends if they are expecting convoys in tonight and are full.

Sunday, January 24th, 5 AM, Versailles. They've had a pretty good night most of them. If you see any compartment, you have only to say cheerfully "how are you getting on in this dugout" for every man to brighten visibly and there is a chorus of "if our dugouts was like this I reckon we shouldn't want no relieving" and a burst of wit and merriment follows. You can try it all down the train, it never fails. They are all in 1st class coaches, not 3rds or 2nds. 9:30 AM. There is a mist and a piercing north wind, and lots of mud. They told me another story of a man in the Royal Scots who was sunk in mud up to his shoulders, and the officer offered a canteen of rum and a sovereign to the first man who could get him out. For five hours thirteen men were digging for him, but it filled up always as they dug, and when they got him out he died. 6 PM. Just getting to Rouen, probably to load for Havre. They do keep us moving. We just had time to go and see the Palais Trianon with the French Sergeant (who is nearly a gentleman and an artist). Is there anything else quite like it anywhere else? It was *defense d'entrer* so we only wandered round the grounds and looked in at the windows, down the avenues and round the ponds and hundreds of statues, and went up the great escalier. Louis Quatorze certainly did himself proud. It was a long way to go, and we were walking for hours until we got dog-tired after the long load from Bailleul, and after lunch retired firmly on to our beds. I don't think we shall take patients on tonight. *Tuesday, 26th January*. A dazzling blue spring day. As we were not going in to load at Rouen until 3 PM, we went for the most glorious walk in this country. We crossed the ferry over the Seine to the foot of the steep high line of hills which eventually overlooks Rouen, and climbed up to the top by a lovely winding woody path in the sun. (The boatman congratulated us on the sinking of the *Blucher*, as a naval man, I suppose.) At the top we got to the Church of Le Bon Secours, which is in a very fine position with a marvelous view. We had some lovely cider in a very clean pub with a garden, and then took the tram down a very steep track into Rouen. I was standing in the front of the tram for the view over Rouen, which was dazzling, with the spires and the river and the bridges, when we turned a sharp corner and smashed bang into a market cart coming up our track. For the moment one thought the man and woman and the horse must be done for, the horse disappeared under the tram, and there arose such a screaming that the three Tommies and I fell over each other trying to get out to the rescue. When we did we found the man and woman had been luckily shot out clear of the tram, except that the man's hand was torn, and the old woman was frantically screaming "mon cheval, mon cheval, mon cheval" at least a hundred times without stopping. The others were out by this time and the two tram people, and the French clack went on at its top speed, while the Tommies and a very clever old woman out of the tram tried to cut the horse clear of the broken cart, and I did up the man's hand with our hankies, the only one concerned least was the horse, who kept quiet with its legs mixed up in the tram. At last the tram succeeded in moving clear of the horse without hurting it, and it was got up smiling after all. The outside old woman went on picking up the fish and the harness and the man was taken off to have his hand bathed, and the poor old woman of the cart stopped screaming "mon cheval, mon cheval" and went off to have a drink, and we walked on and found a train at Rouen. That sort of thing is always happening in France. I hope the overworked people at the heads of the various departments of the British Army realize how the men appreciate what they try and do for them in the trenches. If you ask what the billets are like, they say "barns and suchlike, they do the best they can for us." If you ask if the trench conditions are as bad for the Germans, they say "they're worse off, they ain't looked after like what we are." 9:30 PM. On way to Havre. I was just going to say that from the Seine to Le Havre there is nothing to report, when I came across a young educated German in my wards with his left leg off from the hip, and his right from below the knee, and a bad shell wound in his arm, all healed now, done at Ypres on 24th October. And I had an hour's most thrilling and heated conversation with him in German. He was very down on the English Sisters in hospital, because he says they hated him and didn't treat him like the rest. I said that was because they couldn't forget what his regiment (Bavarians) had done to the Belgian women and children and old men, and the French. And he said *he* couldn't forget how the Belgian women had put out the eyes of the German wounded at Liege and thrown boiling water on them.

I said they were driven to it. I asked him a lot of straight questions about Germany and the War, and he answered equally straight. He said they had food in Germany for ten years, and that they had ten million men, and that all the present students would be in the Army later on, and that practically the supply could never stop. And I said that however long they could go on, in the end there would be no more Germany because she was up against five nations. He said no man has any fear of a Russian soldier, and that though they were slow over it they would get Paris, but not London except by Zeppelins, he admitted that it would be *sehr schwer* to land troops in England, and that our Navy was the best, but we had so few soldiers, they hardly counted. He got very excited over the Zeppelins. I asked why the Germans hated the English, and he said "in Berlin we do not speak of the English at all, it is the French and the Russians we hate." He said the Turks were no good *zu helfen* and Austria not much better. He was very down on Belgium for resisting in the first place and said the *Schuld* was with France and Russia.

They were very much astonished when England didn't remain neutral. He had the cheek to say that three German soldiers were as good as twenty English, so I assured him that five English could do for fifty Germans, and went on explaining carefully to him how there could be no more Germany in the end because the right must win and he said "so you say in England, but we know otherwise in Deutchland, and I am a German." So as I am English we had to agree to differ. His faith in his *Vaterland* nearly made him cry and must have given him a temperature. I felt quite used up afterwards. He is fast asleep now. There is also an old soldier of sixty-three who says General French and General Smith-Dorrien photographed him as the oldest soldier in the British Army. He has four sons in it, one killed, two wounded. He was with General Low in the Chitral Expedition, and is called Donald MacDonald, of the King's Own Scottish Borderers. "Unfortunately I was reduced to the ranks for being drunk the other day" he said gaily. "But the Captain he said 'don't lose heart, MacDonald, you'll get it all back.' " *Saturday, January 30th.* We got up to Merville at one o'clock last night, and loaded up only forty-five, and are now just going to load up again at a place on the way back. We have been completely done out of the La Bassee business, haven't been near it. Two more of my General Hospital friends were, had to be evacuated in a hurry, as several orderlies was killed in the shelling. One of my badly wounded says "the Major" (whose servant he has been for four years) asked him to make up the fire in his dugout, while he went to the other end of the trench. While he was doing the fire a shell burst over the dugout and a bit went through his left leg and touched his right. If the Major had been sitting in his chair where he was a minute before, his head would have been blown off. He said "when the Major came back and found me, he drove everybody else away and stayed with me all day, and made me cocoa, and at night carried my stretcher himself and took me right to Headquarters." His eyes shine when he talks of "the Major" and he seems so proud he got it instead. I asked a boy in the sitting ups what was the matter with him. "Too small" he said. Another said "too young" he was aged fifteen, in the Black Watch. A young monkey, badly wounded in hand and throat (lighting a cigarette—the shatter to his hand saved worse destruction to his throat—though bad enough as it is) after we'd settled him in, fixed his eye on me and said "are you going to be in here along of us all the way?" "Yes" I said. "That's a good job" and he is taking good care to get his money's worth, I can tell you. Some of them are roaring at the man who made a gallant attempt to do justice to all his Xmas presents at once. There is a Sergeant-Major of the Royal Scots very indignant at having been made to go sick with bad feet. Any attempt to fuss over him is met with "I need no attention whatever, thank you, Sister. I feel more like apologizing for being in here. Only five weeks of active service" he growled.

Thursday, February 4th. For once we unloaded at Boulogne and went to bed instead of taking them on all night to Rouen. Moved out of Boulogne at 5 AM, breakfast at Saint-Omer, where we nearly got left behind strolling on the line during a wait. We are going to Merville in the mining district. 3 PM. We have just taken on about seventy Indians, mostly sick, some badly wounded. They are much cleaner than they used to be, in clothes, but not, alas, in habits. Aeroplanes are chasing a Taube overhead, but it is not being shelled. Guns are making a good noise all round. We are waiting for a convoy of British now. It is a lovely afternoon. The guns were shaking the train just now, one big bang made us all pop our heads out of the window to look for the bomb, but it wasn't a bomb. A rosy-faced white-haired Colonel here just came up to me and said "you've brought us more firing this afternoon than we've heard for a long time." We are filling up with British wounded now on the other half of the train. It is getting late, and we shan't unload tonight. *Later.* We were hours loading up because all the motor drivers are down with flu, and there were only two available. The rest are all busy bringing wounded in to the Clearing Hospital. The spell of having the train full of slight medical cases and bad feet seems to be over, and wounded are coming on again. Three of my sitting up Indians have temperatures of 104, so you can imagine what the lying downs are like. They are very anxious cases to look after, partly because they are another race and partly because they can't explain their wants, and they seem to want to be let die quietly in a corner rather than fall in with your notions of their comfort.

At Bailleul on our last journey we took on a heavenly white puppy just old enough to lap, quite wee and white and fat. He cries when he wants to be nursed, and barks in a lovely falsetto when he wants to play, and waddles after our feet when we take him for a walk, but he likes being carried best. Some Tommies on a truck at Railhead brought him up for us, they adore his little mother and two brothers. *Friday, February 5th, Boulogne.* We did get in late last night, and got to bed at 1 AM. They are unloading during the night again now, and also loading up at night.

One boy last night had lost his right hand, his left arm and leg were wounded, and both his eyes. "Yes, I've got more than my share" he said "but I'll get over it all right." I didn't happen to answer for a minute, and in a changed voice he said "Shan't I? Shan't I?" Of course I assured him he'd get quite well, and that he was ticketed to go straight to an eye specialist. "Thank God for that" he said, as if the eye specialist had already cured him, but it is doubtful if any eye specialist will save his eyes. Today has been a record day of brilliant sun, blue sky and warm air, and it has transformed the muddy, sloppy, dingy Boulogne of the last two months into something more like Cornwall. We couldn't stop on the train (there were no orders likely), in spite of being tired, but went in the town in the morning, and on the long stone pier in the afternoon, and then to tea at the buffet at the Maritime (where you have tea with real milk and fresh butter, and jam not out of a tin, and a china cup—luxuries beyond description). On the pier there were gulls, and a sunny sort of salt wind and big waves breaking, and a glorious view of the steep little town piled up in layers above the harbor, which is packed with shipping.

Sunday, February 7th. This is a little out-of-the-way town called Blendecque, rather in a hollow. Army Transport has been here before and the natives look at us as if we were Boches. There are 250 Royal Engineers inhabiting a long truck train here. We have given them all our mufflers and mittens, they had none, and the officer has had our officers to tea with him. Our men have played a football match with them—drawn. We went for a splendid walk this morning uphill to a pine wood bordered by a Moor. I've now got in my bunky hole (it is not quite six feet square) a polypod fern, a plate of moss, a pot of white hyacinths, and also catkins, violets, and mimosa. I suppose we shall move on tonight if there is a marche. Many hundreds of French cavalry passed across the bridge over this cutting this morning, they looked so jolly. 9:45 PM. We are just getting to the place where all the fighting is—La Bassee way. Probably we shall load up with wounded tonight. There's a great flare some way off that looks like the burning villages we used to see round Ypres. It is a very dark night. *Tuesday, February 9th.* Again they unloaded us at Boulogne last night, and we are now, 11 AM, on our way up again. The Indians I had were a very interesting lot. The race differences seem more striking the better you get to know them.

The Gurkhas seem to be more like Tommies in temperament and expression, and all the Punjabi Mussulmans and the best of the Sikhs and Jats might be Princes and Prime Ministers in dignity, feature, and manners. When a Sikh refuses a cigarette (if you are silly enough to offer him one) he does it with a gesture that makes you feel like a housemaid who ought to have known better. The beautiful Punjabi Mussulmans smile and salaam and say Merbani, however ill they are, if you happen to hit upon something they like. They all make a terrible fuss over their kit and their puggarees and their belongings, and refuse to budge without them. Sister found her orders to leave when we got in, but she doesn't know where she is going. So after this trip we shall be three again, which is a blessing, as there are not enough wards for four, and no one likes giving any up. It also gives us a spare bunk to store our warehouses of parcels for men, which entirely overflow our own dugouts. As soon as you've given out one lot, another bale arrives. We have had every kind of infectious disease to nurse in this war, except smallpox.

The Infectious Ward is one of mine, and we've had scarlet fever, measles, mumps, and diphtheria. 7 PM. We got to the new place where we wait for a marche, just at tea time, and we had a grand walk up to the moor, where you can see half over France each way. There is a traveling wireless station up there.

Each pole has its receiver in a big gray motor lorry by the roadside, where they live and sleep. The road wound down to a little curly village with a beautiful old gray church. On the top of the moor on the way back it was dark, and the flash signals were Morse [coding] away to each other from the different hills.

It reminded me of the big forts on the kopjes round Pretoria. I had my first French class this afternoon at Saint-Omer, in the men's mess truck. There were seventeen, including the Quartermaster Sergeant and the cook's boy. I'd got a small blackboard in Boulogne, and they all had notebooks, and the Quartermaster Sergeant had arranged it very nicely. They were very keen, and got on at a great pace. They weren't a bit shy over trying to pronounce, and will I think make good progress. They have a great pull over men of their class in England, by their opportunities of listening to French spoken by the French, such a totally different language to French spoken by most English people. My instruction book is [Victor] Hugo's, which is a lightning method compared to the usual school books. They are doing exercises for me for next time. *Friday, February 12th, 6 AM.* We did a record loading up in fifty minutes last night, chiefly medical cases, and took eight hours to crawl to Boulogne.

Now we are on the way for Havre, but shall not get there till about 10 PM tonight, so they will have a long day in the train. A good many of the lying downs are influenza, with high temperatures and no voice. It is a bore getting to Boulogne in the night, as we miss our mails and the *Daily Mail*. 7 PM. This is an interminable journey. Have not yet reached Rouen, and shan't get to Havre until perhaps 2 AM. The patients are getting very weary, especially the sitting ups. The wards run like a hospital.

Some of the orderlies are now getting quite keen on having their wards clean and swept, and the meals and feeds up to time, and the washings done, but it has taken weeks to bring them up to it. When they do all that well I can get on with the diets, temperatures, treatments, and dressings and etc. On the long journeys we take round at intervals smokes, chocolate, papers, hankies and etc., when we have them. The Victoria League has done me well in bales of hankies. They simply love the affectionate and admiring messages pinned on from New Zealand, and one of them always volunteers to answer them. We shall be up in shifts again tonight. We are all hoping to have a day in Rouen on the way back, for baths, hair washing, shopping, seeing the Paymaster, and showing the new Sister the sights. For sheer beauty and interestingness it is the most endearing town, you don't know which you love best—its setting with the hills, river, and bridge, or its beautiful spires and towers and marvelous old streets and houses. *Saturday, 13th February, Havre.* It is four months today since I joined the train. It seems much longer in some ways, and yet the days go by very quickly—even the off days, and when the train is full the hours fly. We went into the familiar streets this morning that we saw so much of in August "waiting for orders" and had a look at the sea. The train moved off at tea time, so we had the prettiest part of the journey in a beautiful evening sunlight, lighting up the woods and hills.

The palm is out, and the others saw primroses. We have also seen some snowdrops. After a heavy journey, with two nights out of bed, you don't intend to do any letter writing or mending or French classes, but look out of the window or sleep or read *Dolly Dialogues*. You always get compensation for these journeys in the longer journey back, with probably a wait at Rouen or Sotteville, and possibly another at Boulogne.

We have been going up and down again very briskly this last fortnight between Boulogne and the Back of the Front.

Ash Wednesday, February 17th, 6 AM. We took on a very bad load of wounded at Poperinge, more like what used to happen three months ago in the same place, they were only wounded the night before, and some the same day. The Clearing Hospital had to be cleared immediately. We have just got to

Boulogne, and are going to unload here at 8:30 AM. Must stop. Hope to get a week's mails today. A brisk air battle between one British and one French and two Taubes was going on when we got there, and a perfect sky for it. Very high up. A wounded major on the train was talking about the men. "It's not a case of our leading the men, we have a job to keep up with them." It was a pretty sad business getting them off the train this morning, there were so many compound fractures, and no amount of contriving seemed to come between them and the jolting of the train all night. And, to add to the difficulties, it was pouring in torrents and icy cold, and the railway people refused to move the train under cover, so they went out of a warm train on to damp stretchers in an icy rain. They were nearly all in thin pajamas, as we'd had to cut off their soaking khaki, they were practically straight from the trenches. But once clear of trains, stretchers, and motor ambulances they will be warmed, washed, fed, bedded, and their fractures set under an anesthetic. One man had his arm blown to pieces on Monday afternoon, had it amputated on Monday night, and was put into one of our wards on Tuesday, and admitted to Base Hospital on Wednesday. But that is ticklish work. One boy, a stretcher bearer, with both legs severely wounded, very nearly bled to death. He was pulled round somehow. About midnight, when he was packed up in wool and hot water bottles and etc., when I asked him how he was feeling, he said gaily "quite well, delightfully warm, thank you." We got him taken to hospital directly the train got in at 4 AM. The others were unloaded at 9 AM. We are now—5 PM on our way to Etaples probably to clear the General Hospital there, either tonight or tomorrow morning. It hasn't stopped pouring all day.

  It took me until lunch to read my enormous mail. Major has heard today that the French railway people want his train back again for passenger traffic, so the possibility of our all being suddenly disbanded and dispersed is hanging over us, but I believe it has been threatened before. *Friday, February 19th.* We left Boulogne at 5 AM today, and were delayed all the morning farther up by one of the usual French collisions. A guard had left his end of a train and was on the engine, so he never noticed that twelve empty trucks had come uncoupled and careered down a hill, where they were run into and crumpled up by a passenger train. The guard of that one was badly injured (fractured spine) but the passengers only shaken. At Saint-Omer there was a wild stampede, the Khaki Train had all its doors locked, and we had miles to go inside to get out. Their orderlies shouted to ours to pull the communication cord—the only way of appealing to the distant engine, so it slowed down, and we clambered breathlessly on. We are sidetracked now at the jolly place of the Moor and the wireless lorries, probably move on in the night. *Saturday, February 20th, 9 PM.* We've had a very unsatisfactory day, loading up at four different places, and still on our way down. I'm just going to lie down, to be called at 2 AM. Now we're four, two go to bed for the whole night and the other two take the train for half the night when we have a light load, as today. If they are all bad cases, we have two on and two off for the two watches. We have some Indians on today, but most British and not many *blesses*. The other day a huge train of reinforcements got divided by mistake, the engine went off with all the officers, and the men had a joyride to themselves, invaded the cafes, where they sometimes get half poisoned, and in half an hour's time there was a big scrap among themselves, with fifty casualties. So the story runs. A humane and fatherly orderly has just brought me a stone hot water bottle for my feet as I write this in the rather freezing dispensary coach in the middle of the train, in between my rounds. All the worst cases and the Indians were put off at Boulogne, and the measles, mumps, and diphtherias, so there isn't much to do, some are snoring like an aeroplane. *Monday, February 22nd.* We got a short walk yesterday evening after unloading at Rouen. There was a glorious sunset over the bridge, and the lights just lighting up, and Rouen looked its most beautiful. We slept at Sotteville, and this morning Sister and I walked down the line into Rouen and saw the Paymaster and the Cathedral, and did some shopping, and had a boiled egg and real butter and tea for lunch, and came back in the tram. Sister is in bed with influenza. The lengthening days and better weather are making a real difference to the gloom of things, and though there is a universal undercurrent of feeling that enormous sacrifices will have to be made, it seems to be shaping for a step farther on, and an ultimate return to sanity and peace. It is such a vast upheaval when you are in the middle of it, that you sometimes actually wonder if everyone has gone mad, or who has gone mad, that all should be grimly working, toiling, slaving, from the firing line to the base, for more destruction, and for more highly finished and uninterrupted destruction, in order to get peace. And the men who pay the cost in intimate personal and individual suffering and in death are not the men who made the war.

Thursday, February 25th. Moved up to the place with the moor during the night. Glorious, clear, sunny morning. Couldn't leave the train for a real walk, as there were no orders. This time last year the last thing one intended to do was to go and travel about France for six months, with occasional excursions into Belgium. The *Times* sometimes comes the next day now.

9 PM. The ways of French railways are impenetrable, in spite of orders for Bailleul before lunch, we are still here, and less than ever able to leave the train for a walk. This is the fourth day with no patients on—the longest "off" spell since before Christmas. It shows there's not much doing or much medical leakage. *Saturday, February 27th, 9 PM, Hotel at Boulogne.* All the efforts to get my seven days leave have failed, as I thought they would. *Wednesday, March 3rd, Boulogne.* There is not a great deal to do or see here, especially on a wet day. *Friday, March 5th, 5 PM.* On way down from Chocques—mixed lot of wounded, medicals, Indians, and Canadians. I have a lad of 24 with both eyes destroyed by a bullet, and there is a bad "trachy."

Nothing very much has been going on, but the German shells sometimes plop into the middle of a trench, and each one means a good many casualties. 10 PM. We've had a busy day, and are not home yet. My boy with the dressings on his head has not the slightest idea that he's got no eyes, and who is going to tell him? The pain is bad, and he has to have a lot of morphine, with a cigarette in between. We shall probably not unload tonight, and I am to be called at 2 AM. The infectious ward is full with British enterics, diphtheria, and measles, and Indian mumps.

Saturday, March 6th, Boulogne. Instead of being called at 2 for duty, was called at 1 to go to bed, as they unloaded us at that hour. Last night we pulled up at Hazebrouck alongside a troop train with men, guns, and horses, just out from the Midlands. Two lads in a truck with their horses asked me for cigarettes. Luckily, thanks to the Train Comforts Fund's last whack, I had some.

One said solemnly that he had a "coosin" to avenge, and now his chance had come. They both had shining eyes, and not a rollicking but an eager excitement as they asked when the train would get "there" and looked as if they could already see the shells and weren't afraid. *Sunday, March 7th*. We are stuck in the jolly place close to General Headquarters, but can't leave the train as there are no orders. I've been having a French class, with the wall of the truck for a blackboard, and occasional bangs from a big gun somewhere. *Tuesday, March 9th, 12 Noon*. We are passing through glorious country of wooded hills and valleys, with a blue sky and shining sun, and all the patients are enjoying it. It is still very cold, and there is a little snow about. They call their goatskin coats "Teddy Bears." One very ill boy, wounded in the lungs who was put off at Abbeville, was wailing "Where's my Mary box?" as his stretcher went out of the window. We found it, and he was happy. *Friday, March 12th*. We came straight through Boulogne in the night, and have been stuck halfway to the Front all day, I don't know why. *Saturday, March 13th*. We woke at the railhead for Bethune this morning, and cleared there and at the next place, mostly wounded and some Indians. It was frightfully interesting up there today, we saw the famous German prisoners taken at Neuve Chapelle being entrained, and we could hear our great bombardment going on—the biggest ever known in any war. The feeling of Advance is in the air already, and even the wounded are exulting in it. The Indians have bucked up like anything. We are on our way down now, and shall probably unload at Boulogne. No time for more now. 11 PM. We unloaded at Boulogne by 10 PM, and are now on our way up again, shortest time we've ever waited—one hour after the last patient is off.

Army Transports have been tearing up empty and back full all day, and are all being unloaded at Boulogne, so that they can go quickly up again. Boulogne has been emptied before this began. They were an awfully brave lot of badly wounded today, but they always are. Just now they don't mind anything—even getting hit by our artillery by mistake. Some of them who were near enough to see the effect of our bombardment on the enemy's trenches say they saw men, legs, and arms shot into the air. And the noise—they gasp in telling you about it. "You could never believe it" they say. An officer told me exactly how many guns we used, all firing at once. And poor fat Germans, and thin Germans, and big Germans, and little Germans at the other end of it. A man of mine with his head shattered and his hand shot through was trepanned last night, and his longitudinal sinus packed with gauze. He was on the train at 9 this morning, and actually improved during the day. He came to in the afternoon enough to remark, as if he were doing a French exercise. The next time he woke he said it again, and later on with great difficulty he gave me the address of his girl, to whom I am to write a postcard. I do hope they'll pull him through. *Tuesday, March 16th*. We loaded up very early this morning with 316 Indians, and are just getting into Boulogne. I expect we shall be sent up again this evening. One of the Sikhs wailed before, during, and after his hand was dressed. A big Punjabi Mussulman stuffed his hanky between his teeth and bit on it, and never uttered, and it was a much worse one. What was he to do with crying, he said, it was right for it to be done. May God bring blessings on my head whereas it was full of pain, lo, now it was atcha. *Wednesday, March 17th*. I didn't tell you that yesterday a kind Indian Medical Service colonel at the place where we took the Indians on showed us a huge pile of used shell cases near the station, and we all had some. I've got a twelve-pounder and a sixteen-pounder, like my pom-poms, only huge. Next time he's going to get us some Gurkha's kukries. On the way down a little Gurkha happened to get off the train for a minute, and when he looked round, the train had gone past him. He ran after it, and perched on one of the buffers till the next stop, when he reappeared, trembling with fright, but greeted with roars of amusement by the other Gurkhas. We had some more today, including twelve with mumps, and one who insisted on coming with his mumpy friend though quite well himself. We woke this morning at Merville, one of the railheads for Neuve Chapelle, and loaded up very early, guns going as hard as ever. Mine were a very bad lot—British (except the twelve native mumpers), including some brave Canadians. They kept me very busy till the moment of unloading, which is a difficult and painful business with these bad ones, but the orderlies are getting very gentle and clever with them. I had among them eight Germans, several mere boys. One insisted on kissing my hand, much to the orderly's amusement. (A truckful of pigs outside is making the most appalling noise. 11 PM. I am writing in bed. We generally move up about 11:30 PM.) Every journey we hear thrilling accounts, rumors, and forecasts, most of which turn out to be true. We have had a lot of the Saint Eligius people. There were several versions of a story of some women being found in a captured German trench. One version said they were French captives, another that they were German wives. In one compartment were five Tommies being awfully kind to one German, and yet if he had a rifle, and they had theirs, he'd be a dead man. The hospitals at Boulogne are so busy that no one goes off duty, and they are operating all night. We had time for a blow across the bridge after unloading, and I happened to meet my friend (who was at Havre). She is on night duty, and they are grappling with those awful cases all night as hard as they can go. Four were taken out of the motor ambulances dead this week, the jolting is the last straw for the worst ones, it can't possibly be helped "but it seems a pity." In all this rush we happen to have had nights in bed, which makes all the difference. The pigs still squeal, but I must try and go to sleep. *Tuesday, March 23rd, 9 PM.* Waiting all day at General Headquarters, things are unusually quiet, one train has been through with only ninety, and another with a hundred. We went for a walk along the canal this morning with the wee puppy, and this afternoon saw over the famous jute factory Convalescent Home, where they have a thousand beds under one roof, it is like a town divided into long wards—dining rooms, recreation rooms, dressing station, chiropodist, tailor's shop and etc.—by shoulder high canvas or sailcloth screens, they have outside a kitchen, a boiler, a disinfector for clothes, and any amount of baths. They have a concert every Saturday night. The men looked so absolutely happy and contented with cooked instead of trench food, and baths and games and piano, and books and writing and etc. They stay usually ten days, and are by the tenth day supposed to be fit enough for the trenches again, it often saves them a permanent breakdown from general causes, and is a more economical way of treating small disablements than sending them to the Base Hospitals. Last week they had five hundred wounded to treat, and two of the Medical Officers had to take a supply train of seven hundred slightly wounded down to Rouen with only two orderlies. They had a bad journey. I had a French class after tea. We are now expecting today's London papers, which are due here about 9 PM. Have got some Hindustani to learn for my next lesson, so will stop this. *Wednesday, March 24th.* Moved on at 11 PM and woke up at Chocques, a few smallish guns going. Loaded up there very early and at two other places, and are now nearly back to Boulogne, mostly wounded and a few Indians, some of them are badly damaged by bombs. The men in the Neuve Chapelle touch were awfully disappointed that they weren't allowed to push on to Lille. According to the men, we shall be busy again at the end of this week. *Midnight.* On way to coast near Havre. Put all worst cases off at Boulogne, the rest mostly sleeping peacefully. Passed a place on coast where six hundred British workmen are working from 7 AM to 10 PM building hospital huts for 12,000 beds, a huge encampment, ready for future business. Have seen cowslips and violets on wayside. Lovely moonlight night. Train running very smoothly. *Thursday, March 25th.* There is a great deal of very neat and elaborate glass market gardening going on round

Rouen, it looks from the train an unbroken success, thousands of fat little plants with their glass hats off and thousands more with them on, and very little labor that can be seen. But the vegetables we buy for our mess are not particularly cheap.

9 PM, *Rouen*. There are three trains waiting here, which means a blessed lull for the people in the firing line. There was a day or two after Neuve Chapelle when the number of wounded overflowed the possibilities of "collection" the stretcher bearers were all hit and the stretchers were all used, and there were not enough medical officers to cope with the numbers (extra ones were hurried up from the Base Hospitals very quickly), and if you wanted to live you had to walk or crawl—or stay behind and die.

We had a Canadian on who told me last night that he should never forget the stream of wounded dragging themselves along that road from Neuve Chapelle to Estaires who couldn't be found room for in the motor ambulances. Two trains picked them up there, and there were many deaths on the trains and in the motor ambulances. The "evacuation" was very thorough and rapid to the bases and to the ships, but in any great battle involving enormous casualties on both sides there must be some gaps you can't provide for. *Tuesday, March 30th*. This cold wind has dried up the mud everywhere, and until today there's been a bright sun with it. The men clean the train and play football, and the Medical Officers take the puppy out, and everybody swears a great deal at a fate which no one can alter, and we are all craving for our week-old mails. *Wednesday, March 31st*. We actually acquired an engine and got a move on at 4 o'clock this morning, and are now well away north. Just got out where we stopped by a fascinating winding river, and got some brave marsh marigolds. 5 PM. Just getting into Boulogne. *Good Friday, April 2nd*. We got into Boulogne on Wednesday from Sotteville at 5 PM, and as soon as the train pulled up a new Sister turned up "to replace Sister" so I prepared for the worst and fully expected to be sent to Havre or Etretat or Rouen, and began to tackle my six and a half months accumulation of belongings. In the middle of this the Matron-in-Chief arrived with my Movement Orders "to proceed forthwith to report to the Officer in Charge of Field Ambulance for duty" so hell became heaven, and here I am at Railhead waiting for a motor ambulance to take me and my baggage wherever it is to be found. The Railway Transport Officer at Boulogne let me come up as far as Saint-Omer (or rather the next waiting place beyond) and get sent on by the Railway Transport Officer there. We waited there all yesterday, lovely sunny day, and in the evening the Railway Transport Officer sent me on in a supply train which was going to the railhead for Field Artillery.

The officer in charge of it was very kind, and turned out of his carriage for me into his servant's, and apologized for not having cleared out every scrap of his belongings. The "Mess" saw me off, with many farewell jokes and witticisms. This supply train brings up one day's rations to the 1st Corps from Havre, and takes a week to do it there and back. This happens daily for one corps alone, so you can imagine the work of the Army Service Corps at Havre. At Railhead he is no longer responsible for his stuff when the lorries arrive and take up their positions end on with the trucks. They unload and check it, and it is done in four hours. That part of it is now going on. When we got to Railhead at 10:15 PM the Railway Transport Officer said it was too late to communicate with the Field Ambulance, and so I slept peacefully in the officer's bunk with my own rugs and cushion. We had tea about 9 PM. This morning after a sketchy wash in the supply train, and a cup of early tea from the officer's servant, I packed up and went across for breakfast, many jeers at my having got the sack so soon.

11 AM. Had an interesting drive here through a village packed with men billeted in barns and empty houses—the usual aeroplane buzzing overhead, and a large motor ambulance convoy by the wayside. We are in the town itself, and the building is labeled Dressing Station for Officers. The men are in a French Civil Hospital run very well by French nuns, and it has been decided to keep the French and English nurses quite separate, so the only difference between the two hospitals is that the one for the men has French Sisters, with Royal Army Medical Corps orderlies and Medical Officers, and the other for officers has

English Sisters, with Royal Army Medical Corps orderlies and Medical Officers. There are forty-seven beds here, all officers. One Army Sister in charge, myself next, and two staff nurses, one on night duty. There are two floors, I shall have charge of the top floor. We are billeted out, but I believe mess in the hospital. All this belongs to the French Red Cross, and is lent to us. The surgical outfit is much more primitive even than on the train, as Field Artillery may carry so little. The operating theatre is at the other hospital. As far as I can see at present we don't have the worst cases here, except in a rush like Neuve Chapelle. It will be funny to sleep in a comfortable French bed in an ordinary bedroom again. It will be rather like Le Mans over again, with a billet to live in, and officers to look after, but I shall miss the Jocks and the others. *Later*. Generals and "Red Hats" simply bristle around. A collection of them has just been in visiting the sick officers. We had a big Good Friday service at 11, and there is another at 6 PM. The Bishop of London is coming round today.

Still Good Friday, 10 PM. Who said Active Service? I am writing this in a wonderful mahogany bed, with a red satin quilt, in a paneled room, with the sort of furniture drawing rooms have on the stage, and electric light, and medallions and bronzes, and oil-paintings and old engravings, and blue china and mirrors all about. It is a huge house like a Chateau, on the Place, where Generals and Officers are usually billeted. The fat and smiling caretaker says she's had two hundred since the war. She insisted on pouring eau-de-Cologne into my hot bath. It is really a lovely house, with polished floors and huge tapestry pictures up the staircase. And all this well within range of the German guns. After last night, in the Army Service Corps officer's kind but musty little chilly second class carriage, it is somewhat of a change. And I hadn't had my clothes off for three days and two nights. This billet is only for one night, tomorrow I expect I shall be in some grubby little room nearby. It has taken the Town Commandant, the Officer in Charge of a French interpreter, and an Royal Horse Artillery officer and several Noncommissioned Officers and orderlies, to find me a billet—the town is already packed tight and they have to continue the search tomorrow. This afternoon I went all over the big French hospital where our men are.

The French nuns were charming, and it was all very nice. The women's ward is full of women and girls *blesses* by shells, some with a leg off and fractured—all very cheerful. One shell the other day killed thirty-one and wounded twenty-seven—all Indians. I am not to start work until tomorrow, as the wards are very light, nearly all the officers up part of the day, so at 6 PM, I went to the Bishop of London's mission service in the theatre. A staff officer on the steps told me to go to the left of the front row (where all the red hats and gold hats sit), but I funked that and sat modestly in the last row of officers. There were about a hundred officers there, and a huge solid pack of men, no other woman at all. The Bishop, looking very white and tired but very happy, took the service on the stage, where a Padre was thumping the hymns on the harmonium (which shuts up into a sort of matchbox). It was a voluntary service, and you know the nearer they are to the firing line the more they go to church. It was extraordinarily moving. The Padre read a sort of liturgy for the war taken from the Russians, far finer than any of ours, we had printed papers, and the response was "Lord, have mercy" or "Grant this, O Lord." It came each time like bass clockwork. Troops are just marching by in the dark. Hundreds passed the hospital this afternoon. I must go to sleep. The Bishop dashed in to see our sick officers here, and then motored off to dine with the Quartermaster General. He's had great services with the cavalry and every other brigade. *Easter Eve*, 10 PM. Have been on duty all day until 5 PM. They are nearly all "evacuated" in a few days, so you are always getting a fresh lot in. Another Army Sister turned up today in a motor from Poperinge to take the place of the two who were originally here, who have now gone. At six this morning big guns were doing their Morning Hate very close to us, but they have been quiet all day. Two days ago the village two and a half miles southeast of us was shelled. I found my own new billet this morning before going on duty, it is in a very old little house over a shop. It is a sort of attic, and I am not dead sure whether it is clean on top and lively underneath but time will show. The shop lady and her daughter Maria Therese are full of zeal and kindness to make me comfortable, but they stayed two hours watching me unpack and making themselves agreeable. And when I came in from dinner from the cafe, where we now have our meals (quite decent), she and papa drew up a chair for me to *causer* in their parlor, to my horror. At 8 PM the town suddenly goes out like a candle, all lights are put out and the street suddenly empty. After that, at intervals, only motorcyclists buzz through and regiments tramp past going back to billets. They sound more warlike than anything. Such a lot are going by now. *Easter Sunday, 3 PM*. The service at 7 this morning in the theatre was rather wonderful. Rows of officers and packs of men. We have been busy in the ward all the morning. I'm off 2-5, and shall soon go out and take chocolate Easter eggs to the men in the hospice. The officers have any amount of cigarettes, chocolates, novels, and newspapers. A woman came and wept this morning with my billeter over their two sons, who are prisoners, not receiving the parcels of *tabac* and *pain* and *gateaux* that they send. They think we ought to starve the German prisoners to death. This morning in the ward I suddenly found it full of Gold Hats and Red Tabs, three Generals and their Aide-de-Camps visiting the sick officers. *Easter Monday*. It is a pouring wet day, and the mud is Flanderish. Never was there such mud anywhere else. A gunner major has just been telling me you get a fine view of the German positions from the Cathedral tower here, and can see shells bursting like the pictures. He said his guns had the job of peppering La Bassee the last time they shelled this place, and they gave it such a dusting that this place has been let severely alone since.

    He thinks they'll have another go at this when we begin to get hold of La Bassee, but the latter is a very strong position. It begins to be "unhealthy" to get into any of the villages about three miles from here, which are all heaps of bricks now? I'm leaving my billet tomorrow, as they want us to be in one house. And our house is the Maire's Chateau, the palatial one, so we shall live in the lap of luxury as never before in this country. And have hot baths with eau-de-Cologne every night, or cold every morning. And the woman is going to faire our cuisine there for us, so we shan't have to wait hours in the cafe for our meals. There is only one waiter at the cafe, who is a beautiful, composed, silent girl of 16, who will soon be dead of overwork. She is not merely pretty, but beautiful, with the manners of a princess. An officer was brought in during the night with a compound fractured arm. He stuck a very painful dressing today, and said to me afterwards "I've got three kids at home, they'll be awfully bucked over this." He had said it was "nothing to write home about." Another was awfully impressed because a man in his company—who had half his leg blown off, said when they came to pick him up "never mind me—take so-and-so first"—"just like those chaps you read of in books, you know." It was decided that he meant Sir Philip Sidney. Yesterday afternoon I had a lovely time taking round chocolate Easter eggs to our wounded in the French hospital. The sweetest, merriest *Ma-Sceur* took me round, and insisted on all the orderlies having one too. They adore her, and stand up and salute when she comes into the ward, and we had enough for the *jeunes filles* and the grannies in the women's ward of *blessees*. They were a huge success. Those men get very few treats.

Thursday, April 8th. Talking of billets, a General and his Staff are coming to this Chateau tomorrow and we three have got to turn out, possibly to a house opposite on the same square, which is empty. We live in terror of unknown powers-that-be suddenly sending us down. Everyone here are very keen that we should be as comfortably billeted as possible. He said today "later on you may get an awful place to live in." Of course we are aiming at becoming quite indispensable. If you can once get your Medical Officers to depend on you for having everything they want at hand, and for making the patients happy and contented, and the orderlies in good order, they soon get to think they can't do without you. There are two nice tea shops where all the officers of the 1st and 2nd Divisions go and have tea.

Saturday, April 10th, 10:30 PM. It is difficult to settle down to sleep tonight, the sky is lit up with flashes and star shells, and every now and then a big bang shakes the house, above the almost continuous thud, thudding, and the barking of the machine guns and the crackling of rifle firing, they are bringing in more today, both here and at the Hospice, and we are tired enough to go to sleep as if we were at home, I shouldn't wonder if the Night Sister had a busy night. We had to rig up our day room for an operation this evening. We couldn't manage to get any food today, as our rations hadn't come up, so we went back to the cafe. The dead silence, darkness, and emptiness of the streets after 8 o'clock are very striking. *Monday, April 12th.* No mail today. This has been a very quiet day, fewer columns, aeroplanes, and guns, and the three bad officers holding their own so far. The others come and go. *Tuesday, April 13th.* There is something quite fiendish about the crackling of the rifle firing tonight, and every now and then a gun like "Mother" speaks and shakes the town. Last night it was quite quiet. All leave has been stopped today, and there are the wildest rumors going about of a big naval engagement, the forcing of the Narrows, and the surrender of Saint-Mihiel, and anything else you like. These Medical Officers have always hung on to the most hopeless, both here and at the Hospice, beyond the last hope, and when they pull through there is great rejoicing. It doesn't seem somehow the right thing to do, to undress and get into bed with these crashes going on, but I suppose staying up won't stop it. *Wednesday, April 14th.* Very quiet day, it always is after exciting rumors which come to nothing. But it has been noisier than usual in the daytime. I rested in my off time and didn't go out. The Victoria League sent some awfully nice lavender bags today, and some tins of Keating's, which will be of future use, I expect. Just now, one is mercifully and strangely free from the minor scourges of war. The German trenches captured at Neuve Chapelle, and now occupied by us, are full of legs and arms, which emerge when you dig. Some are still caught on the barbed wire and can't be taken away. We are not being at all clever with our rations just now, and manage to have indescribably nasty and uneatable meals. But we shall get it better in time, by taking a little more trouble over it. We had scrambled eggs tonight, which I made standing on a chair, because the gas ring is so high, and Sister holding up a very small dim oil lamp. But they were a great success. And then we had soup with fried potatoes in it and tea. *Friday, April 16th.* At about 7:30 this evening I was writing the day report when the sergeant came in with three candles and said an order had come for all lights to be put out and only candles used. So I had to put out all the lights and give the astonished officers my three candles between them, while the sergeant went out to get some more. The town looks very weird with all the street lamps out and only glimmers from the windows. It was kept pretty darkened before. It may be because of the Zeppelin at Bailleul on Wednesday or another may be reported somewhere about. This afternoon I saw a soldier's funeral, which I have never seen before. He was shot in the head yesterday, and makes the four hundred and eleventh British soldier buried in this cemetery. I happened to be there looking at the graves, and the French gravedigger told me there was to be another buried this afternoon. The gravedigger's wife and children are with the Allemands he told me, the other side of La Bassee, and he has no news of them or they of him. It was very impressive and moving, the Union Jack on the coffin (a thin wooden box) on the wagon, and a firing party, and about a hundred men and three officers and the Padre. It was a clear blue sky and sunny afternoon, and the Padre read beautifully and the men listened intently. The graves are dug trenchwise—very close together—practically all in one continuous grave, each with a marked cross. There is a long row of officers, and also seven Germans and five Indians. The two Zeppelins reported last night must have gone to bed after putting out all our lights, as nothing happened anywhere. The birds and buds in the garden opposite make one long for one's lost leave, but I suppose they will keep. We have only nine officers in today, everything is very quiet everywhere, but troop trains are very busy. 10:30 PM. It is getting noisy again. Some batteries on our right next the French lines are doing some thundering, and there are more star shells than usual lighting up the sky on the left. They look like fireworks. They are sent up in the firing line to see if any groups of enemy are crawling up to our trenches in the dark. When they stop sending theirs up we have to get busy with ours to see what they're up to. It's funny to see that every night from your bedroom windows. They give a tremendous light as soon as they burst. When I went into the big church for benediction this evening at 6:30, every estaminet and cafe and tea shop was packed with soldiers, and also as usual every street and square. At seven o'clock they were all emptying, as there is an order today to close all cafes and etc., at seven instead of eight. All lights are out again tonight. Another aeroplane was being shelled here this evening. *Sunday, April 18th, 9:30 PM.* It has been another dazzling day. A major of one of the Indian regiments came in this evening. He said the Boches (Germans) are throwing stones across to our men wrapped in paper with messages like this written on them "why don't you stop the War? We want to get home to our wives these beautiful days, and so do you, so why do you go on fighting?" The sudden beauty of the spring and the sun has made it all glaringly incongruous, and everyone feels it. One badly wounded officer got it going out of his dugout to attend to a man of his company who was hit by a sniper in an exposed place, one of his subalterns told me. His own account, of course, was a rambling story leaving that part entirely out. This next shows how the Germans had left nothing to chance. They have about twelve machine guns to every battalion, and are said to have had 12,000 when the War began. Passing through villages they pack ten of them into an innocent-looking cart with a false bottom. We captured some of these empty carts, and some time afterwards found them full of machine guns. Gold hats and red hats have been dropping in all day. They do on Sundays especially after Church Parade.

Saturday, April 24th. We were watching hundreds of men pass by today, whistling and singing, on their way to the trenches. News came to us this morning of the Germans having broken through the trench lines north of Ypres and shelled Poperinge, which was out of range up to now, but it is not official. The guns are very loud tonight, I hope they're keeping the

Germans busy, something is sure to be done to draw them off the Ypres line. *Sunday, April 25th.* The plum pudding was "something to write home about" and the Quartermaster sent us a tin of honey today, the first I've seen for nine months. A General came round this morning. He said the Canadians and another regiment had given the Germans this gas fumes business north of Ypres, got the ground back and recovered the four guns. The beasts of Germans laid out a whole trench full of Zouaves with chlorine gas (which besides being poisonous is one of the most loathsome smells). Of course everyone is busy finding out how we can go one better now. But this afternoon the medical staffs of both these divisions have been trying experiments in a barn with chlorine gas, with and without different kinds of masks soaked with some antidote, such as lime. All were busy coughing and choking when they found the Assistant Director Medical Services of the — Division getting blue and suffocated, he'd had too much chlorine, and was brought here, looking very bad, and for an hour we had to give him fumes of ammonia till he could breathe properly. He will probably have bronchitis. But they've found out what they wanted to know—that you can go to the assistance of men overpowered by the gas, if you put on this mask, with less chance of finding yourself dead too when you got there. They don't lose much time finding these things out, do they? On Saturday I shall be going on night duty for a month.

Monday, April 26th, 11 PM. We have been admitting, cutting the clothes off, dressing, and evacuating a good many today, and I think they are still coming in. There is a great noise going on tonight, snapping and popping, and crackling of rifle firing and machine guns, with the sudden roar every few minutes. The thundery roll after them is made by the big shell bounding along on its way. Two officers were brought in last night overpowered by carbon monoxide. Three of them and a sergeant crawled along it to get out the bodies of another officer and a sergeant who'd been killed there by an explosion the day before it leads into a crater in the German lines, and reaches under the German trenches, which we intended to blow up. But they were greeted by this poisonous gas last night, and the officer in front of these two suddenly became inanimate, each tried to pull the one in front out by the legs, but all became unconscious in turn, and only these two survived and were hauled out up twenty feet of rope ladder. They will get all right. The wounded ones are generally in "the excited stage" when they arrive—some surprised and resentful, some relieved that it is no worse, and some very quiet and collapsed. Captain showed me his periscope today, you bob down and look into it about level with his mattress, and then you see a picture of the garden across the road. He has seen one with a magnifying lens in it so good that you can see the moustaches of the Boches in it from the bottom of your trench.

Tuesday, April 27th. Have been busy all day, and so have the guns. It is a stupendous noise, like some gigantic angry lion. The official accounts of the second dash for Calais reach us through the *Times* two days after the things have happened, but the actual happenings filter along the line from Saint-Omer General Headquarters as soon as they happen, so we know there's been no real "breaking through" that hasn't been made good, or partially made good, because if there had, the dispositions all along the line would have had to be altered, and that has not happened. The ambulance trains are collecting the Ypres casualties from the convoys at Poperinge, as we did at Ypres in October and November, and not through the Clearing Hospitals which I believe have had to move farther back.

Wednesday, April 28th. Here everything is as it has been for the last few days (except the weather, which is suddenly hot as summer), rather more casualties, but no rush, and the same crescendo of heavy guns. Some shells were dropped in a field just outside the town at 8:30 yesterday evening but did no damage. *Thursday, April 29th, 4 PM.* The weather and the evenings are indescribably incongruous. Tea in the garden at home and before one's eyes and ears are motor ambulances and stretchers and dressings, and the everlasting noise of marching feet, clattering hoofs, lorries and guns, and sometimes the skirl of the pipes. One day there was a real band, and everyone glowed and thrilled with the sound of it. I strayed into a concert at 5:30 this evening, given by the Glasgow Highlanders to a packed houseful of men and officers. I took good care to be shown into a solitary box next the stage, as I was alone and guessed that some of the items would not be intended for polite female ears. The level of the talent was a high one, some good part songs, and two real singers, and some quite funny and clever comic, but one or two things made me glad of the shelter of my box. The choruses were fine. The last thing was a brilliant effort of the four part singers dressed as comic sailors, which simply made the house rock. Then suddenly, while they were still yelling, the first chords of the "King" were played, and all the hundreds stood to attention in silence while it was played—not sung—much more impressive than the singing of it, I thought. We have had some bad cases in today, and the boy with the lung is not doing so well. My second inoculation passed off very quickly, and I have not been off duty for it. *Thursday, May 6th, 3 AM*. It was a very noisy day, and I didn't sleep after 2 PM. There is a good lot of firing going on tonight. A very muddy officer of 6 feet 4 was brought in early yesterday morning with a broken leg, and it is a hard job to get him comfortable in these short beds. Yesterday at 4 AM. I couldn't resist invading the garden opposite which is the Royal Artillery Headquarters. It is full of lovely trees and flowers and birds. I found a blackbird's nest with one egg in. From the upper windows of this place it makes a perfect picture, with the peculiarly beautiful tower of the Cathedral as a background. *Friday, May 7th, 10 PM*. A pitch-dark night, raining a little—and only one topic—the attack tomorrow morning. The first Royal Army Medical Corps barge has come up, and is lying in the canal ready to take on the cases of wounds of lung and abdomen, to save the jolting of road and railway, it is to have two Sisters, but I haven't seen them yet, shall go in the morning, went round this morning to see, but the barge hadn't arrived. There are a few sick officers downstairs who are finding it hard to stick in their beds with their regiments in this job close by. There is a house close by which I saw this morning with a dirty little red flag with a black cross on it, where thirty commanders of the 1st Army met yesterday. The news today of Hill 60 and the gases is another spur to the grim resolve to break through here, that can be felt and seen and heard in every detail of every arm. "Grandmother" is lovingly talked about. The town, the roads, and the canal banks this morning were so packed with men, wagons, horses, bales, and lorries, that you could barely pick your way between them.

Since writing this an aeroplane has been circling over us with a loud buzz. The sergeant called up to me to put the lights out. We saw her light. There is much speculation as to who and what she was, she was not big enough for our big "bus" as she is called, who belongs to this place. No one seems ever to have seen one here at night before. We are making flannel masks for our men. Our fat little Gabrielle makes the most priceless soup out of the ration beef (which none of us are any good at) and carrots. She mothers us each individually, and cleans the house and keeps her wee kitchen spotless. 4 AM. Here is a true story. One of our trenches at Givenchy was being pounded by German shells at the time. A man saw his brother killed on one side of him and another man on the other. He went on shooting over the parapet, then the parapet got knocked about, and still he wasn't hit. He seized his brother's body and the other man's and built them up into the parapet with sandbags, and went on shooting. When the stress was over and he could leave off, he looked round and saw what he was leaning against. "Who did that?" he said. And they told him. They get awfully sick at the big print headlines in some of the papers. "There's nothing thrilling about plowing over parapets into a machine gun, with high explosives bursting round you—it's merely beastly" said a boy this evening over shrapnel splinters. *Sunday, May 9th, 1:30 AM.* The Lions are roaring in full blast and lighting up the sky. Have been busy tonight with an operation case who is needing a lot of special nursing, and some admissions—one in at 11 PM, who was only wounded at 9 o'clock. I hope these magnificent roars and rumblings are making a mess of the barbed wire and German trenches. There seems to be a pretty general opinion that they will retaliate by dropping them into this place if they have time, and pulverizing it like Ypres. 5:25 AM. It has begun. It is awful—continuous and earthquaking.

9:30 AM. In bed. The last ten minutes of "Rapid" did its damnedest and then began again, and we are still thundering hell into the German lines. It began before 5 with a fearful pounding from the French on our right, and hasn't left off since.

Had a busy night with my operation case and the others (he is doing fine), and in every spare second getting ready for the rush. Must try and sleep. But who could yesterday and today? *Monday, May 10th, 9:30 AM.* We have had a night of it. I got up early yesterday and went down to the barge to see if they wanted any extra help (as the other two were coping with the wounded officers), and had a grim afternoon and evening there. It was packed with all the worst cases—dying and bleeding and groaning. After five hours we had three-fourths of them out of their blood-soaked clothes, dressed, fed, hemorrhage stopped, hands and faces washed, and some asleep. Two died, and more were dying. They all worked like bricks. At 11 PM the place was unrecognizable, every corner of every floor filled with wounded officers—some sitting up and some all over wounds, and three dying and others critical, and they still kept coming in. They were all awfully good strewing about the floor—some soaked to the skin from wet shell holes—on their stretchers, waiting to be put to bed. One had, had "such a jolly Sunday afternoon" lying in a shell hole with six inches of water in it and a dead man, digging himself in deeper with his trench tool whenever the shells burst near him. He was hit in the stomach. One officer saw the enemy through a periscope sniping at our wounded. 4 PM. In bed. It seems quiet today, there are so few guns to be heard, and not so many ambulances coming. All except the hopeless cases will have been evacuated by now from all the Field Hospitals. There was a block last night, and none could be sent on. The Clearing Hospitals were full, and no trains in. Those four Sisters from the base had a weird arrival at the barge last night in a car at 11 PM. It was a black, dark night, big guns going, and a sudden descent down a ladder into that Nelson's cockpit. They buckled to and set to work right off. The cook, who had been helping magnificently in the ward, was running after me with hot cocoa, and promised to give them some. One wounded of the Munsters there said he didn't mind nothink now—he'd seen so many dead Germans as he never thought on. As always, they have lost thousands, but they come on like ants. They have only had about seven new cases today, but two of last night's have died. A Padre was with them. They had no market this morning, for fear of bombs from aeroplanes. There's been no shelling into the town.

Wednesday, May 12th, 6:30 PM. Slept very well. My little room is crammed with enormous lilac, white and purple, from our wee garden, which I am going to take to our graves tomorrow in jam tins. *Thursday, May 13th, 11 AM.* Can't face the graves today, have had an awful night, three died during the night.

I found the boy who brought his officer in from between the German line and ours, on Sunday night, crying this morning over the still figure under a brown blanket on a stretcher. Of the other two, brought straight in from the other dressing station, one only lived long enough to be put to bed, and the other died on his stretcher in the hall. It seems so much nearer, and more murderous somehow in this Field Ambulance atmosphere even than it did on the train with all the successive hundreds. 9 PM. Everything very quiet here. A gunner just admitted says there will probably be another big bombardment tomorrow morning, and after that another attack, and after that I suppose some more for us. Another says that the charge of the Black Watch on Sunday was a marvelous thing. They went into it playing the pipes.

The Major who led it handed somebody his stick, as he "probably shouldn't want it again." It is very wet tonight, but they go up to the trenches singing Ragtime, some song about "We are always—respected—wherever we go." And another about "sing a song—a song with me. Come along—along with me."

11 PM. Just heard a shell burst, first the whistling scream and then the bang—wonder where? There was another about an hour ago, but I didn't hear the whistle of that—only the bang. I shouldn't have known what the whistle was if I hadn't heard it at

Braisne. It goes in a curve. All the men on the top floor have been sent down to sleep in the cellar. 12:15. Just had another, right overhead, all the patients are asleep, luckily. 1:30 PM. There was one more, near enough to make you jump, and a few more too far off to hear the whistling. The sky on the battle line tonight is the weirdest sight, our guns are very busy, and they are making yellow flashes like huge sheets of summer lightning. Then the star shells rise, burst, and light up a large area, while a big searchlight plays slowly on the clouds. It is all very beautiful when you don't think what it means. Two more—the last very loud and close. It is somehow much more alarming than Braisne, perhaps because it is among buildings and because one knows so much more what they mean. Another—the other side of the building. An ambulance has been called out, so someone must have been hit, I've lost count of how many they've dropped, but they could hardly fail to do some damage. 5 AM. Daylight—soaking wet, and no more shells since 2 AM. We have admitted seven officers tonight, the last—just in—says there have been five people wounded in the town by this peppering—one killed. I don't know if civilians or soldiers. That bombardment on Sunday morning was the biggest anyone has ever heard—more guns on smaller space, and more shells per minute. Nine officers have "died of wounds" here since Sunday, and the tenth will not live to see daylight. There is an attack on tonight. This has been a ghastly week, and now it is beginning again. The other two Sisters had quite a nasty time last night lying in bed waiting for the shells to burst in their rooms. They do sound exactly as if they are coming your way and nowhere else. I rather think they are dropping some in again tonight, but they are not close enough to hear the whistle, only the bangs. There is an officer in tonight with a wound in the hand and shoulder from a shell which killed eleven of his men, and another who went to see four of his platoon in a house at the exact moment when a percussion shell went on the same errand and the five were wounded—none killed.

Monday, May 17th, 10 AM. Another night of horrors, one more died, and two young boys came in who will die, one is a

Gordon Highlander of 18, who says "that's glorious" when you put him to bed. It was a long whirl of stretchers, and pitiful heaps on them. The sergeant stayed up helping until 3, and a boy from the kitchen stayed up all night on his own, helping. In the middle of the worst rush the sergeant said to me "You know they're shelling the town again" and at that minute swoop bang came a big one, and we looked at each other over the stretcher with the same picture in our mind's eyes of shells dropping in amongst the wounded, who are all over the town. I hadn't heard them—too busy—but they didn't go on long. The Boches have been heavily shelling our trenches all day. One boy said suddenly, when I was attending to his leg "Aren't you very foolish to be staying up here?" he said "Oh sorry, I was dreaming you were in the front line of trenches bandaging people up." Our big guns have been making the building shake all night. The Germans are trying to get their trenches back by counterattacking. *Saturday, May 22nd, 6:30 AM*. Things have been happening at a great pace since the above, and we are now in our camp beds in an empty attic at the top of an old chateau about three miles back. Just as I was thinking of getting up yesterday evening they began putting shells over into the town, and soon they were raining in three at a time. My little room is a sort of lean-to over the kitchen with no room above it, so I cleared out to dress in one of the others and didn't stop to wash. At the hospital, which was only about 200 yards down the road, the wounded officers were thinking it was about time Captain moved his Field Ambulance. One boy by the window had got some *debris* in his eye from the nearest shell, which burst in my blackbird's garden, or rather on the doorstep opposite. The orders soon came to evacuate all the patients.

    Everybody got the patients ready, fixed up their dressings and splints, gave them all morphine, and got them on to their stretchers. The evacuation was jolly well done, their servants appeared by magic, each with every spot of kit and belongings his officer came in with, and the place was empty in an hour. The din of our guns, which were bombarding heavily, and the German guns, which are bombarding us at a great pace, and the whistle and bang of the shells that came over while this was going on was a din to remember. Then we went back to our billet to hurl our belongings into our baggage, and came away with the Assistant Director Medical Services and his Staff Major in their two touring cars. The Division is back resting somewhere near here. We got to bed about 2 AM after tea and bread and butter downstairs, but slept very little owing to the noise of the guns, which shake and rattle the windows every minute. We don't know what happens next. At about four this morning I heard a nightingale trilling in the garden. 2 PM. In the Chateau garden. It is a glorious spot, with kitchen garden, park, moat bridge, and a huge wilderness up-and-down plantation round it, full of lilac, copper beeches, and flowering trees I've never seen before, and birds and butterflies and buttercups. You look across and see the red brick Chateau surrounded by thick lines of tents, and hear the everlasting incessant thudding and banging of the guns, and realize that it is not a French country house but a Casualty Clearing Hospital, with empty—once polished—floors filled with stretchers, where the worst cases still are, and some left empty for the incoming convoys. Over two thousand have passed through since Sunday week. The contrast between the shady garden where I'm lazing now on rugs and cushions, with innumerable birds, including a nightingale, singing and nesting, and the nerve-racking sound of the guns and the look of the place inside, is overwhelming. It is in three Divisions—the house for the worst cases—and there are tent Sections and the straw sheds and two schools in the village. We had our lunch at a sort of inn in the village. I've never hated the sound of the guns so much, they are almost unbearable. It is a good thing for us to have this sudden rest. I don't know for how long or what happens next. The General of the Division had a narrow escape after we left last night. The roof of his house was blown off, just at the time he would have been there, only he was a little late, but an officer was killed, six shells came into the garden, and the seventh burst at his feet and killed him as he was standing at the door. I'm glad they got the wounded away in time. Aeroplanes are buzzing overhead. 10 PM. In bed. We have now been temporarily attached to the Staff here. *Wednesday, May 26th*. No time to write yesterday, had a typical Clearing Hospital Field Day.

The left-out-in-the-field wounded (mostly Canadians) had at last been picked up and came pouring in. I had my Tent Section of eighty beds nearly full, and we coped in a broiling sun until we sweltered into little spots of grease, finishing up with five operations in the little operating tent. The poor exhausted Canadians were extraordinarily brave and uncomplaining.

They are evacuated the same day or the next morning, such as can be got away to survive the journey, but some of the worst have to stay. In the middle of it all at 5 PM orders came for me, but I didn't leave until this morning at nine and am now on to old Boulogne again. *Later*. These orders were afterwards cancelled and I am for duty at a Base Hospital.

Afterword

The books used for this collection were written by people who lived extraordinary lives throughout various eras of American and European history. Some were famous and others unknown—yet *all* their stories were compelling regardless. Reliving the past through their eyes takes the reader back in history where it almost seems like we are witnessing the events they experienced and feeling what they felt even though several centuries have slipped by. Many of the accounts featured in this collection are gut-wrenching and hard to read. As I relived what happened to John Knight and John Slover while I read their accounts it was difficult to get through either story knowing what happened was one of many, and that much of these events went undocumented by those who saw with their own eyes such horrors. Often enough I've heard individuals say what happened in the frontier during the years following the American Revolution wasn't as bad as it was described in published accounts—often because they who made such ignorant statements haven't read firsthand accounts of those who were there and saw what they did. On the other hand I've listened to Native American historians pretend that these accounts were made up and that their ancestors were the victims and not the monsters they were described to be by witnesses like Knight and Slover. Well, in actuality they were both. No one is denying Native Americans were attacked and wrongly killed by the US government and had their ancestral lands stolen from them simply because of greed. But it should also not be denied that *not* all Native Americans were victims. Some chose their lot in life and their greed got the better of them as well. There are plenty of stories that can verify both accounts as factual, so pretending centuries later that *all* Native Americans were helpless innocents is as credible as present-day white historians stating that Native Americans were not mistreated and their lands wasn't stolen.

The same statements have been made about American and British slavery since today it's easy to choose what one can read based on one's own choices. Henry Whiteley's account of the unspeakable horrors against enslaved human beings he witnessed in Jamaica during the early 1830s led to the abolition of slavery in British colonies throughout the Caribbean islands and elsewhere. Nevertheless there have been clueless historians and armchair readers who refuse to believe his account simply because they feel a kinship with the slave owners despite their endless denials that they don't share the same beliefs.

In many books written by someone recounting their life or the life of someone else, a writer can make what was initially interesting seem dull. Too many times when a personal diary or journal is published we see a much more raw version of what life was like for its author rather than if it was sanitized in order to make the storytelling more easy to understand. With this collection of writings I tried to piece together a collection of personal memoirs that I think made a significant difference to world history—whether from the era of the Pilgrims—to the frontiers of North America—leading up to the *Titanic* tragedy of April 1912—and ending in the bloody battlefields of Europe which made heroes of ordinary people during the first World War.

The brief endnotes following for each of the people whose stories made up this book were sourced from verified material.

Edward Winslow

Edward Winslow was born in 1595 and traveled on the *Mayflower* in 1620. He was a Separatist and author of several books about the early days of Plymouth Colony. Winslow also helped write *Mourt's Relation* with William Bradford of which has an account of the First Thanksgiving in November 1621. In 1655 he died of a fever while in the Caribbean on behalf of the British government. Winslow is also credited with establishing Marshfield, Massachusetts as a separate settlement in 1632.

William Bradford

William Bradford was born at Austerfield, England in 1590 and is credited with being one of the original founders of Plymouth Colony in 1620. He was also the author of the celebrated memoir *Of Plymouth Plantation* which covered the adventures and early history of the Pilgrims in America from 1620 until his death in 1657. Bradford is buried at Burial Hill overlooking the present-day town of Plymouth just outside of Boston.

John Knight

John Knight was a doctor and Continental Army Officer whose gripping account of his capture and torture by Delaware Indians in present-day Ohio during the ill-fated Sandusky Expedition of 1782 and daring escape made him a frontier legend in his lifetime. After his escape he worked as a surgeon at Fort Pitt in Pennsylvania until the end of the Revolutionary War and then moved to Kentucky and started a family. Knight was originally born in Scotland and died in Kentucky in 1838.

John Slover

John Slover escaped with his life from the hands of hostile Indians after he was taken to a village called Macachack in present-day Ohio to be burned alive. Naked and afraid he stole and horse and rode it as far as he could before he made his way on foot to Fort Pitt on July 10th 1782. He was one of the few survivors to return after seeing many of his fellow captives tortured and killed. He later settled in Henderson, Kentucky.

Daniel Boone

Daniel Boone was born in 1734 and through his exploits became a legendary figure in his own time—often considered the father of the modern frontier by historians. He was one of the first settlers in Kentucky and eventually founded the village of Boonesborough. He later moved further west with his family to Missouri in 1799. Boone attempted to publish his story several times but failed. He died in 1820. Boone's co-writer John Filson was born in Pennsylvania and worked as a schoolteacher in the Kentucky frontier. In 1784 he published a book detailing the early history of Kentucky which included Boone's brief autobiography. John Filson was attacked and killed by Shawnee Indians in 1788 near present-day Cincinnati. His body was never found.

George Washington

In his youth George Washington tried to figure out what his goal in life should be. As an adult, he found his place in history by being an effective leader during the Revolutionary War. He was born in February 1732 in relative obscurity—but died in December 1799 as one of the most respected figures in American history. Washington is buried in a private tomb on the grounds of his former home—Mount Vernon—in Virginia next to his wife.

Tobias Lear

Tobias Lear was born in New Hampshire in 1762 and attended Harvard instead of joining the Continental Army. Lear is best known as the personal secretary of George Washington. He served Washington from 1784 until the former President's death in December 1799. He later served as Thomas Jefferson's envoy to Haiti (then Saint Domingue) as well as peace envoy in the Mediterranean during the Barbary Wars. He was married three times and widowed twice. His second wife was the widow of Washington's nephew and his third wife was the niece of Martha Washington. Lear dealt with several controversial situations during his life, including accusations (never proven) that he destroyed some of Washington's personal writings following his death in 1799. In October 1816 Lear apparently took his own life but left no suicide note to explain his actions. Lear was apparently found alone in his home by his son still holding a bloody gun in his hand. He was known to suffer from headaches and bouts of severe depression but it remains unclear exactly what caused him to kill himself. His death remains a mystery to this day.

Henry Whiteley

Henry Whiteley barely escaped from Jamaica with his life and upon his return to England he testified at what he'd seen in the short time he was in the Caribbean. Through his brave testimony and the work of determined abolitionists, slavery was abolished forever throughout the British Empire. Whiteley did not seek fame or money for his heroic behavior but lived long enough to see his daring efforts change how people viewed slavery initially. Though slavery was abolished in 1833 it wasn't until 1838 when slaves in Jamaica were emancipated. Slavery continued for many more years in the Danish and French West Indies as well as in the United States until 1863 when Abraham Lincoln ended slavery for good during the Civil War. Many of the people who were mentioned in Whiteley's scathing memoir have descendants today throughout Jamaica and in the United States—both white and biracial—as it was a known fact that many slave owners had relationships with female slaves, many of which were against their will if truth be known based on archived historical records, which resulted in biracial offspring that were still considered slaves despite their white heritage and obvious Caucasian appearances. One of those alleged descendants, through her Jamaican father, is noted American politician Kamala Harris, who is a direct descendant of Hamilton Brown—one of the people that knowingly participated in the barbaric mistreatment of slaves in Jamaica as stated by Whiteley in his memoir.

Abraham Lincoln

No one could have guessed back in 1809 that a child born in the Kentucky frontier would not only become President of the United States but would be remembered over a century later for what he achieved in such a short time despite the odds against him. He never set out to change anyone's minds—he only wanted to do the right thing—even if it meant not doing what others expected him to do. Today when weak-willed politicians need someone to look up to—Lincoln looms large—no one needs to wonder what he stood for when it came to right and wrong—you knew by his words and actions—of which he has no equal.

Abraham Lincoln was born in Kentucky in February 1809 to a mother who craved education and a father who was dedicated to hard work required on the frontier. Young Lincoln could never have imagined the legacy he'd one day have as part of the history of the United States of America. His life was touched by an unending amount of tragedy during his childhood and later during his adult years but he persevered nevertheless and achieved greatness despite what must have seemed to of been an impossible task to overcome. The death of his mother Nancy Hanks Lincoln in October of 1818 changed everything for him and guided by her determined belief that education was the key to success he set out to make sure his life wasn't forgettable. He married Mary Todd in 1842 and fathered four sons.

In the following years he dabbled in politics until he found his footing and decided to take the ultimate gamble and threw his hat into the Presidential race of 1860. Upon winning the Presidency of the United States, Lincoln publicly remembered his beloved mother and said all that he was and could ever be—he owed to her because of her devotion to the necessity of education. Lincoln dealt with the tragedy of the Civil War by holding on to the belief that it was his duty to hold the country together even in the face of impossible odds. In 1863 he wrote one of the most important documents in American history.

The Emancipation Proclamation ended slavery forever and ushered in a new future for many who had never known happiness in their lives. Lincoln's words have been repeated endlessly over the years yet never seems to lose its potency.

Lincoln's life plays like a movie that even the most accomplished scriptwriters in their wildest dreams could never have fashioned such an incredible rags to riches tale that inspires over two centuries after the actual events took place. When someone needs to look for someone to admire they need not look further than this simple man. He's in a class by himself.

Martha Morgan

The whereabouts of Martha Morgan after her trip reached its conclusion remains elusive. Except for a few scant notices there seems to be no record of what happened afterwards to those mentioned in Morgan's diary. It can be assumed they blended into pioneer life in California and lived out the rest of their lives in obscurity. Most of the diaries and journals found that were written by travelers on their way westward were lost or placed in trunks after the journeys ended. Sometimes decades would slip by before they were found by family members.

James Akin Jr.

The journal James Akin Jr. is a rare look into the lives of several pioneer families traveling westward on the famed Oregon Trail. Though brief in its descriptions of the events that occurred, it provides a vivid image of the experiences and dangers faced by brave pioneers seeking a new life in Oregon in the middle of the nineteenth century. Akin's brief journal, first published in 1919, detailed the experiences of James Akin Jr. who was about eighteen years of age at the start of his journey westward. It described specific events and briefly detailed the extreme hardships experienced by his family and several others as they traveled together on the Oregon Trail in the early 1850s.

Frances Sawyer

Frances Horr Lamar Sawyer's account of her overland trip to California was first published in 1894 in a Kentucky newspaper called *Breckenridge News*. Sawyer's journal covering her trip across the Plains was also published in numerous narrative collections over the years as well. During the nineteenth century many pioneers ventured across the Plains and a brief journal of her experiences and those of her fellow pioneers throughout their journey from Kentucky to California in 1852 details their everyday lives and the hardships they endured during their adventurous quest. Born in 1831, she married Thomas Sawyer in 1848 and later ventured westward in 1852 to California. Frances Sawyer died in March 1915 at the age of eighty-three surrounded by her surviving children and grandchildren. She was buried next to her husband at Cloverport Cemetery in Cloverport, Kentucky.

James Richey

James H. Richey most likely settled in California after his trip across the Plains in 1854. Not much is known about his life from this point due to lack of historical records but it is assumed that he and his family remained in Northern California.

Chief Joseph

Chief Joseph was a legend in his own time due to unforeseen events in his life that were beyond his control. His heroism and bravery earned him a respected place in nineteenth century United States history among whites and Indians alike as a peacemaker and humanitarian—but few know the real man behind his legendary persona or his prolific views on his own people as well as the rest of the United States. In his own words (as dictated to a writer from the North American Review on a trip to the nation's capital in 1879) Chief Joseph tells his incredible story about his life and times as well as his hope for the future despite how bleak things seemed at the time for his people.

This simple narrative is the story of a man whose actions and character inspired not only his own people but many others and continues to do so long after his voice was silenced by death in September 1904. Long before there was noted social activists like Rosa Parks or Martin Luther King Jr. there was Chief Joseph. He was a legend in his own time, his voice, though not as powerful as polished politicians of the time had a successful and more far-reaching effect upon the future than he could have ever imagined while he was alive. Very few people have made a greater impact on nineteenth century American history than this quiet and unassuming man, yet his legacy continues to inspire others long after his passing. Though he was famous during his lifetime, it did him little good in his brave fight for equality of his people, of which his notable trips to the nation's capital made him a household name even to those who never gave much thought to the plight of American Indians. Chief Joseph was also known for his many quotes of which not only were sensible advice spoken aloud at the time but remain true even today.

One such example of a quoted comment is his notable "It does not require many words to speak the truth." This simple statement made by Chief Joseph over a century ago is still true presently as when it was first spoken. Sometimes long-winded comments made by better educated types have no value or effect on those that witness or read it because it was written without emotion or real conviction despite the fancy wording—yet short but accurate comments such as those made by Chief Joseph during the nineteenth century have long outlasted other more detailed and notable writings of the era—continuously inspiring the present with advice which is sorely needed in a modern world where no one seems to take responsibility for their actions.

Chief Joseph's legacy continues to this day as his life and times inspires not only historians but anyone looking for what is expected from a true humanitarian who achieves results not by empty talk but by example. Would he have appreciated the lavish praise being lapped upon him today if he were alive? I think he would—though I'm certain he would've lectured continuously on the importance of using such notoriety for the betterment of society rather than searching needlessly for more self-importance by saying whatever seems popular at the moment and of which may look good on paper but it accomplishes nothing in actuality as many public figures today do with their endless need for publicity. Chief Joseph became famous for refusal to be forcibly removed to a reservation during the nineteenth century—but he was also known as a humanitarian and peacemaker during his later years. He died in September 1904 at the age of 64.

Nancy Hunt

Nancy Zumwalt Cotton Hunt was a pioneer in the early days of the founding of California. She and her second husband later operated a dairy for many years. She died in 1904 and was buried at the Sacramento City Cemetery in Sacramento, California. Her son, Rockwell D. Hunt was a California historian as well as a professor at the University of Southern California and the University of the Pacific. He edited his mother's memoirs for publication in 1916 and was also an author of several notable books, including a recollection of his life and times. He died in 1966 at the age of ninety-seven and is buried at Inglewood Park Cemetery in Inglewood, California, a suburb of Los Angeles.

Frederick Walker

Frederick Dunbar Walker was born in Dublin, Ireland and eventually made his life in Honolulu. He became a naturalized citizen of Hawaii in 1906. His memoir has been reprinted in numerous book collections focusing on the Hawaiian Islands.

Frank Allen McCurdy

Frank Allen McCurdy was born in 1876 and served as one of Theodore Roosevelt's famed Rough Riders as a Volunteer in Troop F during the Spanish American War. He died in 1912.

John Kirk McCurdy

John Kirk McCurdy was born in 1878 and was one of Theodore Roosevelt's Rough Riders from Troop F Volunteer Cavalry during the Spanish American War. He died in 1945.

Harold Bride

The sinking of the *Titanic* on April 15, 1912 was one of history's most notable maritime disasters—and while there were many eyewitness accounts of the events that took place that terrible night—most were written long after the fact. All except one—that of a wireless operator named Harold Bride. His account of the events that took place before and after the "unsinkable" *Titanic* sank beneath the icy waves of the North Atlantic Ocean after striking an iceberg as related to a reporter from *The New York Times* shortly after his rescue remains one of the best accounts of the tragedy. Bride's brief memoir about the events leading up to and after the sinking of the *Titanic* is probably the most accurate account about what happened aboard the "unsinkable" liner by one of its own crew members. Though other accounts have contained more details about events that took place as the *Titanic* hit an iceberg on April 15, 1912 and began taking on water, the fragmented narrative by Harold Bride provides the most detailed view of how the sinking affected the crew and passengers alike. Bride also bares his soul about his own behavior that night of which could be considered morally wrong by less forgiving types today. But yet, given the circumstances of that tragic event which forever is etched indelibly into the pages of history, he somehow remained unfazed by his own mortality as the world he knew began to slowly slip away from his grasp. Throughout the decades that followed, the events of that April 1912 night so long ago have been scrutinized over and over again by historians looking for answers, where there are none. What should be remembered only is that many lives were lost due to human error of which was preventable. Bride never sought to be noticed as a hero, but he was a hero simply because he not only did his job facing the harsh reality he might lose his own life in the process, but because his actions saved countless lives that would have been lost without his diligent efforts and those of the *Titanic's* other equally heroic wireless operator, Jack Phillips, who sadly, perished in the tragedy after saving so many others.

Today, finding heroes is an almost impossible task. People seek to call themselves heroes without having done anything truly heroic—while others are glorified as heroes simply because they are famous but have done nothing important. But a true hero is someone who is willing to risk their life for others without being asked to do so, or being paid for their efforts after the fact. How many people today would be willing to do something like that? How about only a few? And yeah, no one is really willing to admit this is reality—except until they are forced to prove it in a crisis—and fail miserably when they can't live up to specific expectations of which they claimed or thought they could handle beforehand. It *is* a fact, true heroes such as Harold Bride and Jack Phillips exist only in a handful of human beings today, which isn't anything to be really proud of by any means if truth be told.

Following the sinking of the *Titanic* the public's fascination with the doomed ship began. Immediately, questions about exactly what happened on the *Titanic* arose and the United States Senate appointed a committee to oversee an investigation on the tragedy. 82 passengers, 4 officers, and 34 members of the crew were interviewed which eventually filled 1,145 pages of text. The conclusion resulted in changes to the amount of lifeboats a ship was allowed to have as well as more knowledgeable manning of the wireless equipment. England also held its own investigation into the disaster but unlike the American inquiry which focused on the "how" it happened, the British focused on the "why" it had occurred and how it could be prevented from happening in the future. The White Star Line was held liable for everything and was never the same again. The bad luck that began with *Titanic* continued with the other White Star ships during the following years. In 1916 the *Britannic* struck a mine off the coast of Greece and sank. However, almost all the passengers survived due to lessons learned because of the *Titanic* tragedy. The *Olympic*, another of the White Star Line's pride and joy survived the First World War but never regained its former glory and was scrapped in the 1930s. White Star Line was eventually bought by its rival Cunard Line and renamed Cunard White Star but was renamed again Cunard Line in 1950. In September 1, 1985 the wreck of the *Titanic* was located in the North Atlantic Ocean where it had remained hidden from view for the better part of seventy-five years. Though the discovery was applauded, the issues of what resulted in the years following, concerning the recovery of items from the doomed liner would have been better served had the wreck never been found at all since it was considered by most to be a burial site and should have been left undisturbed forever. A fact which has been carelessly ignored by individuals seeking fame, money, and, or, control of recovered items which rightfully do not belong to them—now or ever. Nevertheless books, films, magazines, documentaries and websites dedicated to what happened on April 15, 1912 have guaranteed that the memory of the *Titanic* will never be forgotten despite the passage of time.

Harold Bride continued working as a wireless operator during World War I and later became a salesman. He shunned publicity, choosing to live life out of the spotlight. Bride died in April 1956 in Glasgow, Scotland of cancer and was cremated.

Bride has been mentioned in numerous books about the sinking of the *Titanic* and portrayed on screen multiple times in such films as the British film *A Night to Remember* (1958) the CBS television miniseries *Titanic* (1996) and popular film *Titanic* (1997) as well as the short film *Last Signals* (2012). He was also a major character in the Broadway musical stage version *Titanic* which ran throughout 1997 and won several awards, including a Tony.

Kate Evelyn Luard

Kate Luard's diary was originally published anonymously in the midst of the First World War and was an immediate classic which has not lost its power over its readers even after a century. The rich details about the horrors of war that Luard brought to life in her memoir was effective in 1915 and still echoes today for someone wanting to experience what it was like to live life under such situations. The fact that Luard wasn't a professional reporter or seasoned writer makes her words even more appealing. During her lifetime Luard never acknowledged publicly she was the author of *Diary of a Nursing Sister on the Western Front* for whatever reasons. Nevertheless it remains one of the most reprinted war memoirs. Luard was born in 1872 and served as a nurse during the Second Boer War and later the First World War. She was later awarded a Royal Red Cross in January 1916.

During World War I she worked in various hospitals and was well-known among soldiers. From what we can gather from reading her diary, her life was in danger more often than not, yet she managed to continue her work helping those who needed it most. Her bravery is clear in her writings and rereading it a century later one can only imagine how many times she feared for her life yet never once thought of letting those she served down. Upon the aftermath of Armistice Day she resigned from the Queen Alexandra's Imperial Military Nursing Service (Queen Alexandra's Royal Army Nursing Corps) in order to devote her time and nursing skills to her father who was ill at the time.

Luard later worked at the South London Hospital for Women and as a matron for a boys school. She retired after a long career of service and died peacefully in August 1962 at 90. In 1930 extracts from her diaries was published in a new collection encompassing more material and later years during the First World War. The book was republished in 2014 with new material for the one hundredth anniversary of World War I. In recent years her story has reached a farther audience due to Internet sites focusing on soldiers and those who helped them—as well as publications of newly-found writings from victims and survivors of the First World War which mentions Luard and her services to soldiers on the brink of death. Many of these accounts have finally been published in compilations of first-person accounts of soldier life on the Western Front and elsewhere. Like so many women her era, Luard was a hero whom never thought she was doing anything other than her job and probably never realized how valuable her services was to those who were injured and to those who were dying and comforted in their last moments by Luard and others like her. Seeing what she and others saw (for years) and living with fear every day the way she and her contemporaries must have done makes one appreciate today that reading about what she encountered is much easier than actually having to live through such a horrifying experience.

Source Notes

Material used for this collection can be found online at the library listed below in unedited downloadable PDF editions. Books were scanned from existing public library copies in the United States and Europe.

www.nancyhankslincolnpubliclibrary.org

Cape Cod Journal of the Pilgrim Fathers was first published in 1920 by the Advocate Gift Shop Press. Edited by Lyon Sharman from journal entries by Edward Winslow and William Bradford of Plymouth Colony. It was published to specifically coincide with the three hundredth anniversary of the landing of the Pilgrims in the New World. The original entries were modernized from old English to modern English in order to make it easier to read by present-day readers. An original version was published in 1622 under the title *Mourt's Relation*. Several versions of *Mourt's Relation* has been reprinted several times in various editions.

Narratives of a Late Expedition Against the Indians was first published in 1783 by Francis Bailey in Philadelphia. John Knight's and John Slover's accounts of their capture and escape from their Native American captors were published together with other material. Both Knight's and Slover's narratives were dictated to writer Hugh Henry Brackenridge. This book has been reprinted several times and published within other book collections.

Autobiography of Daniel Boone was originally published in 1784 in a book called *Discovery, Settlement and Present State of Kentucke* by John Filson. Boone's brief memoir was dictated to Filson and published as part of the appendix. Boone's detailed account of his life has been reprinted over the years in other collections.

Washington's Diary at the 1787 Constitutional Convention was first published in 1887 by the *Pennsylvania Magazine of History and Biography*. Extracts of the original MS diary was included in a noted biography of George Washington by Jared Sparks.

Last Words of General Washington was first published in a special pamphlet edition in 1892 from the private writings of Tobias Lear, who was George Washington's personal secretary in his later years. It was distributed initially by the Library of Congress.

Three Months in Jamaica on a Sugar Plantation was published in 1833 by J. Hatchard and Son under the title *Three Months in Jamaica in 1832 Comprising a Residence of Seven Weeks on a Sugar Plantation*. The book was responsible for the abolition of slavery in the British colonies throughout the Caribbean region.

Autobiography of Abraham Lincoln was first published in 1905 in a limited edition by the Francis D. Tandy Company. It was originally published in 1894 as part of the *Complete Works of Abraham Lincoln* which was edited by John G. Nicolay and John Hay.

A Trip Across the Plains in the Year 1849 with Notes of a Voyage to California by Way of Panama was first published in 1864 in a limited edition by the Pioneer Press in San Francisco. This book is considered a rare book with few copies still in existence. The Newberry Library is Chicago has one of the existing copies.

Journal of James Akin Jr. was first published in 1919 by the University of Oklahoma Bulletin and edited by Edward Everett Dale. It was initially published in a limited pamphlet edition.

Frances Sawyer's account of her adventure across the Plains was first published in 1894 in a serialized format in the now-defunct newspaper *Breckenridge News* in six parts. Later a typed copy was distributed to public libraries around the United States.

A Trip Across the Plains in 1854 was first published in 1908 in a limited edition pamphlet. It is assumed James H. Richey dictated his memoir but the editor and actual writer remain unknown.

Chief Joseph's Own Story was first published in April 1879 in the *North American Review* and in 1907 by the McClure Company (later Doubleday) as part of *Northwestern Fights and Fighters* by Cyrus Townsend Brady. A special edition was published in 1925 by Great Northern Railway Company with additional info.

By Ox-Team to California was first published in April 1916 as part of the *Overlook Monthly* in a limited pamphlet edition. The personal narrative of Nancy Hunt was edited by her son Rockwell D. Hunt from Hunt's writings that was completed prior to her death. Hunt's narrative has been republished several times in book collections and material dealing with pioneer studies.

Log of the Kaalokai was first published in 1909 in Honolulu by the Hawaiian Gazette Company. This detailed maritime memoir covered the experiences of Frederick Dunbar Walker and his crew in the waters off the Hawaiian Islands during the early 1890s.

Two Rough Riders Letters from the McCurdy Brothers was first published in 1902 under the title *Two Rough Riders Letters from F. Allen McCurdy and J. Kirk McCurdy* by F. Tennyson Neely.

Thrilling Story by Titanic's Surviving Wireless Man was written by Jim Speers from Harold Bride's dictated account after Bride was rescued from the Atlantic Ocean. The story first appeared in *The New York Times* on April 19 1912. It has been reprinted in numerous book collections and online sites over the years.

Diary of a Nursing Sister on the Western Front was first published anonymously in 1915 by William Blackwood and Sons of Edinburgh, Scotland. Kate Evelyn Luard was eventually credited as its writer several decades after her death in August 1962.

About the Series Editor

Gary Brin was born in 1965 and has lived in the United States Virgin Islands, Hawaii and California. He has edited numerous original literary works over the years—both new and revised. In 2019 he established Standish Press to bring forth interesting fictional and historical material usually ignored by mainstream publishers because of specific views or content. In addition to publishing books, he also created the Nancy Hanks Lincoln Public Library (named after the mother of Abraham Lincoln) in 2014 to make available hard-to-find books to a worldwide audience.

Production Notes

Manuscripts edited by Gary Brin
Front cover design and book layout by Gary Brin
Cover layout and additional design by Victoria Valentine
Additional help provided by Carlton J. Young
Material compilation by Gary Brin

For free public domain books please visit
www.nancyhankslincolnpubliclibrary.org

Marie Laplace
February 13, 1892
August 16, 1981

Robert J. Questel
June 22, 1911
August 4, 1990

Marie Anicia Berry Questel
January 13, 1912
April 9, 1997

Eugene Albery Brin
March 21, 1932
May 26, 1977

Lucille Questel Brin
February 21, 1940
December 10, 2000

They never got to have the dreams they wanted or expected but their lives were important nevertheless.

Self Portraits

Published by
Standish Press

www.ingramcontent.com/pod-product-compliance
Lightning Source LLC
Chambersburg PA
CBHW071953110526
44592CB00012B/1069